STO

ACPL ITEM
020.8
DISCARDED SO-CBH-591

LIBRARY LIT. ... THE BEST ..

ALLEN COUNTY PUBLIC LIBRARY
FORT WAYNE, INDIANA

DEMCO

LIBRARY LIT. 17- The Best of 1986

edited by

BILL KATZ

The Scarecrow Press, Inc.
Metuchen, N.J., & London
1988

Allen County Public Library
Ft. Wayne, Indiana

ISBN 0-8108-2089-7
Library of Congress Catalog Card No. 78-154842
Copyright © 1988 by The Scarecrow Press, Inc.
Manufactured in the United States of America

CONTENTS

INTRODUCTION

Here is number seventeen, heading towards twenty. As most people
know, the idea is to reward good writers by granting them immortality
in this collection of the 30 best 1986 articles about libraries and related areas. After the twentieth gathering, we probably will go back
and pick the best of the best--this at the suggestion of several
friendly critics such as George Bobinski. Meanwhile, the present
group indicates once again the high character of the profession.

There are numerous tests for inclusion here. The first is that
the article keep the audience awake. Experience indicates this may
be as important as the notion we have about the author's grasp of
the realities of present day libraries. While no one would think of
this material as entertaining, for it has no reason to do more than
pleasantly inform, at least the writer is expected to make a gesture
towards transmitting the message in such a way as to keep us alert
and involved.

Repetition, rhythmical or otherwise, is the stuff of the more
than 180 periodicals which we currently search for the present collection's winners. One expects to find the appreciative piece on
computers, new approaches to cataloging rules and sometimes incom-
prehensible formulas for collection development in almost every other
publication. These types of articles undoubtedly contain elements
of originality, if little suspense or surprise.

The virtue of repetition is that sooner or later the ordinary
casual reader will get the idea, no matter how uninteresting or un-
inspired. The myth is that repetition is necessarily symbolic of
thought. So, one hunts among the 180 journals for the militant individual whose virtue is not only failure to sound the same message
again, but the ability to become the knight-errant of an original
idea.

Since most original articles have ideas which can be described
as benevolent or malevolent--depending on your point of view, experience and natural inclination to favor the right or the left or
center--there is a need for a jury to insure balance of selection.
The worthies who make up the jury agree on the necessity of pass-
able style and new approaches to library problems and ideas, but
there is far from consensus about what is a playful, wicked or downright inspired set of ideas. (This is not to suggest there is always

total agreement about either style or degrees of originality, but at least they are somewhat more objective and easier to evaluate than the spirit of the piece.)

Given a generous number of articles which are preselected by the editor and librarians during the year, the judges individually choose their favored 30. They then do battle with one another until the pieces you find in this collection are decided upon. It is hardly the type of struggle one imagines at the Iceland summit, or at a typical library staff meeting, but it can arouse rather violent emotions. True, one is tempted from time to time to wish fellow jury members were less disagreeable, at least about a particularly loved article which is deleted, but this is not a world in which all wishes are magically granted. The content of this volume represents compromise, but it is precisely because of compromise that we are sure the 30 articles selected truly are the best which have appeared in numerous periodicals from 1 October 1985 to 1 October, 1986.

In addition to style, originality and philosophy, articles are evaluated at another level. An effort is made to reach balance between different types of libraries, different areas of interest and, finally, between periodicals. The latter is important in that the judges would hope the reader would depart this collection with a new respect for the numerous journal editors who may not be as well known as those who head Library Journal, Collection Building, College and Research Libraries, etc.

It would be misleading to say there are not other barriers the candidates must pass through to win a place here. A work may justly be condemned, for example, because it fails to make its point or points. Put another way, even the most labored research project is not insurance of a creditable result, no matter how logical the conclusion may be to the writer. Sometimes this is hard to ascertain, particularly when the conclusion is drowned in jargon, or ferried across the pages by dramatic solecistic phrases. Fortunately, the judges are past experts, in discovering the unpleasant truth that too many articles have a beginning and a middle but no logical end.

Then, of course, a perfectly worthy candidate may have been overlooked. This has, and will continue to happen. Unhappily there's no solution for it, although over the past 17 years the pursuit of excellence seems to be generally rewarding and few truly fine articles have missed the jury's consideration.

Meanwhile, all readers are urged to suggest candidates for next year's collection. They may be sent to the editor at the School of Information Science and Policy, State University of New York, 135 Western Ave., Albany, NY 12222.

The 1986 Jury

John Berry, editor-in-chief of the Library Journal; Mary K. Chelton, co-editor of VOYA (Voice of Youth Advocates); Arthur Curley, editor of Collection Building; Norman Horrocks, Vice President, Editorial of Scarecrow Press; Pat Schuman, President, Neal-Schuman Publishers; and the undersigned.

Special thanks to Peggy Barber, Associate Executive Director of Communications, American Library Association for her assistance in compilation of consensus; and to Nancy Slater, my assistant, who did so much to insure the success of this work.

--Bill Katz

Part I

LIBRARIES AND LIBRARIANS

SMALL LIBRARIES--NO SMALL JOB!*

Diane Gordon Kadanoff

There are more small public libraries in the United States than any
other type of size, according to the National Center for Educational
Statistics of the Department of Health and Human Services. While
the center defines a small public library as one which serves a population under 100,000, my own opinion is that those libraries serving
populations of less than 25,000 are what truly qualify as small public
libraries.

I cite this information because I just want you to know that
there are more of us out there in small public libraries than in any
other type and I think it is time that we received some recognition
and respect for the terrific job we do. We are the most overlooked
and underrated segment of the library profession and I want to speak
out for all of us who work in the small public library.

Academic Library Condescension

Regardless of the size of the library they work in, all public
librarians have had the experience of being snubbed by our academic
compatriots. Many academic librarians tend to think they are the
Crème de la crème of the profession--that they do the important and
significant library work. Please understand that I am not damning
all academic librarians; some of my best friends work in the groves
of academe and we have lively exchanges of information and share
a mutual respect for each other. But these friends of mine are the
exceptions not the norm. You have only to go to an Association of
College and Research Libraries (ACRL) program at an ALA Conference and state that you are a public librarian. You will probably
be informed that you won't understand the program or be asked why
are you interested in whatever topic it is if you work in a public
library. Someone who knows you and knows you are a public librarian

*Reprinted by permission of the author and publisher from Library
Journal, III: 4 (March 1, 1986) 72-73. Published by R. R. Bowker,
a division of Reed Publishing, USA; Copyright © 1986 by Reed Publishing, USA, a division of Reed Holdings, Inc.

will surely say, as you both enter the room, "What are you doing here?"

Look around your state association meetings. How many academic librarians are ever present? I have been told by one of my academic librarian friends that the state association conference never includes anything that interests her. She has said this about conferences in two different states in which we both have worked. Possibly it does occur to her that collection development, planning for computers, personnel issues, or most other topics cut right through those type of library distinctions; but I think her assumption is that she can't possibly learn anything from public librarians or else she assumes that the discussions will somehow be on a lower level because they also deal with the public library.

"Quaint, Cute, and Second-rate"

If we who work in small public libraries don't get any respect from our academic colleagues, at times we get even less from our friends who work in large public libraries. They tend to think we are quaint, cute, and/or second-rate. One librarian expressed these sentiments to me this way, "Oh, I thought you were much further along in your professional career."

The size of the population I serve obviously nullified the involved conversation we had had about evaluating personnel. On another occasion, a middle manager from a library in a very large southwestern city asked me the amount of my book budget. When I told her it was $30,000, she responded that I couldn't have a very good collection for that amount. Our library has an excellent collection that has been selected with great care, thought, and skill. While it is true that it may not have the depth of a large library collection, instead of 30 to 40 titles on the same subject, my collection has only three or four titles on one subject, but you may be sure those three or four titles are the most inclusive and the best choices for the community I serve.

From all of this you sometimes get the feeling that your peers think you are in a small public library because you can't get a better job. I am totally confident that I could run a large system but I have no desire to do so. It would mean giving up opportunities which I value such as the day-to-day interaction with the public.

We find the same type of attitudes when we turn to professional literature. For example, in the table of contents of Dorothy Sinclair's Administration of the Small Public Library, 2d ed., (ALA, 1979), we find this heading: "I, the small community: an opportunity for the young librarian." I am not denying that small public library work does attract people fresh out of library school. I know that many librarians use the training they get in a position in a small

public library to move on to a larger library and often to move into
more specialization.   But Sinclair makes no mention of the thousands
of us who love what we do and continue to work in the small public
library, by choice, throughout our careers.

Unlimited Librarians

Discussing the small public library, Sinclair says:

> The word "small" is a comparative one, implying the exist-
> ence of something larger and perhaps more complex. In the
> case of libraries, it suggests a smaller collection, staff, build-
> ing, and community than those of larger public libraries.
> Inevitably, therefore, it presupposes services, or degrees
> of service, the large library can give that the small one can-
> not. "Small," thus, implies the existence of limitations.

It is my contention that while "small" may imply limitations imposed on the library itself, it does not necessarily mean limitations
on the skills, talents, creativity of the professional staff. Librarians who work in small public libraries must be innovative and adapt-
able. They learn to do everything with a degree of expertise that
sometimes astounds me. In many cases they are the only professionals that library has; so necessity forces them to become proficient
experts in children's services, cataloging, microcomputers, reference
work, outreach to senior citizens, and, in their primary function,
library administration. That means they must also be proficient in
budgeting, writing grant proposals, scheduling, hiring, and sometimes firing.

If they are lucky enough to have other professionals on the
staff, as I am, the small public library situation still demands that
every professional always be ready to take up the slack. If your
children's librarian is sick, you have to fill in as the storyteller at
story hour. If your cataloger resigns, you have to do the cataloging until you can replace her. When your custodian doesn't show up
and the walk is covered with snow, you have to shovel it--even
though it isn't in your job description.

No Plumbing at Library School

At my library, we currently employ a morning custodian and
an evening and night watchperson who locks up the library and does
some custodial chores. So why, in the middle of the afternoon when
we are without custodial help, does the urinal in the men's room begin
to flush continually? Off I go with a wrench to fix it; plumbing
was not a duty they taught me at library school but it is a necessity
in a small public library with a very small maintenance budget. I
am not declaring that my ability with a wrench enhances my professional

skills but it probably does add to my empathy for patrons who are looking for how-to-do-it information.

Teaching for Service

Speaking of library school reminds me that some of us in small public libraries also function as library educators, and we do that in a small but vital way. In my first directorship, I had a staff of three, all with only high school educations. I could not possibly be present in the library every hour that it was open so it was necessary to train those three clerks in some basics of reference work. Out came my copy of Winchell, and once a week we held a staff meeting to learn the difference between an almanac and an encyclopedia, what you could expect to find in the Americana as opposed to World Book, and how to conduct a reference interview.

I do not pretend to be a library educator nor do I think that the staff who received our training could then qualify for the MLS, but I do believe that the library patrons received more effective reference service, and that was our goal.

Be Proud, Enjoy the Work

The profession has been talking about the need to develop horizontal career ladders for some time. If you are a children's librarian who enjoys your work and performs in a superior fashion, there should be some way to reward you, both financially and with recognition, without your having to give up what you do best in order to move ahead. The same applies to all the librarians working in small public libraries who face the daily challenges of frontline library work. You should know that you are the backbone of the profession. Be proud of the excellent job you do and continue to enjoy your work.

FINANCING LIBRARY AUTOMATION:
SELLING THE BENEFITS AND THE BUDGET*

Murray S. Martin

Libraries are costly, labor-intensive institutions. Moreover, their costs tend to rise rapidly.[1] The suggestion that automation should be super-imposed on rising operating budgets is likely to meet with considerable resistance. Plans for automation need to be presented as an expression of the library's concern for cost containment, increased productivity, fiscal responsibility, and resource management.

Automation, as discussed in this article, refers to the purchase and installation of a "turnkey" system, rather than the inhouse development of a system or the adoption of various automated service contracts. While this article will follow the form of a case study loosely based on the experience of Tufts University in seeking such a system, the concepts and guidelines presented are useful for academic libraries in general. As background, Tufts University has about 7,200 students (4,500 of them undergraduates) on three campuses, a decentralized library system with eight locations, a collection of about 650,000 volumes and about 500,000 transactions annually.

Groundwork and Stage Setting for Automation

In preparing for automation there are two products to sell--first the idea of automation itself, second the actual automation proposal. The first requires setting a suitable climate before the second can even by contemplated. Preparing statements of goals and their benefits for different audiences is a time-consuming and frequently frustrating task. Library service benefits are dispersed and notoriously difficult to quantify. Most of those who have to be convinced are not regular library users and may not even have much idea of how libraries operate. One must also have in mind the ultimate sources of funds--tuition, capital reserves, grants, loans--each of which requires a different strategy to bring them into the project.

*Reprinted by permission of the author and publisher from The Bottom Line, Charter Issue (Fall 1986), 11-16; copyright © 1986 Neal-Schuman Publishers, Inc.

Not everyone is convinced by the same kind of argument.
For example, competing with other colleges can be a strong incentive
for those concerned with future admissions of students, but the financial people want to be convinced that any added cost is going to
bring in adequate returns. Some will argue that improving the library's productivity is well and good, but what does that do for the
students. Others will want to know what the visible differences will
be and how they can be sold to potential donors. Some are fasci-
nated by the technology and see it as a way of meeting their private goals. Finally, nearly everyone has some other more important
priority; some will support the project to further their own ends,
while others will oppose the diversion of funds. Given this background of conflict, any march towards automation must be a mix of
strategy and tactics. It is seldom a straight line and, indeed, may
more closely resemble a cross-country steeplechase.

Automation and Reduced Costs

No automation project yet has resulted in decreased total cost
of library operation. This must be made clear. There will be shifts
in staff and expenditures and there will be efficiencies. Over time
there will be reductions in what would otherwise be unavoidable cost
increases. The principal benefits, however, arise from the increased
flexibility which allows shifting resources to activities more in need
of them, and from the added productivity of staff members.

Smaller institutions seldom have much to spare in their library budgets and to deliver major offsetting savings requires some fantastic
legerdemain. There will indeed be costs avoided such as OCLC
charges for catalog cards, but these are relatively small in relation
to the total added cost. Arguments based on such savings will have
very little impact. They are, however, useful as ways of indicating
the impact of automation on library operation.

Instead of promising savings, it is better to attempt two things.
First, separate capital and operating costs. Capital costs, though
substantial, can be found more readily because they are clearly identifiable and separable. Strange as it may seem in view of the totals
involved, continuing operating costs loom larger in financial planners'
thinking because these are usually paid for by tuition increases.
Second, emphasize ongoing benefits to the principal library users--
faculty and students. All benefits, of course, have associated costs
and the goal should be to show that the costs are outweighed by
the benefits.

Depending on the sophistication of the audience it is also possible to point out the ways in which automation can hold down the
otherwise inevitable cost-increases associated with library growth.
Here is where the shift of personnel from maintenance to service
activities can be used for telling effect. Instead of filing cards, both

in the public catalog and the various circulation files, staff can be used to add services. Even quicker reshelving is a benefit that can easily be understood. Better control of overdues and loss can be stressed, since these losses represent real money. Further, any increases in income or decreases in costs can be seen as reducing the added overhead caused by automation.

Benefits and Budgets

The principal public benefit--enhanced bibliographic access-- is little understood and will not be evident until the system is in operation. Nevertheless, particularly in a decentralized library setting, i.e., where services emanate from a number of sites, this improvement is very real and can be related directly to improved support for study and research. The reduction in travel time represented by such a change is substantial. When accompanied by an increased level of satisfaction in retrieval because of prior knowledge of whether specific books are on reserve or otherwise in use, the improvement in library-user activities is dramatic.

Care must be taken to avoid the implication that the actual contents of the library will be available online. Much current writing about electronic publishing has led partially knowledgeable faculty and administrators to confuse access to the bibliographic record with access to the information they represent. While online access to full text is becoming an economic possibility for libraries, it is not yet feasible on any large scale. Existing library automation systems do not provide such a linkage. They do provide the first step, particularly if the necessary wiring is undertaken with that development in mind. So this venture can be presented as offering a double return on the investment, first enabling the library to install an automated system and then allowing access to a larger electronic communications network.

The principal library benefits will be understood most by those who have had to deal over the years with library budget requests. Increases in services and activities most frequently require increases in staff. The relationship between size and cost has been amply demonstrated by several ARL studies [2] though it is not yet entirely clear whether such relationships are true for all sizes of libraries. Automation can address only some of these factors. Added books still require added shelving. Increased circulation results in increased reshelving. So far these continue to be human activities. Reference continues to be a one-on-one activity, though even here automation can increase the speed of finding pertinent information. Online access to dictionaries, encyclopedias, even the library's own database, eliminates the need to leave the desk to find information.

It is mostly in the "back room" activities that automation can increase productivity. Acquisitions, serial check-in, cataloging, and

processing can all be speeded up and the personnel resources dedicated to filing can be redirected. Libraries have seldom calculated
the actual cost of maintaining all the files they must have in a manual setting. Because it is mostly a part-time activity all costs cannot
be eliminated directly, only redirected to more productive activities
in service terms. Speed in turnaround for circulated materials and
more accurate records will influence a library's finding rate which,
while it does not guarantee dollar savings, certainly reduces user
frustration.

Expenditure Alternatives

The question will always be raised as to whether the money
might not be spent more wisely on added acquisitions or more space.
These are complex arguments to counter because all libraries require
both--in addition to automation. Most faculty and administrators
have difficulty in understanding the ramifications of additions to
the book budget--added processing costs and added collection space.
These facts can be used to demonstrate that automation helps librarians utilize book funds better and plan more adequately for meeting
actual, rather than perceived, needs. In fact, the money spent on
automation would buy very little space at $100 or more per square
foot. Rather, the proper use of the managerial data retrieved via
computer can assist in the better use of space in collection management. Space for study is not an issue that should be linked with
automation, but it is the principal issue for students, and the need
is to demonstrate that automation can actually assist them by improving basic services like reserve reading and circulation.

Diverse Perceptions and Funding

How then do these diverse perceptions affect the financing of
automation? Mostly they affect the ways in which it must be presented in order to show the link between cost and benefit. Automation costs big money and the results must be worth it. The financial presentation must show this clearly.

From a set of requirements developed by the librarians, an
RFI (Request for Information) can be generated both to determine
if prospective vendors can meet the requirements and to obtain a
preliminary fix on costs. The first determination helps to set the
limits on any proposed system, based on feasibility. In this case
the search is for an integrated (i.e., all-purpose) turnkey system
with minimal university systems involvement. The second enables
the development of a generalized cost statement which can be used
to determine whether the system is financially feasible.

Several elements are required:

Capital cost--central installation, terminals, printers, etc.; communications, which is particularly important for a dispersed institution; installation.

Maintenance--hardware and software costs, staff.

Preparation--cost of record conversion, item preparation, labeling.

It is important to note that, if it is necessary to borrow money for the capital purchase, there will also be interest charges.

The distribution of library sites requires a higher number of terminals than would be the case in a more centralized university, in this case 100 to 125 terminals. This also affects the size of the central computer installation.

The result is a system with the following preliminary financial profile:

Capital cost:	$750,000-800,000
Maintenance:	$100,000-125,000 (annually)
Preparation:	$600,000-700,000

Once these figures are established with some credibility, they must be presented in a cost-benefit package to those who will have to pay for it. When library budgets are decentralized, it requires a wide variety of approaches; to the central administration as a general benefit to the university's image; to those with the biggest direct interest as a long-term investment in improvement; to those with more modest commitments as not being an unmanageable burden; to all of them as a shared project none of them could afford independently. Potential sources of funding need to be identified, which means a lot of work with the development staff. The computer staff should be involved, particularly since they are going to be asked to look after the installed system. Likely faculty supporters need to be rallied. And all of this must be approached with the knowledge that most outsiders have little specific knowledge of library use or library management.

Establishing the Financial Context

Libraries are seldom seen as capital investments, largely because their collections are paid for from current income. Yet over the years the capital investment represented by the library can be vast. For academic libraries, it is often greater than for any other segment within the university. The annual library budget at Tufts is approximately $4,000,000. This expenditure is distributed thus:

Collections	$1,500,000
Processing	800,000
Administration	200,000
Services	1,500,000

The accumulated value of the collection is $70,000,000 at replacement cost. Library buildings represent a further $16,000,000 in capital investment.

In this context, the added capital value of automation at $1,500,000 represents the addition of less than 2 percent to the existing capital investment. The operating costs of $125,000 represent only a 5 percent increase which can be diminished by generated savings.

The point to be made is that the added value of automation, represented by time-savings and added productivity, represents a highly desirable return. Via automation the libraries can double their capacity for such operations as circulation and cataloging, without added staff. The return to users comes in quicker access to information, faster turn-around in circulation, and better use of collections. All this can be achieved without having to promise to reduce current personnel costs.

An even greater return results from better record control. The added value of online catalogs is not readily understood. In most libraries, because the collections are scattered through several physical locations, it is impossible to provide copies of the entire card catalog. The cost of duplicating the card catalog, which is the equivalent of installing terminals with access to the online catalog, is so great as to be out of reach of any library system. From this flows not only the difficulty of ensuring that users find what they need, but the necessity of duplicating both books and serials. No one can pretend that all such duplications can be foregone, but they can certainly be reduced, especially older runs of serials, saving money for their purchase, housing, and maintenance.

Financial Impact

The result of this process is a kind of impact study. Its tentative nature must be stressed, and care must be taken not to overestimate savings. In view of the continuing importance of operating costs, a period of five years is recommended. This represents the likely period during which the system is expected to be stable. Table 1 illustrates this. Transferable, direct costs represent expenditures for all items, such as catalog cards, which are no longer required. Reassignable savings occur through tasks replaced such as filing.

A listing of ways in which the system can help improve and

TABLE 1
FISCAL IMPACT OF AN INTEGRATED LIBRARY SYSTEM
(Preliminary Figures)

	Year One	Year Two	Year Three	Year Four	Year Five
Capital	$ 750,000	$ 50,000	--	--	--
Quasi-Capital	450,000	250,000	--	--	--
Operating	75,000	100,000	$125,000	$125,000	$125,000
Total	$1,275,000	$400,000	$125,000	$125,000	$125,000
Transferable Direct Costs	6,000	15,000	25,000	30,000	30,000
Net Impact	$1,269,000	$385,000	$100,000	$ 95,000	$ 95,000
Reassignable Savings	$ 10,000	$ 30,000	$ 35,000	$ 40,000	$ 40,000

simplify library operations emphasizes the added nonmonetary value
of automation:

- Total catalog record access at all locations simplifies library
  activities in support of study or research. Particularly
  important for branches and separated campuses.

- Simplified circulation and better control over losses and
  overdues.

- Simplified and improved communications between libraries,
  easier borrowing of materials, consultation on new purchases,
  actual savings on OCLC costs for interlibrary loan.

- Internal simplification of acquisition and cataloging procedures
  to ensure faster processing.

Acquiring the Funds

At this stage a number of questions are sure to be asked:
Where will we get the money? Does the university have capital reserves? Are there funds set aside for automation? What is the current state of fund raising? Is a library building planned or contemplated? What is the university's attitude to bond issues? Is an
issue planned? Are there interested donors? What is the university's track-record with known major donors, such as the Pew Trusts
or Kresge Foundation? Are there local or regional foundations with
a known interest in libraries? Does the university possess collections
that might be of national importance that would qualify for grant
sources such as Title II-C?

At Tufts, the final purchase cost was about $800,000. Asso-
ciated costs of about $200,000 were for site preparation and elec-
tronic networks. The initial impetus came from a federal building
grant for a new health sciences learning center, which included
money for library automation. To this $400,000, as the proposal
developed, were added $500,000 from the Pew Trusts, smaller founda-
tion grants of about $40,000, and, finally, agreement to provide
$400,000 from capital reserves. Actual site preparation was met from
loan funds. The Pew Trusts Grant included $300,000 for data pre-
paration to which was added about $200,000 from library operating
budgets. Cobbled together as it may seem, the total represents
commitments from across the university. The range of possible direct
annual savings is from $10,000 to $50,000; the reassignable operating
costs exceed $60,000 per year.

The fact that this was the first university-wide venture into
electronic communications on such a scale made some of the initial
cost estimates soft, to say the least. It did, however, require the
university to come to grips with the subject and more parts of the

broader communication network are now under active consideration. The library has gained from this the recognition that it is an integral part of the university's information system.

The answers to most questions are likely to be ambiguous. A library considering automation needs to jockey for position with other known fund-attracting activities, like athletics or scholarships. The best situation to be in is to have a portion of the funding assured via a building project, or in association with some other goal, such as curriculum improvement. Sad to admit, libraries are not, in the words of one fund raiser, "sexy." They are simply necessary and frequently taken for granted. The object of the activities outlined earlier in this article has been consciousness raising. With any luck some of the pace-setters within the university will have been convinced that library modernization is an important measure of the university's commitment to a better future.

The Catch-22 in financing automation is that fund seeking cannot effectively precede agreement to automate, but that commitment frequently depends on having the finances in hand. Breaking from this cycle is usually dependent on having convinced one of more of the prospective financial supporters that the project is worthwhile. This is as much a matter of political skill as practical skill. Sounding out the ambitions and goals of the leadership can pay dividends.

If approval is given to go ahead with a full bidding process, guarded by the proviso that final approval will be given only if funding can be assured, it is possible to seek external funding even though it must proceed in parallel with the actual bid process. The first product, the RFP (Request for Proposal) weeds out actual contenders from prospective suppliers and derives firmer cost figures with which to approach possible donors. It also provides a firmer base for internal cost calculations.

Fund Raising

Armed with these figures (for the purpose of this discussion we'll use $850,000 for hardware and software and a direct annual cost of $100,000), and a fairly clear idea of the probable vendors, requests for funding can be sent out. Multiple approaches to foundations for system purchase are unwise; select a major target and subordinate requests to other donors. Target foundations may well differ from region to region, particularly where there are local foundations with a long history of institutional support. Strategy sessions with financial and development officers pay off here.

Institutional Support

All fund raising should be undertaken with a healthy dash of

realism; donors are not usually falling over themselves to give money.
They need to be assured that any project has full institutional support and will result in substantial benefits. Moreover, libraries are
seen as activities the institution itself should support. It is, therefore, highly beneficial to be able to demonstrate institutional commitment. Since foundations and corporations are seldom willing to provide all the funds, and are more willing to support a joint venture,
the goal should be to present a project with multiple financial sources, so that each donor can feel he or she is providing a distinct
part of the whole. It has also to be remembered that some donors
require a visible product for their money and others are willing to
fill in the gaps or support data conversion.

Full-back Position

    A lengthy funding campaign can be fatal. Major foundations
usually take some months to decide, and do not always give prior
indication of interest. They also wish to be assured that the rest
of the cost is covered. A fallback position is necessary. In most
cases this turns out to be postponement. A better position is to
gain consent to include library automation in a bond issue. This
incurs interest costs, spread over several years, but enables fund
raising to be pursued aggressively rather than diffidently, because
any funds so raised will reduce potential debt, always attractive to
the financial administrators. In Tufts' case, funding success was
assured when The Pew Trusts made a major grant towards capital
and quasi-capital costs.

    Simpler goals are equally useful. A Friends Group can make
it part of their program to fund specific items. It is possible to
seek from alumni and parents small sums to be identified with individual terminals, thus allowing public recognition. Interest in the
project can be generated by news releases on retrospective conversion, where students are involved. The object of such an approach
is to place the project in a positive context--even if one has private
nightmares. Nevertheless, the work involved is substantial. Only
one approach in five is likely to result in a real accession of funds.
But the first major donation leads to others. People more naturally
support something that others believe in.

Rallying Internal Support

    When a university is decentrally organized--a frequent arrange-
ment in private universities--it is important to bring all the constituencies on board. This requires the development of a kind of cost-
benefit statement for each unit. What do they get from the system,
what must they contribute to it? Do they participate in any savings?
Will they benefit from fund raising? Unless the system has been
poorly conceived, all these questions can be answered, and positively.

Don't understate costs nor overestimate savings. The latter should
only be those resulting from direct cost transfers, e.g., OCLC costs.
Stress the benefits to study and research of having direct access
to all library records. Use-statistics can be valuable here. There
is always more interlibrary use than the separate constituencies realize. For the largest library in the system the principal benefit is
increased efficiency, and therefore, improved service. For smaller
libraries it is as if their collections were quadrupled. Sharing is
not a much-touted virtue in a decentralized system, but it is possible
to point out the costs of independence as against the fruits of co-
ordination.

The Cost Projection

    When a system has been selected a five-year cost projection
should be prepared, and not only for the system chosen but for the
runnersup, so that the total costs can be compared.[3] This is the
point at which the benefits of lower maintenance or specific savings
become obvious. The choice should, of course, be based primarily
on functionality, but there is frequently little to choose functionally
between systems and the bottom line will make the difference. It
may be necessary to point out problems associated with cheapness.
In the old adage, good may be cheap, cheap is never good.

    If an entire subsystem is lacking, alternatives will have to be
paid for; perhaps by the maintenance of files that would otherwise
have been closed. Some advantages or disadvantages are difficult
to put a price on, partly because there is no easy way, for example,
of making up for the absence of cross-linked subjects, but the attempt must be made. Tables can show clearly how the long-term
advantages of less costly maintenance or directly attributable savings
offsets highter capital expenditure. As Table 2 (page 18) shows,
the greater savings from System 2 arise from the substitution of
access to LC tapes for OCLC cataloging. Deficiency costs represent
funds that would be expended for missing elements until they are
available, for example, costs of maintaining the union catalog until
the bibliographic data is online.

Cost Allocations

    Distribution of cost by college can be made with accuracy only
following system selection. Presuming that the System 2 recommendation is approved, a tentative allocation can be made. There are no
ground rules for such an allocation since these will be affected by
existing precedents. Student numbers are frequently used, though
it must be pointed out that faculty use the library, individually,
more than undergraduate students. The capital cost should reflect
the numbers of terminals, which can be costed directly to each unit,
since these relate directly to the size of CPU needed. Arguments

TABLE 2
LONG-TERM SYSTEM COSTS

	System 1	System 2	System 3
Capital Cost			
Hardware	605,000	700,000	760,000
Software	95,000	65,000	80,000
Installation	50,000	60,000	60,000
Sub-total	750,000	825,000	900,000
Direct Maintenance Costs (5 years)	600,000	500,000	500,000
Direct Savings (5 years)	-40,000	-150,000	-50,000
Deficiency costs (variable periods)	50,000	10,000	10,000
Sub-total	610,000	360,000	460,000
TOTAL (5 years)	$1,360,000	$1,185,000	$1,360,000
Functional preference	3	1	2
Cost preference	2=	1	2=
Timing to installation	9-12 months	4-6 months	4-6 months
General order of preference	3	1	2
Recommendation	System 2.		

Sources of Funding:	Foundation Grant	200,000
	Smaller donations	100,000
	Capital Reserve	400,000
	Bond issue (prospective)	125,000

Setting up costs are covered by a combination of grant and operating funds. Effects of direct annual operating costs on student tuition (7,500 students)

System 1	$15 per year per student
System 2	$10 per year per student
System 3	$12 per year per student

will be made that smaller libraries should contribute in proportion
to their holdings. In fact, the benefits are in inverse proportion
to input. In the long run, therefore, capital costs can best be
distributed by number of terminals.

Operating costs are much more difficult to allocate in advance.
Since projections of use have already been computed to estimate the
size of system needed, some proportional allocations can be made,
but it is just as likely that an existing formula for the allocation of
central costs can be used. A good argument can be made for a mixed
distribution, directly allocating terminal maintenance costs and sharing
the remaining costs according to a formula. Transaction based cost
allocation is complex, uncertain and, in any case, cannot be contemplated until a complete year's transactions are accumulated. Table
3 (page 20) illustrates a more useful method. Schools B, C, D,
and E are all professional schools with significant research, hence
the different faculty ratios.

Continued Fund Raising

Fund raising should not stop. In fact it can be redoubled because there is a real product to offer. Further, actual contract negotiations may change or reduce some of the costs--not all terminals
need be installed immediately, for example. Small though it may seem,
there are real savings in substituting a general terminal for a circulation terminal plus light pen, where the number of circulation transactions does not justify a dedicated terminal, and vendors, when
making actual site inspections prior to installation, are willing to
make recommendations resulting in greater efficiency. The goal here
would be to eliminate the funding gap represented by the prospective
bond issue.

A process as complex as this takes a great deal of time. Selling the need for a system within the institution can take at least one
year. The process of selection and negotiation will also take a year.
Fund raising will probably take more than a year--for example, foundations frequently take six to eight months to respond--and should,
therefore, be preceeding parallel to the other aspects of the project.
Then, of course, it is time to start planning for the next stage.
Since at least four years are likely to elapse between initiation and
realization of automation, it is extremely important to think in terms
of the future to avoid having to re-estimate goals and costs to meet
changed conditions.

References

1. D. Kent Halstead, Higher Education Prices and Price Indexes
(Washington, D.C.: G.P.O., 1975).

TABLE 3
SYSTEM COST DISTRIBUTION

	School A	School B	School C	School D	School E
Library Collections	400,000	100,000	80,000	(see A)	20,000
Students	5,000	250	1,800	200	250
Faculty	400	40	500	10	50
Terminals	63	10	40	2	5
Capital Cost (based on # of terminals)	52.5%	8.3%	33.3%	1.7%	4.2%
Operating cost:	(Equal Weighting to All Factors)				
Terminals	52.5	8.3	33.3	1.7	4.2
Students	66.7	3.3	24.0	2.7	3.3
Faculty	40.0	4.0	50.0	1.0	5.0
Collections	66.7	16.7	13.3	–	3.3
Average (div. by 4)	56.5%	8.1%	30.2%	1.3%	4.0%

2. William J. Baumol and Marcus Matityahu. The Economics of Aca-
    demic Libraries (Washington, D.C.: A.C.E., 1973) and Kendon
    Stubbs. The ARL Library Index and Quantitative Relationships
    in the ARL (Washington, D.C.: ARL, 1980).
3. Joseph R. Matthews, Choosing an Automated Library System
    (Chicago: ALA, 1980), pp. 50-51.

THE INFLUENCE OF REFERENCE PRACTICES
ON THE CLIENT–LIBRARIAN RELATIONSHIP*

Joan C. Durrance

In a recent editorial in <u>College & Research Libraries</u>, writing in the context of evaluation of reference performance, Charles Martell raised a number of important questions; one of them was "How does the environment in which we work discourage ... [the] assessment [of reference performance]?"[1] Questions like this, which call for an examination of the basic reference model, have seldom been asked by librarians and researchers and certainly have not been answered by them.[2] One study that raises a similar question, "What effect does the environment of reference service have one the reference interview?" was done by Mary Jo Lynch. She sketched the differences between our professional model and other models:

> Other professionals do not usually operate in such an atmos-
> phere. Clients commonly make appointments to see them and
> even when appointments are not made the professional works
> in a private or semiprivate place and admits clients one at
> a time. Reference librarians, by contrast, wait in a public
> place for any client that may come along.... The implications
> of this situation must be taken into account in any considera-
> tion of the reference interview.[3]

Although her study found that library users are not well served by the public practice of reference she suggested that it "may be neces- sary because ... of the way that people use libraries."[4] I would argue that people use libraries the way they do because they are encouraged to do so by the environment created by librarians.

This paper attempts to apply empirical data to the concerns that Martell, Lynch, and others have raised.[4] It addresses these concerns by breaking them into several component questions: (1) Does present practice limit the ability of library users to distinguish between librarians and other staff members? (2) Does it make it

*Reprinted by permission of the author and publisher from <u>College & Research Libraries</u>, 47:1 (January 1986) 58-67; copyright © 1986 by the American Library Association.

difficult for library users to see librarians as information intermediaries? (3) Does present practice discourage library users from becoming clients of librarians? (4) Does it make it difficult for librarians to function as professionals?

This paper addresses these questions within the framework of two concerns that have reappeared with disturbing regularity in the literature of librarianship. The first is the problem of librarianship as a profession, in particular the image that the public has of librarianship as a profession.[6] The second concern, is a component of the first: librarianship's inability to develop an adequate theoretical framework. In a recent paper on professional issues, Michael Winter noted that "the lack of an adequate theoretical body of knowledge is ... a serious obstacle to the professional development of an occupation."[7] Winter goes on to say:

> The various dimensions of professionalization are interdependent. Thus problems in the knowledge base, combined as they are with low public recognition and complicated by structural constraint, are probably more serious in librarianship than the same problems are in other disciplines.[8]

A better understanding of the effect of the reference environment on the user will add to the theoretical base required for optimum practice of reference. In addition, it will make it easier for librarians to communicate more clearly their role to the public and should permit the field to evaluate reference performance more effectively. The literature devoted to the evaluation of reference service is both extensive and inadequate, perhaps because it does not adequately analyze the limitations of present practice.[9]

In a 1983 review article on reference theory Richard Danner found that "despite continuing interest in the problem of reference theory ... librarians have been unable to reach a consensus on a definition of library service or on a characterization of the activity."[10] Thelma Friedes reached a similar conclusion in her review of trends in academic libraries.[11] Danner posits that the articulation of a theory of reference service is "of crucial importance to the future of the profession" in light of current trends in the development of information technology.[12] Although for more than a decade researchers have examined the interaction that occurs between the librarian and the library user in the reference transaction, the affect of present identification practices on the professional-client relationship, per se, has not been adequately examined.[13] Communication concepts such as the reference interview have been defined and explained within the context of present professional practice, but without discussion of the effect that present practice might have on the library user.[14]

Librarians have assumed that the distinctions necessary to

distinguish between them and other staff can be made by library
users. Yet, a quarter of a century ago, William Goode reported that
the public's perception of librarians as clerks posed a serious problem
for librarianship as it sought professional status.[15]   In 1977, Peter
Hernon and Maureen Pastine found that "students perceive the role
of librarians, clericals, and student assistants as being the same."[16]
They also found that although 87 percent of the university students
in their study thought that librarians and other library staff members
differed in their backgrounds, most students believed that librarians
sat behind desks, and were older, more knowledgeable and competent
than other staff.[17]

The present study examines the perceptions that library users
have about library practitioners and the effect these perceptions have
on their behavior both as library users and as clients.

THE CLIENT PROFESSIONAL
RELATIONSHIP IN REFERENCE

The perceptions library users have about the library practitioner
will influence the nature of the professional-client relationship that
they develop. If a norm for the professional-client relationship has
been developed and transmitted to library users, it is that the user
should approach an anonymous staff member of unknown credentials
who is behind one of several public desks and who is often simultaneously engaged in some other activity. Since these unidentified,
uncredentialed staff members rotate days and times, the library user
is required to initiate contact with any one of several desk staff.
If the user is referred to another source of information, the referral
is likely to be to another location and not to a staff member. Most
academic libraries adhere to this pattern.

Certain conditions must be present before a client engages
a practitioner in a professional relationship. It is the argument of
this paper that the traditional practice of reference may transmit
indistinct messages to library users about the role and practice of
librarianship, making it difficult for library users to become clients
of librarians. The paper asks the question "Does this practice produce a set of conditions conducive to the development of a true
client-professional relationship?"

Method

Major variables in this study include: (1) user knowledge of
staff differentiation, (2) user ability to recognize specific staff members, (3) the inclination of users to look for and return to particular staff members, (4) the inclination to avoid specific staff members,
and (5) the criteria that are used as the basis for a decision to return to or avoid a staff member.

This study was conducted with users of three academic libraries that are similar in size and user composition: The Eastern Michigan University (18,880), Bowling Green State University (16,866), and the University of Toledo (21,489). Since there were no major differences in responses among the three universities, the data from all sites were combined. Interviews were conducted with 429 library users as they left each library during morning, afternoon, evening, and weekend hours for the months of May and June 1984.

Interviewers were stationed inside near the exit gates. With the exception of the principal investigator, interviewers were University of Michigan graduate students in library science and political science; both male and female interviewers were used. Eight two-hour blocks were spent interviewing at each site by a rotating team of two; an average of thirty-two hours was spent on interviews at each institution. Based on use data provided by staff at these institutions, interview hours were weighted toward more heavily used afternoon and evening hours. Each interview took between two and seven minutes.

The interview elicited detailed information from the user about a recently asked reference question. This question was used as a critical incident around which the interview was structured. To distinguish between a reference and a directional question, and to establish a reasonable time frame, the interviewer inquired if the user had asked a library staff member for assistance in getting information about a topic or help in locating library materials within the six past months. Each library user was placed into one of three categories by type of assistance sought: reference question, (including title-author questions), directional-equipment request, or no question.

USER KNOWLEDGE OF STAFF
DIFFERENTIATION

Does present practice make it difficult for library users to identify librarians? This question was tested by analyzing three related factors: (a) the extent to which library users were aware of staff differentiation; (b) the categories assigned to library staff members by interviewees, coupled with the degree of uncertainty expressed; and (c) the reasons given for indicating that a staff member was a librarian, a library assistant, or a student assistant. Although nearly 84 percent of the users were aware that several categories of library staff work in academic libraries (a finding similar to Hernon and Pastine), they were not always able to identify professional staff.

When all library users who knew that different categories of staff worked in libraries and who had requested assistance were asked to indicate the category to which they would assign the staff member

who had assisted them, the certainty dropped from 84 percent who
were sure of the category of the person who had assisted them.
Over one-third were uncertain about the category.

The Ability to Identify Library
Staff Members by Name

In most professions, those who interact directly with the client
are known by name. Seventeen percent of the users who asked questions knew the staff members by name. Those who recognized or
knew the name were likely to be more intensive library users than
those who did not. They were more likely to report that they typically used several types of materials. They were twice as likely to
report regularly seeking assistance than those who didn't know the
name of the staff member (19.2 percent to 10.1 percent). Finally,
they were far more likely to return to the staff member they consulted (74 percent) than those who didn't recognize or know the name
of a staff member (47.9 percent).

A 1980 study of citizen-group leaders showed that if they knew
the name of a library staff member, they were likely to have a higher
library success rate.[18] However, the present study showed that
recognition of a staff member or knowledge of the name did not assure that the library user knew the category to which the staff member belonged. Nearly a third of the respondents who could recognize
or name a staff member were not sure to which category he or she
should be assigned (see table 1, page 27).

Rationale for Selecting
Specific Staff Categories

The reasons given by the 256 library users who were sure of
the staff members' status fell into five categories: (1) appearance
and environmental clues, (2) expertise, (3) bibliographic instruction
or some other practice that facilitated identification, (4) personal
knowledge and, (5) "no reason" or "don't know" (see table 2, page
27).

The reasons are strong indicators that users are unsure how
to differentiate between librarians and other staff members. The
evidence suggests that the knowledge users have about how to identify the different categories of staff is based not on information,
instruction, or other assistance, but on appearance and supposition.

Appearance and Environmental Clues

Over half of the users who asked a reference question relied
on clues provided either by the environment or by the staff member's

TABLE 1

CATEGORIES ASSIGNED TO LIBRARY
STAFF MEMBERS BY THOSE
WHO HAD ASKED FOR ASSISTANCE

Category	Number	Percentage
Librarian	115	37.8
Librarian, not sure*	36	11.8
Library assistant	28	9.2
Library assistant, not sure*	15	4.9
Student assistant	47	15.4
Student assistant, not sure*	11	3.6
Other/Don't know	50	16.4
Totals	302	100.0

*Respondent indicated the category with hesitation, i.e., "I think
she must have been a librarian," or, "I'm pretty sure he's a student."

TABLE 2

REASONS GIVEN FOR ASSUMING
THAT A STAFF MEMBER SHOULD BE ASSIGNED
TO A PARTICULAR CATEGORY

	Category Selected							Totals
	Librarian		Assistant		Student			
Reason Given	N	%	N	%	N	%		
Appearance	80	58.8%	20	14.7%	36	26.5%	=	136 (100%)
Expertise	61	89.7%	6	8.8%	1	1.5%	=	68 (100%)
ID Practice	15	62.5%	5	20.8%	4	16.7%	=	24 (100%)
Bib. Inst.	10	100%	0		0		=	10 (100%)
Knew Before	9	39.7%	4	17.4%	10	43.4%	=	23 (100%)
No Reason	12	38.7%	7	22.6%	12	38.7%	=	31 (100%)

Note: All reasons given by respondents were recorded. Some respondents gave more than one reason for assigning a staff member
to a particular category. This table is a combination of six cross-
tabulations (one for each reason given).

appearance to make a decision on staff category. Librarians were
identified primarily as older and as behind desks. Most younger
staff were assigned to the student category. Users generally relied
on appearance and location rather than on any other method for determining the categories to which a staff member was assigned.

Expertise

Expertise was associated almost exclusively with the librarian
category. However, it is interesting to note that although sixty-
eight (27 percent) of the respondents recognized expertise as a
reason for assigning a staff member to a category, library users
cited appearance twice as often (168 responses). Although appearance and environmental clues are only circumstantial evidence, they
are the most common means used to determine professional status.

Personal Knowledge

Twenty-three users said that they were sure of the category
of the staff member who assisted them because they knew the person
outside of the library. Nearly half were fellow students; the others
were known in another context. The categories assigned to staff
by those who are acquainted with one another are more likely to be
accurate than the categories assigned based on appearance or expertise.

Bibliographic Instruction and
Other Practices That
May Result in Staff Identification

Only thirty-five users based their rationale on what appears
to be a fairly accurate method to identify library staff categories--
previous contact through bibliographic instruction (BI) or other practices used by librarians, which may result in more accurate identification of credentials and/or status. The other identification practices
include self-identification by or referral to another staff member by
name. These factors were mostly used to place the staff in the librarian category. All ten users who noted that the staff member
had spoken to a class placed the staff member in the librarian category.

No Reason

Finally, thirty-one library users said that they did not know
and/or had no reason to think that the staff member belonged to the
specific category to which they had been assigned.

The first part of this paper has shown that present practice makes it difficult for library users to distinguish librarians from other library employees. It must be recalled that users were asked these questions not about any staff, but about library staff who had answered reference questions. Overall, these data show that although library users may be aware that there is staff differentiation in libraries, they are not able to distinguish with any certainty between librarians and other library employees when asking for assistance in obtaining information or materials.

The final portion of this paper returns to the questions and concerns raised in its opening paragraphs. Does present practice make it difficult for library users to perceive librarians as information intermediaries? Does it discourage most library users from becoming "clients" of these information intermediaries? Does it make it difficult for librarians to function as professionals? The final portion will discuss different modes of client behavior that result from the present anonymous practice of reference. It will examine the differences among four types of library users—those who do not seek assistance, those who ask only directional questions, those who seek assistance from library staff members, and those who not only seek assistance but also look for particular staff members when they need help.

INCLINATION OF THE USER TO SEEK ASSISTANCE

Given the anonymous practice of reference at an open desk, any relationship developed by the user and the practitioner is likely to be shaped by the user. Several variables may lead the user to recognize that a staff member may function as an information intermediary, e.g., the inclination of the user to seek assistance. Figure 1 (page 30) outlines possible client-professional relationships; table 3 shows the number of users who asked a question in each category and the recency of these questions.

1. Users Who Do Not Seek Assistance. Seventeen percent of the users in the sample made no contact with a library staffmember within the six months prior to the study. Yet over half of them used the library several times a week. Half reported using the library as a place to study and three-fourths reported using library materials regularly. The fact that these users had made no contact with library staff but reported heavy building and materials use is an indicator that they perceive the library as a useful building. But either they do not recognize that staff may function as information intermediaries or they have no need to interact with the staff.

2. Users Who Ask Only Directional or Equipment Related Questions. Nearly one in five users had asked only directional questions.

FACTOR	TYPES OF QUESTIONS ASKED			
	Asks No Questions	Asks Only Directional Questions	Asks Reference Questions (Includes both reference and title/author requests)	
Library Use (Building/Materials) Patterns	Building use only; Building use and materials use	Building use only; Materials use	Building use; Materials use	Building use; Materials use
Recognition Factor	Not known	No indication of staff recognition	No indication of staff recognition	User reports recognizing staff; Recognizes only or knows name
Intermediary Use Patterns	No questions	Asks directional questions	Asks directional questions; Asks reference questions of any staff	Asks directional questions; Asks reference questions of any staff, but may also seek particular staff
Preference Factor	Not applicable	Goes to anyone	Goes to anyone	Inclined to look for particular staff; May avoid specific staff
Inclination to Return	Not applicable	Either return or no preference	May return	More likely to return
Client-determined Relationship	No contact	Relationship limited to single inquiry; Not professional in nature	Relationship limited to single question	Prefers particular practitioners; Relationships extend over time
Type of Relationship	No relationship	Relationship not professional	Aware of intervention capability of library staff	True client-professional relationship

FIGURE 1: TYPOLOGY OF CLIENT-DETERMINED RELATIONSHIPS WITH LIBRARY PRACTITIONERS BASED ON TYPE OF ASSISTANCE SOUGHT

TABLE 3

TYPES OF QUESTIONS ASKED IN THE PAST SIX MONTHS

Recency of Question	None %	Type of Question Directional %	Title/Au. %	Reference %
Day of the Interview	0	23%	26%	24%
Less than 2 Weeks	0	31	30	35
2 Weeks to 1 Mo.	0	17	15	9
1-3 Months	0	18	21	27
4-6 Months	0	11	9	6
Over 6 Months or None	%	100%	100%	100%
Total N = 426 N =	71	83	110	162

Sixty-five percent reported that their typical library use included facility use e.g., computer terminals and study tables. The majority were frequent users; nearly 58 percent reported using the library several times a week. Sixty-six percent reported using the library as a place to study on the day of the interview and about half-reported using library materials regularly.[19]

These users expressed greater uncertainty about the different categories of staff in libraries than other users; 22 percent were not aware of staff differentiation in libraries. When users who asked directional questions are combined with those who asked no questions, the study shows that one-third of the users had not asked any questions that required the assistance of a librarian.

Users who asked directional questions differed from users who asked no questions in that they were inclined to seek, but had not made use of the professional skills of librarians. A number of studies have raised questions about those who use libraries but do not call on the professional capabilities of librarians.[20] This study compares the behavior of those who are inclined to see librarians as intermediaries with those who do not.

3. Users Who See Library Staff as Intermediaries. The inclination to view the library staff member as an intermediary is a prerequisite for the development of a professional relationship. Nearly two thirds of the users questioned, or 275 persons, had sought assistance. These users can be divided further into two distinct but disproportionately sized groups. The vast majority of those who asked questions (85 percent) said that they would go to any staff member when they had a question. The remaining 15 percent preferred to look for particular staff members. The principal difference between these two groups will be discussed below.

a.   Users Who Go to Any Staff Member.   Those who ask questions but who do not look for particular library staff members represent the largest category of library users.   These individuals conform
to the client norm expected by present reference practice.   Nearly
62 percent reported using the library several times a week.   Their
library materials and building use was similar to those who asked no
questions or who asked only directional questions.   About two-thirds
had used the library as a place to read or study on the day of the
interview.   Only 13 percent reported seeking assistance regularly.
These users ask questions but do not seek out particular staff.   Although they did not customarily look for particular staff members,
55 percent said they would return to the person who had assisted
them if help was needed at another time.   Findings show that this
large group does not engage in a true client relationship.   Their
contact with librarians as information intermediaries is likely to be
limited to single, isolated encounters.

b.   Users Who Act as Clients--Those Who Seek Out Particular
Staff Members.   All library users were asked, "When you use this
library do you usually look for particular people when you need assistance?"   Only 10 percent of all users look for particular staff.
The library-use patterns of this minority follow: their frequency
of use and library building and materials use patterns are not substantially different from the patterns shown by other users; less than
19 percent reported seeking assistance during their typical use patterns.   It is not surprising to find that these and all other library
users in this study report heavy materials and building use and minimal assistance seeking; library users spend far less time as clients
than as library users.   However, those who have recognized the
value of the intermediary role do use the professional expertise of
librarians.   The next section of this paper examines the client behavior of these individuals.

The Client Mode--The Inclination to Look for Particular Staff

The 15 percent of users who looked for particular staff members were far less likely to say they were unsure of the category
of the staff member (16.3 percent) than those who did not look for
particular staff (33.7 percent).   In addition, they were more likely
to say that they selected a staff member on the basis of expertise
(26.8 percent) than those who did not look for a particular staff member (20.9 percent).   They were much less likely to say that they
would go to whomever was at the desk (14.6 percent) than those with
no preference (27.4 percent).   Library users who looked for particular staff members were also much more likely to say that they avoided
certain staff members (22 percent) than those who did not (8.6 percent).

Individuals who look for particular staff when they seek assistance act like the clients of other professionals.   They select the

professional and return to him or her when they need assistance. They do not prefer to go to just anyone. In the process of selecting, they may also make a conscious decision to avoid a particular practitioner. They may learn the name of the staff member with whom they have developed a relationship, but if not, they will return to the staff member through recognition alone. Users who have learned the name of a practitioner benefit by having the ability to reestablish communication with a professional at a later time.[21]

Criteria Used to Select the Library/Information Professional

Only those users who have engaged in client behavior develop criteria to select staff. They constitute a small minority of library users; in this study only forty-one qualified. In librarianship the absence of obvious credentials or specialties known to the client-- such as family practice or obstetrics in medicine, or divorce or taxation in law--requires the clients to develop their own criteria.

These criteria allow the client to develop the qualities later sought in the practitioner. Expertise was the criterion most often used by the respondents in this study; half of those who looked for a particular staff member said that the staff member was selected for expertise or knowledge exhibited in a past encounter. Thirty-nine percent of those who looked for a particular staff member said that they selected the staff member because they recognized that person. Finally, sixteen did so because the staff member seemed friendly or approachable.

The Inclination to Return

The inclination to return is a strong indicator that the user has established a client relationship with a staff member. In this study, the 360 users who asked questions, and would return to the staff member who had assisted them, were more likely to know that different categories of staff worked in the library (89 percent) than those who didn't care if they returned to the staff member (79 percent). They are more than twice as likely to recognize or know the name of the staff member (26 percent) than those who didn't care (13 percent). None of those who said they would prefer to go to someone else the next time knew the name of the staff member who had assisted them. Those who return are twice as likely to say that a library staff member had spoken to their class (12 percent) than those who had no preference (6 percent). Finally, they are twice as likely to cite expertise as a criterion for selection than those who had no preference (25 percent to 12 percent).

Criteria Used to Avoid Staff

Library users who avoid particular staff members have client behavior in common with those who seek out staff. They distinguish among staff members and they exhibit preferences. Fourteen percent of those who asked questions reported that they avoided specific staff members. Library users who sought specific staff members were more likely to avoid particular staff (22 percent) than those who did not (9 percent).

The reasons for avoidance were grouped into two main categories: (1) negative style of the staff member, based on past experience or perception; and (2) past experience unrelated to expertise. About half of the users avoided particular staff members because they were unpleasant to approach. Although some users avoided a particular staff member because they thought that person was a student or a nonprofessional, 56 percent of the staff members avoided were thought to be librarians. Forty-four percent avoided certain staff members because in a past experience the staff member had appeared to be too busy to deal with their inquiry, had given no help, or had given more help than the user needed.

Summary and Implications

The introductory section of this paper raised questions about how present reference practices keep users from recognizing the professionalism inherent in this activity. The data show that library users: (1) do not easily distinguish between librarians and other staff members; (2) have only a vague notion of staff differentiation; (3) are unaware of the credentials of librarians; and (4) environmental clues or other circumstantial evidence are used to identify staff by category.

Without doubt, misperceptions influence the ability of librarians to practice their profession, because librarians cannot serve effectively those who understand neither their purpose nor their expertise. If users cannot distinguish between professionals and other staff, they may respond inappropriately to the profession. Inappropriate responses may include (1) a misunderstanding of the role of the librarians as an information intermediary, (2) assuming all staff have the same credentials and provide the same level of service, (3) developing invalid criteria about whom to consult when assistance is needed, or (4) thinking of staff as merely custodians of material. Professional practice that places anonymous staff members behind the reference desk not only lacks a theoretical basis but also is dysfunctional.[22]

Present practice produces users who have little contact with librarians, usually ask only directional questions, and show little preference for who answers their questions. Most users are not true clients: their relationship is limited by present reference practice to an isolated encounter. A few users have overcome the constraints of the environment and developed a true client relationship with willing professionals or other staff.

In recent years libraries have made greater use of information desks to respond to the directional questions that make up such a large percentage of the reference work load. These desks have been staffed by nonprofessionals or students trained to answer directional questions, to provide simple bibliographic information, and to filter questions.[23] It does not appear that those who have created these desks have taken into account the limited knowledge that library users have of staff differentiation in libraries. (This statement is equally true of the presently configured reference desk.)

The information desk has great potential as a cost-effective method for providing directional information and for refering true reference inquiries to the professional staff member with the appropriate credentials at a time that is convenient for both the user and the librarian. Libraries need to experiment with models that underscore the professional functions of librarians and staff differentiation in libraries.

Altering the present reference configuration to make it more client-centered or user friendly is not a task to be undertaken lightly. Charles Martell, who recommends a total restructuring of the academic library from its traditional functional design--acquisitions, cataloging, circulation, and reference--to a number of client-centered functional work groups, believes that a new client-centered approach would require two to five years in the prototype development stage before the model could be evaluated.[24] However, prior to implementing a reformed model of client-centered reference practice, planners should consider research findings that will promote the development of a true client-professional relationship. Librarians who devise client-centered models need to examine the messages currently sent to library users by existing reference and other public service desk policies and practices.

A reconfigured reference service should exploit the benefits brought to the client-professional relationship by well-designed bibliographic instruction, online searching, faculty liaison, and other practices that highlight the expertise of librarians. It should eliminate aspects of present reference practice that confuse the public. In all likelihood, a client-centered reference model will effectively use nonprofessionals just as other professions effectively use auxiliary staff. A reconfiguration may include the provision of various physical changes in the library building and in service, e.g., clearly visible private or semiprivate offices for professional staff, methods for identifying information intermediaries by name and general area of expertise. It might also include methods that will help the user become a client and facilitate the client's ability to find the right intermediary. Such a reconfiguration should provide the basis for more accurate assessment of reference performance.

REFERENCES AND NOTES

1. Charles Martell, "Editorial: Performance at the Reference Desk,"
    College & Research Libraries 46:4 (Jan. 1985).
2. See Charles A. Bunge, "Interpersonal Dimensions of the Refer-
    ence Interview: A Historial Review of the Literature," Drexel
    Library Quarterly 20:4-23 (Spring 1984).
3. Mary Jo Lynch, "Reference Interviews in Public Libraries,"
    Library Quarterly 48:136 (April 1978).
4. Ibid.
5. A number of questions about the professional aspects of refer-
    ence are raised in Mary Biggs and others, "Replacing the Fast
    Fact Drop-In with Gourmet Information Service: A Symposium,"
    Journal of Academic Librarianship 2:68-78 (May 1985).
6. For a discussion of the issue, see Michael F. Winter, "The Pro-
    fessionalization of Librarianship." Occasional Papers no. 160
    (Urbana: University of Illinois, Graduate School of Library and
    Information Science, July 1983).
7. Ibid., p. 36.
8. Ibid., p. 37.
9. For a critical review of the evaluation of reference services,
    see Ellen Altman, "Assessment of Reference Service," in The
    Service Imperative: Essays in Honor of Margaret E. Monroe,
    ed. Gail A. Schlachter (Littleton, Colo.: Libraries Unlimited,
    1982), p. 169-85.
10. Richard A. Danner, "Reference Theory and the Future of Legal
    Reference Service," Law Library Journal 76:217 (Spring 1983).
11. Thelma Friedes, "Current Trends in Academic Libraries," Li-
    brary Trends 31:457 74 (Winter 1983). Theme issue, entitled
    "Current Trends in Reference Services."
12. Danner, p. 218.
13. See Mary Ann Swope and Jeffery Katzer, "The Silent Majority:
    Why Don't They Ask Questions?" RQ 12:161-66 (Winter 1972);
    see Bunge for a review of the literature.
14. Social psychologist Erving Goffman has examined a number of
    social interactions from the perspective of their affect on the in-
    dividual. In particular, see chapter 4 of Relations in Public
    (New York: Harper, 1971).
15. William J. Goode, "The Librarian: From Occupation to Profes-
    sion?" Library Quarterly 31:313 (Oct. 1961).
16. Peter Hernon and Maureen Pastine, "Student Perceptions of
    Academic Librarians," College & Research Libraries 38:132 (Mar.
    1977).
17. Ibid.
18. Joan C. Durrance, "The Generic Librarian: Anonymity Versus
    Accountability," RQ 22:278-83 (Spring 1983).
19. Paul Kantor's studies show that, normally, only 20 to 25 per-
    cent of academic library users are reading library materials at
    any given time. (Interview with Paul Kantor, President of
    Tantalus, Oct. 10, 1985).
20. In particular, see Swope and Katzer, Hernon and Pastine.

21. Joan C. Durrance, "Citizen Groups and the Transfer of Information in a Community" (Ph.D. Diss., University of Michigan, 1980), p. 170-74.
22. Several authors have called attention to the dysfunctional nature of presently configured reference from the perspective of the user; see Lynch, Swope and Katzer, Hernon and Pastine, and Friedes. The findings of Haack and others suggest that the reference environment contributes to burnout. Mary Haack and others, "Occupational Burnout Among Librarians," Drezel Library Quarterly 20:46-72 (Spring 1984).
23. See Martin P. Courtois and Lori A. Goetsch, "Use of Nonprofessionals at Reference Desks," College & Research Libraries 45:385-91 (Sept. 1984); Egill A. Halldorsson and Marjorie E. Murfin, "The Performance of Professionals and Nonprofessionals in the Reference Interview." College & Research Libraries 38:385-95 (Sept. 1977); Laura M. Boyer and William C. Theimer, Jr., "The Use and Training of Nonprofessional Personnel at Reference Desks in Selected College and University Libraries," College & Research Libraries 36:193-200 (May 1975).
24. Charles R. Martell, The Client-Centered Academic Library: An Organizational Model (Westport, Conn.: Greenwood, 1983), p. 102.

WHEN A LAME DUCK QUACKS:
REFLECTIONS UPON A RETIREMENT*

Martin Erlich

"When was the last time that anyone took me at my word."--
Attila the Hun to Snow White after massacring six of the
seven dwarfs.

PROLOGUE

On January 14, 1985, after months of wrestling with the pros and
cons of retirement, I submitted a letter of resignation to our new
city manager. Effective April 1, 1985, after a brilliant career span-
ning more than 37 years, mostly as a public librarian, at almost age
61, I decided to take the pension check and run. Why? Were there
too many seasons of discontent? Was the computer making a terminal
man out of me? Was the latest employee grievance about to add the
peptic to the ulcer? Would you call it "burn out" as so many do?
Reading the names of library colleagues in the obituary columns didn't
help matters either. I would say that any of the above plus a ple-
thora of ill-conceived scenarios would suffice. But way back in left
field where the grey matter gathers that stuff that dreams are made
of, there was one more fantasy looming. It goes like this.

The city manager, upon receiving my letter of resignation,
drops everything that he is doing, picks up the red phone and says,
"Martin, what is this nonsense I see before my very eyes. A letter
of resignation! Forsooth, has flipped thy lid? A man in the pride
of his prowess--a veritable lion amongst cubs. Surely thou jests!
Surely there must be some way to cause thee to change thy mind?"
Well, damn it all, surely there was a way to make me change my mind.
All of my life I had but one commodity for sale--my labor. It always
was for hire; it is now for hire; and a year from now if the price
is right, I can still be bought several times over. What would you
expect from a child of the Great Depression? But did I hear two

*Reprinted by permission of the author and publisher from The
U*N*A*B*A*S*H*E*D Librarian,tm the "How I Run My Library Good"sm
letter, no. 54: 18-21, 1985.

coins jingle? Did I hear the rustle of green paper? Did I hear a
deafening silence? You bet! The city manager and the city council
didn't even have the courtesy to offer me a fistful of dollars as an
inducement to change my mind. In general, they never hold that
high a regard for libraries, let alone librarians. Where police and
fire are concerned, the sky seems to be the limit, but libraries--
no dice. And disability awards seem to be built into their retirement
systems. Libraries--forget it!

For me to change my mind it would take at least $5,000 or a
city car, (for personal use) whichever comes first. Alas, as it was
explained to me by my friends--"Erlich, they took you at your word.
You said you were going to retire, and they believed you. They
never thought you would resort to a ploy to extort a few extra bucks."
If you ever want to play at this game, $5,000 is the right asking
price. I have seen lesser city employees get more than a $5,000
raise in one year for reasons far less worthy than mine. Anyhow,
to make a short story long (after all, I am retired now) the powers
that be accepted my resignation and so it became necessary to get
on with the show. This is the heart of the article; the do's and
don'ts or retirement.

REPEAT AFTER ME: I AM NOT INDISPENSABLE

I would advise all readers to take the following with a pillar
of salt. It is, however, predicated on the assumption that you want
to do what is best for your library. That was, indeed, my intention.
For example, though our sick leave policy leaves something to be
desired, I would never abuse it. I have seen some of my colleagues
rationalize the last sick leave day away, to their everlasting shame.

The Letter of Resignation

The crux of the matter is, how much notice to give before you
depart the scene? I can offer you the best answer, all things considered. Give three months--no more or no less. If you give less
than three months notice, the Personnel Department will never have
your replacement on deck before you leave. And a week's break in
period between the old and the new is highly desirable. Figure it
will take the Personnel Department four months to have the new librarian aboard. Why so long, you might ask? Most people forget
that the replacement should give at least one month's notice to his
or her boss. Then the city is always on the lookout to save a few
bucks at the expense of an acting interim. After all, the library runs
by itself--nicht wahr? But the reason why you must give three months
notice is for your own benefit. It takes the pension folks that long
to process your papers. Suppose, just for the sake of supposing,
that you change the date of your retirement, or you might change
your mind altogether! I have seen that happen more than once. In
my case there was no turning back. I had to save face.

RETIREMENT ...

The prime consideration for giving three months notice turns
out to be a highly practical one. I have actually seen one department
head give eighteen months notice. He lasted less than three months.
In another instance I witnessed a department head give a year's notice
of his intended retirement, and what followed was utter confusion.
Employees do not know how to react to such news. The brighter
and more perverse employees take the news with reams of glee. It
gives them the license to give the illusion of work--but in reality
they know you are a lame duck whose quack is worse than his bite.
So, don't tip your hand until you must. Three months is all you
should allow for games employees play.

Make sure that your letter of resignation is mild in tone. You
wish to spend more time with grandchildren; you wish to travel; you
wish to write the great Chinese novel; and with deftness indicate
that you are in glowing health, and willing to change your mind if
the price is right. (If that is your intention.) Don't put down dumb
things like "burn-out" or "this chicken ... outfit." You may rue
putting such sentiments on paper, especially if you ever need a letter
of recommendation, or if the powers-that-be really ask you to stay
on for a bit longer. And woe to the employees who rejoice prematurely and loudly upon learning of your intended retirement! You
get my drift.

The State of the Library Message

In addition to a letter of resignation there should also be a
State of the Library Message, addressed to the city manager. This
should cover such matters as the physical condition of the facilities;
where you have hidden grant funds in your budget; not a fink list,
but the status of library personnel; and the need for additional staff
if such is indeed the case; a word about the Library Board, the
Friends of the Library; the status of the computer and automation;
long range library plans and other matters that require the serious
attention of the city manager. A budget statement would be in order.
Are you on target for the year? going in the red? Now is a good
time to tell the city manager that you need a bigger book budget.
Always need a bigger book budget!

Will the Real Interim Please Sit Down

Before too long it will occur to you that your heir apparent
will never be on deck before you have shuffled off into retirement
land. So, it becomes imperative that you send a memo to the city
manager telling him that you need his blessings, in writing, to appoint
an interim manager. He will agree and in all likelihood, he will approve
of your choice. The interim should be the most logical, qualified

person to run the library after you have gone. Make sure you keep
the interim person apprised of your intentions. This is not a mere
exercise in gamesmanship. The transition of "power" is no joking
matter. The interim must sign many official documents, time cards,
purchase orders, claim vouchers, pick up pay checks, remove my
name from bank accounts and adding the interims, etc. Of course,
the choice of the interim gives this employee a leg-up on the internal
and external competition to succeed to the throne. (In this case,
the interim did not succeed to the throne.) And please keep sight
of the fact that after you are gone the interim really has to run the
library, sometimes for as long as two months before the issue is resolved. Now you must perform the painful duty of informing the
entire world, including the press, of your impending resignation and
the naming of the interim.

After 18-and-a-half years of steering the library ship of state,
it was obvious that I would form some fast friendships; some luke-
warm relationships; and a smattering of deep resentment, some quite
deserved, from a few. In my memo to the staff I quipped that staff
should give all possible support to the interim because she might become the real thing. I also said that from henceforth the staff could
address me as Martin, or Your Majesty, instead of Mr. Erlich. And
"if you are ever in need of money, look in the yellow pages under
Savings & Loans."

In the month that followed I worked very closely with the interim. I told her where the funds were secreted; she attended all
the meetings that I would normally attend; and she got a good dose
of evening meetings, budget preparation, getting on a first name
basis with other city department heads, the city manager, a stray
city councilman or two, fellow library directors, various vendors,
the Friends of the Library, the Library Board, and the Santiago
Library System personnel. Since the interim had been an employee
for the past 15 years there was no need to tell her who to be wary
of. She already knew. This period of divestiture was no picnic
for me either. But for me, at last I could see the dark at the end
of the tunnel.

The King Is Dead--Long Live the Queen

Without seeming to be piqued, try if possible to remove yourself as far as possible from the final selection process. You must
avoid the slightest suspicion of having a vested interest in the outcome for obvious and for some not so obvious reasons. First, there
might be other in-house contenders to the throne. Second, you have
already tipped your hand by choosing an interim and thereby giving
the interim a leg-up in the selection process. Try to avoid the writing of the job description flyer, the placing of the job advertisement
or how long it is to run; what constitutes "administrative experience";
the educational requirements and desirable background such as computer

know-how, cable tv smarts, languages, and salary. Avoid like a
plague the culling process. We had a goodly number of applicants
despite minimal advertising and getting down to a precious few was
no easy task. If you hear the term "assessment center" pretend you
have gone entirely deaf. You have nothing to gain in the selection
of your successor except the emnity of the library staff, city manager,
and city council--if your successor turns out to be a nerd. If you
help pick a winner the aforementioned get the kudos. Though you
might be tempted to play the role of king-maker, don't get carried
away by your ego. You don't need it! Let the personnel department
handle all aspects of the recruitment. That is what they get paid
to do.

"Nobody Lives Forever"--A quote from the diary Al Capone

        Don't, please don't, if humanly possible, leave your successor
with your unfinished business. Resolve any outstanding employee
grievances. Employee transfers should have been made months ago.
If you are about to initiate a new policy or procedure, like, say,
50 cents a day for an overdue book, don't do it. Don't begin an
automation project and leave in mid-stream. Don't start a collection
service for the recovery of overdue materials; don't install a new book
security system; don't initiate an employee-of-the-month program or
an ambitious series of programs for your community room. Don't
commit a huge chuck of Friends of the Library money to one of your
last pet projects like a Spanish fountain or a framed art reproduction,
or a piece of sculpture that bears a striking resemblance to you.
Such things are best left undone. Let the new Library Director make
such decisions. For all that, I did saddle my interim and eventual
successor with an enormous undertaking, but I had no alternative.
We were deep in the planning stages for a massive celebration of the
100th anniversary of library service in the City of Orange. I had
started too many committees in motion and there was no way to impede
their progress. Literary costume parade, apple pie contests, literary
essay contest, book-marathon run, Dixieland Jazz Band, all day ba-
zaar, dignitaries from the city, county and State of California would
all be there. And that was the tip of the centennial iceberg. Sorry
about that, chief.

The Captains and the Kings Depart

        On a lighter note, when you depart the scene, go like a
"mensch." This is a German word and it means, "like a real person."
With dignity. I tried very hard to go out the back door with as little
fanfare as possible. This was stupid in light of the fact that I was
a real favorite with the city. It gave staff an enormous amount of
work anyway, what with invitations, food preparation, clean-up before and after, and money. And the room where my "roasting" was
held was woefully inadequate. I knew I must have made some friends

after 18-and-a-half years of service because they couldn't all be
enemies who showed up (some 300 plus or minus). So, let it be done
the right way and stop fighting your secretary because she does know
better than you how to plan an affair in your honor. Let them pass
around the money bag and the get-well cards; arrange for a nice
restaurant; let the staff take you out to lunch if they so desire; the
City Council, the Friends of the Library, the Library Board, a vendor
or two--why deprive them? How many times do you expect to retire
in one lifetime? And if at your "roast" they wish to capture these
moments (three hours believe it or not) on video--let it be! The loot
I got! It makes me cringe with pride. VCR, Samsonite luggage, a
Pentax camera that even I can operate, enough plaques to gladden
the heart of every dentist in Orange County, resolutions commending
me for services I never remember performing, the pomp and the circumstances. I was overwhelmed with such a display of kindness and
affection for me. So, make sure that after the shouting dies, and
how soon it does, that you thank all concerned, or at least try to
get your secretary to do it for you as your last official act. God,
how I miss the smell of my office in the morning, the ringing phone,
my secretary, the photo-copy machine (A Minolta and a gem and I
don't care who knows it now), the three-ring hole punch, 3 by 5
cards, white typewriter goo. What have I done!

THE POLITICS OF INFORMATION:
LIBRARIES & ONLINE RETRIEVAL SYSTEMS*

John M. Haar

No more profound development has occurred in the information field of information science than the expansion of online retrieval systems. Begun as a government-sponsored effort to establish a fast and efficient computerized method of searching bibliographic databases and spurred by cost-reducing technological improvements, online retrieval has become the biggest growth industry in librarianship.

Most important for the future, it is now an industry firmly lodged in the private sector and dominated by profit-oriented companies.[1] The big three companies to emerge in the last decade are Lockheed Information Service of California, which markets its software under the name DIALOG; Systems Development Corporation, another California concern, which sells ORBIT; and Bibliographic Retrieval Services of New York, which calls its software by the acronym BRS.

The big three all operate in essentially the same way. They do not create their own databases; rather they buy databases, mostly indexing and abstracting services, from producers and then sell access to the cumulated data to libraries and other information agencies. There are other vendors of online retrieval systems, such as the New York Times Company and the Institute for Scientific Information, who sell their own databases, but most of the business in the field is done by the "wholesalers," who act as middlemen between database creators and users.

Online Growth

The growth of the online retrieval industry has been phenomenal, both in number of databases available in an increasing variety

*Reprinted by permission of the author and publisher from Library Journal, 111: 2 (February 1, 1986) 40-43. Published by R. R. Bowker, a division of Reed Publishing, USA; copyright © 1986 by Reed Publishing, USA, a division of Reed Holdings, Inc.

of subject areas with over 500 already available as early as 1979,[2] and more added every year since (some estimate over 2000 currently). The number of libraries purchasing database services has grown at the same rate. Commentators almost universally and quite fairly refer to it as a revolution.

While several underlying factors help explain this growth, such as our society's accelerating fascination with and dependence on computers and the almost compulsive tendency of libraries to avoid the appearance of losing their "competitive" edge to other libraries, the primary reason is apparent. The automated systems hold the promise and often even the reality of providing faster, more thorough, and more accurate bibliographic searches than the old manual method of painstaking delving through print indexes and abstracts.

As rapid as the development of the industry has been, the future appears to offer the opportunity for even more astounding expansion. A much greater variety of information sources will surely be added to the system. At least one new encyclopedia is already online; it is not hard to imagine other basic reference items and even newspapers following suit. As the various systems provide more generalized types of information it seems likely their markets will expand from academic and special libraries, where it is now centered, to public libraries and eventually into the home.

Dramatic as all the revolutionary technological capabilities of the online systems are, however, they should not distract us from addressing some very fundamental political implications of the online retrieval industry. Stripped of the glamour and allure of computer virtuosity, the basic function of the industry is to trade in the access to and manipulation of information. And information is by its nature an essential component of power in our society or any other. If this were not true, dictatorial governments would not expend so much effort to restrict access to it. Thus, how we deal with the provision of information to all our citizens has everything to do with how truly open and democratic our political system is.

Pressing Political Questions

The online retrieval industry raises pressing political questions by virtue of its very existence and growth potential because it is both privately owned and profit oriented. It has already begun to limit the public availability of information in two important ways.

First, it retains ownership of the databases involved and merely provides customer libraries with temporary and limited access to them. This is a critical departure from the traditional mode, in which libraries purchase databases (indexes, abstracts, books, or whatever) directly from vendors or publishers and can therefore provide public access to the data (i.e., information) as they wish.

Secondly, the industry has fostered restrictive access to information on the basis of cost. Because online systems are expensive, most libraries pass part of their cost on to the patron in the form of search fees. This effectively diminishes or even denies the opportunity to acquire information to those who cannot afford the charges. Though online systems are not the only service for which libraries charge, they represent the biggest threat yet to the concept of free libraries.

These matters take on even greater import when we consider-- as we must--their larger implication. In doing so we must unavoidably ask ourselves whether we as a society should treat information as a private product to be bought and sold or as a public asset equally accessible to all?

The User Fee Debate

The issue of cost has become a special center of controversy among librarians. A scan of almost any major library journal over the past few years is sure to turn up articles debating the merits or demerits of fees for library services in general and computer-based services in particular. If the articles can be counted as an informal poll, it seems that most librarians oppose charging patrons.

In 1977 the American Library Association Council branded levying fees for information as discriminatory and staunchly advocated equal access to information in principle.[3] Practice, however, is quite another matter; charging for online retrieval appears to remain much more the rule than the exception among libraries.

A point that should be repeated in this context is that libraries have long charged for a variety of nonautomated services, such as interlibrary loan or photocopying. Thus the debate over user fees is one with broad ramifications. Nonetheless the development of online retrieval systems has made the issue more acute than ever among librarians.

At the core of the argument made by those in opposition to user fees is an irrefutable assertion: that such fees confer greater access to information upon some patrons than upon others solely on the basis of ability to pay. It is hard to avoid the conclusion that the result is nothing less than an economic form of censorship.[4] Wealthier patrons can simply afford to buy more information than poorer ones, an equation of inequality that applies to independently wealthy congressmen as opposed to welfare recipients, full professors as opposed to graduate students--even large corporations as opposed to small businesses.[5]

If the product involved were merely hamburgers or television sets, this situation might be tolerable. When the product is information, however, so closely tied to power, what occurs is a rigidifying of social and political inequities that democracies are supposed to ameliorate.

The irony in all this is that as more sophisticated tools are developed to access information, it well could become less accessible to more people. At present the problem is limited in scope if only because most online databases contain predominately esoteric information of interest to a relative few scholars, researchers, and technologists. It is sure to become more critical when information with broader appeal, the 1980 census for example, goes online.

The fact that most online databases are currently available in print also seems to lessen the impact of computer charges. It is clearly possible that the future will bring fewer print alternatives as database producers go exclusively online or as libraries cut back on orders for print copies in response to tighter budgets. Unequal access is a problem that will not be avoided easily.

Proponents of user fees for online retrieval most frequently justify their position through the simple dictum that online service is unavoidably expensive. They maintain that libraries, already strapped by rising costs and inadequate financial support, have to subsidize their expenses for computer hardware and software and even the staff time required for assistance to online patrons.[6] Advocates are also quick to note that fees for online services do not represent a new concept, merely an extension of an old one.[7]

That online retrieval systems are expensive is an arguably valid point, but expense alone hardly seems a sufficient reason for providing the systems on a fee basis.

Maintaining an adequate book collection is also an enormously expensive undertaking for most larger libraries, yet few would ever think of compensating for this through the imposition of user charges for the entire collection. The mere fact that online systems involve a different mode of information delivery--one that easily lends itself to billing for finely specified units[8]--is no cause to provide them through an economic rationale different from that used in the provision of books.

Another defense of user fees holds that they are actually beneficial in that only those using the online service will pay for it, while those who have no need of it will not have to bear the expense.[9] Beyond ignoring the very real possibility that some who have need of the service may not be able to afford to pay, this argument has another fundamental weakness. Carried to its logical extreme, it advocates the end of all tax subsidies to libraries since many, if not most, of those paying taxes make no use of any library service.[10]

After considering all the arguments, libraries will have to

recognize that there is no compelling justification for charging for
online retrieval. On the other hand, providing such services free
of charge appears the only sensible approach, particularly if we remember that the library's chief service is providing information and
that restricting access to information by price or any other means is
politically repressive to democracy.

Information Ownership

The other political issue generated by online retrieval systems
is the matter of who owns them. This is an even more serious concern than user fees. Like fees, it raises the question of whether
information is to be treated as a public or private commodity, only
it does so much more pointedly. The potential dangers of the present trend to private ownership are much more awesome to contemplate
than the abuses of patron charges. It is, therefore, surprising--
even appalling--that so little has been written about the significance
of the ownership of online databases in library literature.

One consequence of the arrival of regional and national online
systems is that individual libraries already have less control over
various databases and the means of gaining access to them, a situation likely to become even more pronounced in the future. It is the
database producers and, increasingly, the database vendors who
retain more and more of such control. In the traditional chain of
transactions, each library purchases data--the Readers' Guide, for
instance--from a vendor and controls it to the extent of determining who may use it and with what types of finding aids users will
be provided.

If the same library becomes a DIALOG subscriber, however,
it purchases only access to a database controlled by the vendor,
who can terminate access at almost any time. It gains that access
only through finding aids (software) provided by the vendor. Furthermore, unlike the Readers' Guide, which libraries pay for once
and use forever, access to DIALOG, even repeated access for the
same information, costs repeatedly.[11] Clearly libraries are political
and economic losers in the transition from print to online data.

But what of patrons? Do they gain through the allocation of
information through private corporations as opposed to libraries?
This seems highly unlikely. Some libraries are, of course, more
service oriented than others, but almost all academic and public libraries are motivated by some sense of public good. The corporate
vendors of databases, on the other hand, are motivated solely by
profit and self-interest, objectives which leave little room for a sense
of social obligation to provide equally for the information needs of
everyone.

The Danger of Manipulation

Whatever the current inequities, they pale before the potential for abuses in this area. The greatest danger lies in the realization that the control of databases carries with it the power to manipulate them. In the past sheer numbers prevented this from being problematical. If thousands of libraries own thousands of copies of the same controversial political tract, this alone serves at least as protection against its universal expurgation or confiscation. What would happen, however, if this same document existed only on a few machine-readable tapes unowned by any library?

We may not be so far away from a future in which not only indexes and abstracts, but also encyclopedias, newspapers, periodicals, and even monographs will exist exclusively online.

Material included within them could be modified or deleted without the control or even the knowledge of libraries or librarians, to the detriment of good library service. Encyclopedias, for instance, regularly undergo revision. With print copies libraries can retain older editions as a matter of historical interest to serve as a means of tracing changing scholarly or societal attitudes. Will this be possible when the revisions are made on magnetic tape?

There are more sinister possibilities to consider. Online systems present no safeguards, other than the good will of the producers and vendors, that databases and software will not be manipulated, in fact censored, for political purposes.

Can libraries afford--for that matter can society afford--to be smugly confident that corporations would not be tempted to tamper with news reports critical of their activities or detrimental to their profit margins? The same technological dexterity that makes online systems so popular, also confers upon their owners unparalleled power to prejudice public opinion or rewrite history.

Libraries would do well to keep this power from falling exclusively into the hands of the online retrieval industry. Even if vital political concerns were not at stake, self-interest is motive enough. Private control of the new technology presents an unmistakable threat to the library's survival as a major purveyor of information.

The online systems vendors are surely looking beyond the library and into the home as the lucrative market of the future. Experiments in home-computer information delivery have already begun, and one can easily visualize a giant online industry selling DIALOG, ORBIT, BRS, and much more directly into living rooms before too long. At best, such a turn of events would leave libraries with a vastly constricted range of services to offer to a shrinking clientele. At worst it would leave the public completely unprotected against the mismanagement of information.

Libraries as Marketers

Ironically the online vendors are currently using libraries to develop their markets, and libraries, wittingly or not, are subsidizing these efforts.[12]   The typical subscriber library provides space and facilities for the retrieval system's hardware.   More importantly, it provides staff members to assist or perform searches, at considerable salary cost.   Despite this the library still pays the vendor a rental fee!   All the while the vendor continues to cultivate a growing body of customers which it can later lure away from the library through the tempting attraction of convenient database searches in their own homes.

Library Action

If libraries are to help prevent the online retrieval industry from monopolizing information storage and delivery they must take action very soon.   Otherwise the industry may well have established such an overwhelming economic and political momentum in its favor that resistance will be all but impossible.   There are signs that this process is already underway.

In 1979 database producers reported that their sales of print abstracts and indexes in the United States were either static or declining,[13] perhaps an indication that the availability of print alternatives to online systems had begun to diminish.

A recent government pronouncement on the foundations of U.S. information policy, though recognizing some of the inequities involved, touts information as a free market good,[14] which can only be an encouragement to those who would treat online data as a commodity useful for yielding profits.

For any action to be successful, libraries will have to be prepared to make a strong case to the public and to themselves that information is too precious an asset and too important a political instrument to be distributed in a discriminatory manner.   They must further argue that they, not profit-oriented companies, represent society's best guarantee against the unequal dissemination and the imprudent and even malicious manipulation of information.

Along these lines they would do well to reform some of their own discriminatory practices, such as levying user fees for online searches or other services.

There will also need to be some sort of consensus among librarians on how to remedy the economic and entrepreneurial problems online databases present.   Some have suggested government ownership of database vending services as a kind of public utility, but this presents obvious political dangers of its own.[15]

A favorite proposal of vendors is to erect a two-tiered access structure, in which patrons who can afford to pay will be charged, while those who cannot will be allowed free searches.[16] It is hard to conceive of a method to determine who can afford fees without invading patrons' privacy. Others speak of using vouchers similar to food stamps for library services,[17] yet this system, aside from being cumbersome, still amounts to charging fees and allots only certain limited increments of service to those who cannot pay.

A Library Database Consortium

Perhaps the best long-term solution is for libraries to form a nonprofit consortium to vend databases, a system that would assure them of control of the data and methods of access to it. Until such an organization is feasible, individual libraries might consider other means of retaining as much control as possible over information.

One possibility is to insist that producers of online databases also produce the same data in print. This would mean a refusal to buy the online version if no print version were available.

All of these options, from dropping user fees to forming a consortium, would be unquestionably expensive. They are expenses that libraries will have to carry, even if it means cutting back in other areas. The issue is no less than the open and democratic provision of information, one that cannot be irresponsibly sloughed off on the grounds of economic expediency.

References

1. By 1977 the government produced only 41 percent of the databases available online. Martha E. Williams, "Databases, Computer-Readable," in The ALA Yearbook 1977, American Library Assn., 1977, p. 109.
2. Williams, Martha E., "Databases, Computer Readable," in The ALA Yearbook 1980, American Library Assn., 1980, p. 128.
3. Kent, Allen, "The Potential of On-Line Information Systems," in The On-Line Revolution in Libraries: Proceedings of the 1977 Conference in Pittsburgh, Pennsylvania. ed. by Allen Kent & Thomas J. Galvin. Dekker, 1978, p. 21; and "Council and Membership Step into Action," American Libraries, July/August 1977, p. 378.
4. Horn, Zoia, "Charging for Computer-Based Reference Services: Some Issues of Intellectual Freedom," in Charging for Computer-Based Reference Services. ed. by Peter G. Watson. Reference and Adult Services Division, American Library Assn., 1978, p. 17.
5. Wessel, Andrew E. The Social Use of Information--Ownership and Access. Information Sciences Series, Wiley, 1976, p. 88-89.

6. Cooper, Michael D., "Charging Users for Library Service,"
    Information Processing & Management, 1978, p. 419; and Carlos
    A. Cuadra, "Potential: Commentary," in Kent, The On-Line
    Revolution, p. 57.

7. Cooper, Ibid., "Charging Users," p. 420.

8. Ibid., p. 419.

9. Ibid., p. 426.

10. There are, indeed, some who make this argument. See Marilyn
    Killebrew Gell, "User Fees II: The Library Response," LJ.
    January 15, 1979, p. 172.

11. Kent, op. cit., "Potential of On-Line Information," p. 20.

12. Schiller, Anita R., "The Potential of On-Line Systems: The
    Librarian's Role," in Kent, The On-Line Revolution, p. 33;
    and "The Prostitution of Information: Fees for Service," Amer-
    ican Library Association Social Responsibilities Round Table
    Newsletter, no. 45, 1977, p. 1.

13. Williams, op. cit., "Databases, Computer Readable," in The
    ALA Yearbook 1979, American Library Assn., 1979, p. 98.

14. Bushkin, Arthur A. & Jane H. Yurow, "The Foundations of
    United States Information Policy," Information Hotline, October
    1980, p. 16.

15. Wessel, op. cit., Social Use of Information, p. 60.

16. Cooper, op. cit., "Charging Users," p. 426; and Samuel A.
    Wolpert, "Potential: Reaction," in Kent, The On-Line Revolu-
    tion, p. 29.

17. Zurkowski, Paul G., "Information Control and Marketplace Feas-
    ibility," in Information Systems and Networks: Eleventh Annual
    Symposium. ed. by John Sherrod, Greenwood Pr., 1975, p. 198-
    199.

DEFINING THE ACADEMIC LIBRARIAN*

Edward G. Holley

Fifteen years ago, when I was still director of libraries at the University of Houston, I addressed the Southeastern Library Association on "What the Modern Library Expects of the New Graduate."[1] This was before I became a dean and therefore was very certain about what a library director ought to expect from our professional schools. Like those directors of academic and public libraries whom Herbert White surveyed recently, my expectations didn't always square with what other directors wanted.[2] I particularly remember one distinguished librarian taking me to task for stating that a modern foreign language wasn't high on my list for most beginning librarians. Other participants found different points of view with which to disagree. Included was one vigorous faculty member from the institution where I subsequently became dean. I was cheered by Lester Asheim, later to join me at Carolina, who had just completed the "Library Education and Professional Utilization Statement," now more familiarly known as the "Asheim Statement." Asheim had also addressed the Southeastern librarians. In our friendly chat afterwards, he remarked, "We don't really disagree, do we?" We really did not. As I look back on that conference, I am amazed at how brash I was-- brash and independent. I'm a little less brash today, but no less independent. I am also amazed, as I re-read my remarks, at how relevant they sound today.

Enough, though, of this southern chronicle. One of my strongest points then, as it is today, was that academic librarians need to know far more than the technical skills they learn in library school. They need to know especially the social, economic, and political context in which the library operates. That seemed such a simple view, coming as it did three decades after the Louis Round Wilson years at the Graduate Library School of the University of Chicago, but it is one which seems so difficult to convey to librarians--actual and

*Reprinted by permission of the author and publisher from College & Research Libraries, 46:6 (November 1985) 462-468; copyright © 1985 by the American Library Association. This paper was presented at the ACRL University Libraries Section program, ALA Annual Conference (Chicago, 1985).

potential. Here are some of my actual statements on the kind of
orientation I thought the academic librarian needed:

> Some background in the history and development of higher
> education ... an appreciation for the history of scholarship
> and learning and the way knowledge is obtained in various
> disciplines ... and the ability to evaluate research findings.

After more than thirty-five years in academia, I believe even
more strongly today that these characteristics should define the academic librarian. For one of the truly appalling facts about faculty
in colleges and universities (not just librarians) is the widespread
ignorance of how our colleges and universities became what they are
today, what constitutes their general mission, and how the political
milieu, on and off campus, affects all of us. That general ignorance
often leads to counterproductive efforts both by librarians and teaching faculty. Let me cite an example.

After a recent University of North Carolina (UNC) Faculty
Council meeting, in which our faculty legislative body passed a number of pious resolutions with no chance of implementation, I discussed the faculty's irresponsibility with a senior historian colleague.
My friend, who had been secretary of the Faculty Council for fifteen
years, shook his head sadly and remarked, "Yes, you're right. I've
noticed the faculty increasingly evade their responsibility in this
area. The net result is that they have no credibility with the administration or the trustees. The trustees dismiss such resolutions
out of hand. Ultimately such behavior is very harmful to the university." Of one thing you can always be sure, though. In any
list of priorities, faculty salaries and fringe benefits always rank
first, sabbatical leaves second, libraries third or fourth, and educational policies far down the list. One could be cynical about this.
Nonetheless, our faith in scholarship and learning persists, even
among those of us who are aware of how far short we fall in our
attempts to promote that great triad of teaching, research, and public
service for which American universities are noted. One sometimes
wishes he could remind various faculty groups of a statement by
Herbert Putnam, Librarian of Congress, who in 1904 admonished
ALA members to "Let no guilty ignorance escape." Lack of knowledge
about how our own institutions operate and what is their function in
society must surely be included among "guilty ignorance."

One general ignorance among faculty is the role of the university administrator. Having just finished a six-month stint as
chairperson of the search committee for UNC's dean of the general
college and the college of arts and sciences, I assure you that views
of faculty about what they want in a dean are as diverse as the
qualities librarians want to find in library directors and those qualities library directors want to find in beginning librarians. There
are some common threads, however, and it is those common threads
I will discuss.

Let me start by renewing my faith in the need for academic librarians to possess four kinds of knowledge in addition to his or her professional library skills:

1. A background in the history and development of higher education

2. An appreciation for the history of scholarship and learning

3. An understanding of how knowledge is obtained in various disciplines

4. An abilty to evaluate research findings

Many of you will recognize that these views are not very different from those Louis Round Wilson enunciated in an article, "What Type Research Librarian?" thirty-five years ago at a University of Pennsylvania symposium on "Changing Patterns of Scholarship and the Future of Research Libraries."[3] In part, they have been repeated recently by Patricia Battin and by David Weber during an interview with Russell Fischer.[4,5]

As a historian I could even go back fifty-five years to Charles Harvey Brown's chapter in the U.S. Office of Education's Survey of Land Grant Colleges and Universities.[6] Brown held an exalted vision of the academic librarian's role in the college and university, one from which he did not waver during his long and productive life, though he recognized that many individuals fell below the ideal.

Let me now address each in turn, and try to assess why the academic librarian needs each.

1. Background in the history and development of higher education. Colleges and universities intrigue me, just as their libraries intrigue me: not necessarily because I am a library historian, although that may help. My intellectual curiosity is aroused by such diverse questions as "How did the American university come to adopt the pattern of an English undergraduate college as its base and place the Germanic professional and graduate schools on the top?" "Why did the University of Illinois develop, in the middle of the corn fields, one of the greatest Milton collections in the world?", and "Why did Iowa State University, where Charlie Brown served so well, develop as a research institution long before other separate land grant colleges emerged as significant research institutions?" These are not questions just for the historian. Answers to such questions will provide new insight into the nature of the institutions where we work.

The politics of higher education also interests me. Externally, these questions seem pertinent. "What impact has the development of state boards of higher education had upon the development of libraries and the research function of universities?" "What long-range

impact will result from that fact that 85 percent of the North Carolina legislators serve on one or more trustee boards of private colleges and universities?" (The answer may well be self-evident as
North Carolina approaches a budget of $25 million annually in state
subsidies for private institutions.) "How can the librarian influence
decisions made by board staff at the Coordinating Board, Texas College and University System, or the Illinois Board of Higher Education?" Answers to these questions affect libraries in very important ways. An understanding of the broader picture of higher education would help us formulate strategies for achieving our goals.

On a campus the following questions are relevant. "What is
the organizational structure through which decisions are made?"
"Why is it that over the past twenty-five years the head librarian
no longer reports to the president but reports to a vice-president
sometimes for academic affairs, sometimes for support services?"
"Does it make any difference?", "What is the path for appointment,
promotion, and tenure recommendations at this particular college or
university?", "Do librarians have the same review path and are decisions partially governed by a campuswide advisory body as are other
faculty appointments?"

I fear that we often graduate from library schools students
who have not wrestled with these questions. Yet I know that we
are not alone on campus. I once knew a dean who never understood
the basis upon which his worst cases were regularly rejected by a
personnel committee over a period of years. His political naivete
served him and his school poorly. Librarians can ill afford the
luxury of such ignorance. Anyone who believes that multimillion-
dollar operations can function without involvement in the political
process or an understanding of fairly well-defined structures that
reflect basic academic values is surely living in a dream world. Ultimately, the campus political situation is dominated by the arts and
sciences faculty, the largest and most influential group on campus,
whose power is enormous when they choose to use it. We ignore the
fact at our peril.

2. An appreciation for the history of scholarship and learning.
I assume that the reason most of us are academic librarians as opposed to being public, school, or special librarians is that (1) we
enjoy the academic life, (2) we want to be a part of the learning
process, (3) we have some modest or active interest in research,
and (4) we value the place of the library in learning and scholarship.
The life of the mind, especially in our information-based society, ex-
cites us, and we want to be a part of institutions critical to the functioning of our democratic society. To participate fully in these intellectual endeavors we need to know something about the history of
scholarship, how learning takes place, what role our institutions play
in higher education, and how both scholarship and learning are
changing. While we do not necessarily have to be scholars ourselves
(many faculty are not, whatever the pretense), we have to be schol-

arly persons, with keen intellectual curiosity and have something to contribute to the enterprise beyond what we learned in liberal arts colleges or graduate professional schools ten, twenty, or thirty years ago.

3. The way knowledge is obtained in various disciplines. In an earlier period, or maybe I should say in the period when I entered higher education, the way knowledge was obtained in various disciplines was fairly well established. In the humanities we researched in libraries and archival repositories. In the social sciences we used both libraries and field work, especially number-crunching through calculators but also through survey instruments of a rather primitive kind. In the sciences we depended upon the laboratory, with strong back-up services such as Chemical Abstracts, Chemisches Zentralblatt, or the Bibliography of North American Geology.

But as Charles Osburn has pointed out in his excellent book, Academic Research and Library Resources: Changing Patterns in America, the ways in which knowledge is obtained, at least for research purposes, has changed markedly in the years since World War II.[7] "In an increasing number of disciplines, the library is no longer the most important repository."[8] Agencies and avenues other than the library have become involved in the exchange of information on an increasingly large scale. Chief among these ... is the computer center."[9] These new agencies, with the help of federal grants, support reasearch that emphasizes social relevance, service to contemporary society, quantification (even in library study), a cross-disciplinary approach and team-project research, extensive use of the invisible college, and an intensification of laboratory and field work. Such research puts a high premium on current literature and rapid access to it. Experimental research is often narrowly focused with little need for the historical approach that resulted in massive collection building in an earlier period. Access to a hard core of literature and to a more carefully targeted search of that literature seems more important to some faculty than large collections. Manipulation of enormous quantities of statistical data is essential for an increasing number of disciplines. The question of coordinating these information agencies and libraries is certainly a major issue for many institutions in addition to my own. I am not sure that many librarians, directors included, are as sensitive to these changes as they need to be.

Librarians, if they are to serve their faculties and students well, must be attuned to the new ways in which researchers handle data. We take the use of the computer for granted. It helps us in numerous ways besides number-crunching or administrative chores. In the future, the computer will assist the researcher in ways not yet imaginable. Fortunately, we are developing our own research skills to investigate the uses of research literature, published and unpublished, through citation analysis studies, bibliometrics, sophisticated statistics, and other means. Search strategies for use of

computerized data are the equipment of all new reference librarians.
Improved subject access to databases is a constant plea. The aim
of all this activity is to understand the way knowledge is obtained
in various disciplines so that the academic librarian can help users
do their research work better.

    4. <u>An ability to evaluate research</u>. These three kinds of
knowledge cumulate in the need of the librarian to evaluate research.
Citation analysis is a wonderful tool, but it must be used with care.
Bibliometric techniques tell us a lot, but they don't tell us everything. Statistics are important, despite Disraeli's admonition about
the three kinds of lies: "Lies, damned lies, and statistics." Even
as a person with a modest knowledge of statistics and computers, I
discover that I know when the numbers don't tell us what they purport to tell us. Yes, even multiple regression analysis is not the
whole answer. Just because some of our literature represents the
worst of research techniques (e.g., the Houser-Schrader volume or
Ralph Conant's book on library education) doesn't mean that there
hasn't been remarkable progress in adding to our store of knowledge
about our profession and its activities in the last forty years. If
we believe that knowledge is cumulative (and as a historian I could
hardly argue with that!), then we have to rejoice that the knowledge
base of our profession has expanded at a gratifying pace in recent
years.

    I pause here to note two important pieces of good advice Hugh
Atkinson gave twelve library educators at our Research Libraries Institute in Chapel Hill last summer: "Don't put the profession down"
and "Don't put the professional literature down." To those who tell
me how pedestrian and dull library literature is, I invite you to examine the major journals in the disciplines of English, history, so-
ciology, and even, God help us, theology that line the periodical
shelves in your libraries. Yet these are journals that report basic
findings upon which further knowledge can be built. As an editorial
board member of several journals, I am often amazed at how many
manuscripts reveal that the author has not searched the relevant
literature. Our students need to be taught that an important part
of their professional obligation is to search the research record.
We can hardly ignore the need for doing what we encourage in others.

    These four kinds of knowledge seem to me basic in any defini-
tion of the academic librarian. Now I want to turn to the question
of academic credentials which the academic librarian ought to have.
You will not be surprised to learn that I am strongly committed to
a basic liberal arts education and an M.L.S. degree as the foundation for professional practice.

    In the last couple of years I have attained some sort of repu-
tation (notoriety, some would say) for defending the M.L.S. degree
as an entirely reasonable standard for the <u>beginning</u> professional
librarian. I stress that "beginning" because I certainly don't regard

the M.L.S. as the "ending" point either for formal or informal study.
While my mother didn't raise her son to be an expert witness, I felt
a strong professional obligation to defend the M.L.S. degree in the
case of Glenda Merwine v. Mississippi State University. Needless
to say, I was elated when the U.S. Fifth Circuit Court of Appeals
affirmed Judge Charles Powers's decision, in every particular, in the
Merwine case. What pleased me most, aside from the ignoble feeling
of personal triumph, was a belief that the court had ruled in favor
of "logic and common sense," to use Judge Powers's happy phrase.
For if the library profession, and if academia generally, cannot defend its M.L.S. degree on the basis both of logic and common sense
as the principal credential for entry into our profession, then our
claim to professional status and social usefulness is indeed called
into serious question. Let me quote from some of the Fifth Circuit's
key phrases:

> The evidence presented by Merwine, with all reasonable
> inferences drawn in her favor, does not persuade this Court
> that Lewis' adherence to the ALA-MLS degree requirement
> was pretextual. All this evidence, viewed favorably to Mer-
> wine, points without hestitation to the opposite conclusion.
> The uncontradicted evidence establishes that the ALA-MLS
> degree is a legitimate nondiscriminatory standard for hiring
> academic librarians. It is a standard widely recognized and
> utilized by academic and professional employers, including
> the United States Supreme Court. In addition, as the par-
> ties stipulated, at the time Merwine's application was under
> consideration, six applications were before the hiring com-
> mittee. Three of the applicants, two females and one male,
> possessed the required degree and only these three were
> interviewed for the position. None of the applicants without
> the degree was even considered. Lewis' uniform application
> of the degree requirement is indicative that his denial of
> Merwine's application for the same reason was not pretextual
> in nature*....

> We agree with the magistrate's finding that no reasonable
> jury could find that the preference for such a degree was
> a pretext in view of the total lack of any credible evidence
> indicating the preference for such a degree was not a legiti-
> mate, nondiscriminatory factor uniformly applied to all appli-
> cants. Accordingly, we hold that the magistrate did not err
> in granting judgment for Lewis notwithstanding the jury's
> verdict....

> ... We believe that MSU's preference for an objective degree

*Note: On October 7, 1985, the U.S. Supreme Court denied Merwine's
petition for a writ of certiorari, therefore affirming the ruling of the
lower courts.

requirement that is widely recognized by academic and professional employers and that is required by approximately
eighty percent of college and university libraries is supported
as a valid business necessity. Our review of the record indicates that the magistrate was not clearly erroneous in concluding that the ALA-MLS degree requirement had a manifest
relationship to the position Merwine sought.[10]

The Merwine case was surely one of the significant attacks
upon academic credentials in recent years. If one agrees with the
courts, then it is clear that both the courts and professional practice in academic libraries have sustained the M.L.S. degree as a
basic requirement for academic librarians. Yet the court case does
not answer all the questions, nor does it provide comfort for those
who also contend that the M.L.S., by itself, is the only credential
an academic librarian needs. In a college or university where the
doctorate in most disciplines is regarded as the "terminal degree,"
and lack of it constitutes grounds for dismissal from the teaching
faculty, the librarian who aspires to faculty recognition still has a
problem. In political terms, the problem is how one navigates among
the minefields laid by promotion and tenure committees in the absence
of the common understanding of the phrase, "terminal degree." (Surely
"terminal degree" is an inappropriate term in these days of rapid
changes, though one can agree that there are some faculty in academia for whom it has been terminal in a very real sense.) We should
note here that our insistence, through the ACRL guidelines, that the
M.L.S. is the "terminal degree" for librarians has not achieved wide
acceptance on most campuses and, in my opinion, is likely to be even
less persuasive in the future.[11]

In overtenured universities, personnel committees have tightened
standards for tenure and look with jaundiced eyes at the record of
teaching, research, and service of all faculty appointments. As librarians, we do better on teaching (broadly defined) and service
than we do on research. In the absence of the doctorate, one's record has to be extraordinarily strong to convince our other university
colleagues that our records are indeed equivalent to theirs and our
contributions as significant.

Recent research indicates that more and more academic librarians
either possess, or are working on, subject master's or doctoral degrees.
John Olsgaard's study of success among academic librarians indicated
that more than one-third of the persons in this study possessed a
second master's degree and an additional 10 percent held doctorates.[12]
Terrence Mech's study of directors of small college libraries in the
Midwest indicated a similar pattern.[13] Mech added, "Holding graduate degrees in addition to the M.L.S. is almost a universal requirement to obtain a director's position in any size college."[14] A study
by Robert Swisher, Peggy Smith, and Calvin Boyer in 1978 found
that 29 percent of academic librarians held a second master's degree
and another 7 percent were pursuing that degree; 8 percent held

the doctorate and another 6 percent were pursuing it.[15]   Dorothy
Anderson's recent study of Council on Library Resources (CLR)
Senior Fellows provides additional confirmation of the importance of
additional graduate work for leadership success.[16]   The evidence
that educational qualifications for the academic librarian are rising
seems clear. I would predict that they will continue to rise in the
future. The data in these four studies, incidentally, indicate that
the courts were right about the M.L.S. being held by most academic
librarians. Olsgaard's study showed 92 percent holding the M.L.S.
plus 5 percent with the old B.L.S.[17]   Mech and Swisher, et al.,
indicated that the fifth year professional degree was held by more
than 90 percent of academic librarians.[18,19]

What does all this say about defining the academic librarian?
Realistically, the academic librarian today must have an M.L.S. degree.
That degree is assumed to provide a student with the professional
and technical skills he or she needs to begin the practice of academic
librarianship. Included in formal study for the M.L.S. should certainly be those core elements Dean White discovered in his survey:
basic reference, collection development, academic libraries, personnel
and human relations, introduction to information science, and organization of materials.[20]   Hopefully, either in these courses or elsewhere in the curriculum, the student will be introduced to the four
types of knowledge I have discussed. The broader the training, the
more likely the individual will have these understandings, as well as
the professional skills so necessary in today's libraries.

Is there life beyond the M.L.S.? Yes, but in the words of
the old business school slogan, "The future belongs to those who prepare for it." We must take into account the political context of higher
education, not only as it exists today but as it will probably exist
tomorrow. In academia, courses and degrees are the coin of the realm.
In that context the M.L.S. is crucial for most positions, but it is
only the beginning point. The trends are clear. To plan one's career
so that one can compete successfully in an academic world with fewer
but more sophisticated librarians, academic librarians will need all
the education they can obtain. One may view such additional preparation either pragmatically (as the union card for status among one's
colleagues), or nobly (as a means of participating in the intellectual
challenge of teaching and research). For me, after equally long
years both in the practice and the teaching of librarianship in colleges and universities, I prefer to stress the latter. I still view the
academic library as a place of intellectual excitement, basic and continued learning, and professional growth and development. The best
libraries, in my opinion, can continue to be such places. To do so,
however, they will need politically astute librarians with strong professional credentials and solid research interests. Such librarians
will not only benefit personally from such preparation; they will also
make even greater contributions to learning and scholarship--which
is, after all, what our colleges and universities are about.

References

1. Edward G. Holley, "The Librarian Speaks: What the Modern Library Expects of the New Graduate," Southeastern Librarian 20:222-31 (Winter 1970).
2. Herbert S. White and Marion Paris, "Employer Preferences and the Library Education Curriculum," Library Quarterly 55:1-33 (Jan. 1985).
3. Louis Round Wilson, "What Type Research Librarian?" Changing Patterns of Scholarship and the Future of Research Libraries; A Symposium (Philadelphia: University of Pennsylvania Press, 1951), p. 112-22.
4. Patricia Battin, "Developing University and Research Library Professionals," American Libraries 14:22-25 (Jan. 1983).
5. Russell Fischer, "Managing Research Libraries: An Interview with David Weber," Wilson Library Bulletin 59:319-23 (Jan 1985).
6. Charles Harvey Brown, "Library," in Survey of Land-Grant Colleges and Universities, USOE Bulletin, 1930, no. 9, v. 1, p. 679-93.
7. Charles B. Osburn, Academic Research and Library Resources: Changing Patterns in America (Westport, Conn.: Greenwood, 1979).
8. Ibid., p. 91.
9. Ibid., p. 148.
10. U.S. Court of Appeals, Fifth Circuit. Glenda Merwine vs. Board of Trustees for State Institutions of Higher Learning et al; Defendants-Appellees. no. 84-4036, March 8, 1985.
11. John Budd, "The Education of Academic Librarians," College & Research Libraries 45:19 (Jan. 1984).
12. John N. Olsgaard, "Characteristics of 'Success' Among Academic Librarians," College & Research Libraries 18:5-14 (Jan. 1984).
13. Terrence Mech, "Small College Library Directors of the Midwest," Journal of Academic Librarianship 11:8-13 (Mar. 1985).
14. Mech, p. 10.
15. Robert D. Swisher, Peggy C. Smith, and Calvin J. Boyer. "Educational Change Among ACRL Academic Librarians," Library Research 5:195-205 (Summer 1983).
16. Dorothy J. Anderson, "Comparative Profiles of Academic Librarians: Are Leaders Different," Journal of Academic Librarianship 10:326-332 (Jan 1985).
17. Olsgaard, p. 5-14.
18. Mech, p. 8-13.
19. Swisher, p. 195-205.
20. White and Paris, p. 1-33.

NATIONAL PLANNING AND THE IMPACT OF ELECTRONIC TECHNOLOGY ON DOCUMENT PROVISION AND SUPPLY*

Maurice B. Line

Introduction

In this paper I shall use the term 'document provision and supply,' in preference to the increasingly old-fashioned 'interlending.' Much interlibrary traffic involves photocopies of articles sent by one library to another. Some articles are obtained direct from publishers or commercial document suppliers. Most important, interlending is of no use unless the material is there to be supplied. What countries need is not simply a document supply system, but a provision and supply system.[1]

The growing importance of document provision and supply systems is not due mainly to an increase in the volume of publications, nor does it seem that on-line bibliographic searching does much to increase interlibrary loan demand; what evidence there is suggests that only about one eighth of interlibrary document requests are generated as a result of on-line searches.[2] The crucial factor is that the budgets of libraries have not been able to keep pace with increases in the price of library materials.

Requirements of National Document Provision and Supply System[3]

The most obvious requirement is a high fill rate--the proportion of demand satisfied. However, quite a high fill rate can be achieved with a poor system, because it may attract very little demand, and that only for items virtually certain to be supplied. The fill rate is therefore meaningful only if it is taken together with the volume of demand, which is one measure of the success of a system.

An equally obvious requirement is fast supply.

*Reprinted by permission of the author and publisher from Libri, 35:3 (1985) 181-190; copyright © 1985 Munksgaard International Publishers, Ltd., Copenhagen, Denmark.

A less obvious requirement is ease of use. People will tend to use an 'easy' system in preference to a 'difficult' system even though they know the latter is likely to perform better. Also, a system that is difficult to use costs money in staff time. Another requirement is ability to monitor performance, to enable the system to be responsive to changing needs.

A further requirement is the ability to access the utility of documents in advance of requesting. Many items must be requested that prove on receipt to be unnecessary.

Finally, the system should be such as to fulfill the necessary requirements at minimal cost. Costings of document supply systems should take into account not only the total costs of the requesting or supplying institution, but the construction and maintenance of union catalogues, money spent on additional acquisitions in cooperative schemes, and so on.

The Performance of Traditional ILL Systems

How do existing systems perform against the above requirements?[4]

The fill rate tends to be low, perhaps in the region of 70%. There may be several reasons for this: The items wanted may never have been acquired in the country; their owners may not be willing to supply them; or they may be in use already. Fill rates can be improved by more comprehensive national provision. In a decentralized system, libraries may cooperate in their acquisitions to achieve better total provision than they could by working independently. However, cooperative acquisition schemes require either plentiful funds, which are a thing of the past, or special additional funding, which is rarely forthcoming. The administration of an effective cooperative acquisition scheme is inevitably complex, and the cost may be quite high. Moreover, materials acquired for the general good rather than the local good constitute a special responsibility on the libraries that acquire them. Cooperative acquisition schemes have had a sad history in general; when money is plentiful they are less necessary, and when it is short libraries find it very difficult to spend some of their diminishing resources on material that they do not need for their own clients, but that the clients of some other library may want some time.[5]

As noted above, the fill rate has to be taken together with the volume of demand. A comparison of two such countries in Europe and at a similar stage of development of a similar size shows that one has four times the volume of demand that the other has; this is not due to superior collections or acquisitions in the libraries of the second country. Demand is largely a function of supply.

Speed of supply is usually poor--perhaps typically three weeks between requesting and receipt. This is not generally due to delays in actual transmission, which are rarely more than two or three days in most developed countries. One reason is that many requests have to go to two, three or more libraries before they are satisfied; another is that supply to other libraries inevitably take a lower priority than service to the library's own clients, so that requests from other libraries often have to wait.

Most systems are not easy to use. There may be several union catalogues to have to be searched; searching them and locating holding libraries can take some time; requests for, say, 20 items may have to be sent to 20 different libraries; and each supplying library may have slightly different rules and procedures. As for monitoring performance, this is virtually impossible except by conducting frequent and extensive surveys.

Utility can be assessed to some extent by consulting abstracts in the case of journal articles, but libraries rarely have time to search secondary services for every item that is requested, and users are most unlikely to do so.

The cost of cooperative interlending systems may appear to be quite low, unless additional resources are poured into a cooperative acquisition scheme. However, union catalogues are not cheap to construct, maintain and use, and the costs of requesting and supplying are substantial; the operating costs incurred in libraries are usually much higher than the costs of actually transmitting the material, whether by mail or by other means. The above criticisms apply even when access to a country's library resources is total. In fact this is never the case. At best, union catalogues give only partial coverage, and whatever their attempted coverage they are never completely up to date, whether with new acquisitions or with withdrawals of material that has been dicarded or lost.

This catalogue of deficiencies applies much less when provision and supply are centralized.[6] A central collection dedicated to supply, with large acquisition funds and comprehensive coverage of published materials, can achieve high fill rates, partly because it can acquire material that is wanted, usually in advance of demand, partly because it can acquire material that is wanted, usually in advance of demand, partly because since its function is remote supply there is no conflict with service to local clients. It can, and from the experience of the British Library Lending Division does, attract a very large volume of demand: demand in the UK grew by a factor of four between 1961, when the National Lending Library for Science and Technology came into operation, and 1981. It can achieve a fast speed of supply because its systems and procedures can be designed specifically for this purpose. It is very easy to use because all or most requests can be directed to it, and it is uniquely able to monitor demand if it attracts the majority of interlibrary loan demand in the country. The cost of a comprehensive central collection is undoubtedly high, and can be justified only if demand is also at a high level; when this is the case, as it is in the UK, unit costs per request work out actually lower than for a decentralized coopera- tive system able to achieve a roughly similar performance. However, a centralized system is no better able to allow the assessment of utility for items in advance of demand than any other system.

Automation and Telefacsimile

Conventional automation can do much to improve matters. It makes union catalogues much easier to construct and maintain, and entry of new acquisitions into union catalogues can be more or less automatic; in fact, it can be as up to date as the cataloguing of contributing libraries (which may or may not be up to date). Access to union catalogues is easier and faster with an automated system. Requests derived from searches in bibliographic data-bases should be more accurate; this saves time in both requesting and supplying libraries. Requests can be transmitted to holding libraries quickly, and rapidly switched to other libraries as necessary. Failure to supply, or delays in supplying, can be notified immediately to the requesting library. Loan periods can be easily controlled, and re- calls automatically sent. Accounting can be done automatically, and routine surveys can be carried out.

Thus, several of the stipulated requirements can be achieved more fully than with non-automated systems--in particular, ease of use and ability to monitor performance. Costs can also be substan- tially reduced, and so can some of the delays. However, automated systems, while they improve the speed of requesting, do not improve the speed of actual document supply. More seriously, they do not extend provision--the total amount of material available--unless union catalogues are used also as aids to cooperative acquisition. While the management of cooperative acquisition may be made rather easier by automation, the other disadvantages of such schemes are inherent.

Telefacsimile ought to be able to achieve much faster supply, and various attempts have been made to do so. However, since trans- mission times are not the main elements in delays, at best the im- provement is relatively small. Two or three days can nevertheless be critical for some requests, and at best only an hour or two need elapse between the transmission of a request by computer (or telex, or telephone, or for that matter telefacsimile) and the receipt of a copy of the document. Unfortunately, telefacsimile is still very ex- pensive, both in visible costs and in staff time, and the quality of copy, although improving, is not always perfect by any means. The library that receives the request must be prepared to give it high priority, perhaps even sacrificing some of its service to its own users in the process. If, as is often the case, external requests take a low priority because of the staff time they require, telefac- simile requests will intensify this problem because they take even

more time. As a result, either local service may suffer, or transmission may have to be delayed, thus defeating the whole point of
the exercise. Telefacsimile is best treated not as a routine or standard service but as a special service for truly urgent requests.

Is There a Need for Electronic Technology?

To review the present situation, then, even with the help of
automation and telefacsimile, existing document provision and supply
systems tend to be very imperfect, except in three sets of circumstances. The first is where there is a comprehensive central collection able to supply the great majority of requested items. Secondly, a deliberately planned and nationally supported system of
large subject specialized libraries can achieve good performance.
Thirdly, where there are very large numbers of libraries, including some very big ones, excellent total provision can be achieved,
and with the help of automation fast and efficient access can also be
achieved. I can think of only one country for each of these sets
of conditions. Only the United Kingdom has a comprehensive central
collection; the British Library Lending Division handles on average
over 11,500 requests per working day, that is nearly three million
a year.[7] Only the Federal Republic of Germany has a really effective subject specialization system, although a few other European
countries, notably in Scandinavia, are planning rather similar systems.[8,9] And only in the United States is the third set of conditions fulfilled: in all other countries the total resources available
without any special planning fall well short of comprehensiveness,
and only in the United States is there such an efficient system as
OCLC to provide access to them.[10] It is known that the UK can
achieve a better performance on all criteria than the Federal Republic
of Germany; how it compares with the United States would make an
interesting subject of research.

While a comprehensive central collection and a subject specialization scheme both require deliberate national plans and extensive
national funding, the third system is a result of natural circumstances; it constitutes a de facto national provision and supply system,
but an essential feature is that there must be an organization large
and powerful enough to put it together.

Three questions now need to be asked. What is wrong with
a good system on one of the foregoing lines? Can electronic technology help? And might electronic technology do any harm?

The first question is quickly answered. Not very much is
wrong with a good national document provision and supply system
aided by automation; it is possible to achieve by more or less conventional means a very good performance, except in advance assessment of the utility of documents.

Electronic Storage and Transmission of Documents

The answer to the second question, whether electronic technology can help, must be 'Yes'.[11,12] Once documents are stored
electronically, whether on digital optical discs or in some other form,
document provision and supply take on a different aspect. Provision
can be extended in several ways. Items need never go out of print;
and provision within a country need constitute neither a practical
nor an economic limit to access, since electronics can transcend national boundaries. Since electronic masters will not be lent, the
fill rate should be very high.

Supply can be very fast, indeed instant. There is nothing in
principle to prevent a system being designed for maximum ease of
use. Monitoring of demand can be automatic. What is more, an
electronic system can do something that even the best conventional
system cannot, that is allow scanning of documents to assess utility
in advance of requesting the entire item.

There is no doubt therefore that an electronic system can perform outstandingly on all the requirements stipulated. What would
the cost of an electronic storage and transmission system be? There
are two questions here--the actual costs, and the prices charged.
Many of the earlier predictions of a paperless society were economically far too optimistic. The economics and the rate of advance depend on several factors: technology, the ability to invest in it, and
the market. The price to users can be whatever the suppliers make
it, but this must be influenced by what consumers will pay.

The application of electronic technology to document storage
and transmission is not driven by any wish on the part of publishers
to help libraries to move documents among themselves, or indeed to
help libraries at all. To see electronic technology as a sort of knight
errant rescuing interlending damsels in distress is to be out of touch
with reality; in any case, medieval knights errant often left damsels
in worse distress than they found them. Electronic technology is of
interest to publishers because they hope it may solve some of their
problems, in particular the problem of a market that is either shrinking or not expanding in line with their costs.

The belief that there is an ever-expansible market for scientific
and scholarly publications dies hard. Until very recently journal
publishers were still doing very well indeed. When their growth
began to slow down they put the blame not on economic factors that
were affecting nearly every other industry but on libraries for photocopying their journals--for purchasing which they were often charging
them two or three times as much as they charged individual subscribers. As well as the packages of articles called journals that they
were selling to libraries, who then abused them by copying articles
from them, they felt they ought to be able to sell articles direct to
individuals or to libraries that were not subscribing to the full

journals. Moreover, publishing on demand from a high-density electronic master would solve their problems and costs of maintaining back stocks. With the aid of electronic technology they should be able to obtain payment for every use of their products, whether they were printed out and sent to the user or transmitted electronically and read or printed out at the user's end. Libraries would either act as intermediaries or be cut out altogether--either way they would no longer be making many publications available to their users free.

Document provision and supply in an electronic world, therefore, would take the form of a market economy.[13] Or would it? Scholarly and scientific publishing is far from a market economy at present. Articles published in learned journals are very rarely paid for by the publishers--they are more likely to be paid for by the authors. The market for learned journals consists largely of libraries supported from public funds. If publishers want a full market economy, and if they want to cut out libraries or use them merely as channels for getting money from users, they could well be cutting their own economic throats. Why should an author pay for using articles if he receives no payment for his own? Why should libraries cooperate with a system that may be hostile to the interests of their users and inimical to the function they have always served of helping to equalize access to information?

The question is further complicated by the medium term need for 'parallel publishing'--making the same articles available both in conventional printed journals and as electronic separates. It is doubtful if there will always be a double market for secondary services; it must be still more doubtful for full text data-bases, which occupy far more storage and incur much higher costs. Moreover, while a parallel system operates there is nothing to stop libraries from acquiring printed journals as now and supplying copies of articles within the terms of copyright legislation. To compete with this publishers would have either to subsidize their on-line versions or give a much superior supply to what libraries can give.

If publishers cannot continue parallel publishing for long, and have to choose, they can go back to conventional publication, but this would not solve their long term economic problems. If they go for electronic publication only, they run the risk of losing their present markets and not replacing them by a market for individual articles. They could almost certainly run an economic system by concentrating on high-use articles, but insofar as these are contained mostly in a limited number of high-use journals the existing system of conventional publication is in no danger whatever--it is not these journals that are threatened.

The temptation to restrict publication to articles likely to receive high use may be a strong one, particularly if, as is possible, scholarly publishing begins to fall into the hands of large corporations

that have the money to invest in the appropriate technology and that
think there is a quick buck to be made from scholarly articles--and
if there isn't, they needn't be published at all. If this happens,
publishers will be pushed into applying the same criteria to acceptance of articles as they do to books, especially if they are eventually
obliged to pay authors. The end result would be that many articles
would never be made available at all, unless some sort of electronic
dump were established on public funds or at the author's expense.

Another question concerns the way in which documents in an
electronic system would be made available. Individual publishers are
not likely to want to supply documents direct. They will want to use
intermediaries--data-base hosts--in the same way as secondary services do. These intermediaries could supply individual users direct
or through libraries. Publishers might be willing to sell data-bases
to libraries, whether as complete journals or as packages of articles
specially oriented to the interest of the parent institution, but in
this case they would require either high initial payment or payment
per subsequent use. In principle libraries could still achieve equal-
ization of access by users, but his depends on how well they are
funded. Certainly unless the data-bases themselves are collected by
libraries, or the documents in them are all printed out and kept by
libraries, they could disappear completely if their publishers went
out of existence--yet another threat posed to availability by electronic
technology.[14]

To my third question, whether electronic technology might
harm document provision and supply, the answer, as to the question
whether it can help, must be a definite 'yes.'

The Need for National Action

The situation seems then to be that efficient national document
provision and supply systems can be designed without the application
of electronic technology to the storage and transmission of documents.
Electronic technology can undoubtedly help, especially in countries
that do not have efficient conventional provision and supply systems,
but unless great care is taken electronic technology may not only
restrict access, especially for the less wealthy, but also reduce the
amount of material actually available. The greatest danger is the re-
movel of scientific and scholarly publication and availability entirely
from the public sector. It is true that very many libraries, in particular special libraries, are in the private sector, but it is also true
that such libraries benefit from the fact that the present system works
on the assumption of a large public sector market.

How can we reap the benefits of electronic technology without
risking the dangers? Publishers may be tempted to put the long
term future of publication and access at risk because of what they
see as necessary to their prosperity in the short or medium term.

I believe not only that attempts to achieve a full market economy
for scholarly and scientific publication are liable to damage publication, but that they are inimical to the public and national good. It
is possible that market forces might in the end produce a satisfactory
result, but the risks are too great. Scientific communication is too
important to be left to the commercial sector.

The balance between public and private sectors that has evolved
over a long period is already being disturbed, and needs to be restored, or rather redesigned, to fit new circumstances. This could
be done by mutual agreement between the sectors--between publishers, data-base hosts, libraries, and authors/users, but it would be
a great optimist who could see satisfactory agreement being reached
among these parties. A good information and document provision and
supply system is as much a matter of national interest as defence
or the national economy--both of which indeed depend to an extent
on information and document provision and supply. The state thus
has a legitimate and vital interest in the matter. To the argument
that the state should not interfere, I would respond that it is already
involved in document availability: it legislates on copyright, and
most major libraries in most countries are supported from public
funds.

Many countries are now developing national information policies,
or constructing national information plans. Document provision and
supply must be part of such plans. This is necessary with conventional, non-electronic, systems if they are to be effective and efficient: it is even more vital as we move into an electronic world.

What can be done immediately by libraries, other than to press
for national involvement in document provision and supply in the light
of electronic technology? It is imperative that some practical experience is gained with electronic systems. Some journals are already
accessible on-line, and libraries should examine the pros and cons of
such access compared with conventional journal use. Involvement on
a larger scale is all but impossible except for a few large and wealthy
libraries, and these carry a special responsibility. The Library of
Congress has a very ambitious programme of electronic data capture,
storage and access,[15] and the National Library of Canada is also
concerned with digital optical discs. The British Library has an
interest ranging from conservation at one end to document supply
at the other. All this involvement requires the investment of money
and staff, and not all of it will prove in the course of time to have
yielded tangible benefits. However, there are two less tangible benefits that the libraries concerned can hardly fail to reap, and that
must also be felt indirectly by other libraries: hands-on experience,
and close cooperation with the private sector. A little practical working together can be worth a great deal of discussion, and this sort
of involvement may do a lot to work towards the new public-private
sector balance that I believe to be so vital.

It is on these two fronts, then, that progress can and must be made: in national planning, and in practical experimentation involving both public and private sectors. The two questions of document provision and supply, and of the balance between public and private sectors, are critical to the future, not only of libraries but of the functions of information availability and access that libraries exist to serve. They need to be treated with all the seriousness and urgency we can devote to them.

References

1. Vickers, Stephen and Line, Maurice B.: Improving the Availability of Publications: a Comparative Assessment of Model National Systems (Wetherby: IFLA International Programme for UAP, 1984).

2. Stevenson, Jean.: 'The Impact of Computerized Bibliographic Searches on Interlibrary Loan Demand.' Interlending and Document Supply, 12 (1984): 18-20.

3. Line, Maurice B.: 'Performance Assessment at National Library Level,' in Blagden, John (ed) Do We Really Need Libraries? (Cranfield: Cranfield Press, 1983), p. 25-42.

4. Line, Maurice B. and others: National Interlending Systems: A Comparative Study of Existing Systems and Possible Models. (Paris: Unesco, 1980).

5. Collins, Judith and Finer, Ruth: National Acquisition Policies and Systems: A Comparative Study of Existing Systems and Possible Models (Wetherby: IFLA International Office for UAP, 1982).

6. Line, Maurice B.: 'The National Supply of Serials--Centralization versus Decentralization.' Serials Review, 8 (1982): 83-85.

7. Line, Maurice B.: 'The British Library Lending Division.' Journal of Information Science, 2 (1980): 173-182.

8. Kefford, Brian and Line, Maurice B.: 'Seminar on Interlending in Western Europe: A Report,' Interlending and Document Supply, 12 (1984): 35-41.

9. Landwehrmeyer, R." 'A Planned Decentralized Solution for National Document Supply: The Federal Republic of Germany.' Interlending Review, 9 (1981): 122-127.

10. Dodson, A. T. and others: 'Electronic Interlibrary Loan in the OCLC Library: A Study of Effectiveness,' Special Libraries, 73 (1982): 12-19 (January 1982).

11. Line, Maurice B.: 'Document Delivery, Now and in the Future.' Aslib Proceedings, 35 (1983): 167-176.

12. Russon, D.: 'The Impact of New Technology on Present Document Delivery Systems.' Electronic Publishing Review, 2 (1982): 131-136.

13. Line, Maurice B.: 'Some Implications for Publishing of Electronic Document Storage and Supply.' Communication, Technology, Impact, 5 (1983): 1-7.

14. Neavill, Gordon B.: 'Electronic Publishing. Libraries, and the Survival of Information.' <u>Library Resources and Technical Services</u>, 28 (1984): 76-89.

15. Hahn, Ellen A.: 'The Library of Congress Optical Disk Pilot Program. A Report on the Print Project Activities.' <u>Library of Congress Information Bulletin</u>, 42 (1983): 374-376.

URBAN LIBRARIES IN THE SUNBELT*

Lowell A. Martin

I flew into Phoenix from Portland, Oregon, where I am conducting
a study of the public library. We have not seen the sun for two
weeks in Portland. Before that I was at my home in upstate New
York, where we were having one of the most dismal winters of recent years, with any sight of the sun being a rarity. So, you see,
I am not very well acquainted with the sun--and therefore not well
acquainted with the Sunbelt and much less knowledgable about Sunbelt libraries. You can blame what I am going to say on lack of
sunshine--you have before you an old and withered plant that hopes
to be revived at this conference.

But I have studied some Sunbelt libraries--in Los Angeles,
Atlanta, Tucson, and Mobile. I don't know where you draw the line
separating sun from frost, but Memphis, when I was there, had more
of the former; so perhaps you will permit me to mention that city
and its library along the way. I won't drag in Baltimore because I
remember having to walk from the railroad station to the library, a
distance of almost two miles, in a foot of snow, because no vehicles
were moving.

Contrasting Views of Present Service

Let me lay down a proposition at the outset. What many librarians believe should be done about libraries--our degree of satisfaction or dissatisfaction--depends on our appraisal of the present
performance of the institution. There are those who are satisfied,
relaxed, and see little reason for change or new directions in these
next years before the turn of the century; they rest on past accomplishments and present strength and wonder what all the harping is
about. On the other hand, there are those who are critical of library service today, uneasy that we may be on a plateau, marking
time, or idling in neutral, and these people look for the fresh lead
and the opportunity ahead; they see the library in 2000 as somehow

*Reprinted by permission of the author and publisher from Public
Libraries, 29:3 (Fall, 1986) 79–84; copyright © 1986 by the American
Library Association.

different and better than the agency of today. Most of us lean one
way or the other and either defend the library or criticize it.

My problem is that I wobble, leaning both ways. With my friends
I sing the praises of the public library; with my professional colleagues
I find fault and make doomsday pronouncements--sort of a case of pro-
fessional schizophrenia. I would like to think of you as friends as
well as colleagues, so you are in for some of both--the sunshine of
Phoenix and the storm clouds of Portland.

I would like first to make the case on each side, to remind
you of the virtues and accomplishments of the institution to which
we devote our lives, and then turn around and tell you what is
wrong with it, at least in one person's view. How you judge these
two cases, pro and con, will pretty well determine what you think
should be done.

Here is the defense of the institution. I had a head count
made of the persons entering the central building of the Multnomah
County Library in Portland on Saturday, February 1. There were
forty-one hundred individuals from 10 a.m. to 5:30 p.m. Here are
twelve people at the desk in the audiovisual department; I suspect
that many of them want videocassettes for the weekend. A family
with three children burst through the door and scattered in several
directions as though they were picking up their favorite food in a
supermarket. This middle-aged man is checking out ten easy-to-
read children's books; what is he going to do with them? Four high-
school students have preempted a reading table and are having an
animated discussion; are they discussing world peace or the local
basketball team? You can't get a seat at the table marked "Consumer
Products; What to Buy" that holds the various consumer guides.
Want to listen to a good piece of music; you will have to wait until
one of the dozen players is free. There is a bum sleeping; there is
a man who seems to be getting ready to make a killing in the stock
market and a woman who has three books by Barbara Pym in front
of her. I was not surprised to see her nodding when I walked
through a little later.

The public library is a unique and notable achievement. Public
money is spent to provide people, free of charge, with the accumulated wisdom of humanity, with the record of factual information,
and with entertainment in printed, graphic, and visual forms--but
the public and its legislators approve of this expenditure. The library organizes the vast range of material and provides personal
guidance in its use. It extends access by means of branches, book-
mobiles, and telephones. In the face of sharply different views in
the society on social, political, and moral issues, the institution has
retained an enviable objectivity, resisting censorship and providing
materials on all sides of problems. When questioned, most users
report satisfaction with the library, and the general public, including
people who never enter the building, considers it a desirable community resource.

And all this has been true for a hundred years. How many public services have endured essentially the same through war and peace, through prosperity and depression, through the print expansion and the information explosion, into the time of the computer and nuclear power?

Given this benign view, the strategy indicated for the future is clear enough: continue as we are; librarians simply need to perform professionally, and all will work out well for 2000. To fall back on two cliches, "We must be doing something right" and "If it works, don't fix it."

I do not think this is enough; I don't think we can coast to 2000. To explain my view we must shift to the other side, to the increasing criticism that has been directed toward the public library.

I have been keeping a record of articles in the literature that challenge the public library and question its efficacy. Here are a few recent titles: "Will the Public Library Be Obsolete in the 1980s?"; "Disestablishing the Public Library"; and "Long Day's Journey into Night." I was asked to do one piece entitled "The Late Great Public Library; May it Rest in Peace" and another under the title "Middle-age Crisis or Old Age?" When I did a study of the Chicago Public Library, I found the most impressive of the library trustees to be a man named Louis Lerner, who because of his outstanding work as a trustee was appointed a member of the National Commission on Libraries and Information Service, and who said shortly: "I think the public library in its present form is absolutely finished and will be dead within the next twenty years." At least as applied to his own institution in Chicago, this pessimistic statement was not too far off the mark.

That is the other side, the charge of the prosecution. Most of us rise up in indignation on hearing such condemnation, but it might be good discipline to sit still for a moment and listen to the indictment.

Yes, the critics say, the public library had its day--it served a clear purpose when the nation needed it, but that day is gone. The public library was the means of education for generations with limited formal schooling, but that is not the situation today. Now we are an educated people, most having completed high school and many having gone on to college. The condition that brought the community library into existence no longer prevails. Not many people seek out the institution with conscious educational motives. The People's University is an agency that had its rise and decline. The library itself has pulled back on its educational activities such as the reader's adviser. Young adult service, with its informal educational purpose, appears to be a nearly dead issue represented now by a few cases of little-used books in a corner. In fact, the agency has pulled back on such an elementary educational tool as the book list of recommended readings; you don't find it in libraries nearly as much as you did ten years ago. The People's University has become more the free bookstore and, now, the free videocassette rental agency.

Well, perhaps the People's University is no longer needed. But what of the other library missions, say the provision of wholesome recreational materials? To the vast increase in popular, diversional reading after the turn of the century, the library responded. In a period of relative print scarcity--the number of bookstores then was small, the circulation of magazines modest, the paperback still in the future--the library stepped in and performed a valuable service by providing literature for relaxation before the time of radio and television. But the period of scarcity is gone. We live now in a time glutted with entertainment, wholesome and otherwise, in print form and in forms carried over the airwaves. If the public library was in the forefront among the providers of recreation, it is now well back in the parade.

But hold on, the library will say, what about the function that was part of the library mission from the beginning and that is still needed now, that of furnishing background and knowledge for individuals to perform as citizens. We are told constantly that voters who understand are the requisite of a democracy. In your library, how fares the circulation of books on social and political issues? In the libraries I have studied, these topics constitute one of the least used parts of the collection. At your reference desk, what is the proportion of questions asked for civic understanding? The answer, in most cases, indicates that it is very small. Wherever citizens get their voting information, it is not primarily from the public library.

Well, then, what about the many other kinds of information, for business and career, for health and family affairs, for hobbies and travel, for almost every topic under the sun that comes to a reference desk? Here it may be possible to mount a defense against the indictment, for reference use is increasing in many libraries. But, outside the library, information inquiry and delivery are increasing even more rapidly, via newspaper and news telecast, via journal and database. The library was among the first in the field--reference service appeared in the early 1900s--but it has been overtaken and bypassed. The public library is not the information center: it is one node in a vast and growing complex, an alternative for those who have not yet worked out more direct sources. The public library gathers and waits; the commercial providers disseminate. Small wonder that a very small part of the population turns to it for information.

So let's try another tack. If the public library is no longer a continuation of the educational system, a means for plain people of limited background and economic level to get the knowledge and training they need, what about its service to the leaders of the

society? If not the agency for the followers, what is its role for
those up front, the government officials, business moguls, cultural
pacesetters, and sports and entertainment stars? A commissioned
poll in Portland concludes flatly: "The leaders think the library is
fine, but they do not use it themselves." How long has it been since
your mayor, state legislator, chamber-of-commerce head, or chair of
the orchestra or drama society used your library?

All that may be true, the witness will respond, but the fact
remains that libraries are still quite busy. This is so but not as
much as in the 1960s, except where population has increased markedly. Many public libraries had their highest circulation in the
1960s--Memphis is down 20 percent from that time; Mobile, 25 percent; even Atlanta, 10 percent. Yet these last twenty years have
been a time when the sale of books has more than doubled.

Another consideration. Have you looked sharply at the age
of your patrons lately? Students aside, they are getting older on
the average. You have not been bringing in the twenty- and the
thirty-year-olds.

Public library users these days are remnants of former larger
publics--the small number who are following subject interests systematically, the modest number who have learned that the library is
a reservoir of information, and those who follow popular literature
but elect to take a chance on what they can get in the library rather
than to buy the title they actually want from a commercial source.

Fresh Approaches

Let me try to make the point in a different way. Clear from
your mind the image and structure of the public library as we know
it, the fine, substantial, central unit and the pleasant branches
scattered in communities. Start over again with a clean slate, as
though we were designing the agency from scratch. The first question is what is this service for, what is it seeking to do? Let's start
with what users most frequently say they come for: entertaining material for relaxation, particularly current and recent publications.
Would you build a large central building, in one location, holding a
half-million or a million volumes for this purpose? No, you would
recognize that we have a distribution or marketing problem, requiring
very convenient access to a product with a relatively short shelf
life. You would plan for fairly small installations in frequently used
locations. Minibranches in small stores in shopping centers come to
mind, and newsstand-like arrangements in the lobbies of large office
buildings, even kiosks in local squares and parks. What about de-
posits in the largest apartment buildings and housing projects?
Here is a way to reach the people if this is your mission. Push this
concept, and your circulation would be several times what it is at
present.

Or adopt a very different mission, that of information center, providing people with the data they need for making practical decisions, whether in the business office, kitchen, workshop, or government office. In this case, your strategy would be quite different if you were starting from scratch. You would assemble information sources in depth in one location, in print form and, increasingly, in machine-readable form. The information must be accessible, at the fingertips of the searchers when needed, so you would not expect individuals to come to your storehouse but would utilize modern electronic communication to get it to them--the telephone today, the cable connection tomorrow, the online computer contact the day after tomorrow--no big central library with hundreds of seats. And even as the model I visualized a moment ago for popular reading would increase your circulation of books severalfold, so this model for information provision would substantially increase your reference count.

Are the models too farfetched? Note that the plan I outlined for recreational reading already exists--in the commercial world. There are paperback racks in every supermarket and drugstore, and between them they supply far more diversionary reading than the public library; we serve a remnant, a fringe group of this public. Similarly, the online information system I described also is coming into place--once again in the commercial arena. Business people, professionals, and specialists increasingly utilize databases for their fields. Just within the past few weeks I have encountered a database for the insurance industry and another for those in the forest products industry. This information network outside the library is growing rapidly and will shortly reach into most aspects of human endeavor, while the library rocks along with its rows and rows of reference titles.

But hold a minute, you say--we subscribe to Dialog. It has come to the point where I am sorry to hear this response, not that there is anything wrong with Dialog, for what it seeks to do, but because it suggests a lack of understanding of what we are talking about. Dialog is essentially a bibliographic database. It does not provide facts but, rather, citations to sources in which the facts sought may or may not be found. It is not a computerized form of a broad reference collection but only of the indexes and bibliographies within that collection. Obvious as this is, it is not fully understood. As a consequence, I note a growing feeling of disappointment on the part of staff, as well as the public, with this first venture into computerized information. This was to be a bold entry into a new world, and it proves to be another fringe service used a few times a month while automated information provision marches steadily forward outside the library.

Note, if you will, that neither of the models I projected includes a large subject-organized central library or even large branches with collections of one hundred thousand volumes or more. I am not trying to avoid or disparage such facilities--on the contrary, my

personal philosophy of library service inclines me towards resources
of some depth. My purpose was simply to show that some of the missions we most often claim--providing the recreational literature that
people seek and providing utilitarian information--are not best achieved
by the institutions we have built and now maintain.

Education as the Mission

I have mentioned a few offbeat models for library service.
Let me try just one more, this one really from high off the wall.
From the discussion thus far, you may well inquire about good old-
fashioned educational service, which is where the public library
started. Is not this the reason we have our substantial collections
and trained librarians? Yes, historically, the public library took its
present form because it began as an extension of the schools for a
populace with limited educational background and a desire for knowledge that would advance their careers and enrich their lives, thus
the need for a broad subject collection and an active readers' advisory service of the kind that impressed me so when I first began
shelving books in the Chicago Public Library in the 1920s. Where
does educational service fit in today?

Assuming you consider this mission important and still relevant,
consider a different pattern of educational service, more in line with
the way other professional services have developed. We would still
need a strong central collection, even broader and deeper than we
have now. But many of the librarians would be scattered through
the city and metropolitan areas in small offices, as are doctors and
lawyers. They would see their clients--there is a word we don't
use anymore--in the offices. Of course, they would have a full
record of the library's holdings at their fingertips. They would
prepare prescriptions for their advisees, as do doctors and lawyers,
in this case in the form of reading and media sequences. The individual would go to the central collection to get the prescribed materials, as a doctor's patients go to the pharmacy or hospital, or
the materials could be delivered to the same location the next day;
before too long, they could be accessed electronically. One large
central collection--librarians as guides and specialists with many offices close to people--materials disseminated directly into homes--a
very different pattern from what has evolved.

I suspect that by this point I have lost you entirely, but I
remind you that one of the driving forces behind the emergence and
growth of the public library--the stimulation and guidance of reading--
has all but disappeared from our quick-stop, fastfood type of contact
at the service desk. The only place where I see reading guidance
going on to any extent is in the children's room, and children's
service remains one of the most impressive of the library's activities
and a service that I suspect carries a considerable weight when we
ask for funds at budget time.

The hardheaded realist may well call me back to Earth. Face the fact that this is a different time, the realist would say; we are for the most part an educated country--adults are not pursuing subjects as they did formerly--there is no need for intensive advisory service, and it would be little used if it were provided. That may be true, but remember that if it is, it is also an argument against the substantial central collection, for it is those who are engaged in systematic self-learning who need and use that collection.

Bear with me for just a few moments more on this old-fashioned educational purpose. Self-learning on the part of adults spans the complete spectrum of human interests, and I don't think it has disappeared from the earth. On the contrary, rather than people no longer seeking to learn, I think it is the other way around, with libraries having grown away from serving the natural desire to explore, question, examine, appreciate. We have grown away from this part of our public.

Two quotations from the past echo this time-honored purpose. Here is one of the early sentences in the Material Selection Policy Statement of the Enoch Pratt Library in Baltimore, a document that has influenced book selection statements of other libraries, but usually with this sentence omitted: "The Library recognizes that a major objective is the stimulation and development of concern, learning and understanding." That does not sound like a particularly passive statement, not the credo of an insitution waiting to see what comes down the road and then latching on to it--" development of concern, learning and understanding."

The other quotation is older still, coming from an early statement of the Minneapolis Public Library, which was that the aim of the agency was to make people "happier, wiser and better able to discharge their duties." In that brief phrase there are three ideas we don't use much anymore: happiness, wisdom, and duty. The term I find myself using is self-realization, the development of one's desires and capacities as a human being.

I am convinced that self-realization is still a widespread motive--indeed it may actually be stronger than in the past--and that it will be prevalent in 2000. We have come through the period when the dominant motive of people was simply getting ahead. When one gets ahead--and more people are doing so at an earlier age--what next? Either boredom or self-realization.

How does one achieve self-realization? By every activity and interest that the human imagination can devise. But won't many of these activities have little if any connection with library materials? Do you know that I sat for several minutes trying to think of non-intellectual adult interests for which library materials would have no relevance? Motorcycle racing, mountain climbing, spearfishing, cave exploration? These had many other outdoor activities led me within

82   Library Lit.--86

a few seconds back to the library. So I tried avocations around
the house, such as cooking, gardening, woodworking, or antique
collecting. Again I was back in the library collection--the arts,
stargazing, community work, travel--back again to the library. What
about gambling, if that is the way one wants to express oneself? My
best advice to gamblers is to study the library's resources on probability, or they will soon run out of money. Turn around, reach
out, try to find out who you are, develop your unique qualities--
and you are back in the library.

But libraries are not well tuned to people in this basic phase
of their lives. We are there if you want to relax, if you want to
advance your career, or if you want to prepare for a course, but
librarians have not thought in terms of the motives of individuals
as individuals. Just when the natural desire of the human animal
to explore, examine, experience, question, and taste has mounted,
and just when people have time and means to exercise these interests, the public library has grown away from them in its playing down
of stimulation and guidance services.

The much maligned Yuppies are one group that is searching.
What do we do for them--have we reached them? Young adults are
another group trying to find themselves. Do we respond effectively?
Then there are the seniors, seeking purpose after retirement. Once
again we have seldom made the connection.

Information as the Mission

So much for trying to put a little depth and zest into educational service. What is the prospect for information provision? I
referred earlier to the many specialized and computerized databases
that exist, and I criticized most libraries for just putting a toe in
the water of this whole new development. From this, one might conclude that the new information age has bypassed the library. Everyone will have a home computer, and will simply flip the switch to get
any information they need. This does not necessarily follow--and
particularly not for the millions of nonspecialists in our society.
Even as we have provided books for many nonscholars, so we have
the opportunity to provide information for nonspecialists.

To begin with, every home may not have a personal computer.
This trend has definitely slowed down because more people are asking exactly what the computer will do for them; someone has said
that the sale of home computers will not pick up again until one is
invented that does the dishes. Furthermore, even where home systems exist, now or in the future, information will not appear automatically and without charge. Each database must be subscribed to,
and the cost will be more than nominal--this for a source that in
most homes will be used only occasionally.

This is where the library comes in. I foresee a situation similar to that for the acquisition of books. The advent of the bookstore did not put an end to the library. You know the book procurement practices of your friends and acquaintances--some do buy all their books and never enter the library. At the other end, some seldom go into the bookstores or stop at the paperback rack but depend almost entirely on the public agency. Then there are the many between, who buy some of their titles and borrow others from the library. Commercial and public sources exist side by side, and reinforce each other.

The situation will be the same for automated information sources. Some people will have all the equipment and will subscribe to all the sources they need. Others will not even have the hardware, and many who do will subscribe to one or a few databases and will depend on the library or some other middleman for access to the rest.

Before the end of the century, computer access to factual databases--not just bibliographical bases--will be common in libraries; terminals will be located in branches as well as central buildings, and there will be multiple terminals designed so that they can be used directly by searchers without the intervention of a librarian. The information provided will be produced more rapidly and will be up-to-date. The reference collection will look very different, and much of the annual scramble and cost of replacing outdated sources will be ended. Either this development will occur, or the public library will be out of the mainstream of the information age.

However, automation of information is not all that is needed for the next period. If other changes do not occur, the library will labor under the handicap of being a reservoir or storehouse at a distance, a place the user must go to, in contrast with the immediate availability of the mailbox, the telephone, the button on the TV set, and the computer terminal on the desk. Further, the organization of the library information, unless we change our approach, will be neat and logical but not prepackaged for particular groups.

But how can the library go beyond its walls and deliver neat packets of information? The starting point is a concept: the mission not only of assemblage of resources, not only their organization, but distribution, dissemination--the fountainhead rather than the reservoir. Distribution--dissemination; this is not some far-out prospect depending on satellites or other expensive technology. Taking full advantage of the telephone is the first step, using that marvelous invention that enables individuals to sit at their desks and call the library to them. Of course, all libraries have telephones, but they differ widely in capacity to take and effectively process telephone inquiries. Even before the telephone, there are the mails. How many libraries have mailing lists of people with different interests

and send out information that applies to each group? Think of terminals in banks, providing access to the library's catalog and to a
range of databases, with the bank paying for the installation because
they would see it as a customer attraction in the competition for bank-
ing business. Cable TV offers an opportunity to disseminate. The
library will not compete with sponsored newscasters nor with subsi-
dized dramatic productions--it does not have the capacity to do so--
but it can assemble background on the news and contemporary issues
and project it to people who want to know. It can pull together
from its resources a summary of new tax laws, or the effects of different garden insecticides, and a thousand other topics; it can provide brief background on Ethiopia when its people starve or on the
Phillipines when its people revolt; on a new tennis champion or an
old football hero.

Now I have the librarian not only at the computer, not only
on TV, but at the author's desk digesting information for dissemination. I had better stop there, for fear that the library as we know
it will completely disappear. I know that this will not happen, for
the book--the most thorough and individual of these various media--
will remain with us as will the librarian as the keeper of the book,
standing ready to work with seekers who come in from the fray to
find out what it means for them.

Financial Support

But where will the money come from? I have not forgotten the
bottom line. I no longer have to meet a budget, but I did at one
time, in a commercial setting, and it was well into eight figures.

Public libraries do not get the money they need. But I have
a conviction that they themselves contribute to the problem by seeking to do more than they are able to do with the support they have.
Something for everybody becomes in practice too little for too few,
and the institution fades as an essential facility deserving priority
support.

Sometimes I think that public libraries get the money they deserve. Those that deliver go about $25 per capita. Those that
don't limp along on half that. To those who have, it is given; to
those who lack, it is denied. Even as we have rich people and poor
people, so we have well- and poorly financed libraries. And the
poor you will have with you always, say the Scriptures.

What can the poor do? One alternative is to seek a government
handout. For libraries this would mean going to state or federal
sources. I don't think libraries are going to fare much better than
individuals at such levels in these next years.

So what other alternatives are available? One I hear proposed is more aggressive public relations, but if this means getting the message across, telling the public how good we are when in fact we are weak, I am skeptical. The publicity must come, but only when there is something worth publicizing.

The only promising alternative I know for the underfinanced is somehow, in one or two areas, to show strength, even if this means the temporary neglect of other services, and then to publicize what has been accomplished, pointing to it as an example of what the agency can do in various areas--if it had the money. I don't care what is selected for emphasis, as long as it relates to the city and constituency served--it could be business or children's service, family affairs, or best-sellers. Show that you can do something well, and you are more likely to get money to do other things well. Concentrate and strengthen.

Looking Ahead

Where does all this leave public libraries in planning for 2000? I am not advocating that they adopt one of my far-out models. I presented those only to jerk us out of the familiar pattern that we take for granted and that is likely to leave us marking time in the period ahead.

I have no illusion that the library can drastically change itself. It is an institution, a bureaucracy. It has its ingrained staff to keep things going just about as they have in the past. It has its small publics that do not want change. The library in Portland has just shifted a small selection of current issues of magazines from the Popular Library on the first floor and combined them with the main periodical collection on an upper floor, and the current magazine readers are protesting that they now have to go upstairs.

No, I don't have a grand model for the future. What I am urging is that we get out from behind the service desk and seek to understand the motives of people in these last years of a remarkable century, the motives of those who use us and even more the motives of those who do not. I am pleading for a focus in service that grows out of the dynamics of the time rather than a carryover from a previous day--the people-centered library rather than the resource-centered library.

Application to the Sunbelt

Let's bring all this to the Sunbelt. Perhaps under the sun it will dry up and die, but I hope it will blossom.

Obviously city libraries in the Sunbelt are not all of a kind, in great part because its cities differ widely and are at different stages

of development. This came home to me forcefully when, in succession,
I made studies of libraries--first in Atlanta, then in Memphis, then
in Mobile, less than a year ago--Atlanta: dynamic, exciting, expanding, overbuilding, the sky's the limit; Memphis: at the crossroads,
perhaps to become a major communication and distribution center,
old Southern neighborhoods with Federal Express airplanes weaving
through the sky all night; Mobile: crumbling, missed by Sunbelt
development, waiting, hoping to get a shot in the arm from a new
waterway leading from Mobile Bay into the heartland. If you were
taken blindfold into the central libraries of these three cities, you
would know which city you were in the moment the blindfold was removed, and in the next few moments you would have an impression
of markedly different capacities. Any statement made for Atlanta
and its libraries would have to be reversed for Mobile; any prescrip-
tion for Tucson would have to be modified for New Orleans. Are
we talking about such cities as Houston, San Antonio, or Orlando,
which become different every ten years, or about El Paso, Long
Beach, or Birmingham, which in their different ways have settled
into a mold?

I saw a news release recently that claimed the Phoenix area
would show the second-fastest growth in the country in the next
fifteen years and by the year 2000 would have 2½ million residents.
If library service were unified in this area, that would be the fourth
or fifth largest library in the country in terms of population served.
That scale of growth will draw this and other Sunbelt libraries into
one of the most complex political questions that have long faced large
city libraries--how to structure and pay for systems that are used
increasingly by people living outside the central city in separate
taxing districts. Perhaps this conference should have been called
"Metropolitan Libraries in the Sunbelt."

Besides differences from city to city in the Sunbelt, I also see
similarities to cities in the North. The business-commercial centers
of various metropolitan areas show definite signs of decline and de-
cay--the last department store in central Mobile closed when I was
there. I have not encountered in the South as notable reversal and
rehabilitation of downtown areas as has occurred in such older,
northeastern cities as Boston and Baltimore. Also, outside the central
retail districts, inner-city neighborhoods are appearing in the Sun-
belt--sections of high unemployment and physical deterioration--and
we have not learned to shift out of our standard branch syndrome
and effectively reach these sections. The problem will be with you
more in these next years. In some of the southern metropolitan
areas, it is becoming hard to judge where a central library building
should be located.

In my experience, Sunbelt libraries stand somewhat at the two
extremes in the matter of size of branches. Some of the older cities
that have not been growing rapidly fall on the side of many small
branches spaced fairly close together, while those that are growing

rapidly tend more toward fewer and larger branches--I think of the
Wilmot Branch in Tucson, which annually circulates close to a million
volumes. Which is best--small or large, many or few? That depends
on what you seek to do in branches, and at which users you are aiming. The very large units are more cost efficient per transaction:
they have broader collections and more services; they draw in good,
regular adult users, but they do not reach as many children and
they are not as flexible for serving neighborhoods with people of
below-average education. The starting point is purpose and clientele.

What impresses me about some of the Sunbelt libraries is that
they have not only managed to keep up with remarkable population
growth--5 percent or more a year in some cases--but at the same time
have improved and deepened service in old-fashioned basics such as
collections, and reference service, and community participation. I
don't know whether you brought the energy with you when you came
from the "Frostbelt," or whether you have acquired some kind of
individual solar generator here in the South, but I note that when
people ask me to name exceptional city libraries, I find myself increasingly mentioning southern institutions. Some of our northern
cities are reviving, and their libraries with them. Perhaps the next
conference can be "Preparing for 2001; Sunbelt and Frostbelt Together."

I have talked pie-in-the-sky long enough. We all have the
right to our own dreams. I think the important thing is not to remain sound asleep.

Here are the homely guidelines I draw from all this speculation:

- We are in the most rewarding of work, bar none, but this
  does not make us perfect.

- Over the years we have woven a pattern, built a bureaucracy, and it may not fit in 2000.

- But we have strength inside our walls--and also strength
  outside in the faith that the public retains in libraries--
  the task is to get the two together.

- The way to do this is to go outside the four walls, to identify and empathize with our users, present and potential.

- We can justifiably claim to be service minded; we cannot
  actually claim that we understand our publics.

- In particular, seek to understand people as individuals,
  people searching for self-realization; this could be the pervasive motive of these next years.

- Decide what you are aiming at, what you want your agency to accomplish, what hopes and ambitions you hope to promote in the lives of your patrons.

- Don't be afraid of change--at the same time, don't be afraid of remaining the same.

- Whether similar to the institution of today or not, the library of tomorrow will be more exciting and easier to use.

- The several main sections of the library--for information, education, recreation, happiness, or self-realization--will look and feel different from one another.

- Take a day off: go to the shore or the desert and contemplate what you want your library to be fifteen years hence. When you get there, look for a little high ground, so that you can see ahead and not get mired down in the rut in front of you.

The force that will move your library forward is not many hours of sunshine in Phoenix or many hours of rain in Portland, not increasing population, not even money. It is imagination--creative planning--on the part of the librarian. During the last years of the nineteenth century, our early leaders fashioned the institution that we know today. In these next years, can we repeat that for the time ahead? Or have librarians run out of that plus factor, that extra ingredient that makes and moves institutions? I sincerely believe that librarians are the most service-minded group of workers that exists today. Do librarians, in addition, have the capacity to remake and revitalize their agency?

THE CURRENT TRENDS AND CONTROVERSIES IN THE LITERATURE OF REFERENCE SERVICES AND THEIR IMPLICATIONS FOR THE PRACTICE OF REFERENCE WORK

Carl F. Orgren and James Rice

Reference work by virtue of its nature deals with all kinds of information in all disciplines and attempts to provide it to all sorts of people for all sorts of reasons. While the very definition of reference service is a matter of controversy, we will open with an arbitrary one--the actions, and the administration of those actions, by which we assist patrons in their discovery and use of appropriate portions of mankind's graphic record. Note that the definition doesn't say appropriate to what--appropriate to the education, entertainment, edification, growth, etc. of the patron. These are intentially left out because they are all relevant to our role, and the role of the library. Further, it is very difficult to separate them--who is to say a person well entertained isn't learning something? Who is to say there is not entertainment value in something learned? With this much diversity in the character of reference work, how can its literature be anything but diverse? Therefore we looked at the topic carefully but selectively to provide some semblance of order. Breadth is emphasized more than exhaustive depth. This will not be an enumeration of research studies, publications, or names of all writers on the subject. Instead, it is an overview of the primary issues that have been prominent in the literature and in the field during the last 10-15 years.

Library-Use Instruction

Certainly one of the most significant issues in reference work is library-use instruction and bibliographic instruction. The development of teaching library-use has, as primary foundations, the library college concept and the more general conviction that the library and library-use are central to all education. The movement evolved somewhat slowly during the 1950's and 1960's, with intensified efforts in

*Reprinted by permission of the authors and publisher from The Reference Librarian, 14:XX (Spring/Summer 1986) 10-15; copyright © 1986 by the Haworth Press, Inc.

the 1970's. For the last 10 years it has played a prominent role in
the literature--in one study, around 1/3 of all the literature relating
to reference service in academic libraries.[1]   The practice of library-
use instruction is gaining momentum in all types of libraries in various
ways.

At the heart of the argument in favor of library-use instruction
are two ideas. First is the notion that, while it is nice to teach
people specific parts of any discipline, it is even better to teach them
how to find out on their own--knowing how to catch a fish is better
than receiving the fish. Of course, this is why library-use instruction has been most accepted in educational environments. The other
rationale for library-use instruction is the idea that information is
a valuable commodity in all environments--not just education. Information is power--and libraries have a unique role in the information
explosion. As librarians, we have a responsibility to enable people
to become more self-sufficient in information access. This idea has
also been expanded to indicate a possible advantage for reference
departments. If people have a rudimentary grasp of library-use,
it will relieve us of considerable drudgery.

Both of these ideas rest on the assumption that no one is
better qualified to teach library-use than a librarian. This is where
the rub has come in the profession. Several articulate opponents
have argued that librarians are not teachers--they are information
providers. If finding information for people is our real function then
teaching might detract from our ability to do the best possible job
of what we really should be doing.[2]

Furthermore, users might not want to know how to use the
library, they might just want the information itself. It is even more
of a failure on our part to try to teach someone who just wants direct
information service. Some have argued that it is a mistaken notion
that we can even succeed in library-use instruction--really effective
library use is sophisticated and our real role is that of mediator and
facilitator.[3]   It has been argued that library-use instruction is
necessarily a more conservative form of reference service, and that
it held higher favor among earlier reference theorists is a misread-
ing of those earlier theorists, and a misunderstanding of the relative
roles of instruction and direct provision of information in reference
service.[4]

Meanwhile, study after study confirms the fact students respond well to library-use instruction, they express a desire to have
it, their effectiveness in using the library increases, and library
use itself even goes up.[5]   Thousands of libraries (mostly school
and academic, but other types as well) have implemented library-
use instruction and made it part of the duties of reference personnel.
Thelma Freides has concluded that, as far as academic libraries are
concerned, the advocates of library-use instruction are dominant.[6]
But its popularity has certainly not overshadowed all controversy.

Online Searching

Probably the next most popular topic in the literature of reference services is online searching. This developed in the 1970's
and during the last few years has started to dominate the literature.
It is a different kind of issue from library-use instruction because
the the demand for online searching is unavoidable. The information
industry produces several new electronic databases every month.
The volume of use of online services is constantly increasing. Many
librarians resist promoting their online searching service for fear
they will be deluged with requests beyond their ability to handle
them. But for a reference department which claims to support information access and research not to at least offer online searching
is becoming sheer folly. There are, however, several issues and
controversies concerning online searching which deserve consideration.

The most debated issue in online searching among librarians is
the fee or free issue. It has been intensified by the fact that in
most libraries it is virtually impossible to implement free online searching without drawing budget away from collection development and other
services. Not to have fees robs Peter to pay Paul. However, the
primary argument against fees is that online databases will become
more and more necessary to conduct standard reference work. Already, we see ready reference sources, encyclopedias, statistical
databases, and cumulated runs of indexes, bibliographies, and catalogs appear in online form. It's difficult to justify charging fees for
something which is part of basic reference service.[7] It will become
increasingly cost effective and inevitable that reference work will
rely on these sources. In one recent survey, it was discovered that
a majority of newly implemented online services were offered free.[8]

Another issue is whether online searching should be integrated
into the reference department or a separate related function. To
integrate poses personnel and staffing problems. Training all or
many reference professionals in online searching is expensive. Who
searches and who does the more traditional reference work? If online searching is fully integrated into reference work will this increase the demand for expensive online searching beyond our ability
to handle?

Not to integrate poses problems which are perhaps even more
vexing. In special, research, and academic libraries more of our
clientele are asking us for online services apart from any other reference work. And some library users are even starting to search
on their own--without mediation, notably in chemistry, medicine,
psychology and engineering. Thought provoking statements from
faculty in universities include: "Did you know that the library still
subscribes to a whole bunch of expensive indexes which I can easily
and quickly search from my own desk--and I can store the results
of my search, make bibliographies--the sky's the limit/" "Why should
I go to the library? I just send my T.A. over to check out the

source documents I want." It has been true for some time that many
of our users see libraries only as institutions that store and circulate books, journals, and other materials. Consciously or uncon-
sciously, there is an assumption that pretty much all we do is document delivery. But in the online age, if users can do some reference
work--even ready reference work without help from the reference
department, they will perhaps never discover any of the additional
ways reference departments could help them (either with a specific
topic or in general). Of course there is also a question of how well
users can do online searching without help from reference professionals. Vocabulary control, choice of database, precision and recall of search results are all factors which benefit from an information
professional's attention. Indeed, it is not difficult to support the contention that there is a huge gulf between what users do in practice
and what really should be done--not only with online searching but
with information gathering in general. Where does this leave reference services? It can be effectively argued that if reference departments don't incorporate and integrate online database searching,
then users will simply begin to do it in some other way--and make
even less effective use of reference services than before.

Another interesting trend is that these two most prominent
topics of reference service: online searching and bibliographic instruction are, in a sense, pitted against each other. Online searching (as it is often practiced) encourages the avoidance of use of the
library except for document delivery. Either the research is done
by the librarian or by the client on the computer. It can appear
that there would thus be a dwindling need for a knowledge of library
use. Library instruction advocates respond that online searching is
one more aspect of the library-use spectrum--one more resource
that we should teach about.[9] It should be noted, however, that
the goal of online searching is basically to obtain a bibliography on
a topic. Library-use instruction should involve much more than producing a bibliography on a topic--it should involve methodology for
topic selection, organizational and outline skills, bibliographic style,
the structure of the entire literature--whether electronic or not, and
the procedures for research. In fact, electronic information suggests
a possible benefit to the calling of bibliographic instruction. It can
provide a clerical function removing a lot of the drudgery of library-
use and enable us to concentrate on a broader, more sophisticated
understanding of how information should be gathered and how research should be done.

Special Reference Services

Some other very important developments during the last decade
or two which have had significant impact on reference services can
be grouped under the heading of special reference services. This
category includes such things as I & R services, SDI services, services to the handicapped, custom reference or research services, in-

formation brokering, outreach services and community information services.

The questions that usually arise when considering such services are these: If we offer this service, can we really do a good job of it? Will doing this detract from our normal ongoing reference work and assisting people to use the library? Is it within our basic role and function to offer this service? In answering these and other questions, it should be noted that I & R services, services to the handicapped, various outreach programs, and some community information services have had wide acceptance. Many special libraries have been able to offer SDI services, custom research services, and various high-powered individualized special services.

One recent notion in the literature is that certain special services in reference departments stem from "a misguided philanthropic notion on the part of libraries" and an erroneous feeling that librarians should do more than just provide access to information.[10] After all, we are not really qualified to be counselors, social workers, diagnosticians, etc. It is the opinion of the authors that the services selected for inclusion here do conform to the customary role of librarian--information organizer, provider, and disseminator.

One special service that is interesting is the university based community information service. The prototypical example of this is called PENNTAP--Pennsylvania Technical Assistance Program at Penn State. Many other state universities have implemented or are considering similar programs. Basically it is a program whereby the reference department and a full-time staff of technical experts field questions from all over the commonwealth of Pennsylvania. The PENNTAP staff also disseminates critical scientific or technical information to needy users who may not have even requested it.[11] Some such programs are located in the university reference department while others just use the library as one source of possible answers. In any case, the entire university faculty is also available as a source of answers-- and is therefore harnessed on behalf of the state taxpayer in solving problems. Most such services are free of charge.

Standards and Guidelines

Another ongoing issue in the reference literature is that of standards and guidelines. Since the RASD guidelines were adopted in 1976 and the ethics section was added in 1979, the main issue in the literature seems to be whether or not we can and should have quantitative standards. The RASD has also been working on standards for online searching. One important aspect of the standards is the requirement of a service policy manual in each reference program.[12] This seems to be a recommendation that is uniformly understood and accepted or even applauded in the literature--but not at all consistently done in practice.

There are various questions of ethics that continue to occupy
the literature. Should the librarian recommend purchase of given
titles?--in other words, endorse specific products? Should librarians
give advice? Should the personal views of librarians enter the process at all?[13] Should the librarian help someone build a bomb by
providing the information--or help someone commit suicide? Should
librarians help runaways get married or criminals to find loopholes
in the law? What circuitous information access methods are morally
or ethically appropriate? The RASD statement of commitment--section
6 provides guidance on most of these questions[14] and most of the
current literature seems to accept these ethical standards.

The Impact of Technical Services
on Reference Services

The impact of automated library operations on the reference
function has drawn much interest recently. Of key importance is
the role reference departments must play in online public access catalogs.[15] The responsibility for user awareness and training falls
on the reference department. Public relations, user resistance,
terminal placement and in fact, the very design of the system and its
software ultimately come to roost in the reference department. One
example of this impact is seen in the fact that several libraries have
implemented online catalogs with only a portion of the total collection
in machine readable form. The remainder of the collection is then
still available through the card catalog. Research on subject access
with such catalogs indicates that users will often consult one form
of the catalog--not both.[16] While partial conversion may be expedient from the technical services perspective, from the reference
perspective, it may result in providing only partial access to the
library's collection for many users. This is a very serious problem
and one that deserves considerable attention.

Another interesting aspect of the automation explosion is affecting reference departments--microcomputers. Records management
functions in reference departments that are very well suited to the
microcomputer include vertical file maintenance, ILL record control,
I & R files, word processing, local or special purpose indexes, use
statistics, personnel scheduling, and pathfinder databases to name
a few.[17]

Several libraries have provided public access to bibliographic
utilities such as OCLC, RLIN, or WLN in the reference department.
Patrons can do research, verification, or known item searching, and
even local catalog access through these systems.[18]

Resource Sharing

Always present in the literature is the issue of resource sharing and networking. The literature has taken on an increasingly negative complexion regarding resource sharing in the last few years. Some writers on the subject postulate that, in the final analysis, it is cheaper to buy most requested materials than to locate and borrow them from another library. But also in the literature are many continuing reports of successful cooperation. Many of the large academic and research libraries have increased their commitment to resource sharing--especially through the bibliographic utilities. RLIN, WLN, and LC have developed a basis for linking their authority files and bibliographic records.[19] Most of the states have made progress in developing union catalogs, serials lists, resource sharing arrangements, and automation networks.

Much of the progress, however, relates to document delivery rather than information access. Cooperative reference service providing actual search and discovery of information (including but not limited to bibliographic verification) continues to be practiced in many states and regions.[20] Networks like RLIN, OCLC and WLN, along with online searching are good reasons for optimism about cooperative information service, as machine readability certainly expedites cooperation. However, although the Library of Congress has worked with the state libraries in question referral, the problems of jurisdiction and type of library differences as well as funding have prevented anything resembling the national implementation of a patron's right to access to information beyond his or her own library. The RASD Cooperative Reference Service Committee is presently pretesting a form for communicating information requests from one library to another.[21]

There are many continuing controversies that relate to reference service that we can only mention here. For example, should there be a separate children's reference department in a public library, or one reference service? Should there be a separate undergraduate reference service in college and university libraries? How open or closed should reference collections be not only for access but for circulation? Should continuing education be the responsibility of the library or institution or is it the responsibility of the individual? Should non-professionals work at the reference desk and, if so, to what extent? How should reference departments be managed--and how should managers be developed or selected? The list can go on and on.

Professionalism

But let us move on to what will be the last topic of discussion and what is among the most important of all the issues presented so far. It can be called the issue of professionalism. It can also be identified as a topic which has not been as popular as most of the above subjects in terms of volume of published pages but it has had sporadic and continuing attention for many years--really throughout

most of the history of our profession. What is reference work?
Writers like Wynar, Vavrek, Whittaker, Rettig, Katz and others have
all grappled with this question.[22] Most of the controversies mentioned above come back to this question: just what is reference
work, and what is a professional librarian?

Recently the Office of Personnel Management (OPM) lowered
the civil service classification of librarians in federal libraries so
that people without LS degrees can qualify to obtain these positions.
The Office of Management and Budget (OMB) has adopted a new
policy demanding that information services and research be contracted
out to the private sector rather than performed by government libraries, information centers, and other agencies.[23] Also recently,
Mississippi State University was sued by Glenda Merwine over the
question, does a university have a right to require an MLS degree
as a condition for employment? The case is still in litigation but
ALA has decided not to be involved at this time.[24]

It appears that librarianship is in a bit of an identity crisis.
In the May 1984 issue of American Libraries, there is an article which
basically asserts that current reference practice is in a state of great
confusion and turmoil--certainly very much part of the same identity
crisis.[25] Much of the author's concern is tied in with the fact that
we are doing more than ever before--so much more that we may not
be able to continue doing it well--we're on a tread mill. Unfortunately
there are other writers who have voiced similar feelings of "sturm
und drang." Quite recently, Bernard Vavrek asserted that not only
is the golden age of reference librarianship over but concern must
now be voiced about the future of librarianship itself as a viable
function in a modern society.[26]

What is the answer to this conundrum? Perhaps if we balance
our efforts towards document delivery with provision of information
(making better use of our literature reviewing skills and our knowledge of information transfer in the various disciplines and areas of
interest) we will be more credible in our insistence on rigorous educational and professional standards for those who provide such service.

Are we, indeed, professionals? Let us follow the lead of Pauline Wilson. In an article in September, 1984 American Libraries on
the Merwine Case and OPM decisions, she says simply that we have
used the professional model about which to organize our work for
several decades.[27] We may not be a perfect profession, but by
our own choices we fit that model better than we do others. Given
the variety of trends and controversies, how should a professional
reference librarian act? One of the chief features of a profession is
that the practitioner takes responsibility for some portion of a client's
welfare. For the moment we will avoid such issues as the preparation, body of knowledge, and other aspects of a profession which
give the professional the needed expertise, and emphasize simply that

as professional reference librarians we take responsibility for the information welfare of a client. This is crucial. We do not provide
reference service for the sake of being nice to the patron, or to
make the patron feel good. We do not provide good reference service
by telling the patron what we happen to know, or by telling the
patron what we can readily find. Rather, we take responsibility for
the information welfare of the patron. This requires an active rather
than defensive stance. It does not mean we are slaves, any more
than other professionals are slaves. If we cannot help the patron
because the information need has been brought to us too late, we
need to level with the patron, just as a lawyer may have to tell a
client--why didn't you ask me before you engaged in such and such
behavior, or entered a flawed contract. The long term information
welfare of the patron may be best served by calling attention to what
the patron needs to do this time or next time to be better informed.
That may include some version of the directive--next time bring me
a better question. The most important element, here, though is that
we have accepted a responsibility.

Another characteristic of a professional is the dominance of
conscious activity, based on training, reading, study and research.
To put it bluntly, too often we operate on automatic. Just as one
can identify doctors, nurses and other individual practitioners who
have not kept up to date, who are not "professionally alive" so are
there reference librarians who somehow think they can just show up
at the desk for another day of work and all will be well. All will
not be well. There are new sources to be learned, new developments
in society and in various disciplines, erosion of interpersonal skills
once held, and other factors that only conscious action can remedy.
We must take this responsibility.

As one thinks about acquaintances in various professions, are
they not often individuals who are both plugged into local events
and activities, and at the same time, more so than most people in
the community, tuned into the outside world? Should this not also
be the case with the reference librarian, to assure that the library
is the window to the larger world for those who wish to use it as
such? Notwithstanding the Planning Process' attention to interests
within the community, the library, and its reference service should
provide access to a wider base of information and materials.

The next aspect of professionalism has to do with the fact
that the professional operates in a transparent way in regard to other
professionals in the same field--the work of the individual professional
is subject in some way to scrutiny by others. This is much talked
about in medicine, and ethical committees exist in the legal profession
to oversee behavior of the individual lawyer. Yet why do we resist
oversight of our own reference work? Among the extensive literature
on measurement and evaluation of reference service one usually finds
the notion that such activities are for improvement of service generally, and should not be used to evaluate the individual reference

librarian. It seems to us we should expect to have our work evalu-
ated--the more reference encounters that can be evaluated and in
other ways shared by and with our colleagues, the better will be our
service. The acceptance of such scrutiny would indeed be good evidence of the acceptance of responsibility for the information welfare
of the patron as mentioned above. The true professional communi-
cates in many ways with colleagues and accepts the scrutiny of peers.

Another aspect of professionalism is the responsibility to pro-
tect the resources of the profession so that it can meet its responsibilities. It is not enough to wring our hands and say "We can't
take responsibility for our patron's information welfare. We lost two
lines on the budget last year." We must see that the resources are
there. Do we stand by idly while they are eroded, even to provide
other services within and without the library? Do we know where
we stand in reference service in comparison to five years ago as far
as resources go? It would be interesting to see data across the country on that subject.

Another aspect of professionalism is that of personal quality
control. Are you the reference librarian you used to be, or have
you become something less than you were, or less than you hoped
to become? It seems common to find in our students the opinion that
things must be getting better in reference librarianship, that recent
graduates don't evidence the forbidding tone that they recall in contacts with "old time" librarians. It is our contention that we are
susceptible to becoming reflections of our worst fears, or that of
which we are most critical. Only through discipline (professionalism)
will we be otherwise--and we owe it to ourselves and to our profession to exercise that discipline.

Perhaps it is true that we cannot espouse sound theory on
the nature of reference work. Without well developed theory, a well
ordered philosophy of reference service is impossible to articulate.
Perhaps this is just because of one major, unavoidable, yet truly
exciting fact--reference service, in the end, is passive in the best
sense of the word. While we will prepare ourselves well, discipline
ourselves to provide the best possible services at all times based on
the best available resources, we will do so to topics and information
needs brought to us by our patrons. Until we receive an individual
request, we cannot fully anticipate its nature, and we should so construct our services to best react to the idiosyncratic nature of the
next, unknown request.

But there are some things we can anticipate, and as a profession we have attempted to do so in an official document--the RASD
Committment to Reference Service Guidelines, mentioned above. How
well are these known? Do we care about what they say? Are we
ready to dismiss guidelines we can't reach as unfeasible or idealistic?
The Guidelines say that you must have a professional reference librarian on duty at all times that the library is open. Is that so

outlandish? It is if we see the sine qua non of library service as document delivery or provision of study hall space. But if we believe a library to be more than that--if we believe that as a profession we take responsibility for our patrons' information welfare, it doesn't sound so outlandish. There are many further examples of important policy issues spoken to in this document. We suggest that a good start to a renewed dedication to reference service would be a reading of these guidelines, a commitment to their implementation, and attention to revisions as they occur.

Even if we act as professionals, accepting responsibility, are disciplined in behavior, and attentive to standards, there are still great dilemmas. Prime among these is the boundary of service. What information is appropriate for us to get for patrons--anything? Certainly not. "What's my Uncle Ted doing next Friday?" That question is unanswerable, and it is information, but few libraries would seek the answer. The definition with which this paper opens attempts to ward off this dilemma by stating that we are involved with information that is in some way connected to the graphic record of mankind. This seems somewhat too limiting. Although we cannot solve this dilemma here, it is best to keep the definition as broad as possible, not using false niceties to limit it, such as we often do with medical or legal questions. "Won't I get sued?" Let me quote L.S. Allen in a book on consumer health information: "As far as anyone has been able to determine from reported legal decisions, no librarian has ever been held liable for damages for negligence in supplying or failing to supply information to a patron."[28] In other words, worry about lawsuits and other such worries may mask unwillingness to provide the service we should be providing.

In conclusion, let us emphasize individual and collective professional responsibility. This includes the responsibility not to accept blindly what is put forth here. It should be questioned. One should consciously arrive at defensible professional standards. Only then will we become the professionals we can and want to become.

References

1. Thelma Freides, "Current Trends in Academic Libraries," Library Trends 31 (Winter 1983): 458-59.

2. See summary of arguments and discussion by James Rice, "Library Use Instruction with Individual Users: Should Instruction Be Included in the Reference Interview?" Reference Librarian 10 (Spring/Summer 1984): 75-77.

3. See summary of arguments and discussion by William A. Katz, Introduction to Reference Work, 2 vols. 4th ed. (New York: McGraw Hill, 1982), vol. 2: Reference Services and Reference Processes, p. 59.

4. Robert Wagers, "American Reference Theory and the Information Dogma," Journal of Library History 13 (Summer 1978): 265-81.

5.   See the following for a fairly complete list: Arthur P. Young,
     "Research on Library-User Education: A Review Essay," in
     Educating the Library User, ed. John Lubans, Jr. (New York:
     Bowker, 1984), pp. 1-15. Arthur P. Young and Exir B. Bren-
     nan, "Bibliographic Instruction: A Review of Research and
     Applications," in Progress in Educating the Library User, ed.
     John Lubans, Jr. (New York: Bowker, 1978), pp. 13-28. De-
     borah L. Lockwood, Library Instruction: A Bibliography (West-
     port, Connecticut: Greenwood, 1979). Hannelore B. Rader,
     "Library Orientation and Instruction ... ," Reference Services
     Review 9 (April 1981): 79-89; 10 (Summer 1982): 33-41; 11
     (Summer 1983): 57-65; 12 (Summer 1984): 59-71.
6.   Freides, "Current Trends," p. 459.
7.   James Rice, "Fees for Online Searches: A Review of the Issue
     and a Discussion of Alternatives," Journal of Library Administra-
     tion 3 (Spring 1982): 25-33.
8.   Mary Jo Lynch, Financing Online Services in Publicly Supported
     Libraries: The Report of an ALA Survey (Chicago: American
     Library Association, 1981). See RQ 21 (Spring 1982): 223-26
     for a summary.
9.   Freides, "Current Trends," p. 466.
10. David Isaacson, "Library Inreach," RQ 23 (Fall 1983): 65.
11. For information, contact PENNTAP (Pennsylvania Technical As-
     sistance Program), J. Orvis Keller Building, University Park,
     Pennsylvania 16802.
12. A Commitment to Information Services: Developmental Guide-
     lines 1979," RQ 19 (Spring 1979): 277-78.
13. Mary Prokop and Charles McClure, "The Public Librarian and
     Service Ethics: A Dilemma," Public Library Quarterly 3 (Winter
     1982): 69-81.
14. "A Commitment to Information Services," p. 277.
15. P. K. Swanson, "Reference Librarians and Online Catalogs,"
     RQ 23 (Fall 1983): 23-26.
16. Joseph Matthews, ed., Using Online Catalogs: A Nationwide
     Survey (New York: Neal-Schuman, 1983), p. 85.
17. N. C. Jacobson and Natalie Slurr, "Automated Reference Desk:
     Three Ways Libraries Can Use Computers to Enhance Reference
     Services," American Libraries 15 (May 1984): 324.
18. J. E. Miller, "OCLC and RLIN as Reference Tools," Journal of
     Academic Librarianship 8 (November 1982): 270-77. Swanson,
     "Reference Librarians," pp. 23-26. S. C. Farmer, "RLIN As
     a Reference Tool," Online 6 (September 1982): 14-22. Kathleen
     Low, "RLIN and WLN Databases: Not for Catalogers Only,"
     American Libraries 15 (May 1984): 326.
19. Ray Denenberg and Sally McCallum, RLG/WLN/LC Computers
     Ready to Talk," American Libraries 15 (June 1984): 400-4.
20. For bibliography on the cooperative reference attempts see Mar-
     jorie E. Murfin and Lubomyr R. Wynar, eds. Reference Service:
     An Annotated Bibliographic Guide (Littleton, Colorado: Libraries
     Unlimited, 1977), pp. 214-222 and Supplement (1984), p. 221-25.

21. A copy of this Information Request Form may be obtained by sending a self addressed #10 envelope to The Reference and Adult Services Division, American Library Association, 50 East Huron, Chicago, Illinois 60611.

22. Bohdan Wynar, "Reference Theory: Situation Hopeless But Not Impossible," College and Research Libraries 28 (September 1967): 337-42. Bernard Vavrek, "A Theory of Reference Service," College and Research Libraries 29 (November 1968): 508-510. Ken Whittaker, "Toward A Theory of Reference and Information Service," Journal of Librarianship 9 (January 1977): 49-63. James Rettig, "A Theoretical Model and Definition of the Reference Process," RQ 18 (Fall 1978): 19-29. Bill Katz, "The Uncertain Realities of Reference Service," Library Trends 31 (Winter 1983): 363-374.

23. "Public vs. Private Sector," The Bowker Annual of Library and Book Trade Information: 1984, Julia Ehresmann ed. (New York: Bowker, 1984), pp. 6-7.

24. Edward G. Holley, "The Merwine Case and the MLS: Where was ALA?" American Libraries 15 (May 1984): 327-331. Reader Forum--"More on Merwine, Holley and the MLS," American Libraries 15 (July/August 1984): 482-85. Robert Wedgeworth, "ALA and the Merwine Case: A Word as to the WHYS," American Libraries 15 (September 1984): 561-62.

25. William Miller, "What's Wrong with Reference?" American Libraries 15 (May 1984): 303-06; 321-22.

26. Bernard Vavrek, Introduction to issue, "Current Trends in Reference Services," Library Trends 31 (Winter, 1983): 361.

27. Pauline Wilson, "ALA, the MLS, and Professional Employment: An Observers Field Guide to the Issues," American Libraries 15 (September 1984): 563-66.

28. Luella S. Allen, "Legal and Ethical Considerations in Providing Health Information," in Developing Consumer Health Information Services, ed. Alan M. Rees (New York: Bowker, 1982), p. 45.

PART II

COMMUNICATION AND EDUCATION

SERVICE TO CHILDREN IN GROUPS*

Hennepin County Library Task Force
on Services to Groups

THE REPORT

Planning recommendations and staff discussions over several years
have shown children in groups to be a rapidly growing phenomenon
in need of expanded public library service. Statistics project a large
increase in the number of children, ages 0-4, in suburban Hennepin
County, from 37,338 in 1980 to 41,594 in 1990, an increase of 11.1
percent.

There is an even greater growth in the numbers of children
enrolled in group care facilities. Nationally, more than 70 percent
of all children between the ages of 3 and 5 attend some form of preschool education.[1] Statistics published by the Minnesota Department of Public Welfare in October 1983 indicated that approximately
12,000 children, age 6 weeks to 14 years, are cared for in an estimated 1,000 nursery schools, day-care centers and licensed day-care
homes in suburban Hennepin County. The number of children in
care facilities has increased by 3,455, or 40 percent, since 1979
while the number of facilities has grown by 200, or 38 percent, in
the same period. State officials indicate that this trend is continuing. In addition, an estimated 2,000 children, ages 5 to 14, are enrolled in school district latchkey programs offering before- and after-
school care.[2]

Adult statistics are also changing. In addition to the many
single parent families today, many more mothers are working outside
the home. In 1983, for the first time, half of all mothers with children under age 6 were in the labor force.[3]

These changing forms of modern society create a need for

---

*Reprinted by permission of the Hennepin County Library Task Force
on Services to Groups (Chair, Vicki Oeljen; members: Louis Ander-
sen, Bill Erickson, Holly McDonnell, Gretchen Wronka, Julie Ylinen)
and of the publishers from Public Libraries 29: 3 (Fall 1986) 100-
104; copyright © 1986 by the American Library Association.

changes in library service as well. Traditionally, the individual
child has been well served through reference and reader's advisory
services, story time, and programs. Now, many children do not
come to the library by themselves because they are enrolled in some
type of group care. The groups often do not take advantage of
library services because of lack of awareness, times at which services
are offered, and/or lack of transportation.

Society has placed an increased emphasis on the educational,
social, and cultural growth of children. For example, the ALA Realities: Education Reform in a Learning Society designates as its number one reality, "Learning Begins before Schooling." It emphasizes
a variety of ways library services to parents and day-care staff can
support preschool learning and suggests coalition building, with the
library staff acting as information providers to community groups.

Realities also urges public officials to appropriate funds for
parent education and early childhood education in public libraries
and to establish state and federal regulations requiring books and
library resources in child- care programs.[4] The Minnesota Long
Range Plan for Library Service, 1985 addresses services to children
including school media center funding and communication with child-
care staff.[5]

Also of interest is a recent survey of adult users in small public libraries from upstate New York that shows an 85 percent correlation between those who visited libraries as children and continue to
do so as adults. "Once the library habit has been introduced, it
tends to continue throughout the rest of childhood and adult life."[6]

The public library has the opportunity to become a key element in providing services to a segment of the population that is
growing rapidly, is recognized as of primary importance, and is
greatly in need of the diversity of materials and services necessary
to becoming responsible, productive, knowledgeable members of a
fast-changing, pluralistic society.

Task Force Activities

In the course of establishing recommendations the task force
conducted a literature search; gathered and studied statistics; collected input from HCL children's librarians and suburban Hennepin
County child-care providers through questionnaires, meetings, and
informal conversations; conducted a six-month survey to determine
current service being offered to children in groups in HLC; and
studied projects undertaken by other library systems throughout
the country. Two notable examples of the latter are the King County
Traveling Library Center and the Library Child Care Link of the
South Bay Cooperative Library System.

Statistics gathered from September 1984 through February 1985 showed that 18,293 children and 2,585 adults in child-care groups were served through HCL programs. This was accomplished with no direct library-initiated contact. Inequalities are inherent in service based on patron request rather than library initiation in that only child-care staff who were aware of services and materials make contact. While story times are generally considered to be service to the individual child, the survey showed that 40,000 children who were part of an identified child-care group participated in story times during the six-month period. The group requests that could not be accommodated usually failed due to reference desk and other programs commitments.

Charge

The Task Force was asked to prepare the following documents:

1. A three-year plan of service, 1985-1987, including recommendations, prioritized when applicable, for utilization of staff, collection, and other resources. Recommendations should be evaluated and prioritized with regard for what is realistically feasible in balance with all other services that HCL should continue to provide.

2. Policy recommendations--library board or administrative.

3. Procedures relating to both policies and practices.

4. A 1984 LSCA grant proposal.

To expand on the above: Recommendations are listed in four categories of priorities--very high, high, medium, and low. The task force intends that those appearing in the very high category be established in 1985, those in high be established in 1986, and those in low be reexamined in 1987 to evaluate feasibility and desirability at that time. Adoption of the recommendations must not diminish the responsibility to serving the individual child. [Editor's Note: Only very high and high recommendations are included in this article].

The task force has drafted the Library Board Policy on Service to Children in Groups and has recommended the rewriting of the Library Board Policy on Programming to minimize disparity of programming between groups and individuals.

For the task force, procedures evolved for incorporating into each recommendation the action that should take place and the person who should be responsible for that action. Most of the recommendations assume the development of system guidelines, by agency size, for service to children in groups. See guideline on page 108.

Rather than prepare a grant proposal, the task force investigated grant sources and selected those that seemed the most suitable sources of funds for recommendations. Many of the task force recommendations are suitable for outside funding.

Note: The task force focused almost exclusively on preschool children, as it is in this age range that the proliferation of groups has occurred. However, survey results indicated that half of the groups served during the six-month survey were full-time school students. While the task force set one goal with three attendant recommendations relating to school group service, it should be stressed that school group service was not addressed in depth, but further study is essential. Therefore, it is the strong recommendation of this task force that guidelines for service to school groups be established immediately.

RECOMMENDATIONS SECTION

Policy

Policy is needed as a framework for building a plan of improved service to children in groups. The task force recommends that the following policy be adopted:

> Hennepin County Library is committed to the provision of quality library service for children and seeks to provide equal access to individuals and those in groups. In recognition of the increase in the number of children and the number of children in groups, and the difficulty in reaching persons in groups as effectively as individuals, HCL will actively share information, expertise, materials, and services with children in groups, child-care workers, and the organizations and networks serving those children. Guidelines and sufficient support will ensure fair and uniform service to individuals and groups throughout the library system.

Guidelines

The task force cannot create a system for assigning the responsibilities toward groups in the individual agencies. A process must be implemented for distributing responsibility fairly within HLC and ensuring that all groups receive quality service throughout the system. Guidelines should be developed and adopted according to the following suggestions. These guidelines must precede the implementation of most of the recommendations.

The task force recommends that guidelines for service to children in groups by established according to the size of library (community library 1, 2, 3, and area). Representatives responsible for children's services from each library will meet in groups according to library size with the senior children's librarian and a PSD coordinating librarian. Guidelines will be developed to reflect the service that can be offered by libraries of similar size.

In preparing the guidelines the following factors should be addressed to minimize inequitable service resulting from local option.

Ratio of adults to children:
- take into account ages of children

Services that can be provided:
- take into account group size, age of children, notification time, age range within the group, staff complement, frequency of visits, initial and follow-up visits

Availability of the library during nonpublic service hours

Size of group that can be accommodated

Staffing patterns required to respond to groups:
- take into account group size, service requested.

Notification time requested
- take into account service requested

Visit frequency:
- take into account service requested, number of groups served

Visit duration:
- take into account service requested

Creation of service priorities:
- take into account visit duration, visit frequency, services requested, group size, geographic distance, access to transportation, type of group

Visits by children's librarian to group locations:
- take into account visit frequency, geographic distance, access to transportation

Limits on local option

Extended loan

Establishment of a referral process within HCL for groups that cannot be accommodated at individual agencies

Guidelines should be adopted by December 31 and should be reviewed annually.

Priorities

Many factors must be considered in choosing how best to implement the recommendations. Those that follow suggest some specific means for implementation, but practical application necessitates carrying them out in a variety of ways or to varying degrees. Adoption of some recommendations depends on the completion of others and some cover activities that are currently done at some agencies or that have been tried experimentally. It must be kept in mind that a commitment to serving children in groups will affect the entire library.

As stated in the policy section, providing quality service to children in groups requires the aid and cooperation of child-care staff. Therefore, workshops, printed materials, and network contacts are given high emphasis. This sharing of information, expertise, and materials includes child-care group leaders and staff, networks, group umbrella organizations, HCL staff, and librarians outside HCL.

Whenever practical, library services should be offered within the library setting. Transportation problems of child-care groups require that some services be offered outside the library. The goal is optimal library service to children and the adults working with them, not the number of people in the library.

Some group child-care staff members have expressed a willingness to pay for certain HCL services. Because of the danger of creating unequal service patterns and because charging fees is strongly opposed by the children's librarians, this suggestion was rejected.

The priorities were assigned according to the suggested time of implementation. They are based on suggestions from the HCL children's librarians and group child-care staff. Cost, ease of implementation, current budget, current staffing, and degree of controversy were considered, but the overriding concern was service to children.

GOAL-Regularly inform child-care providers of materials, services, and facilities available at Hennepin County libraries and encourage their use.

RATIONALE-The difficulty of reaching a child in a group as effectively as an individual child requires that librarians work through child-care providers. Many providers are unaware of all that HCL has to offer. Survey information collected by the task force shows that currently all group visits to the library are initiated by child-care staff rather than by librarians.

Very High Priority

Recommendation 1-A committee of children's librarians working

with the senior children's librarian and public information office
(PIO) will develop brochures explaining services available at HCL
for child-care groups and staff.

Recommendation 2-Children's librarians will initiate and annually
renew contact with child-care leaders by personal visits, mail, and/or
telephone to acquaint them with services and materials available. Contact procedures will be determined by individual children's librarians.
These contacts will increase demand and agency staff and collection.
This recommendation is dependent on the completion of recommendation 3.

Recommendation 3-The senior children's librarian will annually
produce an updated list of child-care providers and parenting groups
for use by children's librarians.

Recommendation 4-Children's librarians will provide regularly
scheduled workshops on an area basis for child-care providers covering such topics as orientation to the library and search strategy.
A lower priority option is to videotape presentations. These require
considerable effort to produce and are less effective. In addition,
child-care facilities generally lack playback equipment. Once created,
however, they are a readily available alternative.

Recommendation 5-The senior children's librarian will identify
newsletters of appropriate child-care organizations and will solicit
items and information from children's librarians and others, which
will be submitted on a regular basis to these newsletters through
public information office. Information will be provided about pertinent
materials, book sales, programs, and workshops.

Recommendation 6-Children's librarians with the help of PIO
senior juvenile selection librarian, and the senior children's librarian
will regularly create materials lists ranging from simple bibliographies
to full annotations. Child-care providers indicate that materials
lists are a high priority and have requested lists by age level, subject, and currency (last five years). This recommendation will have
a significant impact on the materials budget.

Recommendation 7-The senior children's librarian will establish
and maintain a staff speaker bureau file consisting of names of staff
members who have prepared presentations and their outlines and materials lists. These speakers and materials may be used to provide
similar workshops to avoid duplication of effort.

Recommendation 8-Children's librarian will offer formal and
informal book talks individually or via speaker's bureau, panels, or
video presentations to child-care providers. Costs are high for staff
preparation time and impact on materials collections.

GOAL--Provide quality service, sufficient materials, and a wel-
coming atmosphere to children in groups while maintaining current
levels of service to individuals.

RATIONALE-There is a need to increase the awareness of the
importance of service to children in groups in all library staff. To
serve groups as fully as possible, while maintaining current levels
of service, additional staff dedicated to children's services and an
increase in the materials budget are necessary.

Very High Priority

Recommendation 16-Staff time devoted to children's work will
be increased. Options include additional agency staff, additional
professional staff assigned to provide service throughout each area,
realignment of agency staff responsibilities to support the increase
in children's services, and additional substitute funding.

Recommendation 17-Juvenile materials budget will be increased
in response to use and circulation.

Recommendation 18-Use of the survey designed by the task
force to measure service to children in groups will be continued after
revision by the children's librarians. Results of the survey, along
with demographic information, will enable the senior children's librarian to make future budget recommendations.

Recommendation 19-Children's librarians will discuss task force
recommendation and their impact on all staff via agency meetings.

Recommendation 20-Professional staff will be encouraged and
given the opportunity to attend continuing education programs to
enhance their knowledge of children's materials and services.

Recommendation 21-Children's librarians, agency heads, and
lead clerks will meet annually to set agency goals for the year for
service to children in groups.

Recommendation 22-Agency heads will be responsible for maintaining a positive staff attitude toward service to children in groups.

Recommendation 23-Staff training and development committee
will provide assistance to inform, motivate, and encourage staff in
serving increased numbers of groups.

GOAL-Provide improved access to programming for children in
groups.

RATIONALE-Groups are often discouraged from attending programs because of space limitations, staff availability and program
costs.

High Priority

Recommendation 24-Additional cultural activities programs will
be provided with the schedule based on the guidelines that will be
established, individual library's facility and staff, number of groups
in the community, frequency of requests, and size of groups. Agency
children's librarians will communicate this information to the program
librarian. In addition to an increase in the cultural activities budget,
staff costs will be affected.

Recommendation 25-Agencies will provide additional in-house
programming, e.g., films, puppet shows, and story times, based
on the factors outlined in the recommendation above. Additional
staffing will be required.

Recommendation 26-Library board policy on programming will
be rewritten to minimize disparity of programming between groups
and individuals.

GOAL-Clarify roles and increase cooperation between HCL and
local school districts.

RATIONALE-Policies and practices of school media centers and
public libraries are often mutually misunderstood and conflicting.
Some schools view the public library as a substitute rather than a
supplement to the school media center, and heavy and inappropriate
demands are being placed on HCL staff and materials.

Very High Priority

Recommendation 31-HCL administrators will initiate discussion
with school administrators to clarify the role of each institution and
encourage school administrators to allocate adequate funding for materials and staff in their school media centers.

Recommendation 32-Administrative policy and guidelines for
practice will be written defining HCL's role in supporting the schools'
curricula, assignments, and special programs, e.g., Book Nook.

Recommendation 33-Children's librarians will regularly contact
school personnel in their community by attending faculty meetings,
making visits, or telephoning in order to facilitate communication and
cooperation.

GOAL-To foster excellent communication with child-care staff
and their organizations and to better understand their needs for
service.

RATIONALE-Libraries and child-care groups do not always

clearly understand one another's goals, needs, communications systems, or bureaucracy.

High Priority

Recommendation 35-Establish an advisory board made up of child-care staff from a variety of types of cares, which will meet on a regular basis with children's librarians to make suggestions and monitor progress. The senior children's librarian will select the board with input from children's librarians, chair meetings, and produce written reports of these meetings.

GOAL-Evaluate HCL's reponse to these goals and recommendations.

RATIONALE-In light of societal changes and the library's response to this report the task force feels a responsibility to assess recommendations and note progress.

High Priority

Recommendation 36-Representatives from the task force will be reconvened by the associate director for public services in eighteen months to prepare a written progress report assessing implementation of the recommendations, evaluating the response of the childcare community and recommending realignment of priorities where necessary.

IMPLEMENTATION

In her letter of January 29, 1986, Wronka lists the following accomplishments.

At this point, $10,000 from the 1986 budget had been allocated for substitute funds to support children's services. Requests for funds will be funneled through the office of the senior librarian for children's services. The money will be used to support

1. service to groups;

2. special services new to a particular library, e.g., toddler story time, evening story time, book talking in elementary or junior highs, etc.;

3. special projects such as collection development; and

4. development of new and innovative programs for a particular library of the system.

The library is also sponsoring a day-care providers workshop. A direct mailing was sent to licensed groups and family day-care providers in the area we wanted to reach. The program will be planned and presented by children's librarians; inservice training credits will be offered through the county day-care licensing agency. The goal is to provide day-care providers with information about the library services and materials available to them for use with their children or as part of their own professional development.

Based on last year's workshop, a fourteen-minute videotape was produced for use by day-care providers as a basic orientation/ introduction to the Hennepin County Library. It can be used in the library or the center. The attempt was to give "rock bottom" information to providers who may not be familiar with library services.

A workshop to inspire the staff is also planned. It will include a prominent child advocate, a member of the governor's Council on Children, Youth, and Families, and a practical approach to how library systems can improve services to day-care providers, both family and group.

REFERENCES

1. Will Manley. Snowballs in the Bookdrop (Hamden, Conn.: Library Professional Publ. 1982), p. 51.
2. Roz Anderson, School District 281, Community Education Latch Key Program, interview with Holly McDonnell, Crystal, Minnesota, February, 1985.
3. Sheila Kammerman, "Child Care Services: A National Picture," Monthly Labor Review 106:35 (Dec. 1983).
4. American Library Association Task Force on Excellence in Education, Realities: Educational Reform in a Learning Society (Chicago: American Library Assn., 1984), p. 3.
5. Issued as Minnesota Libraries 27, no. 11 (Autumn, 1984).
6. Barbara Will Razzano, "Creating the Library Habit," Library Journal 1 10:114 (Feb. 15, 1985).

THESPIANS, TROUBADOURS, HAMS
AND BAD ACTORS*

Larry Amey

As a child, my daughter used to study intensely--almost like an
anthropologist--those weird and exotic creatures called teenagers.
She watched their every move, full of fascination and envy. One
day she concluded her field work and declared: "You can always
tell which of the kids are the teenagers--the ones that giggle all
the time." (I enjoy reminding her of that insight now that she is
fifteen.)

They not only giggle, but laugh and shout and scratch and
shove, and dress and speak provocatively, gather in menacing groups,
disobey or ignore rules, and generally make a nuisance of themselves.
Clearly they are not an easy group to accommodate, and some librarians consider them to be impossible patrons. However, much of what
they do is not done in order to annoy us. To properly understand
and serve adolescents we need to look at their behavior in their
terms, not ours. This is particularly true with respect to the library, where we must see beyond our concern with circulation statistics, peace and quiet, and other professional matters. We might
better ask how the library can become a positive force in the lives
of young adults; how can we aid them in their search for self-reliance
and independence? The answers to these questions will grow out
of our understanding of adolescent developmental patterns.

Adolescents Are Not Children

A good place to start is to acknowledge that adolescents are not
children. While everyone recognizes that there is a bit of a child
in every adolescent, this is not the same thing as saying that adolescents should be thought of and treated in the same way as children.
A whole new social and intellectual agenda is drawn up at the onset

---

*Reprinted by permission of the author and the publisher from Emer-
gency Librarian, 13:5 (May-June 1986) 9-14; copyright © 1986 Dyad
Services.

of adolescence. Adolescents have new goals and new life tasks.
These are very different goals and tasks from those of childhood,
and the adolescent must develop different attitudes in facing them.
We, in turn, must treat teens in a very different way than we do
children. To fail to do so is more than just an oversight on our
part; it is to interfere with the process of growing up.

Some of the developmental tasks of adolescence identified by
psychologist Robert Havighurst are:

- achieving emotional independence of parents and other adults,

- selecting and preparing for an occupation,

- preparing for marriage and family life, developing intellectual
  skills and concepts necessary for civic competence,

- desiring and achieving socially responsible behavior,

- acquiring a set of values and an ethical system as a guide to
  behavior,

- achieving assurance of economic independence. [5:111-156]

These and other tasks of adolescence make up a formidable agenda,
and the voyage from dependence to independence can be a stormy
one. In many ways teenagers are poorly equipped to take on such
tasks. At the very time that they are trying to come to terms with
themselves and their place in society, they find themselves caught in
a double dynamic. From within, their body systems stage a coup
d'etat, releasing a hormonal flood and initiating a growth spurt second
in velocity only to that experienced in early childhood. [8:18] This
internal physiological revolution, and the resultant anatomical mani-
festations which beset adolescents, make young people vulnerable
and uncertain about themselves. Put another way, it is difficult to
know who you are when you are so much taller, bigger and otherwise altered from the person you were a year before.

The Good Old Days

The other half of this double dynamic, the changing face of the
outside world, also presents a problem for a teenager who needs to
define himself or herself against society. All the essential aspects
of society--the family, male and female roles, morality, employment--
are undergoing drastic change. One need only consult that barometer
of the contemporary human condition, the country and western hit
parade, to appreciate the problem. A recent song by the Judds
catches the situation precisely:

> Grandpa,
> Tell me 'bout the good old days.

Sometimes it feels like
This world's gone crazy.

Grandpa,
Take me back to yesterday
When the line between right and wrong
Didn't seem so hazy.

Did lovers really fall in love to stay?
And stand beside each other come what may?
A promise was really something people kept
And not something that they would say
And then just forget.

Families would really bow their heads to pray
Daddies would really never go away
O Grandpa
Tell me 'bout the good old days [10]

Suffice to say that it is difficult for an adolescent to assert fidelity to basic social values when these values are constantly reworked and eroded by an uncertain culture.

A Leap Into Uncertainty

Erik Erikson, a psychologist with much to say about adolescence, speaks of the importance of ego-identity, and we all know that the key question of adolescence is "Who am I?" Why is that such a difficult question to answer? Erikson suggests that we move systematically through stages of personality development, and that at each of the stages we are caught between those forces which act to hold us back, and those that can pull us forward. It is when we reach such a stage, and stand poised at the gap which separates us from the next stage in the process of maturation that we face what Erikson has called an identity crisis. [3:14] A major crisis is faced when the jump is to be made from childhood to adulthood and the adolescent asks: Who am I? Do I have the courage to go forward? Am I worthy to take up life's challenges? These are the questions which must be answered to resolve this crisis and embolden the adolescent to chance the leap across the gap.

The outcome of the identity crisis is greatly influenced by the ways in which adults surrounding teenagers evaluate and encourage their achievements. There is a danger at this juncture of identity confusion or loss of belief in oneself. This is why one of the major tasks of adolescence is achieving a clear perception of oneself as a mature, confident, independent individual.

How is this to be accomplished? What's a teenager to do? A common response is to become a performer: to try on and try out

various identities to see which one fits. Many young people see
themselves as "on stage," with the whole world as an audience. Nature and psychology, however, work in odd ways. Although the
process of self-definition is a lonely task, paradoxically it seems
best accomplished by adolescents grouping together with their peers.
It is useful to regard these groups, or cliques of teens as traveling
road shows, groups of actors in search of a stage and audience in
order for each actor to perform--as much for himself or herself as
for anyone else. Even love at this stage, Erikson theorizes, is a
sort of narcissistic (or negative) projection of oneself on to the be-
loved in order to clarify one's own perception of self. In this view,
the love object, and other people the teenager encounters are used
as a screen or mirror on which to project, in order to study the
response and gain some insight about oneself. Egocentricity is an
obvious characteristic of adolescence. Piaget gives this amusing and
perceptive assessment: "The adolescent in all modesty attributes to
himself an essential role in the salvation of humanity and organizes
his life plan accordingly."

The projection process, however, can be a confusing one. It is
not uncommon for a young person, male or female, to fail to differentiate between what others are thinking about them, and their own
mental preoccupations. That is, they assume that other people are
as obsessed with their behavior and appearance as they are themselves. This, in turn, may lead the adolescent to anticipate the
reactions of other people. Such anticipations, however, are based
on the premise that others are as admiring or critical of him as he
himself is. That is, the adolescent creates an imaginary audience.
Harry Mazer in I Love You, Stupid! gives a good-humored example
of what is going on inside the head of his teenage protagonist, Marcus
Rosenbloom [9:1]:

> Entering the school cafeteria, Marcus imagined that girls all
> over the room were looking up at him. Standing apart this
> way, on the top of the steps, tall, an inch over six feet, made
> taller by a mass of curly dark hair, he observed--and was
> observed (he hoped). "Who's that stunning guy, that senior?"
> Look who just came in ... Isn't he gorgeous?" "Oh, god, it's
> Marcus Rosembloom. He's a writer, you know, only seventeen
> and so brilliant ... Sexy!"

(In real life, of course, Marcus is far from self-assured and
self-confident.) We can all remember such vainglorious day dreams,
"movies" scripted out of our own adolescent attempts at self-analysis,
and acted out on those around us. The library is often just another
"theater", along with the school and the mall and other popular locations, in which the identity crisis is played out. While these
theatrics are amusing (in retrospect!), they also serve an important
purpose. Piaget has cautioned that individuals who do not dream
big dreams, who do not write idealistic "scripts" and become heroes
in their own minds are handicapped in their development. This process

of adolescent role play seems to serve as an audition for a real life
adult existence.

Well, yes. But in the meantime, how do we cope with this band
of thespians, troubadours, hams and bad actors?

Some Modest Suggestions

The Chinese say that understanding is forgiveness. So perhaps
we must begin by reminding ourselves that a good deal of adolescent
behavior, although sometimes bizarre and disruptive, is a necessary
feature of growth and development. Good kids are under those pink
mohawks and that grotesque make-up. (The punk style is, after all,
a perfect disguise from behind which an adolescent actor can observe
the audience reaction.) We must learn to restrain our adult judg-
ments--"why are you reading such junk?"--and save our energy to
become a positive force in the lives of teenagers. Poor self-image
may account for much of the depression, suicide, drug use and other
self-punishing behavior that one finds among adolescents. The library can do its bit in helping young people attain a positive self-
image.

A Place of Their Own

Teens need a place of their own: a relaxed, friendly place that
allows group interaction, a place where they can do homework together
and meet socially. The architectural straitjacket tailored for solitary,
silent reading simply does not fit active adolescents.[13] Donald
Gallo recently surveyed 481 students in different types of schools
throughout Connecticut.[A 738] He was interested to discover what
teenagers thought about libraries. The thing that they disliked most
was quiet. Trying to impose silence on teenage users is likely to be
a frustrating and ultimately self-defeating proposition. It is better
to work toward the creation of a special Young Adult section where
this is not such a high priority.

Many libraries, unfortunately, are too overcrowded to permit
the provision of a proper Young Adult area. The imaginative use
of existing space, however, will pay dividends. Any steps to provide
a "special" place are appreciated by young people. One public library, for example, carved an area out of the lower floor stacks as
a Young Adult department. A well-lit space with tables for group
work was established. The stack shelves act as "walls", and the
facing shelves are devoted to Young Adult books and magazines. A
small rack of records and cassettes has been made available, posters
hung, and (most importantly) a sign posted identifying it as the
Young Adult area. This modest effort has met with considerable
success.

It is commonly believed that the walkman is the most important thing to a teenager. Actually, a far simpler technology--the mirror-- is all-important. Only Snow White's wicked stepmother examined the contents of a mirror with more concentration than the average teenager. Unlike the evil queen, however, this interest on the part of adolescents is guided not by conceit, but from an authentic need to know themselves. In trying to plumb their souls, adolescents begin with what is immediately available--their external appearance. I hasten to reassure you that this is not the basis for suggestion that you line your library walls with mirrors. Rather, I wish to argue that that old standby, the bulletin board, can function as a mirror for adolescents. There is no topic of greater interest to teenagers than teenagers. A carefully crafted, frequently changed bulletin board given over to matters of concern to young adults will act as a drawing card, and it will serve to identify the special YA area. Examples of recent clippings of interest might be:

- "Reaction by Parents Can Harm Grades Study Shows"

- "Teen Drinking and Driving: A Deadly Rite of Passage"

- "A Chart of Teen Spending"

- "The Face at 14: A Top Model"

- "What Makes a Teen Turn Into An Alien in the Family?"

The bulletin board is also a perfect place to display job information, a topic of great importance these days. A high school librarian attracts hundreds of bulletin board readers by clipping and posting the daily horoscope.

Young Adult Specialist Needed

The person designated to work with teenagers must bring to the task an understanding of adolescents, their interests and their needs. The job demands a great deal of patience and forbearance. Too often, however, the Young Adult position is treated as an overflow or overlap to the children's library position. This approach is fraught with difficulty. Adolescents are involved with the task of defining themselves as adults. One of the ways in which they accomplish this is to rigorously distinguish themselves from children. They do not wish to associate themselves with children's services and children's collections. They may very well prefer not to be served by a children's librarian. This is especially true if the children's librarian applies the same approaches and techniques to YA service that he or she employs in serving children. Adolescents strive for independence and they appreciate people who work with them in a way that encourages self-sufficiency. If it is not possible to provide a fully-trained, full-time YA librarian, it is, as a general rule, more appropriate to employ an adult services person to take on the extra duty of young adult services. It should be emphasized, however, that the proper

response is to provide an actual young adult specialist. A recent
survey of over 3000 students asked when they received advice on
their reading.[4:736] The study found that 19 percent of the students in grades 4-6 most often acted on a librarian's suggestions for
good books. This figure fell to 4 percent among the junior high
students, and 2 percent of the senior high students. The researcher
speculated that : "Perhaps one of the reasons older students don't
trust in suggestions of a librarian as much as younger students do
is the quality of the information they are likely to receive. Younger
children are more likely to go to the children's librarian for information and assistance. For teenagers, there is too often no comparable
individual to approach." [4:738]

Forging Links

     The key to successful YA service lies in the link between the
school and the public library. Neither of these institutions can afford to ignore the other if success is to be realized. Adolescents
use both types of libraries, often in different ways. Research on
the information seeking behavior of adolescents, conducted with nearly
300 grade 10 students, found that they made considerable use of both
school and public libraries in their independent learning endeavors.[1]
They used the libraries in somewhat different ways, however. The
public library was used principally for reference materials, encyclopedias and its book collection. The collection was turned to in support of "heavy assignments" such as a term paper or a major project.
School library use, on the other hand, tended to focus on elements
less connected to the collection. The main attractions of the school
library were as a place to study, to meet friends, and to do homework. Respondents recognized the depth of the collection at the
public library and employed it for their research assignments, but
they found the school library to be a friendlier, more comfortable
place to work. These sorts of findings point to rather interesting
differences in user perception and needs.

     In some jurisdictions it is considered politically astute to dis-
courage any link between the school and public library lest the taxpayers and politicians perceive the situation as unnecessary duplication and begin to call for an abolition of service to young people in
one or other of the institutions, or an amalgamation of the two into
a school-housed public library. This strikes fear in the hearts of
some professionals and they elect to ignore the sister institution and
to put as much distance between each other as possible. It is wrong
to insist on rigorous separation. Young adults must be served in
their schools, and in public libraries. In order for such service
to be truly effective, it must be closely coordinated. To do otherwise is to penalize adolescent users. This is not to minimize the
political problem. It is true that some will cry "duplication." It is
up to librarians to make the case for service in schools and in public
libraries. We must document use patterns and educate the public
about the varied information and education needs of adolescents.

The school library-public library link is an under-researched area. Most of the existing literature insists on the value of cooperation, but falls short on specifics. A recent study, however, provides some suggestive data. Barbara Will Razzano describes a survey of adult users in 28 small public libraries in upstate New York.[12] Although the study dealt with adults rather than young adults, the questions were directed at how, when and why the adults, while growing up, had come to use the public library. The responses provide, for example, some information on what initially attracted people to the library. Depending upon the age at which their initial visit had occurred, the major reasons cited for first visiting the public library (after book borrowing, which was the paramount reason in each case) varied from program attendance (22 percent of those who visited as preschoolers), to program attendance and homework assistance (10 percent each of those who visited in the 7-12 age bracket), to homework assistance (26 percent of those who first visited as teenagers). Of particular interest, however, was the information supplied on what has come to be known as "adolescent fallout." Librarians have observed that there is a decline in public library use as children become adolescents. This research, however, reported that 96 percent of the current adult users who first visited the library while under the age of 18 continued to use it throughout their teenage years as well. In fact, 87 percent said that they visited the library weekly or monthly while they were teenagers How, then, can we account for the common perception that many children stop using the library when they become teenagers? The answer suggested by Razzano is that librarians may have been misled by a change in use patterns. It was found that during the teenage years the most important reasons for use become homework assistance and research assignments. Indeed, the teens were found to be the only age group in the whole age spectrum for which the importance of the reference function of the public library equalled or exceeded the importance of the book borrowing function. It is possible, therefore, because reference books seldom circulate, and because those materials meeting young adult homework requirements are often obtained from the adult or non-book collections, that this heavy use of the public library by adolescents would not be accurately reflected in YA book circulation, and would account for why many librarians see their young patrons as "lost" when they reach adolescence. In fact, the New York survey showed an increased but different use of the library during the teenage years.

More work is needed to confirm these findings, but some tentative speculation may be in order. These results suggest that while much attention has been paid to YA fiction, much more research must be done on the non-fiction resource use and information seeking needs of adolescents. Interestingly enough, it is exactly this area in which enhanced cooperation between school and public librarians may be realized. As resource-based learning has been implemented in schools, progressive teacher-librarians have undertaken a systematic approach to the integrated teaching of information skills.

A curriculum embracing a school-based continuum of information skills has become central to the work of the teacher-librarian. Continuous, cooperative teaching with the classroom teachers is now undertaken in regard to student search strategies, use of the catalogue, indexes and reference materials and the acquiring, analyzing, organization and communication of information. The goal is to teach young people the skills necessary to independently access and utilize information. These are skills which have obvious application in the public library domain, and teacher-librarians who have made this their area of specialization have much to share with their public library colleagues.[14]

Young adults as a rule are underserved by all segments of the community. I have chosen to focus on the link between the school and public library, but other opportunities for networking are also possible and necessary. Truly effective YA service will draw upon the expertise of adolescent specialists in the fields of medicine, social work and recreational services.

The Need for Personalized Service

Adolescent information seekers highly value personal contact. The teen respondents in my study identified experts, family and friends in the select category of "most useful resources." My interviewees indicated that they liked to obtain information from other people, and that they found such personal contacts to be an efficient and effective way to gather information.[1:296]

There is evidence, unfortunately, that young adults are often rebuffed in their attempts to use the library. In ranking what they most disliked about libraries, in the Gallo study, quiet came first, followed by librarians.[4:738] The teenagers' reported perceptions of librarians were divided into two lists of positive and negative characteristics. The negative list was four times the length of the positive list. The young adults felt these terms best described librarians: mean, meanlooking, snobby, quiet, cranky, pushy, stiff, grumpy, bitchy, strict, weird, arrogant, short-tempered, old, power-hungry, snotty, inflexible and rude. Not a pretty picture. As Gallo concludes: " ... the findings from ... several surveys suggest that if librarians are unfriendly, arrogant, over-protective of their books more interest in maintaining silence than in creating a pleasant place to visit, and uninformed about YA books, some students will chose to avoid libraries at all costs--and those who must use them will never feel at ease doing so."[4:739]

It is not difficult to uncover library policies and staff attitudes that seem designed to discourage adolescent users. One public library feeling the pressure of student use actually went so far as to stencil signs on the reading room tables prohibiting student occupancy. There is also the problem of the attitude of many non-YA

specialists. Some young adult librarians find that their efforts to
attract teenagers to the library are short-circuited by other staff
members who treat the young people badly when they seek service.
This underlines the need for in-service sessions on young adult service for all personnel. The young adult specialist can use such sessions to explain the nature of the user group and to articulate the
goals of service to teenagers. Everyone must be brought onside in
order to attract and keep young users.

Collection Building

     A recent issue of The Bookmark, the British Columbia Teacher-
Librarians' Association journal, featured a lively discussion on young
adult reading.[11] A well-known Canadian authority was purported
to have told the Vancouver Sun that: "It may be better for teenagers
to read nothing at all than something like Conan the Barbarian--a
pseudo-scientific series about a macho hero who is racist and everything else. It's the ideas that count, not the fact that they're just
reading."[15] I suggested in my rebuttal that we remind ourselves
that librarians are not English literature teachers. A reminder is
necessary because some confusion seems to exist in the profession.
This confusion has been here a long time, and unfortunately, it
seems to persist. The reason for such role confusion may be found
in the fact that many people enter librarianship after undergraduate
work in English. Whatever the reason, this is a pernicious confusion
that must be quashed. Robert Leeson, in a spirited and scholarly
article entitled "Critics' Choice: Child or Book?", explores the roots
of criticism and asks: "What future for the critic? Which critic:
child-centered or book-centered? English-lit critic or "social" critic?
The critic who goes for rigor and respectability or the one who goes
for relevance and response?"[7] These questions are pertinent to
a new Canadian study.

Michele Landsberg's Guide to Children's Books (the title makes me
think of Richard Scarry's Greatest Word Book Ever, but never mind)
has recently appeared to great acclaim.[6] Landsberg's book is
opinionated, argumentative, assertive, perceptive, muddleheaded,
elitist, and oddly prudish--in other words, a very good read indeed.
She knows her children's literature and she argues her case forcefully.
When the Landsberg juggernaut rolls up to young adult literature,
however, it suffers a puncture and comes up flat. In short order
she dispenses with Judy Blume ("The poorest writer of all the problem
novelists") and with S.E. Hinton, Paula Danziger, Robert Cormier,
Paul Zindel, Kevin Major and others who have been found guilty of
popularity. Earnestly applying the traditional Eng.-lit critique to
plot, character development, use of language, and so on Landsberg
finds that popular YA novels are "ungrammatical", "inexpressive",
"cynical", "violent", "cliche-ridden", and "flat". This splenetic exercise completed, Landsberg is left with a puzzling problem: how to

account for the books' popularity? It then becomes necessary to attack the readers and their taste. The books are characterized as "bulk reading", "Kleenex", "Garble", "social glue", and "trash". Blume and Hinton are upbraided because they describe their motivation to write in these terms: "When I was young, I never could find any books about kids like me, and that's what I wanted to read about." Landsberg responds to this straightforward declaration by thundering: "Their almost identical narcissism ... " Narcissism is a very bad word to Landsberg. She manages to completely misunderstand the perfectly normal adolescent concern with self. The egocentrism of adolescence is not a sin, but a natural, needed and important aspect of physical, mental and social development. However, in Landsberg's world, where the book is all, narcissism is evil, and books that cater to the teenager desire for stories about themselves and their concerns will lead, she suggests, to a narrow solipsism. Thus Blume is said to "flatter her young readers by mimicking all their most superficial concerns" (read, real concerns). In an extraordinarily wrong-headed reading of The Outsiders Landsberg asserts that: "Hinton's work flatters the egos of young male readers with its barely subliminal sexual praise and lets them escape into the supposed glory of attention and approval from an older teenage tough." As a final insight, she observes that "Blume's books ... are intended to offer a therapeutic not a literary experience."

A literary experience is clearly a noble and lofty thing. This cool, objective, elevated critical approach has no time for books that speak of pimples, lust, motorcycles and other aspects of the adolescent's world. Better to bathe in the pure waters of imaginative fantasy, folk or historical fiction. Dorothy Broderick has identified this approach to collection building as the "literary excellence syndrome."[2] Its motto is: "Ask not if any kid will want to read it, ask only, is it quality literature." (The last word, Broderick notes, is often pronounced as lit-ter-a-chure.)

Instead of condemning popular adolescent fiction, it is more profitable to attempt to understand why it appeals to teens. Young adult formula fiction is inevitably dismissed as "predictable" and "trite". Isn't it possible, however, that adolescents adrift in personal and societal change will naturally seek out stories which are predictable, which provide comfort and relaxation in their predictability, and which aid them to gain insight by seeing themselves reflected back in the stories that they read? It is important that we do not demean the reading tastes of young people. They read for a reason. The reason may escape the English literature critics, but we as librarians can feel a strong measure of success when we see that teenagers are reading, and that they enjoy reading.

References

1. Amey, L.J. "Information Seeking Activities of Adolescents of

Different Socio-Economic Classes in a Canadian Urban Centre."
Ph.D. dissertation, University of Toronto, 1981.
2. Broderick, Dorothy. "The Literary Excellence Syndrome."
Collection Building. Volume 5 (Fall, 1983), pages 43-45.
3. Erikson, Erik, H. Young Martin Luter, A Study in Psycho-
analysis and History. New York: W.W. Norton, 1958.
4. Gallo, Donald R. "Ask Your Librarian! Four Surveys Reveal
Where Young People Turn for Reading Advice." American Libraries, Volume 16 (November, 1985), pages 736-739.
5. Havighurst, Robert J. Human Development and Education.
New York: Longmans, Green, 1953.
6. Landsberg, Michele. Michele Landsberg's Guide to Children's
Books. Markham, ON: Penguin, 1985.
7. Leeson, Robert. "Critics' Choice: Child or Book?" The School
Librarian. Volume 33 (June, 1985), pages 104-110.
8. Lipitz, Joan. Growing Up Forgotten: A Review of Research
and Programs Concerning Early Adolescence. Durham, NC:
Learning Institute of North Carolina, 1975.
9. Mazer, Harry. I Love You, Stupid!. New York: Thomas Y.
Crowell, 1981.
10. O'Hara, Jamie. "Grandpa (Tell Me 'Bout the Good Old Days)."
Sunbury Music Canada (CAPAC), 1985. Reprinted with permission.
11. "Point/Counterpoint." The Bookmark. Volume 26 (December,
1984), pages 13-27.
12. Razzano, Barbara Will. "Creating the Library Habit." Library
Journal. Volume 110 (February 15, 1985), pages 111-114.
13. There is very little in the literature concerning library architecture and service to young adults. One excellent article,
however, is "Educational and Recreational Services of the Public
Library for Young Adults" by Mary K. Chelton in Library Quarterly, Volume 48 (October, 1978), pages 488-498.
14. See particularly Carol-Ann Haycock, "Information Skills in the
Curriculum: Developing a School-Based Continuum," and Sharon
Walisser "Developing a School-Based Research Strategy, K-7,"
in Emergency Librarian, Volume 13 (September/October, 1985),
pages 11-18 and 19-27.
15. The quote from an article by Douglas Todd entitled "Better Not
To Read At All?" (Vancouver Sun, July 24, 1984, p. B6) was
disavowed by the source, who said she had been misquoted. It
does, however, serve as a nice example of what is all too often
put forth by some critics.

THE EDUCATING OF BLACK LIBRARIANS:
AN HISTORICAL PERSPECTIVE*

Rosemary Ruhig Du Mont

The library school is the "one place where the legitimate claims, the
unrealized ambitions and the unstated needs of all library interests"
are met.[1] It is there that the goals that guide librarianship are
shaped. Consequently, when one wants to identify some of the reasons for the historical underrepresentation of black Americans in
librarianship, one can look to the historical development of professional library science education for some of the answers.

A caveat is in order before this paper begins. It has to do
with the capacity of a white person to understand the black experience in librarianship. Some black librarians would doubt that capacity and resent any such undertaking as this paper by a white
person. The education of black librarians, however, is an issue
that affects, and must be of concern to all American librarians.
Many black librarians realize that if their contribution to the profession is to be fully recognized and respected, whites must be encouraged to learn about the black librarian experience and understand it as best they can from the black point of view. This paper
is one such effort.

The paper will be divided into three major parts. The first
will describe the historical development of library science education
for blacks by chronological periods. The second will discuss the
present situation. The third part will attempt to appriase the historical development of library education for blacks and make recommendations for the future.

HISTORICAL DEVELOPMENT OF PROFESSIONAL LIBRARY
EDUCATION FOR BLACKS

In looking at the secondary source material on the historical

*Reprinted by permission of the author and publisher from the Journal
of Education for Library and Information Science, 26:4 (Spring, 1986)
233-248; copyright © 1986 Association for Library and Information
Science Education, Inc.

development of American library education for blacks, it should be
noted that those historians who have chosen to study the development of American library education have made no attempt to include
consideration of the special nature of library education for blacks
in their investigations. Examination of the major works in the field
show that they virtually ignore the issue.[2] Yet, throughout the
century that professional library science education has been available, the professional education of blacks has been regarded as a
key to progress in the serving of black library patrons.[3] Indeed,
there is much evidence which suggests that it is the education of
black library leadership which has been the critical element in the
progress which has been made in the development of service for
black library users. This conclusion does not suggest that library
science education alone has been the reason for the successes and
failures in service to blacks--it is to say that the condition of library
science education has been a reflection of progress made toward
service goals.

Louisville Free Public Library 1910-1931?

Historically, the development of library science education for
blacks is mainly a chapter in southern library history. Over 90
percent of blacks, were, after all, in the south in the period when
the first library schools were being established at the end of the
nineteenth century.[4] Library resources in the southern states at
this time were extremely limited; there was no free public library
service anywhere in the Southeast before 1895, and no school of library science until 1905. The library facilities and services that
existed were for special groups of those who could afford to pay for
the privilege of using them. Under these circumstances there were
few librarians and fewer still who recognized the need for special
library training.[5]

The concept of "separate but equal," confirmed by the United
States Supreme Court in Plessy vs. Ferguson in 1896, meant that
whatever limited library services were available for whites, were not
necessarily available for blacks. Constitutional authority gave support for separation of the races in virtually every sphere of life.
The facilities and services provided for blacks in all areas of public
life were seldom anything like equal. This included library service
and education for librarianship.

As late as 1913, such large cities as Atlanta, Birmingham,
Dallas, Mobile, Montgomery, Nashville, New Orleans and Richmond
reported having no public library service for blacks.[6] In order
for such service to develop, blacks had to gain entry into the profession through appropriate education and training. This was most
difficult. Blacks were denied admission to southern white colleges
and universities; as a result of the Second Morrill Act they were
relegated to a separate system of federally aided land grant colleges;
and because of inferior education in segregated elementary and

secondary schools, they entered higher education woefully ill prepared.[7] Consequently, blacks were very slow in entering the ranks
of professional librarians.

Following the receipt of a certificate of completion by Edward
Christopher Williams in 1900 from the New York State Library School
at Albany, the next known black graduate was in 1926, when Hampton Institute (Virginia) graduated three professionals.[8] The only
measure taken in the interim to train black librarians was the establishment of an apprenticeship training class for high school graduates in Louisville, Kentucky, as part of the creation of a "Negro
Department" in the Louisville Free Public Library.

Starting in 1910 until the early 1930s, when it ceased to exist,
the apprentice program trained most of the young women who worked
in library branches serving blacks in the South, before the founding
of the Hampton Institute Library School. Twenty-nine local persons
and 12 out-of-town persons (from Houston, Birmingham, Atlanta,
Evansville, Memphis, Knoxville, Nashville, and Chattanooga), took
courses and practice work of four to six months in length.[9]

A paper read by Thomas Fountain Blue, the black director of
the apprenticeship program, at the American Library Association
(ALA) conference in Detroit, in 1922, characterized the apprenticeship training as "a child of necessity." "In those days a public library for colored people in the South was something 'new under the
sun.' Naturally a trained colored library assistant was a rarity ...
The Western Colored Branch of Louisville ... needed assistants, and
so it was decided to train them."[10]

That such a program was the only source of trained black librarians for almost 20 years, reflects the limited nature of library
service to blacks at the beginning of the twentieth century.

Hampton Institute 1925-1939

The founding of the library school at Hampton Institute reflected increased interest in the development of black educational
opportunities after 1920--a development encouraged in large part by
three large and purposeful private foundations--the Rosenwald Fund,
the General Education Board, and the Carnegie Corporation of New
York. These agencies were broadly interested in the improvement
and expansion of education in the South, and within that general
interest, with the improvement of educational opportunities for blacks.[11]
They became most responsible for the direction of black educational
programming.[12]

In the area of library development, in particular, in the 1920s,
the General Education Board gave over a million dollars for black
college library buildings; a half million dollars was appropriated by
the Julius Rosenwald Fund for county library development, which in-

cluded some services for blacks; the Carnegie Corporation built some
branch libraries for blacks and gave money to a couple of black colleges for their book collections.[13]

Library education for blacks also relied on foundation support.
The Hampton library school founded with a grant from the Carnegie
Corporation in 1925 had as its goal the encouragement of "proper
development of library work with Negroes in the South" through the
"preparation of Negro librarians in that environment."[14]

Hampton Institute had opened in 1868, with two teachers and
15 pupils. Founded by General Samuel Chapman Armstrong, with
support from the Freedman's Bureau and northern philanthropists,
it rejected the notion of a traditional literary education for blacks
in favor of instruction in agriculture and simple crafts. Hampton
thus became one focus of the educational dilemma that was to face
black education leaders for more than half a century. In introducing
the idea of vocational education for blacks, it attributed to this type
of training a value superior to that offered by liberal arts colleges
that were also being established at this time. Those interested in
the advancement of black education would be placed in conflict by
the two styles of training: they would debate the merits of one
against the other and find that accepting either would rob them of
some advantage which the other offered.[15]

Hampton's most famous student, Booker T. Washington, became a spokesperson for the concept of industrial education represented by Hampton. Washington pointedly advocated racial separation, the cultivation of friendship with white southerners and industrial, agricultural, and practical education. Industrial education was
not to be a means of propelling blacks into the mainstream of the
total American society: rather it was seen as a mechanism through
which some blacks could be of special service to the growing black
communities around the nation. From this mode of educational development, underwritten by northern philanthropy, emerged the system of "separate but equal."[16]

Hampton was selected as the site of the first library school
for blacks for several reasons: First, it had a significant book collection in a good library building with a trained staff. Second, Hampton allowed a bi-racial faculty and so it could hire qualified white
faculty to teach. Third, Hampton's alumni were placed in black
leadership positions throughout the South and could aid in the placement of the library school's graduates.[17]

A white woman, Florence Rising Curtis, a graduate of the New
York State Library School, was selected as director. She had served
as assistant professor in the University of Illinois Library School
and as vice-director of the Drexel Institute of Library Science. She
had a staff of trained librarians to assist her. Beginning as a junior
undergraduate program, Hampton eventually issued a bachelor's degree in library science and was accredited by ALA.

The establishment of this school came at a time when state and regional accrediting associations were becoming aware of the position of the library in the educational program of the college and were therefore making the library a focal point in the accreditation procedure. With this impetus, the Hampton Library School was able to make a positive contribution to the black college library field. College libraries were the chief employers of its graduates. A 1940 survey showed that 70 percent of Hampton graduates were in college libraries, 15 percent in high school libraries, 12 percent in public libraries, and a few in other positions.[18] The total number of Hampton graduates by the time it closed in 1939 was 183.[19]

Not only did the school furnish trained librarians, but it also promoted black college library interests. Every year, Director Curtis traveled for eight weeks throughout the South with the financial support of first the Rosenwald Fund and later the Carnegie Corporation, interviewing the presidents and faculties of black colleges. She aided them in the development of library facilities and services, providing them with book buying lists, floor plans and any other assistance requested. The expansion of the black college library program, in terms of new buildings, trained personnel, and reorganization from 1925 until 1938, attest to the influence of the combination of accreditation demands and the Hampton Library School.[20] Largely as a result of the work of Curtis, scores of black schools and colleges were accredited.[21]

Unfortunately, during the 1920s and 1930s, public library service in the South did not have adequate financial support, and thus the number of public libraries giving service to blacks was very small.[22] Carnegie grants provided money for black library branches in some seven locations, but the administration, budgets and personnel in too few instances allowed for a vigorous, progressive public library program.[23]

Consequently, opportunities for trained black public librarians were limited. There was no accreditation stimulus to encourage the upgrading of public library service for blacks and little support to hire trained black librarians.

The support of school librarians was somewhat better. A plan for the training of school librarians was proposed by Curtis, to be sponsored by ALA. The General Education Board agreed to finance the program, which resulted in the establishment of four regional centers to offer courses for black school librarians for four consecutive summers from 1936 through 1939. These centers were at Hampton Institute, Atlanta University, Fisk University, and Prairie View A & M University. Basic courses were given in school library administration, book selection, reference, and cataloging and classification.[24] From this effort some two hundred teacher-librarians received the instruction required by the Southern Association of Colleges and Secondary Schools for high school librarians.

Not all black library school students studied at Hampton for
library science degrees during this time. Some did leave the South
to obtain a library school education. A survey reported by Curtis
shows that through 1934, 70 black students had enrolled in library
schools other than Hampton. [25] She noted, however, the difficulties faced by these students. One difficulty encountered was a lack
of suitable lodging places for black library school students within
easy access to campus. [26] A more significant problem was "the
distance [of northern and western library schools] from the South
and the consequent lack of knowledge of positions and success in
placement." [27] Because blacks were generally hired only in "black
institutions" they were restricted to the South for the limited opportunities available. Charlotte Templeton, librarian of the Greenville,
South Carolina, Public Library and president of the Southeastern
Library Association, noted in 1931 that in the South the demand was
very limited for black librarians. [28] Curtis reported in 1935 that
it was not possible to place more than 15 or 20 library school graduates a year, due to limited opportunities, not only in the South,
but in the North and West as well. [29]

As early as 1931, consideration was given to removing the library school from Hampton Institute. In March of that year, a conference was convened at Chapel Hill, North Carolina, by Louis Round
Wilson, in his capacity as Chair of the Board of Education for Librarianship (BEL). Funded by the Rosenwald Fund, the purpose of
the conference was to consider future possibilities in education for
librarianship for blacks. [30] To this meeting were invited representatives of all the foundations working in the South, representatives of
black institutions offering any courses for the training of librarians,
and representatives of the BEL. The discussion at this meeting
covered the need for black librarians and the type of library science
training needed to fulfill that need.

Hampton's role in the education of black librarians was thoroughly reviewed. Although Hampton was credited with meeting "ad-
mirably the demand for college and school librarians" it was perceived
to have "handicaps" for the continuation of this role. [31] Among
these handicaps were the lack of supervised practice and training for
future public librarians and the school's lack of central location for
its potential student body. [32] By far the most serious weakness
identified was the library school's connection with a "vocational school."
This orientation was seen to be a distinct disadvantage to those black
students who desired to take their professional training in a collegiate
institution. [33] The reluctance of such students to go to Hampton
was "in some cases keeping desirable persons from going to library
school." [34] In other cases, students were making the effort to go
to northern schools because degrees from these institutions were
perceived to have more prestige in the South than degrees from Hampton. [35]

Consequently, beginning in 1931, a search was started for a

more propitious affiliation for the one library school for the training
of black librarians that was considered necessary by both library
and philanthropic leaders.

Atlanta University 1941

The new library school affiliation was a number of years in
the making. Hampton continued to operate as a number of new options for the school were considered. Both Fisk University and Atlanta University were evaluated as possible new sites. Either one
was seen to be able to provide more financial support for the school
than was possible for Hampton.[35] All three foundations involved
in the support of library education for blacks, the Rosenwald Fund,
the General Education Board, and the Carnegie Corporation, desired
to find a permanent new home for the library school.[36] The matter
was put on "hold" however, until the Hampton School closed in June
of 1939, due to the decisions by the foundations to cease further
funding of it.

The opening of a new school was not the immediate response
to the Hampton closing. Instead, a survey was done in September
of 1939 to determine if there was enough demand for black librarians
at that point in time to warrant the establishment of "another library
school for Negroes."[37] The BEL asked Tommie Dora Barker, dean
of the library school at Emory University, to prepare a report sum-
marizing the need for a library school "with an estimate of the number and kinds of library positions likely to be open to Negroes in the
next five or ten years."[38] She surveyed the 16 states that main-
tained segregated school systems and concluded that two types of
library education for blacks were needed: some semi-professional
courses for teacher-librarians in secondary schools and a full one-
year curriculum for those who wanted a professional degree to work
in public or academic libraries. The survey noted that "a majority
of Negroes who are reported to be interested in taking or planning
to take full professional training like to have the training in a special school for Negroes in the South."[39] While black institutions
were endeavoring to meet the demand for semi-professional courses
for teacher-librarians (25 such institutions were identified in the
survey[40]), there was no institution endeavoring to give the full
professional curriculum which met the accreditation standards established by BEL.

Special attention was paid to the fact that black students from
the South had difficulty in meeting the entrance requirements of
library schools outside the South "because of limitations of background
and inadequate academic preparation."[41] Consequently, a school
in the South that would be able to recognize and deal with these
difficiencies was seen as necessary.

One black library leader took exception to this recommendation.

Wallace Van Jackson, librarian at Virginia Union University, in commenting on the report, noted that although certain emotional barriers were faced by black students because most library science teachers and students were white, he did not believe that developing a new library school with black faculty for black students was the answer. He saw that the surest way of developing strong black librarians was by being schoolmates of whites in "mixed schools" and having to meet the same academic standards as the white students.[42]

Van Jackson accepted the limited nature of the need for black librarians and estimated, as Curtis had done before him, that only 20 black professional librarians were needed a year. Thus, although most "mixed schools" would only accept one or two black students at a time, the small number of graduates needed could be absorbed by existing programs.[43]

Library education and foundation leaders disagreed. In March of 1940 a conference was held in Atlanta, funded by the Carnegie Corporation and the General Education Board to discuss the development of a school of library science for black students at Atlanta University. It is evident that Atlanta was selected because another library school (Emory) was already in Atlanta, and it was hoped that the two schools would be able to cooperate and perhaps even share some resources.[44] The Carnegie Corporation established an endowment for the new school and at the same time gave funds to the Emory University library school to encourage this cooperative effort. The administrators of the new school thought it best to have an all black faculty,[45] and so it opened in the fall of 1941 under the direction of Dean Eliza Atkins Gleason, and with two faculty members, Wallace Van Jackson and Virginia Lacy. Hampton Institute sent its professional library science collection to Atlanta to get the new school started. Enrollment was restricted to 25 students, who had to be college graduates and in the upper half of their graduating class.[46]

The cooperative arrangements between Emory and Atlanta for the education of these students was slow to develop. In fact, the faculty at Atlanta "did not expect too much" from its proximity to Emory.[47] Rufus Clement, the president of Atlanta University, pointed out in a letter to Robert Lester, president of the Carnegie Corporation, that it was the "existence of the racial situation" that necessitated two schools in the same city and that only limited cooperative activities were feasible.[48]

Thus, library science education for blacks continued to be a thing apart. The Atlanta University School of Library Service was accredited in July 1943; this action made the school the only accredited library school connected with a black institution. It became from the beginning the prime supplier of black librarians, not only for the South, but for the entire United States.

North Carolina Central/Alabama A & M 1941

A second library school for blacks was started in 1941. This
school at North Carolina College for Negroes (now North Carolina
Central University), in Durham, North Carolina, was created in response to a Supreme Court decision made in 1938 which ruled that
the state of Missouri had to give equality in educational privileges
to white and black law students, either by admitting blacks to the
law school already in existence or by establishing a law school in a
black institution. This decision affected the provision of professional
education in all fields in all states that had separate educational
systems for whites and blacks.

The state legislature of North Carolina determined to establish
a separate library school for blacks and so the school of library
science in Durham was begun. Susan Grey Akers, dean of the library school at the University of North Carolina at Chapel Hill was
selected as dean of the school in Durham. She held both positions
simultaneously for the next five years, spending one day a week on
the Durham campus.[49]

Unfortunately few records exist of these early years.[50]
There was an attempt in 1947 to gain accreditation for the school,
but the untimely death of the director, caused postponement of that
process indefinitely.[51] The school was not accredited until 1975.

Alabama A & M University is the third predominantly black institution to have a school of library science. This is a "single purpose" school, emphasizing school library media programs. It was not
founded until 1969, and was also accredited in 1975.

It is significant to note that both Hampton and Atlanta are
private institutions and that no public institution with predominently
black enrollment had an accredited program in library science until
1975. None of the schools reached accreditation status without private funds. The Alabama school was given its push toward accreditation with a grant from the W. K. Kellogg Foundation in 1972. In
1970, when North Carolina Central decided to strive for accreditation
status, a consultant called in to assess the program, said that it
would need an additional one million dollars to reach that goal.[52]
Special funding was not forthcoming from the state. Rather funds
were received from the Carnegie Corporation of New York and the
Andrew W. Mellon Foundation. Substantial contributions were also
received from the Xerox Corporation and the B. Smith Reynolds Foundation.[53]

1954-

On May 17, 1954, the U.S. Supreme Court ruled in the case
of Brown vs. the Board of Education of Topeka, Kansas, that the

principle of "separate but equal" was unconstitutional. The Court
pointed to injustices inherent in racial separation in public institutions and in 1955 ordered the various jurisdictions to embark on
desegregation in education "with all deliberate speed."[54] Now the
problem became one of implementation. In the field of library science,
it was the civil rights movement of the 1960s that caused ALA to
look at the problem and to note that there were few minority representatives in either the profession or coming into it through library
schools.[55] In an attempt to change this situation, the ad hoc Committee on Opportunities for Negro Students in the Library Profession
was established in February of 1966 by the ALA Executive Board,
upon the recommendation of ALA President Robert Vosper. The major
objective of the committee was "to suggest what steps usefully could
be taken by the ALA to identify promising new Negro undergraduates
who might, once identified, be effectively counseled and aided towards
entering library school and securing positions in the library profession."[56] Additional objectives included securing financial assistance for such students as well as appropriate library positions upon
degree completion.

The necessity for taking such special measures became evident
upon analyzing the findings of a report put together by the ad hoc
committee. It found that of the 9,204 students graduating from 25
accredited library schools between 1962 and 1966, only 372 or 4 percent were black. Over half of these had graduated from one institution, Atlanta University.[57]

American library schools were thus encouraged to begin making
an effort to inform black college students of the opportunities in the
library profession, and to motivate and counsel such students to
enter graduate schools of librarianship.[58] Not until the early 1970s,
did library education opportunities for blacks begin to expand dramatically. Library education leaders began to focus on integrating
predominantly white institutions, and the federal government became
a significant force in this effort. The Title II-B Fellowship Program
of the Higher Education Act of 1965 became the vehicle for integration in 1970 when the regulations were changed to provide that funds
awarded be utilized to equalize opportunities for minorities. Before
1970, minorities received only seven percent of the available Title
II-B fellowships; by 1978 minorities received 80 percent of the fellowships.[59]

A survey and evaluation of minority programs in selected graduate library schools for the years 1974-76, done by Herman Totten,
shows some of the initial impact of the availability of financial aid
such as Title II-B for black students. Of the 282 black library
school students he queried, 208 stated that the availability of financial aid was crucial to their choice of school. In addition, the inclusion of minority students in the regular course of study in the
library school as well as the commitment of administrators, students,
and faculty to minority support services, were crucial factors in retaining black students.[60]

A dissertation completed in 1980 by Marva DeLoach substantiated these findings. She examined the impact of Title II-B on minority recruitment into librarianship during the years 1970 through 1977.[61] In the opinion of deans and directors who participated in her study, Title II-B did have an impact on minority recruitment. Title II-B fellowships were considered the prime source of training funds for minorities. She suggests a definite correlation between the availability of fellowships and the number of minority students when Title II-B funds are more plentiful.

DeLoach shows that recruitment efforts for minorities peaked in 1970–71. Title II-B funds were used for that purpose. By the end of the period studied, minorities represented 10.7 percent of graduates reported in 1976 and 12.3 percent of graduates in 1977. Minorities seemed to be making rapid progress at last toward achieving adequate representation in library and information science education.

Recently reported data suggests that the period of rapid progress in the 1970s was temporary. The ALA Committee on Library Service to Minorities reported at the ALA annual conference in June of 1985 "that the minority student population in library schools has decreased substantially, the recruitment of minorities is no longer a priority for the major U.S. library schools, and part of the problem is that scholarship funds have been cut."[62]

It appears that educational parity has not been achieved. Black librarians are not being produced at a rate commensurate with the total population of either the state in which they reside or the nation as a whole. The historical evidence presented here shows that black representation in professional education for librarians has depended on the monumental efforts of a very few white and black library leaders to develop special programs for blacks. They have had to rely on the interest and contributions of foundations and most recently the federal government to provide a full range of opportunities for blacks to study librarianship. The overall effectiveness of the various programs supported by these private and public sources has not been measured. In the end, it seems that the lack of knowledge of effectiveness is also an impediment to equal opportunity. Namely, there appears to be no clearly mandated policy of equal opportunity in library science education; there is only a collection of loosely defined programs. Consequently, measuring and promoting progress for black librarians has been piecemeal: when racial inequalities in one place are dealt with, unseen inequalities emerge in other places.

This situation has been further exacerbated by recent federal policy as expressed in three separate Supreme Court cases: Adams vs. Richardson, DeFunis vs. Odegaard, and The Regents of the University of California vs. Allan Baake. In the Adams vs. Richardson case, nine southern states and the state of Pennsylvania were charged with continually operating dual systems of higher education that effectively channeled black college students into predominantly or historically black colleges and white students into historically white institutions. The unresolved question which still exists currently is the degree to which designated states have complied with specific aspects of a court order handed down in June of 1973 pertaining to the enrollment of black students in graduate and professional schools.[63]

Both the DeFunis case (1974) and the Baake case (1978) challenged the legitimacy of special programs designed to enhance opportunities for minorities and thus rectify the consequences of past patterns of discrimination. The opinion of Justice Powell, writing for the Supreme Court, does not say how racial equality is to be measured and pursued. The Court says simply that it should be neither measured nor pursued on the basis of "race" alone unless stipulated by Congress. Educators may "take race into consideration" in making policy, but they may not use race as the sole criterion for the measurement or remediation of inequality.[64]

Further clarirication of this point of view is found in the currently proposed executive order supported by President Reagan on the issue of affirmative action. Although dealing with hiring practices rather than educational issues, it reflects the notion the federal government, at least, desires no special programs based on race to rectify past discriminatory practice, and in fact, wishes to prohibit such programs in the future.[65] Although the order has not taken affect as yet and its provisions are too ambiguous to permit precise projections of its impact on equal opportunity for blacks, the potential impact in all spheres of national life, including higher education, are enormous. It is apparent that when the federal government pulls back its efforts in affirmative action, so do institutions of higher education.[66]

The problems facing the recruitment of black students into librarianship are thus rooted in Supreme Court decisions and Presidential policy as well as problems inherent in the profession itself. A major problem is suggested in declining enrollments. Librarianship has serious difficulties in competing with professions with earning capacities so much greater than that earned by librarians. In general, librarians are underpaid for the services they perform, and increasing librarian salaries is not a matter of priority in most institutional settings. This poses a major threat to efforts to attract strong individuals of any race to the profession.

The limited or dwindling pool of black applicants suggests that recruitment policy can no longer rely on a potential large pool of college students from the humanities and social sciences. That group of students is declining in number.[67] It is now necessary for schools of librarianship to establish outreach programs and implement stronger recruitment activities in the high schools so that information about the field can be disseminated early to help secondary school students make appropriate career decisions.

There are also problems of retention in some institutions because of the lack of preparation, weak study skills, communication
inadequacies, and writing deficiencies of some students. In addition,
there are problems that relate to alienation and isolation within schools
in which black students are in very small numbers and without psychological support, cultural reinforcements and social bonds, in what
can be perceived as an unwelcome or hostile environment.[68] Of
special note is the role faculty members may play in fostering such
a negative environment. Regardless of the motivating forces that
may cause such a situation to exist, it can only be remedied through
skillful institutional and societal intervention.

The problem of financial aid will also continue to exist as long
as the average income of black families is only 78 percent of the income of white families.[69] Many black students believe they cannot
attend school without financial aid. Yet the $18 billion federal stud-
ent aid budget has fluctuated by nearly $2 billion since 1981, when
Congress began to phase out the educational benefits available under
Social Security programs and put new restrictions on eligibility for
guaranteed student leans.[70] Library schools need to recognize
that to enroll black students, they have to provide generous scholarship assistance. Funds can come from the schools themselves as well
as foundations, business firms, and individual donors. And despite
cutbacks, federal government programs, including Title II-B, can be
utilized by some.

Subsidization of graduate library education should be based,
of course, on both need and merit. But full financing of minority
students should be based most extensively on a professional commitment to seeking out and producing black librarians, as a way of encouraging diversity in the profession.[71]

AN APPRAISAL

Any overall appraisal of the black experience with library
science education is impossible at this stage because large scale participation is so recent. A few general conclusions can, however, be
stated.

On the negative side, from the point of view of blacks, a strong
indictment is surely in order. First, it is a fact that for the one
hundred years in which professional library science education has
been in existence, schools of library science, with the exception of
course of the special schools for blacks, showed little evidence, until
recently, of any sense of responsibility to educate black librarians.

Second, it can hardly be claimed that library science education
for all it has attempted to do recently, has yet achieved a state of
integration. One school is still educating 50 percent of all black librarians. It is not possible in such a situation to gain full respect

for the black librarian experience when the profession at large is so
isolated from that experience.

There are nonetheless, some positive things one can say about
the historical development of library science education for blacks.
There can, for example, be little doubt, that it has been largely responsible for the development of black leadership in the library profession, and this leadership has claimed some of the leadership in
librarianship generally. The visibility of black library leaders can
be used to encourage other blacks to consider entering the library
profession. Such a goal can be realized, however, only if the social,
economic, and educational barriers against access to equal professional
schooling are eliminated. That is most likely to occur with sustained
library leadership, some federal and state support and cooperation
between library schools and private funding sources, combined with
a genuine commitment to equality of opportunity.

Equal opportunity must be a priority at every step of the decision process to recruit, admit, and educate black librarians. This
means doing more than waiting to see what school enrollment figures
look like at the end of an academic year, and responding hastily,
after the fact, to any inequities identified. It is time for library
schools to take an active role in ensuring the equity of all institutional
processes. In the view of this writer, such a step would be a powerful force toward development of better library service for all.

REFERENCES AND NOTES

1. Dalton, J.: Library Education in the Southeast Since World War
   II. In: Library Education in the Southeast Since World War II
   and University Libraries and Change: Proceedings of Two Sym-
   posia Sponsored in Honor of Louis Round Wilson's 100th Birthday.
   Chapel Hill, School of Library Science and University Library,
   1976, p. 22.
2. Vann, S.K.: Training for Librarianship Before 1923: Education
   for Librarianship Prior to the Publication of Williamson's Report
   on Training for Library Service. Chicago, ALA, 1961; Davis,
   D.G. Jr.: The Association of American Library Schools, 1915-
   1968: An Analytical History. Metuchen, NJ, Scarecrow, 1976;
   Carroll, C.E.: The Professionalization of Education for Librarianship With Special Reference to the Years 1940-1960. Metuchen, NJ,
   Scarecrow, 1970; Churchwell, C.D.: The Shaping of American
   Library Education. Chicago, ALA, 1975.
3. See for example Wilson, L.R.: Education for Librarianship--A
   New Opportunity in the South. In: Library Conference Held
   Under the Auspices of the Carnegie Corporation of New York and
   the General Education Board. Atlanta, Atlanta University, 1941,
   p. 17.
4. Pifer, A.: The Higher Education of Blacks in the United States.
   New York, Carnegie Corporation of New York, 1973.

5. Anders, M.E.: The Development of Public Library Service in the Southeastern States, 1895-1950. Dissertation, Columbia University, 1958, pp. 62-63.

6. Yust, W.F.: What of the Black and Yellow Races. ALA Bulletin, 7:159-167, July 1913.

7. Pifer, ref. 4, p. 16.

8. Marshall, A.P.: The Black Librarian's Stride Toward Equality. In: Phinazee, A.L., ed.: The Black Librarian in the Southeast: Reminiscences, Activities, Challenges. Durham, NC, North Carolina Central University, 1980, p. 12.

9. Blue, T.F.: Apprenticeship Training for Negroes in the Louisville Free Public Library. Paper read at the ALA Conference, Work with Negroes Round Table, Detroit, 1922. Quoted in Wright, L.T.: Thomas Fountain Blue, Pioneer Librarian, 1866-1935. Master's Thesis, Atlanta University, 1955, p. 31.

10. Ibid., pp. 34-35.

11. Bowles, F. and De Costa, F.A.: Two Worlds: A Profile of Negro Higher Education. New York, McGraw Hill, 1971, p. 37.

12. Carruthers, I.: Centennials of Black Miseducation: A Study of White Educational Management. Journal of Negro Education, 46:299, Summer 1971.

13. Shores, L.: Library Service to Negroes, Wilson Library Bulletin, 4:311, Jan. 1931.

14. Annual Report of the Board of Education for Librarianship, 1924-25. As quoted in Smith, S.L.: The Passing of the Hampton Library School. Journal of Negro Education, 9:51, Jan. 1940.

15. Bullock, H.A.: A History of Negro Education in the South: From 1619 to Present. New York, Praeger, 1970, p. 33.

16. Meier, A.: Negro Thought in America, 1890-1915: Racial Ideologies in the Age of Booker T. Washington. Ann Arbor, The University Press, 1963, pp. 85-99.

17. Curtis, F.R.: Problems and Conditions which the Librarian Faced and the Progress which has been Made. In: Library Conference ... , ref. 3, p. 67.

18. Jackson, W.V.: Negro Library Workers. Library Quarterly, 10:106, Jan. 1940.

19. Anders, M.E.: The Contributions of the Carnegie Corporation and the General Education Board to Library Development in the Southeast. Master's Thesis, University of North Carolina, 1950, p. 26.

20. Gleason, E.A.: Negro Libraries and Librarianship, 1945. Atlanta University Library School Library vertical file. (typed copy).

21. Jackson, W.V.: Florence Rising Curtis. Library Journal, 69:1060, Dec. 1, 1944.

22. Du Mont, R.R.: Race in American Librarianship: Attitudes of the Library Profession. Journal of Library History, in press.

23. Curtis, F.R.: Librarianship as a Field for Negroes. Journal of Negro Education, 4:94, Jan. 1935.

24. Jones, V.L.: A Dean's Career. In: Josey, E.J., ed: The
    Black Librarian in America. Metuchen, NJ, Scarecrow, 1970,
    pp. 26–27.
25. Curtis, ref. 23, p. 95.
26. See Jones' comments on this problem in A Dean's Career ... ,
    ref. 24, p. 28.
27. Curtis, ref. 23, p. 95.
28. Templeton, Charlotte to Sarah C.M. Bogle, March?, 1931. ALA
    Archives.
29. Curtis, ref. 23, p. 96.
30. Bogle, Sarah C.M. to Louis R. Wilson, Feb. 4, 1931. ALA
    Archives.
31. Templeton to Bogle, red. 28.
32. Ibid.
33. Conference on Training for Librarianship for Negroes. Chapel
    Hill, NC, March 5, 1931. Transcript of meeting. ALA Archives.
34. Ibid.
35. Ibid.
36. Foreman, Clark to Louis R. Wilson, March 26, 1931. ALA Ar-
    chives. According to the Foreman letter, the Hampton Library
    School budget for the 1930–31 academic year included $12,500
    contributed by the Carnegie Corporation, $5,500 contributed by
    the Rosenwald Fund and only $2,450 contributed by Hampton
    Institute. The total income of the school for its 14 years exis-
    tence was $211,922; the Carnegie Corporation gave $155,000 of
    that amount. See Anders, ref. 19, footnote 18, p. 26.
37. Barker, T.D.: Memorandum on the Need in the South for a
    Library School for Negroes. Chicago, Board of Education for
    Librarianship, ALA, 1939. ALA Archives.
38. Ibid.
39. Ibid, p. 4.
40. One of these institutions was Hampton Institute. The Carnegie
    Corporation continued to give financial support to Florence Ris-
    ing Curtis "for the training of Negro librarians" even after the
    library school had officially closed its doors. See Carnegie
    Corporation Annual Report, 1938–1939. 22.
41. Barker, ref. 37, p. 42.
42. Jackson, Wallace Van to Anita M. Hostetter, Feb. 12, 1940.
    ALA Archives.
43. Ibid.
44. Lester, Robert M. to Rufus Clement, Oct. 18, 1940. ALA Ar-
    chives.
45. Clement, Rufus to Florence Rising Curtis, Oct. 31, 1940. At-
    lanta University Archives.
46. Library School File, 1941–42. Atlanta University Archives.
47. Clement, Rufus to Robert M. Lester, Aug. 17, 1940. Atlanta
    University Archives.
48. Ibid. When Atlanta opened, the points of cooperation agreed
    upon with Emory included the shared purchase of expensive and
    unusual material; the shared use of material; the sharing of
    expenses for invited lectures; the sharing of expenses for film

rental and purchase; and the offering of "two lectures by Emory University faculty" at Atlanta. Library School File, 1940-41. Atlanta University Archives.

49. Crumpton, K.: The School of Library Science at North Carolina Central University. In: The Black Librarian ... , ref. 8, pp. 276-277.

50. Phinazee, A.L.: "The Education of Black Librarians in the Southeast." Paper presented to Library History Interest Group, Association of American Library Schools, Jan. 31, 1981.

51. Crumpton, ref. 49, pp. 277.

52. Phinazee, ref. 50.

53. Ibid.

54. Blackwell, J.E.: Mainstreaming Outsiders: The Production of Black Professionals. Bayside, NY, General Hall, Inc, 1981, p. 17.

55. ALA Ad Hoc Committee on Opportunities for Negro Students in the Library Profession Progress Report to the ALA Executive Council, June 27, 1967. ALA Archives.

56. Ibid.

57. Ibid.

58. Ad Hoc Committee on Opportunities for Negro Students in the Library Profession [to graduate schools of library science], May 26, 1967. ALA Archives.

59. DeLoach, M.L.: "The Impact of Title II-B on Minority Recruitment." Paper presented to Library History Interest Group, Association of American Library Schools, Jan. 31, 1981.

60. Totten, H.L.: A Summary and Evaluation of Minority Programs in Selected Graduate Library Schools. Journal of Education for Librarianship, 18:18-34, Summer 1977.

61. DeLoach, M.L.: The Higher Education Act of 1965, Title II-B: The Fellowship/Traineeships for Training in Library and Information Science Programs: Its Impact on Minority Recruitment in Library and Information Science Education. Dissertation, University of Pittsburgh, 1980.

62. A Disparity Exists ... , Library Journal, 110:43, Aug. 1985.

63. Blackwell, ref. 54, p. 30.

64. Morris, L.: Elusive Equality: The Status of Black Americans in Higher Education. Washington, DC, Howard University Press, 1979, p. 2.

65. Davidson, J.D., and Watkins, L.M.: Quotas in Hiring are Anathema to President Despite Minority Gains. Wall Street Journal, Oct. 24, 1985, p. 1+.

66. Evans, G.: Social, Financial Barriers Blamed for Curbing Blacks' Access to College. Chronicle of Higher Education, Aug. 7, 1985, p. 1+.

67. Ibid.

CAN BIBLIOTHERAPY GO PUBLIC?*

Clara Richardson Lack

In times past, the public library has aptly been called "the university of the people," an educational institution dedicated to furthering the democratic way of life. An educational institution is charged with the tasks of transmitting societal values and acquiring knowledge necessary for daily living. Certainly, the public library affirms that all people of the United States have a right to the pursuit of knowledge along with or as part of the pursuit of happiness. Whether or not the library also has some responsibility in assisting patrons in the clarification of societal values and in assisting patrons with life enrichment is not as clear from a historical perspective. That libraries can and should bring literature and books together in reader's discussion groups for enrichment and clarification is the subject of this paper.

The educational services public libraries have provided over the decades reveal certain trends, for instance, moral betterment was a goal from the mid-1850s to 1890. During the depression years, 1930 to 1950, vocational improvement was a major goal. The years 1918 to 1942 have been termed the "emergence of the reader." Along with book reviews and book list distribution, many public libraries established or expanded their advisory service to individuals and groups during this period. Civic enlightenment and personal development goals remained constant during the 1950s and 1960s. One of the most popular of the group services provided by public libraries since the 1950s has been the library-sponsored discussion group. One of the best known programs is the "Great Books Discussions." Developed at the University of Chicago, these great books discussions became library programs in 1954.[1]

What are some dominant themes of this decade? Personal isolation and fear of the future are prominent ones. The struggle to adapt to rapid change with few acceptable social guidelines is another. There is dislocation in every area of modern life, and the public

*Reprinted by permission of the author and publisher from Collection Building (Spring 1985), 27-32; copyright © 1985 Neal-Schuman Publishers, Inc.

library has a unique opportunity to offer the community a neutral
place to meet and to consider our heritage, our present, and our
future as individuals and as society. A balanced library collection
can assist individuals in this exploration. Competent, courteous
reader guidance is necessary. The library can and should do more
to assist readers to connect ideas and models of behavior in literature
with their own lives. One way this connection can be made is to
add reader's discussion groups to the educational service of the library.

What do we want as a society? How do we think and feel about
our individual lives? What values do we feel are important, are worth
preserving? These and countless other questions can be explored
by bringing readers and books together in reader's discussion groups.

The need for stability further underlies the service that literary
artists fulfill by giving us models of behavior to look at, to examine,
to value, or to disregard. Archetypes are clothed in modern dress
for our learning and integration. Virginia Satir said, "I know that
books are not substitutes for people. However, I remember the many
times when a particular book read at a time when I was in a receiving mood, opened up new possibilities which resulted in my taking
new directions for myself."[2] Solitary reading is indeed beneficial
for many individuals. Many thoughtful readers are usually able to
make a connection between the book and themselves. Other readers
may welcome some assistance in making connections between the book
and their own lives. Such readers may enjoy the stimulation and
sharing that takes place in a reader's discussion group.

> Group reading challenges the public library to add the group
> dimension to its individual services, and thus to take the
> radical step from a passive resource to an active agent of
> education.

> What group reading offers to the library is a projection of
> its books into the active thinking of a community. What it
> demands from the library is a reappraisal of its present one-
> dimensional match-making between people and books.[3]

One library's response to the challenge of bringing people and
books together in more than a one dimensional way was for the University of Illinois to set up an experiment in 1951. Its purpose was
to combine the tasks of reader guidance and reference with counseling. Four counselor-librarians were trained in interpersonal skills
involving simple transfer of information, developing individual reading
lists, and in a counselor relationship operating as an agent in attempting to change attitudes and perceptions of a patron. The major
emphasis in counseling was not upon the information to be imparted,
but upon aiding the individual toward self-motivation and self-decision;
it was developmental in character. It was teaching students how to
apply books to themselves.[4] This experiment was short lived, but

it illustrates an assumption by librarians that a trained librarian can
assist patrons in problem solving in other ways than being simply,
or not so simply, a supplier of information.

Library literature reveals only one counselor librarian on a public
library staff. In 1939, the St. Paul Public Library employed a vocational counselor.[5] Reader's Advisors in the 1940s and 1950s would
only approach counselor librarian status.

Because groups reading and discussion are book-centered, such
activities seem as appropriate an activity to the library as story hours
are for children. The public library is a natural setting for informal
learning. People of diverse backgounds feel free to come together.
By reading, thinking, and exchanging ideas and feelings about literature, members of a group obtain better insights into human values.
Participants in a reading and discussion group can clarify their own
values and book beyond their immediate experience to develop a
breadth and depth of outlook. Anthony Burgess speaks of the function of novels:

> A novel ought to leave in the reader's mind a sort of philo-
> sophical residue. A view of life, has been indirectly pro-
> pounded that seems new, even surprising.... The strength
> of a novel, however, owes nothing to its confirmation of what
> conventional morality has already told us. Rather, a novel
> will question convention and suggest to us that the making
> of moral judgments is difficult.[6]

Great Books Discussion Groups were popular in libraries in the
1950s and early 1960s. Two reasons, perhaps, for this public library service to fade from view are the rapid growth of technology--
the necessity to recognize media other than books, and that the great
books used for discussion were chosen primarily from classical literature. With the rapid dissemination of new ideas and themes reflected
in current publications, classical literature appears out of date to
some people, not relevant to modern thought and action. Although
current Great Books Discussions are also taken from modern literature,
their popularity has not been recaptured.

Up to this point, I have avoided using the term bibliotherapy,
but a type of bibliotherapy is what I am advocating. Much confusion
surrounds the term. Some of the confusion is caused by authors
of articles who do not define the term, leaving the reader to guess
which type of bibliotherapy is being discussed. Webster's Third New
International Dictionary defines bibliotherapy within the context of
a medical model: "The use of selected reading materials as therapeutic adjuvants in medicine and psychiatry; also, guidance in the
solution of personal problems through directed reading." For a librarian to carry out this type of bibliotherapy would involve a doctor
prescribing certain books for a client which the librarian would obtain; or a librarian preparing a list of materials on a subject suggested

by a doctor and aiding the client in obtaining the materials. Or a patron could speak of a problem and ask the librarian for suggested reading materials. The librarian's role is reader guidance only; the patrons involved are doctor and client. The medical model in the practice of bibliotherapy has evolved into something more than this special reader guidance and will be discussed in more detail later as clinical bibliotherapy.

Bibliotherapy in an educational context is defined as follows by the Dictionary of Education: "The use of books to influence total development, a process of interaction between the reader and literature which is used for personality assessment, adjustment, growth, clinical and mental hygiene purposes." This educational definition describes the type of bibliotherapy which I am advocating for use in the public or school library, especially the use of literature for total development and growth.

Margaret Monroe comments on another kind of bibliotherapy:

> The developmental mode of bibliotherapy is best described as close to the "education" end of the continuum, but with aspects of "therapy" implicit: goals identified by the facilitator [from which the group could choose] based on knowledge of the typical needs of such persons as the group represented [elderly, adolescent, etc.] and an approach to the discussion based not on knowledge of individual problems in the group, but of the generic development tasks typical of such persons, with a goal of beneficent, benign resolution or prevention of crisis level problems. This ... [is] a complex professional task requiring training beyond that of reading guidance but in no sense a formal therapy.[7]

A homogeneous group with similar goals would utilize this developmental mode of bibliotherapy. Joseph Zaccaria has synthesized some developmental tasks that each individual must face, utilizing the theoretical contributions of Havighurst, Erikson and Super. The general developmental tasks are summarized here:

Infancy--Achieving a Sense of Trust
Middle Childhood--Achieving a Sense of Initiative
Late Childhood--Achieving a Sense of Industry
Adolescence--Developing a Sense of Identity
Early Adulthood--Achieving a Sense of Intimacy
Middle Adulthood--Achieving a Sense of Generativity
Late Adulthood--Achieving a Sense of Ego Integrity[8]

Actual practice of bibliotherapy reveals that not only books but literature of all types are used, as well as film, and participant's creative writing, and song lyrics. Posters and comic strips also have been used successfully. The two dictionary definitions cited give no hint as to the process of bibliotherapy. Neither does much of the

literature on the subject. Several years ago at the close of a conference of librarians and social workers where I had given a demonstration to show how I practiced bibliotherapy, the state librarian
came up to me and said, "None of the articles I've ever read ever
told me how to do it. I never before really understood what bibliotherapy was."

The definition agreed upon by many practitioners of the art of
bibliotherapy is as follows: Bibliotherapy can either be a developmental or clinical process, utilizing selected literature, film, participant's creative writing, with discussion, guided by a trained facilitator for the purpose of integrating feelings and thought in order to
promote self-affirmation, self knowledge, or rehabilitation.

Developmental bibliotherapy is the personalization of literature
for the purpose of meeting normal ongoing life tasks. Clinical bibliotherapy is a mode of intervention in aiding persons severely troubled
with emotional or behavioral problems. Both forms of bibliotherapy
are usually practiced in a group and always with a trained leader
and discussion.

The question has often been asked: How is bibliotherapy different from the reader guidance that a librarian dispenses every day?
There are several opinions about this question. Eleanor Brown thinks
that what distinguishes bibliotherapy from reader guidance is the
presence of a patron with a problem which the librarian knows about
and therefore suggests material which the librarian has read and
believes will allay the patron's disturbance.[9]

Others see bibliotherapy as primarily reader guidance to further
the general personality development of the individual and not necessarily to focus on problems. Kircher focuses upon the aspect of
character formation through books. Books help to form character by
providing catharsis and support which enable the person to glean
principles of conduct which the person can apply to her or himself.
Taba and Crosby focus upon literature as a means for helping individuals build and improve human relations. Rosenblath describes
the use of books for general exploration and cultural insight. Wen-
sel notes that bibliotherapy can contribute to the socialization of the
individual because of its dynamic balance between the intellectual
and emotional components of the content.[10] No mention was made
of any discussion, or follow-up after the books are recommended.

Current thinking and practice of bibliotherapy go beyond this
reader guidance of connecting materials to client-with-problem or
client with a desire for self-growth, and continues the process by
assisting the client in making a personal connection to the materials
through discussion. Hannigan illustrates this further step in her
article: "Narcotic Addicts Take Up Reading."[11]

A reader-guidance transaction may be diagrammed as follows.

1. Patron's request   2. Librarian selects material

The patron requests material from the librarian and the librarian selects material based on the patron's request and gives it to the patron. It is a horizontal transfer between patron and librarian with materials.

In a bibliotherapy transaction there is a partnership interaction between the bibliotherapy-trained librarian and the patron(s) to achieve some synthesis between the materials and the person. A bibliotherapy transaction consists of:

1. The patron(s) and bibliotherapist viewing, listening, reading the materials together in a group or singly. The bibliotherapist has selected the material for potential increase in self-knowledge or enrichment.

Or

The patron(s) write materials singly or in a group for self-expression, self-knowledge, or materials are chosen by the group in collaboration with the bibliotherpaist for the purpose of problem solving, self-exploration, or enrichment.

2. The bibliotherpaist and the patron(s) come together to discuss the materials.

3. The purpose of the coming together is to achieve some integration between the person and the materials whether the materials are individual writing, film, or reading of printed materials.

Possible Personal Integration:

Intellectual stimulation may occur through focusing and interchange.

Universalization may occur by reading about the human condition and by being in a group.

Isolation may be abated by group acceptance and interaction.

A growth in self-esteem may occur as the self is allowed expansion through expression and assurance.

Personal insight may be gained to aid in problem solving or acceptance.

Energizing may occur as one's own cares are laid aside momentarily or the burden lightened through catharsis.

Value clarification may occur as various modes of behavior are
encountered and discussed.

Passage through stages of development may be assisted as one
reads and discusses literature models exemplifying life stages.

Developmental bibliotherapy groups are being conducted in public
libraries, although the groups are not called bibliotherapy because
of the confusion surrounding the term. A more apt description of
groups which focus as much on the reader's expression as on the
book would be "reader's discussion groups."

Santa Clara County Public Library System

One such group led by the author in a branch library of Santa
Clara County Public Libraries in San Jose, California operated with
these guidelines: Selected material--short stories, plays, poetry--
around the theme of "Becoming Human" was read prior to the weekly
meeting. The discussion concerned the content of the literature,
not juicy details about the author's life. Short passages were chosen
to read aloud to illustrate a theme or passages were chosen that
were particularly enjoyable and succinct. Participants told why they
felt certain passages were important or enjoyable. This subjective
response made the discussion personal. People could share or not
share as they chose. Group members in this atmosphere discussed
the ideas presented in the literature experientially as valid or not
valid in terms of their knowledge and of their experience of life.
Goals were to encourage the use of the library and to encourage
self-growth.

The series, planned for six weeks, was extended to eight weeks
by request of the group. Members of the group asked (at a public
meeting convened for community input of library service) that reader's
discussion groups be continued as ongoing library service just as
children's story hours are traditional library fare.

For eight years, under the auspices of Santa Clara County
Public Library System, I directed the Bibliotherapy and Serve Outreach Library Programs. Developmental bibliotherapy groups were
led in convalescent hospitals. Clinical bibliotherapy groups were
conducted in various mental health facilities and the county jail.[12,13]

San Jose City Public Library

At the San Jose City Public Library a series of reader's discussion groups were held as an outreach to seniors in the urban
area surrounding the library. A psychologist donated her time and
used short stories to spark discussion with the group. The seniors
were shy and it took several meetings for the discussion to open up.

Several staff members attended the groups as participants. An unexpected benefit took place as a result of the staff participation in
the group. Some unscheduled in-service training occurred. The
staff found that they were more understanding and responsive to
the needs of older patrons than they had been prior to the reader's
discussion groups with seniors. I believe that developmental bibliotherapy can be used in a scheduled way in staff training.

San Raphael Public Library, San Raphael, California

Library Services and Construction Act funds were obtained to
research whether or not bibliotherapy was a valid part of a public
library outreach program. After two years of ten weekly reader's
discussion groups these recommendations were made to other public
libraries:

> As a public library we were able to extend outreach service
> to people who could no longer use the library in more tra-
> ditional ways. This library service made a change in the
> quality of life of our patrons. Enjoyment, together with the
> enrichment and stimulation of library materials was an ob-
> servable change from the isolation, loneliness and loss of
> belief in one's self which seemed to preclude this possibility
> when we first began ... Had our program been offered by a
> mental health organization, the clinical "therapy" connotations
> would have been unwelcome to many of our participants.[14]

San Raphael Public Library's experience with reader's discussion
groups (developmental bibliotherapy) made it clear that librarians do
need training. San Raphael's facilitators recommended that interested
staff obtain this training in a structured way through classes, reading, and consultation with other professionals, even though bibliotherapy training per se is scarce.

Both developmental and clinical training is offered at St. Elizabeth's Hospital in Washington, D.C. Developmental bibliotherapy training is offered at the Library School of South Florida State University.

At this juncture, something should be stated about the leadership of reader's discussion groups. Reader's discussion groups are
led by a facilitator whose role is to convene the group, select or
mutually select with the group the literature to be discussed, make
sure that each member has a chance to speak, and encourage the discussion with open-ended questions. The facilitator is not to be
viewed as an authority but as one who furthers the group process,
allowing each member to contribute ideas and feelings about the literature. A knowledge of human development and group dynamics is
necessary. Personal qualities are important such as a warm and
friendly manner. Much self-knowledge is necessary. A dominating
leader eager to press his or her viewpoint upon the group can stultify

any group. A leader unsure of her or his authority may be unable
to exert enough leadership to insure that all group members participate fully. Staff already equipped with group leadership abilities
and a love of both people and literature find such service revitaliz-
ing and an opportunity to use professional skills that lie dormant
in performing many managerial tasks.

Reader's Discussion Groups with Children

As a children's librarian, Doris Robinson has led developmental
bibliotherapy groups with special education students.[15] Her ground
rules are: the book must be read in order to take part in the discussion, there are no right or wrong answers, the interaction of the
book characters with each other are commented upon. This discussion
inevitably leads to group interaction and individuals realize that they
have had similar experiences. The children are very excited when
they recognize circumstances or dialog similar to their own situation.

This personal catharsis is viewed as a positive outcome of the
groups. But in no instance is psychotherapy practiced. In reader's
discussion groups (developmental bibliotherapy) remarks are accepted
nonjudgmentally and the group goes on from there. Children evi-
dencing overwhelming tension in the groups are referred to school
counselors by the teacher.

A creativity group in an Alexandria, Virginia, public library
was very popular with the children and without doubt was beneficial
for the children's development. The group stopped short of being
a reader's discussion group because there was no discussion of the
literature, which in this case was the writing of poetry by the children.

Children's librarian, Stella Reed, led a summer series entitled
"Creativity Sessions" and because of interest the sessions continued
throughout the next year.[16] Administrative guidelines were that
reader's advisory bibliotherapy be used, not clinical bibliotherapy.
The children were told that writing poetry involves using their imagination and getting in touch with their feelings. Most of the time,
the children were asked to write about seasons, holidays, colors,
animals or nature. But even then pent-up feelings poured forth:

WINTER

There he is standing in his white suit
Making it hard for us with
     sneezes and coughs
What will become of us
Maybe that's why
Santa brings us toys

WHAT MAKES ME HAPPY

What will make me happy?
Toys on my birthday?
I don't know what makes me gay.
I don't know what to say
I never smile
All I do is frown
I never play outside with my friends
Because they always knock me down
I frown on my way to school
I frown when I take my nap
Oh, I don't know
What will make me happy.

There was no discussion with the children of their feelings. It was a freeing experience to allow them to express themselves without censure or fear of grades. In the practice of developmental bibliotherapy, the leader does not question or probe but acknowledges, in nonjudgmental fashion, the expression of ideas and feelings that do emerge. Writing poetry in the library in a group offers much to the participant. The writing itself offers a form, a vessel of containment. In group discussion of one's own creation or of published literature or film, the materials and the discussion also provide containment and the vicarious experience of feelings. The public place and the group offer boundaries for the expression of ideas and feelings.

A trained leader is able to note individuals who appear to be deeply troubled and may refer such individuals to mental health professionals. School counseling staff and community mental health centers are resources for both advice and referral.

Reader's discussion groups offer enrichment, growth, and stimulation for patrons of all ages and such groups are firmly placed in the tradition of the library as an educational institution. Reader's discussion groups which offer socialization, enjoyment, and boundaries for self-expression are vehicles of preventive mental health and are within the democratic tradition of public service institutions which serve the whole person and the whole community.

References

1. Lee, Robert Ellis. Continuing Education for Adults Through the American Public Library 1833-1964. Chicago: ALA, 1966, p. 114.
2. Satir, Virginia. Making Contact. Millbrae, Calif.: Celestial Arts, 1976.
3. Powell, John W. Education for Maturity. New York: Hermitage House, 1949, p. 175.

4. Maxfield, David K. Counselor Librarianship: A New Departure.
    Illinois University Graduate School of Library Science. Occa-
    sional Papers, No. 38, March 1954, p. 12.
5. Maxfield, p. 26.
6. Burgess, Anthony. "Modern Novels: the 99 Best," The New
    York Times Book Review (Feb. 5, 1984): 37.
7. Monroe, Margaret, ed. Seminar on Bibliotherapy. Library
    School, University of Wisconsin, 1978, p. 80.
8. Zaccaria, Joseph S., Harold A. Moses, and Jeff S. Hollowell.
    Bibliotherapy in Rehabilitation, Education and Mental Health
    Services. Champaign, Ill.: Stipes Publishing Co., 1978, p.
    60-61.
9. Brown, Eleanor Frances. Bibliotherapy and Its Widening Ap-
    plications. Metuchen, N.J.: Scarecrow Press, 1973, p. 225.
10. Zaccaria, p. 59.
11. Hannigan, Margaret and William Henderson. "Narcotic Addicts
    Take Up Reading," Bookmark 22 (July 1963): 1-86.
12. Lack, Clara and Bruce Bettencourt. "Bibliotherapy in the Com-
    munity," News Notes of California Libraries 68 (Fall 1973).
13. Lack Clara and Bruce Bettencourt. "Group Bibliotherapy,"
    Health and Rehabilitative Library Services 1 (Oct. 1975): 19.
14. Allen, Barbara and Lorraine O'Dell. Bibliotherapy and the
    Public Library. San Rafael, Calif.: San Rafael Public Library
    Bibliotherapy Project, 1981.
15. Robinson, Doris. "A Bibliotherapy Program with Special Educa-
    tion Students," Top of the News (Winter 1980): 189.
16. In correspondence with Stella Reed, Librarian, 1984.

GRAFFITI AND SACKING THE HIEROPHANT*

Judith W. Monroe

There is a card in the Tarot called the Hierophant. The person
depicted on the card is a phony, one who wears false authority and
expects to be respected for it--indeed to be worshipped. I once
knew a librarian who played the role of a Hierophant. In search of
dignity or status, he separated himself from young people. He was
in a state called Being Authoritative. He was forever calling upon
the students to understand the power vested in him came from higher
up, because he was part of "the school's administration." He main-
tained this attitude whenever he was at work, the better to keep
young people at bay. All the evidence indicates he would have been
better off replacing the act with a genuine personality, the same one
he used for his friends, colleagues and family. Off duty, he was
really rather nice.

I remember the sister of a friend who worked in a nursery
school and developed a high pitched wheedling voice and a manner
which showed she felt herself to be a little child--even when she was
with adults. Just the opposite of "Being Authoritative" but equally
unhelpful, and falsely powerful, since she used "Babyhood" to get
her way with everyone. Worst of all, beyond this persona, she forgot who she was.

Borrowing a persona may offer a temporary power from other
sources, particularly the power of an institution for which one works.
As tempting as it is to do this it is also dangerous. Institutions
are often careless of individual rights and needs. As such, their
power is as unhealthy for you as for the young.

Escaping from the Hierophat in ourselves can be difficult. It
involves being genuine--a condition commonly believed to be god-
given, easily attained, if not inevitable. Still psychologists have
written whole studies on learning to be "real." Carl Rogers, in
particular, has specialized in assuring faltering humans that it is

*Reprinted by permission of the author and publisher from Voya
8:6 (February 1986) 371-373; copyright © 1986 by Voice of Youth
Advocates, Inc.

better to be honest and open, even if that means being vulnerable.
He has been criticized by people who are uncomfortable with this
deceptively simple concept. Yet those of us who work with kids
know they can detect phonies, and adults are invariably uncomfortable when they sense that children or young adults perceive them
to be two-faced. Adolescents have, as Neil Postman once said, built
in "crap detectors."

The question for many people working with difficult adolescents
is how to get control without relying on some form of power outside
of themselves. The presumption is that outside power is valuable
when working with difficult young people.

Not too many years ago in a large urban school in Maine, a
librarian was having difficulty with graffiti. The usual requests for
it to stop lead nowhere. Every night the janitor complained when
he washed the library tables. The messages were nasty, he said.
The librarian agreed. She gave it some thought and decided to try
to change the students perceptions of graffiti. While she was at it,
she felt it might be a good idea to change their perceptions of her
as a librarian. She knew they presently thought of her as one who
had asked them unsuccessfully to stop defacing the library. She
knew that for the most part they didn't really think about her as
a person at all. She spoke to the janitor the next night. "You have
to wash the tables every night anyway, don't you?" He nodded.
"Then you won't mind if I try to change the style of what is being
written there for a while," she suggested. "O.K." he said, but
she could see he was a little startled. She understood that he believed she should be able to demand the graffiti stop. What was this
about style?

He was not unlike many people who view graffiti as a crime of
defacement. There is another way to view it, as a kind of reaction
to "power over" situations, caused by a need to be heard. The
walls, tables and other spaces in a public place are a kind of plat-
form or forum for the commentary of someone who is otherwise largely
devalued and ignored.

People who write graffiti are seldom caught doing it. Traditional methods of prevention although thought to be of value really
don't work, don't even enter the picture beyond the stage of threat.
But even threat backfires. It sets up a negative environment of
resentment. Everyone who uses the area being defaced is considered a potential vandal rather than innocent until proven guilty,
and then the negative expectations stimulate more graffiti, more un-
dersirable behavior rather than less.

That night, the librarian referred to one of her favorite quotation books and found simple one line quotes. She wrote one of
these neatly in her own handwriting in the center of each clean table.
The next day, she watched for reaction, and saw students reading

what was there. Sometimes, they would glance up afterwards and
see her. She would smile and go on with her work. As the day
went by, she noticed at least one student writing something on the
table, but she said nothing. One of the students stopped her, as
she walked by a table and said, "Did you put this here?" The
librarian responded "Yes, I did." "It's neat," was the response,
and the smile that followed made the librarian hope that perhaps the
madness in her method might yet work. After the students left that
afternoon, and before the janitor came to clean up, she went around
and read what was written on each table. At one, the quote had
been cleaned off, and the table was full of the usual graffiti. On
another table there were large question and explanation marks. On
still another a student had written: "You are not supposed to write
on the tables, Ms....." On a few others there were some amusing
comments responding to the quotes. Most still had their share of
the usual "nasty" words which the janitor had been upset about. She
wondered momentarily if this experiment would only increase the
amount of graffiti in the long run. She decided to chance it.

For a few nights, she alternated the quotes with what she
considered to be validation of students. She wrote simple things like
"Your fortune: You care about others. They care about you," or
"Show the world how bright you are--shine." Sometimes she just
wrote "Good luck." The next day after school was closed and before
the janitor came, she found lots of responses, "You, Too!" "Good
luck, yourself," and the not-yet-annoying remark, "Have a nice day."
Perhaps she was imagining things, but there seemed to be a tiny
bit less of the other kind of graffiti.

She kept this up, building a file of interesting quotes and one
liners, for about a month. Slowly, two things happened. The nasty
writing died down. The other writing became more interesting, and
then, it too began to disappear. It seemed to her that the interest
in writing on the tables lost its iconoclastic flavor. People had said
what they needed to say and they also knew they had been heard.
So she stopped writing messages too. By then everyone knew that
she was the one who had been doing it. She knew it made a difference in the way they viewed her, and it had changed the way she
thought of them as well. When she stopped writing, a number of
students asked her why. Some said they missed her morning messages. Then she explained why she had done it and why she had
stopped. The reaction was gratifying. Students sympathized with
the janitor. Many agreed that the negative comments had been unattractive and crude. Some of these same students now began to
ask her for help in using the library. She knew they would never
have asked before. She felt elated and realized that she learned
two things: She liked most of the students better than she had before, and it made her job much more exciting.

Two days before the Christmas holidays began, the library was
packed with students. None were working. It seemed to the librarian

that faculty gave up the ghost on the last two days before any holiday, but Christmas was always the hardest.

It was impossible to ask students to work as there was no work to be done. It was also against her nature to ask for outside help. Instead of becoming irritated with the students, who were not at fault, she provided them with holiday music, and encouraged a few students to decorate a tree. In the gallery area of the library, the next day there would be a punch bowl with Christmas cookies. Still, she felt, there was all that time and they needed something beyond singing carols, a thing which she noticed over the last few years seemed to have grown unstylish to them.

She decided to return one more time to the graffiti trick. When students arrived the next morning they found ornate drawings and messages of Christmas and Chanukah in the center of their tables. One of the library staff, who was an artist and a few art students, had done the work. In addition, the students found magic markers-- the washable ink kind on the tables. An invitation that was risky she knew. The janitor was going to have to wash these tables and he might think all that color more than he had bargained for. At the end of the day, there wasn't a square inch of room left to draw anything on the tables. The librarian and the staff made a tour and took pictures. Not one negative remark was evident. Every message had to do with the holidays. In addition, the usual hectic atmosphere had been pleasantly controlled.

She was proud of them, and she felt fairly certain that there would be less graffiti in the future. She was right. She used the same technique to deal with book losses, writing positive messages to students and posting them in the stacks. She reminded them that they were honest and basically caring people who wanted to share. She told them the books belonged to everyone and thus could not really be stolen--just kept inconsiderately long. She found that the technique of surprise and validation together worked there as well.

Perceptions and Power

Of the many kinds of power that exist, there are two of particular importance to a librarian working with young people. One which is obvious, lies in the expertise, the knowledge and skills of professional work. Showing the value of being able to locate information, for example, carries considerable weight with many people of all ages, particularly when they have tried unsuccessfully to search and have come up empty handed. Another kind of power is more elusive, and is known as referent power, the power to influence people because they admire or respect who you are as a human being. That is the kind used by the librarian who dealt with the graffiti. Unfortunately, referent power is more difficult to achieve. In fact, in a situation where it might be viewed as adversary, where adolescents think of us as having "power over," it becomes a matter of challenging and changing their perceptions. Students' perceptions of what librarians are like are formed from a variety of sources and can range from the relatively popular notion of Head Husher, or Keeper of Quiet at ALL Costs, to Collector of Useless Information, or the Biggest Bag Lady of Them All. Then there is the less humorous but nevertheless telling perception of the librarian as Spy or Lacky of the Administration. In order to become more valuable in our work, we need to banish these stereotypes, and help young people see us as human first, persons with feelings, attitudes and values. That does take time, but it is time worth spent.

The Element of Surprise

Help is available when surprise is used as a tool to change perceptions. In negotiations where adversaries face each other on tough questions, resolution is sometimes difficult to achieve because of unfair perceptions on both sides. Experts suggest acting inconsistently with the faulty perceptions of the opposite side. This is what the librarian who used graffiti did, and the results can be a kind of wiping away of opposites, and a resolution in which all parties have their needs met. Surprise, however, should never be used to set up false expectations.

Drop the Negative, Punitive Emphasis

Most librarians are interested in building a positive library program which includes lots of intellectual stimulation; as well as respect for property and for individuals as unique beings. There should be much joy arising from reading, viewing, listening and learning. In such a program, the carrot and the stick method of discipline leaves much to be desired. Neither carrots nor sticks give young people an inner-directed sense of values. In addition, busy librarians cannot always be there to hand out rewards, and as for punishment--well, there are those who have already begun to accuse educators of being the "real" child abusers. Fortunately, librarians are less subject to this kind of attack than are classroom teachers, but there is perhaps, a need to look carefully at what tools we do use to exercise control.

Give Students an Opportunity to Save Face

Those who have been involved in an altercation in the library need opportunity, once an initial confrontation has passed, to "Save Face." No one likes to feel defeated, least of all adolescents whose developmental tasks seem to include challenging authority. Some adolescents automatically dismiss the state of adulthood as inherently wrong, which is why the librarian who insisted on Being Authoritative made things much worse for himself.

When young people are reprimanded publicly (which is an error to begin with, but sometimes unavoidable) they will often wait till later to act defensively, resist suggestions for change or generally behave antagonistically when least expected. Although the librarian may see this as revenge or just plain discourtesy, it may, to the individual involved, be a way to salvage dignity in front of peers. Not everyone is ready to forgive and forget what has been perceived as embarrassing or insulting.

Give Young People Part of the Responsibility for Making the Guidelines for Conduct in the Library/Media Center

If they are not involved in what goes on in the governance of the library, adolescents can be very uncooperative when it comes to carrying out guidelines, rules and other standards set by adults. They can and often do recognize the need for rules and will often cooperate readily with those who offer them a part in designing such rules. An opportunity to speak out without interruption (or punishment) and the freedom to vent dissatisfaction about perceived injustices is terribly important.

Power and the Hierophant

Power is neither good nor bad. It just exists, rather like electricity, traveling through but not residing in any one place. It doesn't belong to anyone, and it needs a conductor for it to travel to a particular person. Changing perceptions is a way to set up a conductor, but another conductor of power is genuineness--being real.

Using "power over" is a stop-gap maneuver which lasts while the setting and the props are on hand. Both the child and the adolescent intuitively know what will happen next. That, of course is why adults usually feel faintly defensive when bolstering a position with answers like, "Just because, that's why," or "That's the rule."

There will be times when you may feel powerless and think it necessary to fall back on strength from other sources. But it might also be advantageous to describe what you are feeling about the need to depend on others. It is better in most cases to be honest than to lie. There is nothing wrong with admitting that you need support at times, but the reasons should be valid and explained so that they will be recognized as truthful. Success lies in what others perceive you to be--an enemy, for example, or an honest person trying to get on with the job. Students have been known to rally round an adult who is open enough to admit vulnerability. The young are not as uncaring as some would have you to believe. But to know that you must be brave enough to stand up alone and sack the Hierophant.

WEDNESDAY'S CHILDREN*

Katherine Paterson

I have always known what day my brother was born on. He was a long awaited, greatly rejoiced over baby. By the time I was born he was going on five years old, but my mother was still recalling the happy Sunday on which he came into the world.

The old nursery rhyme she often repeated gives a tag for every day of the week, and if you are as old as I am, you can probably recite it yourself.

> Monday's child is fair of face,
> Tuesday's child is full of grace,
> Wednesday's child is full of woe,
> Thursday's child has far to go,
> Friday's child is loving and giving,
> Saturday's child must work for a living,
> But the child that is born on the Sabbath Day
> Is bonny and blithe, and good and gay.

My mother, having been born in the nineteenth century into a conservative Protestant family, regarded Sunday as the proper Sabbath and had a different interpretation of the word gay than the one in use today.

I also knew what day of the week my older sister was born on. Elizabeth was born on a Thursday. As the rhyme prophetically proclaimed, and my mother reminded us, Baby Elizabeth traveled from Richmond, Virginia, to Huai'an fu, China, before she was six months old.

So how come nobody ever mentioned what day I was born on? I had to assume that I was never told because I would be shattered if I found out, the nursery rhyme being as close to a horoscope as

---

*Reprinted by permission of the author and publisher of The Horn Book Magazine (May/June 1986), 287-294; copyright © 1986 by Katherine Paterson.

a Presbyterian missionary family would have ventured. Obviously,
I thought, I was one of Wednesday's woeful waifs, doomed by the
date of my birth.

One of my sons was born on a Sunday and the other on a Tuesday. Whew. Both very good days. But what about the girls? I
wasn't there when they were born. Whew again. Both of them, as
it happened, were Tuesday babies and therefore full of grace, which
is really quite as nice as being born on Sunday. My husband was
born on a Thursday. It took him nearly twenty years to go more
than a couple hundred miles from the town of his birth, but once he
started traveling, he did, indeed, go far. You can always make
prophecies come true if you're willing to enlarge the parameters.

That left me. Knowing Mother, I must have been born on one
of two days. It had to be either a Monday or a Wednesday. Those
are the only two days that she would have worried about. She
wouldn't have wanted me to think of myself as either fair of face
(likely to make the child conceited) or, as I had always darkly suspected, full of woe (likely to make the child feel sorry for herself).
Weee, as it turns out, my birthday was on a Monday, but since news
of my fair face was a closely guarded secret for nearly fifty-three
years, I have spent most of my life identifying not with the vain,
beautiful people but with those whose lives are full of woe.

Just look at the characters in my books. They all seem to have
been born on Wednesdays. Only three of my central characters live
in homes with their natural families intact. Of those three, two of
them don't realize that their parents do indeed love them, and the
only fully happy child dies at an early age.

After she had read Come Sing, Jimmy Jo (Lodestar/Dutton), a
friend called me on the telephone. "I can't believe it!" she cried.
"You didn't kill off Grandma!" I was immediately nervous. "I wasn't
sure at the beginning whether she would have to die or not, but it
seemed okay to let her live. I mean she only had a minor irregularity.
Lots of people live for years with a condition like that." "Oh, no,
no," she said. "Of course, you didn't have to kill her. It's just
that you always seem determined to do something awful like that."
It reminded me of the librarian who said to me several years ago,
"I always wonder when I pick up one of your books, how's she going
to mess it up this time?"

Actually, after I finished writing Bridge to Terabithia (Crowell)
and being totally washed out emotionally, I decided that the next
time I would write a funny book. "People love funny books," I
thought. "I love funny books. The world needs laughter. I am
known among my family and friends as a moderately funny person.
I could, if I set my mind to it, write a book that would make a reader
laugh."

Well, I laughed a lot while I was writing The Great Gilly Hopkins (Crowell). I remember especially the day I was describing
the grandmother's Thanksgiving visit to Maime Trotter's household.
I was laughing so hard I could barely type. "Could it be that it
was too slapstick? Too Marx Brothers?" I forced myself to sober
up and reread. "No, no," I said. "Perfect. Deliciously funny.
When have I ever read such a lovely scene?" I don't have to be
modest in the privacy of my study or even particularly honest as
long as I'm still working on an early draft.

There were, as always, interruptions in the writing of the book,
but I finally got through the first draft while we were on vacation
at Lake George and turned it over to my husband to read. No one
but me had ever read this book before. I had been working on it
for over a year, and no one even knew what it was about. This
first reading by another human being, was, therefore, of enormous
importance to me. I handed John the stack of messy, typewritten
and scribbled-over pages and tried very hard not to breathe down
his neck as he read each word. My family will wait for a year or
two to find out what I've been up to, but I can't wait a minute to
see how they'll react.

As it turned out, I had to wait. My husband was involved in
something else and didn't seize immediately upon the chance to read
the fruits of my many months of labor. There was nothing I could
do to rush him, so I tried very hard to forget I'd given it to him
and turn my mind elsewhere. A few days later I was sitting on my
towel beside the lake, swimming every now and again, but mostly
reading as the afternoon wore on and on, and still John did not
come down to swim. Finally, it was nearly five o'clock, I could see
him coming, and by the way he was walking, I could tell long before
I could see his face that something dreadful had happened. I checked
the water. Four heads. The children were all right. He was on
his feet, so he was physically safe. All I could think of was that he
had totaled the car on the mountain road and just managed to escape
with his life. "What's the matter?" I cried. "What happened?" "I've
been reading your book," he said. "But, John," I said. "That's
my funny book."

Well, Gilly was published in 1978, and people are still arguing
about whether or not it's a funny book. How can you have a funny
book about a Wednesday's child who is abandoned by her mother,
bounced about in foster care, a child who is so hurt by the woes
the world has heaped upon her that she can't even recognize love
until she's already betrayed it? So it's not the Marx Brothers, but
it is, in the classic sense, not a tragedy, but a comedy.

I wouldn't write a tragedy. I take my job too seriously. I
only write comedies. As you read this you are probably asking yourself, "Bridge to Terabithia a comedy? Rebels of the Heavenly Kingdom (Lodestar/Dutton) a comedy?" And you are wondering what

perverse definition of comedy I've come up with to justify this assertion. The very least you ask of comedy is a happy ending, and
where among all my books is there an ending that an ordinary reader
would recognize as happy?

It reminds me of years ago when I used to go to the movies
in the Japanese country town where I lived. One night I came out
of the theater red-faced and weeping from yet another Japanese heart-
breaker. "I'm never going to see another Japanese movie as long as
I live," I complained between sobs to the Japanese friend with whom
I usually went to the movies. "The endings are always too sad."

She was astounded. "Why, that was a happy ending," she
said. "What do you mean happy ending?" I was equally astounded.
"She died!" "Well, of course, she died," my friend said. "But he
got there before she died." As you see, what constitutes a happy
ending does differ from culture to culture and from person to person.

But I'm not trying to play games with you. I am writing for
and about Wednesday's children. It never occurred to me I could
con my readers or cheat my characters by frosting over the last
chapter with happily ever after. I take very seriously the tragic
dimension of human life. Every human life ends in death. I do not
consider it a kindness to pretend otherwise. Nor do I believe that
our children can be shielded from the world with its infinite store
of wonder and fear and its immense possibilities both for good and
evil.

The ultimate metaphor for this, and would that it were only
a metaphor, is the nuclear threat. Our children have never known
a time when the mushroom cloud did not form the backdrop of civilization. In the eighteenth century, writers of children's books tried
to frighten the young into piety by telling tales of early death. Now
you and I find that kind of book psychic blackmail at its worst, and
yet we all contribute to a system that holds not only our children's
lives hostage but the very life of the planet on which they belong.
But we do not call that psychic blackmail, we call it national security.
Children cannot understand such semantics or how freedom will have
been preserved when everything they love, including their own lives,
has been destroyed.

I addressed this concern in a newspaper essay I wrote by asking the rhetorical question, "How do you write a book for children
who do not know if there will be a world for them to grow up in?"
I got an answer in an irate letter: "Easy, lady. You don't! Leave
the writing to someone who knows that children need to enjoy life
as children and not have their childhood stolen from them. If you
can't do that, then don't write at all." Now I have a lot of problems
with this statement in addition to my obvious reluctance to give up
my life's work. The first problem is with the narrowness of this

gentleman's concern. He is not talking about those thousands of
children who died or who were permanently injured from the noxious
fumes of a Union Carbide plant or those who lie with bloated bellies
in dusty camps in Ethiopia or those children who die daily in a dirty
little war or those children who stand weeping by the ruins of a
Mexican apartment house or even those in our fair land who are
beaten or cursed or neglected.

In August of 1985 I was present for the "Everychild" Awards
Luncheon in New York City. Beverly Cleary accepted the award
for books and told in her acceptance speech of letters she had received from children, including two anonymous letters from children
who were being abused. She called the children's schools and asked
them to try to help these little ones, too frightened even to give
their names to their favorite writer.

Dr. Larry Brown from Harvard University received the award
for child advocacy. Dr. Brown told how in 1967 he had been a part
of the national hunger study that aroused our nation to the point
that children were provided with free lunches and breakfasts at
school, food stamps were provided for the poor, and a special nutrition program was begun to aid women and their children. The
campaign against hunger was a success beyond anyone's wildest
dreams. Ten years later when Dr. Brown and his team went back
to the same sites they had visited, they found that hunger had been
virtually eliminated.

But now, in the last couple of years, physicians once more
are noticing that ominous condition called "failure to thrive," which
in plain language means children are not growing because they do not
have proper nourishment. Dr. Brown's commission found that the
gains of the seventies have been almost erased, as we, as a nation,
have chosen other priorities. The current priorities of the United
States do not include nurturing our most precious resource. We
would rather intimidate our enemies with yet another instrument of
mass destruction than make sure that our children have strong bodies
and alert minds.

When Mr. Rogers stood up to accept the media award, he was
so overcome with emotion that he wept openly at the podium, and the
audience wept with him. What could we be thinking of? How could
we abandon millions of America's children to hunger and the mental
and spiritual crippling which it brings? "I wish," Fred Rogers said,
"I just wish I could reach right through the television set and give
them food." I watched and listened and wept. Somehow we must
learn to love our children more than we fear our enemies.

When a person asks that I let children enjoy childhood, he is
not talking of most of the children in this world or even large numbers of children in this nation. He has forgotten Wednesday's children. He is talking about his dream children: bright, handsome,

winsome, healthy, self-confident; children who have never felt the
sting of prejudice, who laugh freely and bring their parents joy.
A tiny minority of all the children who live out their lives in this
world. And yet, even these, the super-blessed, cannot be left to
enjoy a childhood isolated from the pain and grief and horror of the
real world. The world is too much with us. Even these, our most
cared for and most deeply loved, even our Sunday and Tuesday children, will have their Wednesdays. We have not discovered a vaccine
against fear and grief and pain. I think the reason children like
my books is because they know that I take their feelings and their
fears seriously. But I will not write tragedy for them.

In his wonderful book, Weapons and Hope (Harper) Freeman
Dyson describes the attitude of many Americans to the nuclear pre-
dicament as the "Eeyore Syndrome":

> Eeyore, the old grey Donkey, stood by the side of the
> stream, and looked at himself in the water.
> "Pathetic," he said. "That's what it is. Pathetic."
> He turned and walked slowly down the stream for twenty
> yards, splashed across it, and walked slowly back on the
> other side. Then he looked at himself in the water again.
> "As I thought," he said. "No better from this side. But
> nobody minds. Nobody cares. Pathetic, that's what it is."

But Dr. Dyson maintains that tragedy is not our business.
We must change our attitude toward the state of the world or perish.
In his book Dr. Dyson presents us with new ways of thinking about
the nuclear crisis and lays a foundation for hope--not cheap, wishful
thinking, but hope grounded in responsible and patient endeavor.
One point Dr. Dyson makes, which is particularly important for those
who are concerned about children and their books, is that the best
antidote for the Eeyore Syndrome is comedy.

We who are concerned with books for young people need to
remind ourselves of this truth. There is the real danger that we
will split down the middle--the doom and gloomers on one side and
the sweetness and lighters on the other. Following Dr. Dyson's lead,
let me suggest that the books our children need have three essential
ingredients.

The first of these is sagacity. Wisdom, as Dr. Dyson suggests,
would be ideal, but wisdom is in such short supply in the world that
we must be content with its country cousin, sagacity. Now sagacity
has an honorable heritage in stories for children, whether we go
back as far as Odysseus clinging under the belly of the Cyclop's
ram or the myriad Jacks of folk and fairy fame. In 1985 we celebrated America's most sagacious hero of comedy, Huckleberry Finn.
In comedy the hero may seem stupid, may be regarded as inferior
by everyone, but the hero has perception and judgment that will
not be ultimately defeated by the plastic sophistication of the world.

In a comedy there will also be humor. On the screen, large
and small, a lot which passes for humor is, in fact, gallows humor.
Our laughter becomes a desperate last stand against despair. Today a kind of slapstick exists which is so cruel that we dare not
examine it closely. But this is not the humor of comedy. The humor
of comedy is that which allows us to keep ourselves in perspective.
Stephen Leacock, the great Canadian humorist, speaks of this as the
humor "that reflects through scene or character the incongruity of
life itself," the kind of humor, Leacock says, which "blends laughter
and tears ... intimately together." This is the kind of humor to
be found in the adventures of Don Quixote and Ramona Quimby.

Finally, comedy always issues in hope. Now hope is quite a
different commodity from happily ever after. Happily ever after is
a state of perpetual perfection where there is no room for growth
nor need for forgiveness. Happily ever after has no relationship
to reality as we know it. But in the midst of a most imperfect world,
we still hope, because hope is something that we can do even on
Wednesdays.

"You told me you would never write a book without hope,"
someone complained to me, "but where is the hope in Rebels of the
Heavenly Kingdom?" My critic was right in the large picture. The
Taiping which began in such high hope and with such wonderful
ideals has self-destructed. I could not control that tragic outcome.
But on the last page of the book there remain two, Wang Lee and
Mei Lin, two who bore both the glory and the scars of the movement.
They are living together in peace. They have not bound their daugh-
ters' feet, and they are teaching all their children to read. A miser-
able little remnant of hope to grow out of the scorched and ruined
nation, you might think, but all true hope starts like a tiny seed
that must be nurtured.

Jesse takes May Belle across the rude bridge he has made so
that he can begin to introduce her to the kingdom of Terebithia.
Gilly is finally able to acknowledge her love for Trotter and turn a
few degrees from her self-centeredness to a concern for her grandmother. An adult Louise understands what happened on the day of
her birth and begins, if only barely, to find release from her lifelong resentment of her twin sister. James walks into the spotlight
with his glasses on, and, although he can see all too clearly the im-
perfections of his family and the childishness of his fans, he wants
somehow to care for them and share his gift with them.

Wednesday's children, all. But not, in the end, overcome by
woe. I love these children. Despite their faults and my own deficiencies, I still imagine that I see in each one of them the qualities
of sagacity and humor and hope. I'd like to think their stories are
my birthday gifts to the Wednesday's children who may read them.

BOOK SELECTION IN THE COLLEGE LIBRARY: THE FACULTY PERSPECTIVE*

Mary Sellen

It has been acknowledged in the literature of library administration and book selection that in a college library, the faculty play an important role in the development of the book collection. Lyle, in discussing book selection within the larger context of the administration of a college library, notes that "close cooperation between the librarian and members of the faculty is vital in selecting books."[1] He goes on to state that "in lieu of its own specialist staff, the library leans havily on the faculty."[2] and yet "there is very little factual information on the methods by which faculty go about choosing library materials."[3] Carter et al.[4] spent six pages on the role of the faculty in selection. They theorized about the faculty's role from incidents that had been called to their attention. Broadus[5] acknowledged the role of the faculty but offered no theory or conclusions on their role in the selection process.

Some information about the faculty's role has been reported in studies in which circulation patterns of books were traced to their selectors. Evans, in two related studies,[6] examined which selector's books (faculty, librarians, or approval plans) had the highest circulation. He found that librarians selected a greater number of titles that were used. Bingham,[7] replicating Evans, found that books selected by faculty were circulated more frequently than those selected by librarians, except in the humanities. Geyer,[8] however, found that there was no significant difference in the circulation patterns of books selected by faculty and those selected by librarians.

Two studies were found in which the specific role of the faculty in the selection process was examined. Biskup and Jones[9] sent questionnaires to the faculty at the Australian National University and the Canberra College in order to discover how frequently the faculty selected library materials and what sources they used. They

*Reprinted by permission of the author and publisher from Collection Building (Spring 1985), 4-10; copyright © 1985 by Neal-Schuman Publishers, Inc.

found that a minority of faculty systematically selected materials and that they relied on methods of selection that did not automatically guarantee the quality of the collection. Kim[10] sent questionnaires to faculty in the School of Education at a midwestern university in order to examine selected behavioral factors that were likely to influence the faculty's participation in library book selection. Eleven variables were examined. It was found that years of teaching, publication activity, the amount of professional meetings attended, and the number of professional journals read were significant variables in the faculty's participation. One study was found in which book selection in the college environment was studied. Baughman et al.[11] surveyed a random sample of faculty members at four-year institutions. The librarians and general college administrators of each respective faculty member's institution were also sent surveys. The thrust of the study was to measure the attitudes of these three groups toward collection development policies. They found general agreement on the process of formulating a collection development policy but some disagreement on the issue of an allocation formula. Little information on their selection habits, however, was given.

The following study attempted to add to the literature of college faculty in the book selection process by examining the following questions:

1. What are the attitudes of faculty toward whom should be responsible for selecting books?

2. Is the technical process in ordering books adequate or are there needs that are not being met?

3. What is the role that book selection plays within the larger context of a faculty member's responsibilities of teaching and research?

Methodology

Each faculty member at the Pennsylvania State University-- Behrend College was sent a questionnaire. The research, service, and teaching expectations at this institution were clear enough to elicit adequate responses to the research questions. The first part consisted of two questions in which the respondent was asked to indicate what divisions she/he belonged to. The choices were Business and Social Sciences (BSS), Humanities and Communication (HC), and Science, Engineering, and Technology (SET). The faculty were also asked to indicate the number of years spent in an academic teaching position. The second part consisted of ten statements regarding book selection to which the faculty responded to on a Likert-type scale. The statements focused on the three research questions of 1. who should select the books (statements 1, 2, 3); 2. the process of selection (statements 4, 8, 10); and 3. the role book

selection played in their academic responsibilities of research, service
and teaching (statements 5, 6, 7, 9). The statements were:

1. Book selection should be done by the librarians only.

2. Book selection should be done by the faculty only.

3. Book selection should be done by the librarians and faculty.

4. I could use more help from the library (in terms of book
   catalogs, bibliographies, etc.) in selecting books for the
   library.

5. Book selection is not a high priority in my work for the
   college.

6. Book selection for the library is important for my research.

7. Book selection for the library is important for the courses
   I teach.

8. The monies that are regularly allotted to my department
   are adequate to support the book needs in my discipline.

9. Journals are more important for my work than books.

10. The system for ordering books for the library collection
    (filling out order cards, waiting for months, etc.) is a
    deterrent when I order books for the library.

Two final questions asked the faculty member to rate the frequency of times they sent in book orders and to rank important
sources they used when ordering books. The questionnaire is reprinted at the end of this article. The SPSS subprograms of fre-
quencies and crosstabs are used to analyze the results.

Results

Table 1 presents a general summary of the responses from 44
to 45 percent of the 97 full-time faculty involved in book selection
at the college. The majority of the respondents, 63 percent, rated
themselves "regular" selectors. Thirty-two percent rated themselves
"occasional" selectors, and five percent never participated. An almost equal number of responses was obtained from all three divisions.
The number of years of teaching ranged from 1 to 21+, with the
majority in the category of 1 to 15.

TABLE 1: GENERAL SUMMARY

1. Frequency by Total Percentage:

	Total	Percentage
Regular	28	63%
Occasionally	14	32%
Never	2	5%
TOTAL	44	100%

2. Frequency by Division:

	BSS	HC	SET
Regular	8	9	11
Occasionally	6	6	2
Never	–	–	2
TOTAL	14	15	15

3. Frequency by Years of Teaching:

	1-5	6-10	11-15	16-20	21+
Regular	6	8	7	3	4
Occasionally	8	2	3	–	1
Never	2	–	–	–	–
TOTAL	16	10	10	3	5

Table 2 (page 171) summarizes the responses in regard to the first research question. Faculty were consistent in their response to choice of selector. The responses to statements 1, 2, and 3 were almost identical in agreeing that selection should be done by a combination of faculty and librarians. There was no uncertainty and almost complete agreement that book selection not be left to the librarian alone. Some uncertainty did occur when selection was left to the faculty only or the combination of faculty and librarians. This concern was apparent in the teaching years of 11 to 25+ and the BSS and SET divisions. The greatest dissent to the faculty/librarian combination came from those with 11 to 15 years of teaching experience and the SET division. Those who were "regular" selectors also favored the faculty/librarians combination.

Table 3 (page 172) summarizes the responses to the second research question. A large percentage of respondents expressed a need for more help in the selection process (statement 4). The responses to the statements on the allocated monies (statement 8) and technical system used to order materials (statement 10) were generally even among the three possible responses. Although the expressed need for help was large (47 percent), the majority was either unsure or did not express any need for help (a combination percentage of 53 percent). Faculty in the 1 to 10 years of teaching expressed the most need, while older faculty were either unsure or

TABLE 2: SELECTOR

Statement 1: Book Selection should be done by the librarians only.

TOTAL RESPONSE			YEARS OF TEACHING				DIVISION				FREQUENCY			
A	U	D		A	U	D		A	U	D		A	U	D
2	–	42	1-5	–	–	16	BSS	1	–	13	Regular	1	–	27
(5%)		(95%)	6-10	–	–	10	HC	–	–	15	Occasion	1	–	13
			11-15	–	–	9	SET	1	–	14	Never	–	–	2
			16-20	–	–	3								
			21+	1	–	4								

Statement 2: Book Selection should be done by the faculty only.

TOTAL RESPONSE			YEARS OF TEACHING				DIVISION				FREQUENCY			
A	U	D		A	U	D		A	U	D		A	U	D
4	3	37	1-5	–	–	16	BSS	1	1	12	Regular	4	3	21
(9%)	(7%)	(84%)	6-10	1	2	7	HC	1	1	13	Occasion	–	–	14
			11-15	1	1	8	SET	2	1	12	Never	–	–	2
			16-20	1	–	2								
			21+	1	–	4								

Statement 3: Book selection should be done by the librarians and faculty.

TOTAL RESPONSE			YEARS OF TEACHING				DIVISION				FREQUENCY			
A	U	D		A	U	D		A	U	D		A	U	D
37	4	3	1-5	15	1	–	BSS	12	1	1	Regular	21	4	3
(84%)	(9%)	(7%)	6-10	8	2	–	HC	12	3	–	Occasion	14	–	–
			11-15	8	1	1	SET	13	–	2	Never	2	–	–
			16-20	2	–	1								
			21+	4	–	1								

A--Agree   U--Unsure   D--Disagree

TABLE 3: PROCESS

Statement 4: I could use more help from the library in selecting books for
the library.

TOTAL RESPONSE			YEARS OF TEACHING				DIVISION				FREQUENCY			
A	U	D		A	U	D		A	U	D		A	U	D
21	9	14	1-5	9	3	4	BSS	5	3	6	Regular	11	8	9
(47%)	(21%)	(32%)	6-10	7	2	1	HC	10	3	2	Occasion	8	1	5
			11-15	4	1	5	SET	6	3	6	Never	2	-	-
			16-20	-	2	1								
			21+	1	1	3								

Statement 10: The monies alloted to my department are adequate to support
the book needs in my discipline.

TOTAL RESPONSE			YEARS OF TEACHING				DIVISION				FREQUENCY			
A	U	D		A	U	D		A	U	D		A	U	D
16	14	14	1-5	3	7	6	BSS	6	4	4	Regular	10	6	12
(36%)	(32%)	(32%)	6-10	6	2	2	HC	7	2	6	Occasion	6	6	2
			11-15	4	3	3	SET	3	8	4	Never	-	2	-
			16-20	1	-	2								
			21+	2	2	1								

Statement 10: The system for ordering books is a deterrent when I order
books for the library.

TOTAL RESPONSE			YEARS OF TEACHING				DIVISION				FREQUENCY			
A	U	D		A	U	D		A	U	D		A	U	D
17	14	13	1-5	6	7	3	BSS	4	6	4	Regular	8	9	11
(38%)	(32%)	(30%)	6-10	5	3	2	HC	9	4	2	Occasion	8	4	2
			11-15	5	2	3	SET	4	4	7	Never	1	1	-
			16-20	1	1	1								
			21+	-	1	4								

A--Agree   U--Unsure   D--Disagree

TABLE 4: ACADEMIC ROLE

Statement 5: Book selection is not a high priority in my work for the college.

TOTAL RESPONSE			YEARS OF TEACHING				DIVISION				FREQUENCY			
A	U	D		A	U	D		A	U	D		A	U	D
11	5	28	1-5	2	1	13	BSS	7	2	5	Regular	4	4	20
(25%)	(11%)	(64%)	6-10	2	2	6	IIC	4	2	9	Occasion	7	1	6
			11-15	5	1	4	SET	-	1	14	Never	-	-	2
			16-20	-	-	3								
			21+	2	1	2								

Statement 6: Book selection for the library is important for my research.

TOTAL RESPONSE			YEARS OF TEACHING				DIVISION				FREQUENCY			
A	U	D		A	U	D		A	U	D		A	U	D
26	10	7	1-5	10	3	2	BSS	7	3	4	Regular	18	5	4
(59%)	(23%)	(16%)	6-10	5	2	3	HC	6	6	2*	Occasion	6	5	3
			11-15	7	2	1	SET	13	1	1	Never	2	-	-
			16-20	1	2	-								
			21+	3	1	1								

Statement 7: Book selection is important for the courses I teach.

TOTAL RESPONSE			YEARS OF TEACHING				DIVISION				FREQUENCY			
A	U	D		A	U	D		A	U	D		A	U	D
30	9	4	1-5	9	4	2*	BSS	8	3	3	Regular	21	4	2
(68%)	(21%)	(9%)	6-10	7	3	-	HC	11	2	1*	Occasion	9	3	2
			11-15	8	1	1	SET	11	4	-	Never	-	2	-
			16-20	2	1	-								
			21+	4	-	1								

Statement 9: Journals are more important for my work than books.

TOTAL RESPONSE			YEARS OF TEACHING				DIVISION				FREQUENCY			
A	U	D		A	U	D		A	U	D		A	U	D
19	14	10	1-5	7	3	6	BSS	9	2	3	Regular	11	11	6
(43%)	(32%)	(23%)	6-10	7	2	1	HC	6	5	3	Occasion	7	3	3
			11-15	4	4	1	SET	7	7	1	Never	1	-	1
			16-20	-	2	1								
			21+	1	3	1								

A--Agree   U--Unsure   D--Disagree

in disagreement. Those faculty in the HC division expressed the
greatest desire for help while the SET and BSS divisions were almost
evenly split in uncertainty or disagreement. The "occasional" and
"never" selectors did agree that they needed help and the majority
of "regular" selectors disagreed or were unsure.

The response to the statement on allotments to the departments
(statement 8) was almost evenly divided between the three possible
responses with agreement that adequate monies were allotted only
two percentage points higher than the responses of unsure or disagree. The greatest satisfaction with the monies occurred in the
teaching years of 6 to 15, with the younger faculty in disagreement
or unsure. The SET division was more unsure about the money
amount than the other two divisions, with BSS and HC almost evenly
split between agreement and disagreement. "Regular" selectors were
mostly in disagreement or unsure about their monies. "Occasional"
and "never" were in agreement or unsure.

The majority of respondents, 38 percent, found the system
for ordering books (statement 10) a deterrent when selecting. An
almost equal number were unsure--32 percent, or in disagreement--
30 percent. The dissatisfaction came from those with 1 to 15 years
of teaching and faculty in the HC division. "Regular" selectors were
in disagreement or unsure. "Occasional" and "never" agreed. Faculty
in BSS and SET were more inclined to be unsure or in disagreement
about the system being a deterrent.

Table 4 (page 173) summarizes the responses to the third research question. In general, faculty considered selection a high
priority in their work for the college and important for their research
and teaching. There was also agreement that journals were important
for their work. Most faculty were either in agreement or unsure
about the importance of book selection in their research (statement
6). Faculty in all years of teaching considered selection important.
The SET division was almost unanimous in ranking selection important.
A larger number of respondents in the HC and BSS divisions were
uncertain or disagreed about the importance. The "regular" and
"occasional" selectors agreed that selection was important. There
was, however, more uncertainty or disagreement with the "occasional"
selector than the "regular".

A large percentage considered selection important for teaching
(statement 7). There was little disagreement about this but some uncertainty. The uncertainty was strongest in the younger faculty and
in the BSS and SET divisions. The most noticeable disagreement
came with the younger faculty in the BSS division.

While journals were generally considered important for the
faculty member's work (statement 10), a significant percentage were
uncertain (32 percent). This occurred throughout all years of teaching and in all three divisions. The BSS division rated journal im-

portance the highest while the SET division was split in agreement
and uncertainty.

When ranking sources used when ordering books for the library publishers' announcements, reviews, and advertisements in
professional journals were ranked one most often; references and
citations found in books and articles, and Choice cards were ranked
one less often; conferences and informal sources were not ranked
one at all. Choice cards were chosen as the second ranking source
most often. Publishers' announcements reviews, and advertisements
and references ranked second a number of times also. All choices
were ranked almost equally in the third and fourth rankings.

Discussion

The overall response to this survey indicated that there was
interest on the part of the faculty in the book-selection process.
The characteristics of the faculty selectors covered a large range of
characteristics. "Regular" selectors were found in all three divisions
and in all years of teaching. In general, the faculty felt that the
responsibility for selecting books should be assumed by a combination of faculty and librarians.

Faculty expressed some concerns with the technical process
of ordering materials. Help from the library in selecting books was
a need expressed by a majority of the respondents. The actual
system for ordering was seen as a deterrent by the majority, but
the uncertainty and disagreement about this was significant. The
same was true when faculty responded to the statement concerning
allocated monies. The majority agreed that there was adequate support, with significant numbers unsure or disagreeing.

Book selection was overall viewed as important in the faculty
members' work for the college. Selection seemed to be more important for teaching responsibilities than research, although there was
more uncertainty in the statement about research than in the responses about teaching.

Conclusion

Librarians should not underestimate the interests and concerns
of faculty in the book-selection process. This survey indicates that
selection plays an important role in the faculty members' various responsibilities for the college, a role librarians may not be fully aware
of. The faculty gave indications that they regularly selected books
and desired to work with the librarians in this process.

References

1. Guy R. Lyle, The Administration of the College Library 4th ed.
    (New York: Wilson, 1974), p. 176.
2. Ibid., p. 179
3. Ibid., p. 177.
4. Mary Duncan Carter, Wallace John Bonk, Rose Mary Magrill,
    Building Library Collections 4th ed. (Metuchen, N.J.:   Scare-
    crow Press, 1974), p. 61-66.
5. Robert N. Broadus, Selecting Materials for Libraries 2nd ed.
    (New York: Wilson, 1981), p. 18-19.
6. G. Edward Evans and Claudia White Argyres, "Approval Plans
    and Collection Development in Academic Libraries," Library Re-
    sources and Technical Services 18 (Winter 1974):   35-50 and
    G. Edward Evans, "Book Selection and Book Collection Usage
    in Academic Libraries," Library Quarterly 40 (July 1970):   297-
    308.
7. Robbie Barnes Bingham, "Collection Development in University
    Libraries: an Investigation of the Relationship Between Cate-
    gories of Selectors and Usage of Selected Items," (Ph.D. Thesis,
    Rutgers University, 1979).
8. John Eldon Geyer, "A Comparative Analysis of Book Selection
    Agents and Tools with Student Use at the Long Beach Community
    College Library," (Ed.D. University of Southern California,
    1977).
9. Peter Biskup and Catherine A. Jones, "Of Books, Academics
    and Libraries: Some facts about the Book Selection Habits of
    the Teaching Staffs at Two Canberra Institutions of Higher Learn-
    ing," Australian Academic and Research Libraries 7 (September
    1976):   159-70.
10. Ung Chon Kim, "Participation of Teaching Faculty in Library
    Book Selection," Collection Management 3 (Winter 1979):   333-
    54.
11. James Baughman et al.   "A Survey of Attitudes Toward Collec-
    tion Development in College Libraries" in Collection Development
    in Libraries: A Treatise ed. Robert Stueart and George B.
    Miller, Jr. (Greenwich, Conn.:   JAI Press, 1980).

QUESTIONNAIRE
FACULTY BOOK SELECTION SURVEY

1. Please indicate what division you are in:

    ____ Business and Social Sciences

    ____ Humanities and Communication

    ____ Science, Engineering and Technology

2. Please indicate how long you have been teaching in a college or university:

_____ 1-5 years

_____ 6-10 years

_____ 11-15 years

_____ 16-20 years

_____ 21+ years

PLEASE INDICATE YOUR AGREEMENT OR DISAGREEMENT TO THE FOLLOWING STATEMENTS. THESE QUESTIONS PERTAIN TO THE SELECTION OF BOOKS, NOT JOURNALS.

1. Book selection should be done by the librarians only.

_____ AGREE   _____ UNSURE   _____ DISAGREE

2. Book selection should be done by faculty only.

_____ AGREE   _____ UNSURE   _____ DISAGREE

3. Book selection should be done by the librarians and faculty.

_____ AGREE   _____ UNSURE   _____ DISAGREE

4. I could use more help from the library (in terms of book catalogs, bibliographies, etc.) in selecting books for the library.

_____ AGREE   _____ UNSURE   _____ DISAGREE

5. Book selection is not a high priority in my work for the college.

_____ AGREE   _____ UNSURE   _____ DISAGREE

6. Book selection for the library is important for my research.

_____ AGREE   _____ UNSURE   _____ DISAGREE

7. Book selection for the library is important for the courses I teach.

_____ AGREE   _____ UNSURE   _____ DISAGREE

8. The monies that are regularly allotted to my department are adequate to support the book needs in my discipline.

____ AGREE   ____ UNSURE   ____ DISAGREE

9. Journals are more important for my work than books.

____ AGREE   ____ UNSURE   ____ DISAGREE

10. The system for ordering books for the library collection (filling out cards, waiting for months, etc.) is a deterrent when I order books for the library.

____ AGREE   ____ UNSURE   ____ DISAGREE

11. Check one of the following that applies to the frequency of times you send in book orders for the library:

____ REGULARLY (meaning when you receive a reference for an appropriate book, ordering it for the library is a secondary consideration.)

____ OCCASIONALLY (meaning when you receive a reference for an appropriate book, ordering it for the library is a secondary consideration.)

____ NEVER

12. Please rank (with 1 being the most important) the sources you use when ordering books for the library:

____ Publishers' announcements

____ Reviews and advertisements in professional journals

____ References and citations found in books and articles

____ Informal sources (Ex. conversations, visits to other institutions)

____ Conferences

____ Choice cards

CURRENT ISSUES IN PUBLIC LIBRARY
SERVICES FOR CHILDREN*

Holly Willett

There are several issues grouped under three broad areas that seem
to be having an impact on services for children in public libraries
today. Few localities will escape these trends. Issues arising from
them undoubtedly will influence our working lives over the course
of the rest of the century. While the issues I'm going to discuss
are especially pertinent to the public library setting, particularly
to services for children in public libraries, some of them will also
be pertinent to academic, school, and special libraries, although I
will not draw inferences about these kinds of libraries.

The first of these areas is demographic trends, that is, changes
in the characteristics of the American population. The second set of
issues involves technology, especially electronic information services.
Finally, I want to tie these two areas into our present concern for
reform of public education.

There are at least two demographic trends that are forcing
librarians to look at some issues on which we thought we had already
made up our minds. The first of these population trends is the fact
that our population is aging. Due to improved health care, people
are living longer, and eventually, the baby boom generation, now
approaching middle age, will become senior citizens. In 1960, children
under fourteen accounted for 29.5 percent of the United States' population, while those over fifty-five made up 17.8 percent. By 1982,
children under fourteen accounted for 20.6 percent of the population
and those over fifty-five accounted for 21.1 percent. There are
nearly 5.5 million fewer children now than there were twenty-five
years ago.[1] Whenever there is such a shift in the relative sizes
of age groups in society, somewhere in the library press someone
will suggest that it may be time to diminish the resources devoted
to children's services. Such a suggestion appeared in the Wilson

*Reprinted by permission of the author and publisher from Public
Libraries, 24 (Winter 1985), 137-140; copyright © 1985 by the American Library Association.

Library Bulletin of September 1984.[2] The perception that children's
services is about to disappear may be partly responsible for the fact
that there is a national shortage of children's librarians now.

   Those who think that public libraries will not need to maintain
their commitments of staff and materials to children's services ignore
the fact that people will continue to have children. There is, in fact,
a mild countervailing trend in the birth rates, especially among women
in their thirties who have delayed starting their families for the sake
of their careers. Much of this growth will take place in the Southeast, the mountain states and the Pacific Coast, while very little of
it will occur in the Northeast and the North Central regions according to Regional Diversity.[3] If there are fewer children to work
with, children's librarians will have a greater opportunity to reach
a larger proportion of them. It is a time to maintain services to
young people and improve them, to reach children who are presently
underserved, and to reach more adults who live and work with children. Children's librarians like to say that serving children ensures
the future of public libraries by building a clientele that will support
the library as adults. Even if adults who have used the library in
childhood remain library supporters although perhaps not library
users, there seem to me to be more compelling reasons to support
services for children at the same time that more extensive services
for adults are developed. One of these reasons is that children are
entitled to such services because they are residents of localities that
have public libraries. And another reason is that children have
needs in childhood for which public libraries can provide materials
and guidance.

   It seems most likely that children's librarians will be called upon
to justify their services more often. Just as we find that public libraries are in competition with other units of local government for
funds, departments within the library may have to compete for the
dollars available to them. Library directors are rightly going to
want to know why they should support services for a group that is
not a major portion of the population. And older people themselves
may demand more services. Older people are quite vocal in claiming
public resources for themselves, and they are successful, too. Of
all population groups, their financial well-being has improved the
most in the last twenty years. What evidence can a children's librarian call upon to demonstrate the importance of service to children?

   One area with which children's librarians are becoming increasingly familiar in this regard is child development. What psychologists have to say about the effects of the kinds of materials and
experiences offered by public libraries to children can help us design
more effective programs of service, but also provide evidence that
service to children is an important component of public library work.
Very little experimental research directly involving public libraries
has been done, and there are some problems with the research that

is available. However, even research into general cognitive development and educational attainment is of use in justifying the existence
of a special department devoted to serving children. An example of
highly useful research is Toni Smardo's study of receptive language
skills at the Dallas Public Library. Her results are strong evidence
that reading aloud to preschoolers in the library has a substantial
impact on the acquisition of language skills.[4]

The activities and use patterns of the children's department
are also evidence for justifying its existence. Surprisingly few librarians keep the kind of records that would be most helpful in this
regard unless such records are required by the state library. And
many state libraries do not ask for reports on children's services.
There are only twenty-four states that collect data about children's
circulation, for example.[5] It is simply good management practice
to know what you have done, why you did it, and how well you did
it. Even if the library director does not require the children's librarian to keep track of materials budgets, story hours, class visits,
and activity programs, the librarian should have records for her own
use in planning a total program of service and for collection development. For my dissertation, I conducted a survey of public library
services in California, which asked for statistics from two fiscal years.
One librarian estimated that the children's department had provided
twelve programs of a recreational or cultural nature during fiscal
year 1977-78. Since she also included a copy of the library's annual
report for that year, I read the narrative portion of the report and
counted sixty-eight programs in the summer alone. Similarly, she
reported no educational or information programs for adults, and I
read about forty-four group tours and thirty-five speeches presented
by the library's special collections department in one spring quarter.
While the connotations of this are rather unfortunate for my dissertation, the incident certainly points up the need for improved record
keeping for the purposes of accountability. Even though the lack of
record keeping is as great in adult services, that department is not
in any danger of its operations being downgraded.

Now. On to the second demographic trend that has importance
for children's public library services. None of you will be surprised
to hear that this is the growing presence of mothers in the labor
force. Nationally, in 1982, 46 percent of children under six had
working mothers, and 59 percent of children six to seventeen had
mothers who worked.[6]

What these figures mean is that it is no longer possible to serve
children adequately using the methods that time has honored. The
traditional preschool story hour where individual parents bring their
children to the library will not reach the millions of children in day-
care centers and family day-care homes. Preschool activities now involve planning with day-care agencies and coordinating councils,
travel by librarians to day-care centers, bookmobile visits to day-
care centers, and bringing groups of young children to the library.

All of which requires more preparation time than the traditional forms
of preschool service.

Librarians have much to offer day-care workers as well as
children in day care. Some people involved in day care are college
educated and well trained. Many more are not. Because child care
is a poorly paid occupation, it attracts those whose skills do not
allow them more lucrative employment. These people are aware of
their need to learn about children and to promote child development.
What librarians can pass along to them is our expertise in selecting
quality materials for children and our methods for using materials
with children. Child-care workers also need the assistance of librarians in locating materials to answer specific questions about child
development and the care of children. The most effective means of
presenting information may not always be the kind of individual assistance we are trained to provide and most enjoy providing. Very
often, children's librarians find themselves addressing groups and
organizing workshops. The design and presentation of a formal
educational experience is a role for which many librarians are under-
prepared.

It is crucial, however, that children's librarians make the effort to instruct day-care workers and to work with day-care centers.
Child development studies have suggested that an early and happy
introduction to books has implications for language skills development
so important to future success in school. And we know from the many
commissions and studies of education published in 1983 that illiteracy
continues to be a problem among young people. I will be coming
back to the issue of educational reform later.

What about the even larger group, the 59 percent of children
between the ages of six and seventeen whose parents are not at
home when the children are released from school? Commonly called
latchkey children from the practice of giving them a key to let themselves into their homes, the biggest problem these children have is
supervising themselves. While some children are perfectly capable
of remaining at home alone for those hours when a parent is not
available, other children need more direction. Public libraries report increased "use" of the library after school, not all of it constructive. In New Bedford, Massachusetts, where I was head of the
children's department, roving groups of children aged ten to fourteen made the library one of their regular stops in a daily round of
after-school activities that they had "organized" for themselves.
One winter afternoon, I found one of the circulation clerks wiping
water off the carriage of her typewriter and wearing an expression
of total disgust. A group of boys had found a dead bird frozen in
the snow outside the library. They had climbed the stairs to the
third floor, leaned over the railing, and dropped the revoltingly
semi-thawed object with perfect aim onto the typewriter thirty feet
below. Despite such pranks, I came to realize eventually that it was
better for children to be in the library in semisupervised conditions

than out on the streets. Of course, not everyone on the staff agreed
with me.

For years, children's librarians have told the public and themselves that they are not baby-sitters, and I am not about to suggest that we should become baby-sitters. However, the location of
public libraries, the kinds of hours normally kept by libraries, and
the materials and staff of libraries make them naturally attractive
and useful places for some kinds of after-school activities. But the
library is only one agency within the community that should be involved in planning for the needs of children whose parents must work
while the children are not in school. Obviously, parents have a
great deal of responsibility for their children, but society at large
has a stake in the health, safety, and education of the young. Appropriate agencies for dealing with the after-school care issue include
the schools, the recreation department, and private agencies, such
as the UMCA, as well as the public library. Regular planned programs at specified times in the afternoons are part of an answer to
children's needs, but librarians should also be prepared with drop-
in activities to meet the interests of children who have nothing to do
in particular. Some libraries have found that older school-age children are very happy to help with the chores and have formed groups
of volunteers or Junior Friends of the Library to make constructive
use of youthful energy. Other libraries have set up interest centers,
an idea borrowed from elementary education in which books and materials are set up on display with activities for children to do with
little supervision. Within the scope of the public library's mission
to provide recreation, education, culture, and information, the needs
of school-age children certainly fit. I am advocating a deliberate
policy of cultivating the after-school audience.

Ironically, these two demographic trends--the aging population
and the number of children with working mothers--work against each
other. At the same time that the situation of children is demanding
more intensive efforts at programming and planning with other agencies within the community, the growing proportion of the population
over eighteen also demands and deserves public library attention.
While the economy has recovered from the worst of the 1981-82 reces-
sion, local governments are not going to be any more enthusiastic
about providing for library services than they have been in the past.
The mood of the country is not conducive to expanding public services. It is possible that children's librarians may be able to turn
the aging population to an advantage by using retirees as volunteers
for children's programming. Some libraries are already doing this
with reasonable success. The use of volunteers represents a major
change in philosophy. Previously, only professional children's librarians and their trained assistants were considered capable of providing story hours, book talks, and programs. Today, the demand
is so great and the staffing so limited that such a position is no
longer tenable.

The second area of interest for public libraries is technology.
Computer technology for libraries has been developing for about
twenty years. It has become much more sophisticated, much more
reliable, and much less expensive over that period of time. However, public libraries are still not necessarily using the available
technology to a great degree. For instance, in the area of microcomputers, a recent Bowker survey found that 190,000 micros are
in use in public, school, academic, and special libraries.[7] Of that
number, 100,000 were in elementary, junior high, and middle school
libraries. Less than half the microcomputers in libraries were located
in high schools or the other three types of libraries. The survey did
not count the microcomputers housed in classrooms; however, the implication is clear. Today's youngsters are being raised to view the
computer as a commonplace instrument, as useful and ordinary as
the telephone. When children go to the public library, they may
find that it doesn't meet their expectations regarding technology,
particularly if the library is located in a small town. There is a
potential loss of future support for the public library. But the
serious problem is the question of access.

The electronic databases that are available are commercial en-
terprises that are sold for a fee. Few public libraries are able to
provide free searches for patrons. If libraries are to offer databases
at all, many must charge for a search. Young people in general are
among the groups least likely to have the money to pay for database
searches. Access for children and youth may come to depend upon
the financial resources of their parents and their schools. Children
of relatively wealthy and well-educated parents who can afford to
improve their children's competitive edge will have access to many
data sources through their home computers. Children who attend
school in financially able school districts will have electronic data
available at school. Parents and school districts without the funds
may be unable to offer their children access to databases. Public
libraries, as locally financed institutions, are in the same situation.
As more and more of the information base is placed in electronic form,
the distance between the kinds and amounts of information available
to children of different economic classes will grow.

There is an accumulation of research evidence going back nearly
forty years that is fairly conclusive in finding that the more educated
use the public library the most, despite the fact that public libraries
pride themselves on being available to all. However, this research
has been conducted with adults, and we do not know much about
library use among children of different socioeconomic classes. Studies in Atlanta and Oakland suggest that children may use the library
in disproportionately greater numbers than adults, regardless of
class or race, if there is a library within walking distance of their
homes.[8] But what if that library does not offer the same kinds
of services in poor neighboorhoods as in middle-class neighborhoods,
or asks them to pay a fee for the use of information? Effectively,
the poor of any age will be denied the resources available to those
with a financial advantage.

Americans typically place a high value on individualism and allowing people to work toward their individual aspirations. Indeed, the goal of providing a means for individuals to improve their educations was one of the founding concepts of the public library. The promise is not equal outcomes for everyone, but equal opportunities to shape one's own outcome. In the nineteenth century, free, universal public education was designed to address the question of providing a more equal start for everyone, and it also made good sense economically because of industry's demand for a more skilled work force. Perhaps the question of equality of opportunity for our time will become access to electronic databases as more and more of the world's store of information is coded in electronic form. And it will still be a question of social values and economic advantage.

Despite state funding efforts to equalize local school districts' ability to provide quality programs, the quality of schools varies from locality to locality. The quality of public library services also varies greatly from place to place, and it is unrealistic to expect all libraries to be equally good. However, some consideration should be given to providing a floor under those libraries that especially need assistance to boost them into the information age. Because it seems especially unlikely that the federal government will fund new programs for libraries, we might consider a reorganization of the Library Services and Construction Act to fund the capital outlay necessary to provide public libraries with the technology needed. Then local and state efforts will be needed to provide special funds for the use of databases by those who are unable to afford them, especially children and teenagers who are most likely to be using databases for the purposes of completing homework assignments. Friends of the library groups may be persuaded to set up "information soup kitchens" as a special service to students.

It has been very hard for me to talk about demographic trends and information access for children without mentioning education. Education in public library items usually means an informal learning situation without classrooms, tests, or grades. Usually public library programs are designed as much for pleasure as for the acquisition of knowledge, even when there is specific subject content involved. It is a children's services maxim that learning is fun. (Of course, not all learning in school is formal and not all public library experiences are informal). As Nancy Van House has said, almost any use of the public library by a child can be considered educational because the child can be presumed to be practicing skills and acquiring new information.[9] The argument against allowing the aging-population issue to deflect energy and resources from children's services is that there are personal and social benefits to be gained from maintaining and improving the public library's ability to serve children.

Children, having so much less experience than the rest of us, are constantly learning from their surroundings. The kinds of environments provided by day care for preschoolers and after-school care for older children have implications for social behavior and the acquisition and development of intellectual skills. And I have suggested ways that the public library can assist in improving the quality of day care and after-school services. Much of what goes on in preschools and day care is informal learning, and public library methods and materials are very compatible with the design of such programs. After-school programs for older children also need to be informal learning and recreational environments. At the end of a full school day, children need a change of pace and a relaxation of the pressure to perform. The public library is one agency that can offer activities suitable to their needs and consonant with the library's goals.

Information access is an issue for children and young people because the ability to locate needed information, to understand it, evaluate it, and use it is essential to the conduct of life in our time. Developing the skills necessary to handle information is the job of the schools, and many schools do it well. However, through various indicators, such as S.A.T. scores and illiteracy rates, we know that some schools fail to give children the intellectual tools they need to handle the demands of everyday life. A variety of proposals for improving public education and the public library's contribution to it have been made, specifically in A Nation at Risk and Alliance for Excellence. No one believes that the public library is going to make up for deficiencies of school systems. Public libraries have always viewed their efforts as supplementary to formal education. The time is certainly right to intensify those efforts, and the way to start is to strengthen the cooperation between school libraries and their local public libraries. Areas for cooperation include interlibrary loan, bibliographic networks, deposit collections, and cooperative purchase arrangements.

What I have tried to do here is suggest some particular issues affecting the quality of education in a very broad sense that children's librarians and library administrators need to address and some ways they might go about it. And while implementing changes will require all the management skills we possess, what we need most of all is the will to make changes. I am confident that many good things will come out of the present period of readjustment because one thing has not changed: children's librarians' commitment to children.

References

1. U.S. Bureau of the Census, Statistical Abstract of the United States 1984. (Washington, D.C.: U.S. Govt. Print Off, 1983), p. 31.
2. K. Falcigno and P. Guynup. "U.S. Population Characteristics: Implications for Libraries," Wilson Library Bulletin 59: 23-26 (1984).

3. G. Jackson and others, Regional Diversity: Growth in the United States, 1960-1990 (Boston: Auburn House, 1981).

4. F. A. Smardo and J. F. Curry, "What Research Tells Us about Storyhours and Receptive Language." (Dallas: Dallas Public Library, 1982).

5. M. J. Lynch, "Statistics on Library Services to Youth," Top of the News 41:181-83 (Winter 1985).

6. U.S. House of Representatives, Select Committee on Children, Youth, and Families, U.S. Children and Their Families: Current Conditions and Recent Trends. New York: reprinted by the Foundation for Child Development, 1983.

7. L. Gerhardt, "Editorial: Dreaming Professionally," School Library Journal 31:2 (1984).

8. B. Heyns, Summer Learning and the Effects of Schooling. (New York: Academic, 1978), E.A. Medrich and others. The Serious Business of Growing Up: A Study of Children's Lives Outside of School. (Berkeley: Univ. of Calif. Pr., 1981).

9. N. A. Van House, Public Library User Fees: The Use of Finance of Public Libraries (Westport, Conn.: Greenwood Pr., 1983).

Part III

BIBLIOGRAPHY AND HISTORY

THE BOOK IN HISTORY AND THE
HISTORY OF THE BOOK*

John P. Feather

The history of books is made up of many elements. The
book historian has to analyze the size and composition of the
reading public, the availability of books, the technical history
of book production, the economic history of the book trade,
and the legal and political aspects of publishing. The history of libraries, librarianship, and library education is part
of this wider subject and is a matter of great interest to
the book historian, especially when it puts these matters
into a wider societal context. Book history itself is of fundamental importance to understanding the essentially book-
based culture of the West.[1]

Daniel J. Boorstin wrote recently that "our democracy is based
on books and reading." While it is not my purpose to discuss this
statement in detail, it is a useful reminder of the significance that
is attached to books, far beyond their functional role as containers
of texts. In the National Museum of Ireland in Dublin there are
some exquisite boxes, encrusted in jewels and gold, that at first
glance appear to be reliquaries. In a sense this is exactly what
they are, but they were actually made to contain books. Some of
these books still survive and are among the greatest ever made; the
Book of Kells is only the most famous of a group of manuscripts from
the golden age of Celtic Irish culture. These manuscripts and their
reliquary-like boxes are another reminder of the symbolic significance
that has been attached to books at various times and in various places,
not merely as texts but as objects. In a very different society, William Morris saw the "book beautiful" as the most powerful physical
representation of the ideal medieval world of free craftsmen, which
he claimed to be reviving and which he had actually invented. Bib-
liophiles venerate certain books not for their contents, but for their
physical form. How many of us have read, or would wish to read, or
would even dare to read, a book in a Grolier binding? In the spring

---

*Reprinted by permission of the author and publisher from the
Journal of Library History, 21:1 (Winter, 1986) 12-26, copyright ©
1986 by the University of Texas Press.

of 1985, the British Museum mounted an exhibition entitled "The
Golden Age of Anglo-Saxon Art." On display were artifacts of all
kinds, including some superb manuscripts. Most of the latter were
elaborately decorated or illuminated, but in one case were four rather
ordinary looking books that were attracting very little attention.
They had no rubrications, no drawings, no glistening gold leaf; they
were the unique manuscripts of The Wanderer, The Battle of Maldon,
Wulfstan's Sermon to the English, and Beowulf, four of the masterpieces of Old English literature. As an historical and cultural phenomenon, the book can only be fully understood when we recognize
that it is more than merely a vehicle for a text.

The relationship between text and object is a complex one,
which has rarely been considered, and yet it could be argued that
our understanding of a text is ultimately influenced by the physical
form of its presentation. Consider, for example, the meticulously
edited texts in which we can now read many, if not yet all, of the
major British and American authors. The ideal is that the assiduous
editor should not only print the actual words that the author intended
us to read, but should do so with the spelling and punctuation that
the author used or approved. Yet even in the very rare cases where
this ideal can be fully achieved, it is not, in one crucial sense, what
the author intended. An example will illustrate the point. It is well
known that John Milton, despite his blindness, succeeded in exercising a minute control over the text and orthography of Paradise
Lost. Yet the modern editor who follows this, as one must, does
not reproduce what Milton's first readers saw, or what he knew that
they would see: an octavo, well printed by the standards of late-
seventeenth-century London, but printed on handmade paper in hand-
cast and hand-set type of the design and quality that English printers
of the period accepted without question. Whether the appearance of
the modern edition on clean white paper in neatly photoset typography
affects our reading of the poem is a question for the literary critic
to answer; indeed, it would be agreeable if the question were even
to be asked. I will only venture to suggest that it does so by giving a false air of contemporaneity. My principal point is a rather
different one: that authors can only envisage the dissemination of
their works in the physical form that is the normal product of the
techniques available at the time of writing. When the techniques or
the forms undergo major changes, such as those from the scroll to
the codex, or from manuscript to print, or from print to VDU, the
text itself may be the same, but the reader's perception of it is profoundly different.

The historian cannot ignore these fundamental physical characteristics of the form in which a text reaches its audience. Elizabeth Eisenstein has properly emphasized the uniformity that printing
imposed on the presentation of texts and the far-reaching effects of
this wholly new phenomenon in the fifteenth and sixteenth centuries.
The dissemination of the printed book, and of the art of printing
itself, is, of course, one of the most important phenomena in our

history, but when we attempt to analyze its consequences, and to
draw specific conclusions about them, we are faced with great difficulties. How do we assess the influence of books or of a book?
The literary critic may be able to determine that one author was "influenced" by another. At one level it may be very general, as in
the case of Shakespeare's influence on Keats; at another, it may be
far more diverse, as Lowes found when he looked at how Coleridge's
reading had helped to create Kubla Khan. When we move away from
the individual work or the individual author, the problem is a more
complex one. Most people would agree that three of the greatest
influences on twentieth-century Western civilization are Darwin, Marx,
and Freud, who for good or ill have substantially created the mental
climate in which we all live. All of us have some idea of what they
said, but how many of us have actually read On the Origin of Species,
or the works of Freud, or Das Kapital? Project that question back
into history. It seems probable that few of the Minute Men were intimately acquainted with Locke's Second Essay on Civil Government,
any more than the sans culottes could quote at length from L'esprit
des lois or Le contrat social. In short, when we speak of the influence of the book, we are apeaking, so far as direct influence is
concerned, of the reactions of a small intellectual elite, through whom
knowledge and concepts are transmitted, often transmuted, to the
mass of the people.

It follows from this that the first concern of the book historian
is to define the size and constitution of the audience for books.
Such a task cannot be undertaken without some knowledge of the
extent of literacy and of the means of acquiring it. The book historian is, therefore, vitally interested in the history of education and
of literacy, and while the formal history of educational provision is
a well-ploughed field, historical studies of literacy, despite all the
advances of recent years, are still in their infancy. From my own
studies of the book in eighteenth-century England I conclude that
literacy was far more widespread than has often been supposed, although in other parts of Europe, especially in the Catholic south,
it was far less common among the lower and lower-middle classes.
Mere statistics, however, tell us little. We need to know who the
literates actually were. We can assume that professional men were
literate, and, certainly in eighteenth-century England, so were the
tradesmen. But what of the tradesman's wife or his servant? Too
often the answer is that we do not know, and yet the historian who
seeks to analyze the penetration of society by ideas embodied in
print needs to know as precisely as possible who were the potential
recipients of those ideas.

At the same time, the book historian has his or her own unique
contribution to make to this study. We know, for example, that in
England in the eighteenth century, in communities throughout the
country, groups of professional men and tradesmen came together
to form book clubs and subscription libraries. In many of these
communities there were also bookshops, or at least shops that sold

books; by 1800 there were not fewer than 1,000 of them in England outside London, serving a population of fewer than 8 million. When we know the names of the members of the book clubs, or of the customers of the booksellers, we can put some flesh on the bones of the literacy statistics and begin to understand just how deeply a print-based culture has penetrated into that society.

Another source of great value for such studies, and one that has been increasingly exploited in recent years, is to be found in the lists of purchasers printed in books published by subscription. These lists need to be used with care. They do not tell us who read a book. They do, however, tell us who was sufficiently interested in a book to make a direct financial contribution to its publication, although even that assumption needs to be handled carefully, since some people subscribed from social or political considerations, rather than from intellectual or literary interest. Nevertheless, subscription lists are very valuable to the historian, and indeed to the literary critic. They can help us to delineate a book's audience by occupation, by social status, and by place of residence. There is, for example, a consistent pattern in eighteenth-century England of subscriptions from some parts of the country, but not from others, to works by Methodist and other dissenting theologians, and Pat Rogers showed some years ago how a well-defined group of social and political colleagues and allies formed the main body of Pope's subscribers.

If we can make some advance in assessing the potential readership of printed matter in general, or of particular groups of books, or even of specific titles, we then confront another series of equally difficult questions. What books were available? How did people obtain them?

To discover what books were available is, in one sense, a comparatively simple task, although enumerative bibliographers may disagree with the use of the word "simple." Thanks to the work of generations of bibliographers, we have lists of English and American books down to the end of the seventeenth century; the record for the eighteenth century is nearing completion; and that for the nineteenth century is well advanced. Even though the various short-title catalogs are based only on extant copies found in libraries, we can supplement this information from the book lists that were issued by printers, publishers, and booksellers in increasing numbers from the beginning of the sixteenth century.

To know that a book exists, or has existed, is, however, only the first stage in a study of its availability to contemporaries. At the most basic level, we need to know how many copies were printed, and since we usually lack the documentary evidence that would give us a definitive answer to that question, the book historian has to consider the history of both the printing industry itself and the retail and wholesale trades through which books were sold. If the history of the book is not firmly based in the inky reality of the printing house, it can too easily become a string of vague hypotheses and unjustifiable generalizations. A knowledge of the processes involved in papermaking, typesetting, printing, and binding is as essential to the book historian as is a knowledge of human anatomy to the physician. It cannot be said too often that historical bibliography and the history of the book are not two subjects but one, two parts of a unified whole. Indeed, the tendency of some book historians to ignore or dismiss the technical history of printing has led to the neglect of many important issues in book history. I should like to deal briefly with two of them.

The first is a deceptively simple question. Why was printing invented at all? Successful technological innovation is more than merely a demonstration of the inherent cleverness of inventors. It is a response to social, economic, and political demand. The principles of steam power, for example, were known for decades before economic imperatives made it a viable source of energy for industry and inspired James Watt to develop a more efficient steam engine. The same was true of printing. All the basic principles and techniques had been known and used for generations before the middle of the fifteenth century. Leaving aside the possibility of Oriental influence, we know that woodcuts were probably impressed on paper in western Europe before the invention of typographic printing. The press itself, without the sophistications of the lever mechanism and the hanging platen, had been in use for centuries for pressing grapes in wine-making, and indeed by bookbinders. Engraved metal tools, including letterforms, were also used by medieval binders, as well as by goldsmiths and silversmiths. It is not enough to argue that all of these were brought together by the genius of one man.

In fifteenth-century Europe, the literacy rate was increasing, partly because of the gradual secularization of society, and partly because the plagues, wars, and famines of the previous hundred years had had their most devastating effects on the illiterate classes. On the political front, the three great monarchies of western Europe were all striving for a greater centralization of government. In the economic sphere, Europe's trade was becoming more complex, both internally and in its rapidly developing relations with Asia and Africa. Gutenberg may have been aware of some, or all, or none of this, but, in a sense, that is irrelevant. All his genius, for he was indeed a brilliant innovator, might have been wasted if these conditions had not existed. Even so, Gutenberg might be argued to have anticipated the emergence of the demand for printing, for he was not only the first printer; he was also the first printer to go bankrupt. It was not until the 1480s that printing was established on a sound commercial and financial basis. Printing was ultimately successful not simply because it represented a technical advance on copying by scribes, but because it became available at a time and in a place where it was economically, socially, and politically desirable. Merely to accept the appearance of printing in late-fifteenth-century Europe,

as if it were some newly discovered natural phenomenon, is to miss
the point: the printing press was an agent of change because it
was able to play an important role in the society in which it was invented, and from whose needs it had been developed.

The second important issue that has been neglected concerns
a later period, the late eighteenth and early nineteenth centuries.
From about 1780 onward, a series of technical innovations transformed
the printing craft into an industry. The landmarks are familiar to
all students of the subject: the building of the first iron press by
Stanhope in 1800 and, in the following decade, the commercial ex-
ploitation of the papermaking machine by the Fourdriniers and of
stereotyping by Andrew Wilson, followed, in 1914, by König's first
steam press, built for The (London) Times. These great developments made books and newspapers both cheaper and more plentiful
than they had ever been before. None of them, however, came out
of the blue.

Experiments with papermaking, and with the improvement of
the common press, had been taking place for many years before Robert and Stanhope set to work; stereotyping had been not only invented, but actually used in one or two isolated instances, before
1750, and then abandoned and forgotten. Why then were these revolutionary changes made when they were? Partly because of other
technological developments, which had, for example, brought machine
tools to a point at which a metal platen could be perfectly planed,
or, in another field, made it possible for steam or water power to be
used to drive a Fourdrinier machine. Yet these developments, important as they are, are not the true explanation. Again, the rate
of literacy was rapidly increasing, as indeed was the population as
a whole. The French Revolution, and the reaction to it in Britain
by both its supporters and its opponents, created a huge new demand for books, much of it from people who had never read books
before. Hannah More and other evangelicals started the Sunday
Schools with the intention of strengthening the moral fiber of the
lower classes by teaching them to read their Bible and other improving literature; some did, and as many more read Paine's Rights of
Man. Above all, this was an age of great technological change in
a wide range of economic activities as Britain rushed headlong into
its Industrial Revolution.

Against this background, the changes in the printing industry
in the late eighteenth and early nineteenth centuries not only become
more comprehensible, but also more significant. We can see printing
as only one of many trades that were transformed by new equipment
and new techniques. At the same time, we can see it responding to
society's needs and demands, not only economically, but also in the
cultural and political spheres. Book historians cannot ignore the
technical changes that made possible the proliferation of cheap books
in the early nineteenth century, because these changes themselves,
and the chronology of them, tell us a great deal about the underlying

causes of the revolution in English reading habits between about
1790 and 1830.

I have deliberately chosen two monumental examples of the
intimate relationship between the technical and cultural history of
the book. On a lesser scale, however, technical history, the traditional province of the bibliographer, can inform the book historian
at every point. How many copies of a book were printed? How much
did a copy cost? How did a potential reader discover that a book
existed? How did one actually obtain a copy of a book one wanted
to read? None of these questions can be ignored if we are to trace
the influence of a book, or the penetration of a print-based culture
into a society.

The economic history of the book, like its technical history,
has certainly not been ignored, although it has only two rarely been
related to the broader issues of which it is a part. In particular,
although the history of publishing is now a flourishing and well-
established field of study, the history of the selling of books is a
sadly neglected topic. Compared with the printing house or even
the publisher's office, the bookshop is dull and uninviting; in the
last analysis it is, after all, just a shop. Yet without the bookshop,
at least before the development of mail-order bookselling in the last
hundred years, there would have been no book trade, and the great
majority of the population who had no access to libraries would have
had no access to books. There can be no doubt that an important
factor in the general increase in edition sizes in England in the
eighteenth century was the development of a vigorous bookselling
trade outside London, in response to the growing demand for books,
and the same is true, at other times, of other countries. Publishers'
catalogs, book advertisements in newspapers and periodicals, and
book reviews in magazines were all vital factors in spreading a knowledge of books and in stimulating the desire to own and to read them.
Some excellent work has been done on the history of catalogs, but
there is still no adequate history of newspaper advertising, and very
little on book reviewing before the beginning of the nineteenth century. These vast gaps in our knowledge (and I have not even mentioned such matters as wholesaling, distribution, and the international
trade in books) can only be remedied when we take a view of the
history of the book that looks at more than the minutie of its production or, at the other end of the scale, its alleged societal consequences.

There is one other aspect of the economic history of the book
that deserves our attention, that of authorship. The author is
strangely absent from most histories of the book, yet there were
authors before there was a book trade, and without authors there
would be no books. Only a tiny minority of authors write for simple
reasons. Their motivations are very much the concern of the book
historian, whether that motivation is political influence, artistic expression, academic reputation, or money. It is realistic rather than

cynical to suggest that it is the last of these that has been predom-
inant during the last two centuries.

A good deal of progress has been made in this field in recent
years. We no longer execrate Milton's publisher for paying him what
was, by contemporary standards, a perfectly reasonable fee for
Paradise Lost. We recognize that if hacks did indeed live in garrets,
they did so of choice, and that few, if any, starved. By the middle
of the eighteenth century, and in some cases earlier, authorship
was an established, if not entirely respectable, profession in which
it was possible to make a reasonable living. Yet a whole series of
questions remains unanswered. We know less than we should and
less than we could about the relationships, both personal and financial, between authors and publishers before the nineteenth century.
Most of what we do know is about the major literary writers who,
however important we may judge their works to be, were neither the
majority nor typical of the majority. Reverting to the early days of
printing, it would be interesting to know who was the first author
to write a book with the specific intention that it should be circulated
as a printed book. This is an inquiry of more than merely antiquar-
ian interest, for the answer to it would tell us a good deal about the
acceptance of the printed book and the recognition of its importance
as a cultural phenomenon.

The economic and social conditions of authors are integral to
the history of the book, as indeed are the legal aspects of the author's work. In the most liberal societies authors must take account
of the laws of libel, privacy, and official security. All of those are
matters of concern to the book historian, as are the moral constraints
on authorship whether by social pressures or the law of the land.
In less liberal societies than our own, that is, the great majority
whether in the past or at the present time, the insidious hand of
the censor can never be ignored; nor can the multitude of ingenious
and often entertaining ways in which authors and publishers have
evaded his attentions.

Yet another part of the law that impinges deeply on book history is that of copyright. Indeed, copyright is an issue of central
importance to authors and publishers alike. It is well known that the
first copyright law was that passed in England in 1710, and the modern
concept of "intellectual property" was evolved, not without some difficulty, over the next sixty years. The history of copyright leads
the book historian into all sorts of matters that might superficially
be thought remote. By an historical accident, copyright laws are
generally associated with the compulsory deposit of books in certain
libraries, so that we have to consider the development of the concept
of the comprehensive archival research library. The purchase of
copyrights is the most important investment a publisher ever makes,
so that we cannot understand the economics of publishing without
a knowledge of copyright law. For the author, as for the publisher,
it is copyright law that protects his or her investment, in the author's

case of time and intellectual effort. Indeed, one reason why authorship did become a viable profession in eighteenth-century England
was precisely that the interpretation of the 1710 Act, and the development, in a series of judicial decisions, of the concept of "intellectual
property," gave the author a lever to use against the publisher. As
the relationship between author and publisher became more overtly
commercial, we find parallel development in commissioning, in contracts, and in methods of payment. These mundane financial matters
are integral to a full understanding of the history of the book.

The political dimension of book history has already been mentioned, but it is important enough to deserve some further consideration. One of the many unforeseen consequences of the dissemination
of printing in the fifteenth century was the development throughout
Europe of a more stringent control over what could be written and
circulated. By the end of the sixteenth century, prepublication cen-
sorshop was enforced throughout the continent by a combination of
secular and ecclesiastical authorities, and continued to be so for
centuries. In England there was limited press freedom after 1695,
but it was not finally established, and then by practice rather than
by law, until the 1830s. In France, it was not until 1870 that the
press was finally released from its chains. In what is now West
Germany, freedom of the press, save for the brief interlude of the
Weimar Republic, was unknown until after World War II. The First
Amendment was uniquely enlightened in the guarantees that it offered,
and was for decades the only light of freedom shining over the en-
slaved press of the world.

The speed with which bishops and princes reacted to the growth
of printing in the fifteenth and sixteenth centuries is in itself an
eloquent testimony to its perceived importance. Yet the reactions
of the authorities of western Europe were not wholly negative.
Strong kings like Henry VIII of England and Philip II of Spain recognized that the power of the press, which could be so damaging
to their interests, could also be turned into their servant. Laws
and proclamations could be widely and unambiguously circulated
throughout a monarch's dominions, so that no subject could plead
ignorance of the law as an excuse for breaking it. The arguments
of a monarch or a church or, later, of a political party, could be
circulated far more widely than ever before. Propaganda, like censorship, was one of the growth industries of the age of the printed
book.

By the middle of the eighteenth century, the newspaper was
beginning to displace the pamphlet as the principal organ of propaganda, at least for the great mass of literate people outside the
political elite. At the same time, print was becoming ubiquitous in
every sphere of life. It is, indeed, tempting to argue that it was
not until the eighteenth century that the full force of the printing
press as an agent of change was felt by the societies of western
Europe. Certainly the intellectual movements of the sixteenth and

seventeenth centuries were ultimately dependent upon the availability
of the printed book. It is also true that the effects of these movements, like the influence of Darwin, Freud, and Marx, were felt far
outside the circles of those who were directly concerned with them
or were even consciously aware of them. It was not, however, until
the eighteenth century that print became truly ubiquitous in western
Europe and in those parts of North America that had been settled by
Europeans. Until literacy was comparatively widespread, it was inevitable that news was disseminated and information was gathered by
word of mouth. Indeed, oral transmission remained common for centuries after the invention of printing. There is evidence to suggest
that in rural areas of England literate people would read the newspapers aloud to their illiterate neighbors, while the ballad-singer
continued to be a familiar figure at country fairs until the middle
of the nineteenth century. Increasingly, however, illiterates were
at a disadvantage both socially and economically. It is believed that
in mid-eighteenth-century England, after a change in the law required that the bride and bridegroom should sign or mark the marriage register, young couples learned to write their names so as to
avoid the stigma of illiteracy on their wedding day.

     In economic life, literacy was more than a social convenience;
as the pace of industrialization quickened, it became a necessity.
The pages of Samuel Smiles are full of uplifting stories of poor boys
who learned to read from spelling books propped up on a loom or
a lathe. The most famous product of what would seem to have been
a remarkably dangerous form of autodidacticism was George Stephenson,
the pioneer railroad engineer of the 1820s and 1830s. The ubiquity
of print was, however, fully established half a century before young
George learned his ABCs. By the third quarter of the eighteenth
century, the presses of Europe were producing advertisements, catalogs, packaging material, headed stationery, tickets, and blank forms
at the rate of hundreds of thousands a year. Some material of this
kind had always been produced. There is a famous example of a book
advertisement printed by Caxton, and the STC lists sixteenth- and
seventeenth-century Visitation Articles, which are, in fact, questionnaires. In the eighteenth century, however, there were few areas
of economic life that were untouched by the proliferation of printed
material of this kind. When, after decades of wrangling between
religious factions, primary education in England at last became both
free and compulsory in 1870, the effect of the law was to do little
more than mop up the last few remaining pockets of rural illiteracy.
The great bulk of town dwellers had been literate, of necessity, for
two generations.

     If the imperatives to attain literacy were social and economic,
the consequences were, in part, political. The radicalization of the
urban working class, and the contemporary conversion of the capi-
talists to laissez-faire liberalism, between about 1800 and 1840, were
both achieved largely by the printed word, although the public meeting also played an important part, not least, of course, through the

reports of such meetings that were printed at great length in the newspapers. Something was said earlier of the technological changes in the printing industry that resulted from this increased demand for the written word. At the same time political change on this scale created still further demands for print and underlay the continuing and increasingly rapid changes in printing technology during the rest of the nineteenth century, with the rotary press, the web-fed press, and mechanized typesetting and bookbinding.

As it is portrayed here, book history is a vast, indeed all-embracing, subject. The book historian has something to learn and something to teach at every point at which the printed word impinges on the organization of society or on economic activity. Most difficult of all, however, is the very topic with which we began, the perception of the book, and its force as a cultural symbol.

In one very important sense, our entire culture is based on a book, or rather a collection of books. Christians, Jews, and Muslims have so many ideas and moral standards in common because from the earliest day of Judaism the basic concepts of religion and the behavioral inferences drawn from them were transmitted by the written word. In all three religions the book is treated with great veneration and plays a central part in acts of communal worship. The objects themselves were created to be masterpieces of the bookmaker's art; it is no accident that Western illuminators and Arabic calligraphers reached the highest points of artistic achievement in manuscripts of the Bible and the Qur'an. The text is also treated with special respect. Although the revival of the art of textual criticism in the fifteenth and sixteenth centuries was initially associated with the Greek and Latin classics, it was in the establishment of the text of the Bible, and especially of the Greek New Testament, that it reached its apogée. In Islamic tradition, the text of the Qur'an was treated with such respect that fear of error delayed the introduction of printing into the Muslim world by two and a half centuries, and even today a devout Muslim will read the Qur'an only in Arabic, to avoid the dangers of silent interpretation implicit in the act of translation. In this sense, all the "people of the book" have a very special relationship with it as more than merely an object and more than merely a text: it is a symbol of the most deeply held beliefs, and even among those who no longer adhere to those beliefs the symbolic significance of the book has substantially survived.

The respect that we accord to books has spread far from religion. The anthropologists tell us that in illiterate societies learned people, whether priestesses, medicine men, or witch doctors, were accorded special respect because of their knowledge. They stood outside the hierarchy of warriors and farmers and were not only the advisers of the chiefs but sometimes even treated as their equals. In literate societies the book becomes the symbol of the knowledge that it contains. In medieval and renaissance iconography, the fathers of the Church are portrayed reading or writing or sitting in their

studies surrounded by books. Even today books in the home are a
far more potent status symbol than phonograph records or video-
tapes. When children go to school they learn to read before they
learn anything else. In the developing countries, vast resources
are being poured into primary education programs to reach the goal
of a literate society.

In part, all of this is a recognition that our society is print-
dependent, but it is also an implicit acknowledgment of the primacy
of the printed word. It is, therefore, all the more strange that historians have been so neglectful of this central phenomenon of our
culture. A change of attitudes is, at last, beginning to appear.
From the beginning of this century the history of books was, for
more than fifty years, almost entirely the province of bibliographers
and their uneasy and sometimes unwelcome companions, textual critics.
The great advances in bibliographical scholarship that began with
Bradshaw's studies of fifteenth-century typography in the middle of
the last century reached their climax in the work of Greg and Bowers
a hundred years later. The achievements of that century of effort
laid the foundations upon which the superstructure of the history of
the book can now be built. We know how books were made; we know
how to identify technical difficulties in their making; and we know
something of the effects of technical processes on texts.

It was said earlier that the history of the book must be firmly
based in the reality of the printing house. No apology is needed
for repeating the point: book historians who are not at least aware
of bibliographical techniques are ill equipped for their task, and it
could be forcefully argued that a knowledge of historical bibliography
should be the basis of their training as scholars. We should also,
however, venture outside the confined space of the printing house
into the world in which its products were used. The transition is
indeed inevitable. When Pollard studied the "bad" quartos of Shakespeare, he also laid the foundations of our knowledge of the Elizabethan
book trade. More recently, Robert Darnton's work on the Encyclo-
pédie has taken the reader from the activities of the Société Typo-
graphie de Neuchâtel, through the inadequacies of the European papermaking industry, to the alleged reading habits of the provincial bour-
geoisie during the last years of the ancien régime.

The historian of libraries also has a unique contribution to make
to this history of books. Like the history of the book, the history
of libraries has been transformed in recent years by a more general
historical awareness and a broader social and cultural approach. Library history is no longer a tedious catalog of the good deeds of
benefactors, the enacting of laws, and the opening of buildings.
One of the finest examples of the new style of library history is
Phyllis Dain's history of the New York Public Library, not merely
offering a chronicle of the formative years of one of the world's great
libraries, but also giving fascinating insights into the political and
social history of New York and showing how the early history of

NYPL is inseparable from that of the city and the people it was intended to serve.

There is one aspect of library history that can be particularly
informative to the historian of the book: the study of the use of
libraries. It was suggested earlier that the book historian needs to
know something about who read books, and, although borrowing a
book from a library is no more a guarantee of reading it than buying it from a bookshop, it does suggest at least some minimal interest in, or need for, a book on a particular subject. Studies of the
loan records of libraries, in those few cases where they survive, can
be very illuminating. If we turn again to eighteenth-century England
we find that there is, for example, a consistent pattern of interest
in historical and geographical literature by library users. This interest is also attested by the catalogs and inventories of bookshops,
and some explanation for it needs to be offered. One tentative suggestion might be that, as Britain became a world power, its people
became more interested both in their own history and in the world
beyond the seas that was becoming so important to their destiny. It
would be interesting to know whether a similar phenomenon was ob-
servable in the United States when it stepped onto the world stage
during and after World War II.

Libraries and the history of libraries are important to the historian of the book in another crucial sense. The history of the book
must indeed rest on a sound basis of the technical history of book
production, but the theoretical study of the history of printing, even
when it is supplemented by practical work as enlightening as it is
entertaining, is in itself inadequate. The historian of books, like
the bibliographer, is concerned with the books themselves not only
as tools, like all scholars, but as primary evidence. Library collections are similarly valuable evidence, for the history of their development, use, and perhaps ultimate dispersal can give important insights
into the more general history of books. British examples that come
to mind are the parochial libraries established under the auspices
of Dr. Bray and his associates at the end of the seventeenth century,
and the Miners' Libraries that proliferated in mining communities in
Scotland a hundred years later.

The history of the library as a collection is, however, more
than merely the story of the accumulation of books. The historian
has to study who was selecting the books, the basis on which the
selection was made, and, once again, how the books were obtained
from booksellers or publishers. During the last hundred years, librarians have become the most important single group of customers
for the book trade, and a history of libraries that ignores that trade
and its relationship to library history is as blinkered as a history of
the trade that ignores libraries.

Because the book historian is concerned with all aspects of the
historical role of the book in society, it follows that he or she also

is interested in all of those people who were active in the world of
books. It was suggested earlier that the history of bookselling has
been neglected; so too, until very recently, has been the history
of librarianship and of education for librarianship. John Richardson's
recently published history of the Graduate School of Library and Information Science at Chicago will, we must hope, inspire other scholars on both sides of the Atlantic to look more closely at the history
of the library profession and those who have worked in it.

It should now be clear that the history of libraries is not only
a worthwhile study in itself, but also a part of the larger subject
of book history, never more so than when the book historian ventures,
as is often necessary, into the history of scholarship and education.
Indeed, the distinction between the history of the book and the history of libraries, so often embalmed in library science curricula, is
a false one, and the two subjects should be studied and taught together as a unified whole. They are, in effect, dependent upon
each other, for the books whose history the book historian seeks to
study are very largely the books that have been preserved by generations of collectors and librarians, while the library historian cannot
ignore the books that are, after all, the raison d'être of the library
itself. Just as the history of the book is a vital part of the history
of our culture, so the history of libraries is a vital part of the history of the book.

The history of the book is built up, like all social history, with
bricks, each complete in itself, but each fulfilling its true role only
when it is linked with others. If it is indeed true that the book,
and the written or printed word that it contains, is central to our
history, then it follows that it is also central to the study and writing of history. Our understanding of the past, which is the ultimate objective of all history, will be severely impaired if we do not
recognize this crucial fact. It has been said truthfully that textual
criticism will never prove that Hamlet was a woman or that King Lear
is a comedy; nor will it, but textual critics properly argue that if
words matter, then all words matter, and we should grant authors
the respect of reading what they actually wrote. Similarly, the history of books will not show that the American Revolution began in
1777 or that the Bastille was stormed in 1790, but it may help us to
understand these events, by illuminating the intellectual and spiritual
world of the men and women who participated in them. The perimeters of book history are defined by the perimeters of the printed word
itself, and if we accept, as surely we must, that we live in a culture
whose development has been based on the transmission and understanding of words, then the history of the book is as fundamental
to history as is the book itself to the culture whose history we seek
to learn.

Note

1. This paper was written in response to a request to put library

history into the context of recent developments in book history in general. Without having seen the other papers that were to be presented at the Seminar, I found that I had anticipated both the philosophy and the methodology that underlay many of them. Readers who are unfamiliar with the ongoing debate to which this paper is, in part, a contribution are referred to G. Thomas Tanselle's Hanes Lecture entitled The History of Books as a Field of Study (1981), and my review of it in JLH, 17 (1982): 463-7.

THE FEDERAL WRITERS' PROJECT WORK RELIEF THAT RESERVED A NATIONAL RESOURCE*

William S. Cramer

The Great Depression which ravished the economy of the United States for more than ten years was clearly no respecter of economic class or professional status. White-collar workers, despite their educational attainments and relatively higher income levels, experienced the same miseries of lowered living standards and widespread unemployment that afflicted America's blue-collar forces. Creative professionals, such as writers, musicians, artists and actors, were particularly harmed by the restrictions placed on consumer spending for leisure-time activities and products by the hard economic times.

The plight of the writer was brought about for the most part by three concurrent phenomena. First, book publishing as an industry had suffered severely during the first years of the Depression. In 1929, American publishers had earned approximately $42 million in sales of trade books (i.e. all categories of books except texts), but just four years later earnings had shrunk to $22 million. Not only were far fewer books being published by 1933, but many of those that were sold were consumed by a collective readership rather than by individual buyers. According to the American Library Association, more than four million new borrowers were registered by public libraries between 1929 and 1933, and at the same time many bookstores established circulating libraries from which current books could be rented at modest charge. To the writer paid royalties for each book sold by his publisher, this trend usually meant that, while his works were read by a wider audience than ever before, his earnings decreased considerably.[1]

Second, magazine and newspaper publishing suffered declining advertising revenues and circulation rates. Freelance writers who had earlier found a ready market for their stories and articles with various nationally circulated magazines found these sources drying up, as editors, uncertain of the future, greatly limited their buying

*Reprinted by permission of the author and publisher from Publishing History, 18: 1985, 49-68.

of material. Similarly, newspaper publishers were forced to lay off
reporters and editors as advertising income plummeted during the
early years of the Depression. The mortality rate in the United
States for newspapers increased 48% during the first half of the 1930s,
and those that did survive the hard times paid far from adequate
wages. [2]

The third cause for the sharp drop in income for writers during
the early Depression was competition from such non-print industries
as radio and motion pictures. As earnings from publishing declined,
radio advertising income increased dramatically. Likewise, the movie
industry, by providing passive escapism from the squalidness of
everyday life, enjoyed relative economic success. While both radio
and movies offered employment to some writers, these tended to be
the established cream-of-the-crop and in no way offset the negative
impact that these industries had upon publishing and on those dependent for their livelihoods on the print media. [3]

As their situations deteriorated, writers began to demand assistance from the U.S. government similar to that being contemplated
for other workers. With the election of Franklin D. Roosevelt as
President in November 1932, work relief became a growing topic of
high-level discussion in Washington, and writers as well as other
creative professionals began to express their desire for inclusion in
efforts to improve the condition of the nation's work force.

The earliest relief programmes of the Roosevelt Administration
gave only token recognition to the cultural professions, and almost
none of this was directed specifically at writers. Perhaps this was
attributable to the overall low esteem given to writers by some, or
to the inevitability of adequate reward for writers assumed by others
like the editor of the Saturday Review of Literature who claimed that
'no good story-teller, even in 1932, can fail of a decent reward.'[4]

The first relief measure giving some assistance to writers and
other white-collar workers came in May 1933 with the passage of the
Federal Emergency Relief Act (FERA). This act set up a govern-
mental agency charged with providing $500 million in outright grants
to states, which were required to initiate relief projects. Most of
the projects approved under FERA emphasized manual labour; few
gave any assistance to writers or other professionals. [5] However,
when in November 1933 a Presidential Executive Order created the
Civil Works Administration (CWA) under authority of the National
Industrial Recovery Act, direct responsibility for relief projects shifted
to Federal control Under Harry Hopkins, a Professional and Non-
Manual Projects Section of CWA was established with Jacob Baker as
director, and projects assisting writers eventually were established
in several states. A survey of points of interest in Connecticut,
the collection of historical and social data in Utah, and a project for
unemployed newspapermen in Los Angeles all provided examples of
how work relief could be applied to professional writers. [6] However

such piecemeal efforts didn't have a great deal of impact on the overall desperate condition of the professional writer. A more direct approach would be necessary if this creative natural resource were to
be salvaged out of the human wreckage wrought by the Great Depression.

     Essentially, two approaches had been attempted thus far as
the Roosevelt Administration wrestled with the problem of unemployment. FERA had been a work-relief programme, but had consisted
primarily of short-term projects beyond the control of the Federal
government. The CWA had been an employment programme under
direct supervision from Washington, with $400 million going toward
projects which were intended to result in the hiring of millions of
both relief and non-relief applicants.

     Now, as 1935 wore on, the administration sought a way to com-
bine these two approaches--that is, come up with a programme which
would maintain the relief principle so that the really needy were bene-
fited, but which provided regular, continuous employment at a steady
wage. As President Roosevelt expressed this objective in his State
of the Union Address to Congress on 4 January 1935,

          I am not willing that the vitality of our people be further
          sapped by the giving of cash, of market baskets, of a few
          hours of weekly work cutting grass, raking leaves, or pick-
          ing up papers in the public parks. We must preserve not
          only the bodies of the unemployed from destitution but also
          their self-respect, their self-reliance and courage and de-
          termination.[7]

     In May, a Presidential Executive Order established the Works
Progress Administration (WPA), which was to be 'responsible to the
President for the honest, efficient, speedy and coordinated execu-
tion of the work relief program as a whole.'[8] Its objective was to
place three-and-a-half million people to work on labour-intensive,
socially useful projects. Harry Hopkins, the first WPA administrator,
considered all unemployed and needy Americans, professionals as
well as manual labourers, as potential recipients of assistance under
this new relief programme. Writing just one year after the birth of
the WPA, Hopkins expressed his

          belief that the greatest contributions, not only to American
          life and culture, but to employment, are these less tangible
          ones made by our professional and service workers. If it is
          more ironical for one person to be on relief than another it
          is seen in the fact that scientists, nurses, artists, architects,
          painters, economists, writers, musicians and all the rest of
          those persons, who by virtue of gifts and disciplines have
          arrived in that upper fraction of the people who lead the way
          of history, should find themselves without recognition, liveli-
          hood or any means to continue the benefits which only they
          can bestow.[9]

The WPA had received control of $5 billion as a result of the passage of the Emergency Relief Appropriation Act of 1935. Of this amount, $300 million was earmarked for projects assisting educational, professional and clerical persons, with $27 million set aside for the arts. A WPA Professional and Service Projects Division was established and, after considering a number of possible projects, it approved a half dozen. The first, which included projects assisting writers, artists, musicians and dramatists, became known as Federal Project Number One and received an initial allocation of $6,288,000 in July 1935. Henry J. Alsberg was named national director of the Federal Writers' Project (FWP).[10]

Now that a project to assist America's needy writers finally had been established, two major questions needed to be answered before a functioning organization could be set in place. First, a decision as to what major products should be created clearly was necessary; second, selection of the participants to be engaged in this unprecedented activity had to be undertaken.

Since the FWP had been envisaged as a nationally co-ordinated project assisting writers in all areas of the country, whatever major endeavour was to be attempted had to be large in scope. Of the many proposals put forth, one from a FERA supervisor from Michigan to prepare 'a sort of public Baedeker, which would point out to the curious traveler the points of real value in each state and county' took hold with both Alsberg and Baker. No adequate comprehensive guide book to the United States existed in 1935 (a title in the Baedeker guidebook series had been published in 1893, but the vastness of America did not readily conform to the concise format used so successfully for guides to European countries), but a model of a state-wide book had been completed as a CWA project in Connecticut.[11] Alsberg favoured production of a five-volume American guide series covering the Northeast, Southeast, North Central, South Central and Pacific Coast regions. However, his associate director, George Cronyn, objected that a regional series would inevitably place many states in an inferior light, would be difficult to administer, and would take too long in production to bring the quick results necessary to quiet those already beginning to criticize the Federal arts projects. He suggested a plan calling for individual guides to all forty-eight states, the District of Columbia and the territories. This proposal became the basis of the FWP's major accomplishment, the American Guide Series, and led to an administrative structure consisting of state writers' project offices in each state, territory and in some major cities, all reporting to the central office in Washington, D.C. While the American Guide Series was to be the major focus of the FWP, state offices were encouraged to develop plans for additional publications such as local guidebooks, folklore and ethnic studies, and salve narratives.[12]

Another critical determination that had to be made at the outset of the Federal Writers' Project concerned the selection of participants.

While an estimated 4,500 project jobs were to be available, initial
WPA regulations demanded that 90% of these be filled by persons officially placed on public relief rolls. This requirement infuriated officials of the Authors League of America who had lobbied long and
diligently for a Federal project to assist down-and-out writers, many
of whom for reasons of personal pride refused to undergo the in-
dignity of the 'means test', a prerequisite for placement on the relief
rolls. League spokesman George Creel complained to Hopkins that
'the means test, together with the stupid arrangement by which each
state has been given a certain amount of money regardless of whether
the state has writers or not, has defeated your purpose and our
hope.' Pressure from Creel and others affiliated with various writer
support groups failed to change this regulation, however, so Alsberg was forced to fill his quotas largely from pre-November 1935
public relief rolls.[13]

This requirement resulted in the necessity to broaden the definition of the term 'writer' to include 'almost any other occupation
that involved an understanding of the English language and some
training and observations in the preparation of records.'[14] In addition to persons with training and/or experience as journalists,
novelists, poets, short story writers and other traditional writing
occupations, many state project offices hired historians, librarians,
ministers, lawyers and others whose pre-project employment had required a facility for the English language. In some of the less-
populated states, the mere facts that someone was a college graduate
and was on the official relief roll were sufficient for project employment.

One of the most important steps taken by Alsberg and senior
members of his headquarters staff at the beginning of the project
was the selection of state directors. Since the FWP's very existence
depended upon the quality of the state guidebooks, the selection of
those charged with co-ordinating their production was a critical decision. For the most part, those chosen proved to be effective and
capable, or if not were eventually removed and replaced by those
who were. The majority of state directors came from backgrounds
as college teachers (primarily of history or English), freelance writers
or newspapermen, and tended to have strong organizational abilities.
Assistant state directors were generally appointed to deal with technical duties related to editing the state guides and other project
publications, freeing the state project directors for various politically
sensitive activities. Chief among these was often ensuring the good
will of state WPA administrators, many of whom if not openly opposed
to any project not under their direct control were somewhat suspicious
of a writers' project directed by a Washington-based office.[15]

From the outset, production of the American Guide Series
became the number one priority of the Federal Writers' Project. A
standard format for the guides was adopted by the national office and
rigidly adhered to throughout the project's five-year existence.

Introductory essays dealing with the state's natural setting, history,
government, labour and industry, folkways, architecture, literature,
fine arts and music were followed by descriptive city and town tours.[16]
The latter were of particular importance due to their value as stimu-
lators of local support for the project. Towns and cities vied with
each other for inclusion in guidebook tours, which were intended to
give assistance to motorists driving through the state. Although
writing copy for the tour sections usually demanded less literary
talent than writing the essays, it did offer an opportunity for aspir-
ing authors to include a wide range of scandalous events. 'Controversial subjects could be placed in them. Mining strikes in Harlan,
Kentucky, thus found their way into [tour section copy], as did
company villages, lynchings, demagogues, and the Donner Pass story
of cannibalism.'[17] In some states, the simple collection of data for
guidebook tour sections was in itself an adventure. 'Snow and ice
blocked travel in Montana, Utah and Wyoming ... bad stretches of
dirt road in Texas, old Nevada cow trails and notorious Colardo side
paths made checking a dangerous task at times.'[18]

      The national headquarters efforts to assure that every state
guidebook adhered to this standard format created much friction and
irritation. A stream of technical requirements emanated from Washington to state project offices where they were often ignored, necessi-
tating changes by national headquarters editors after the copy arrived there. This rigid attitude, while it annoyed state directors
and their writing staffs, was necessary due to the uneven calibre
of the writing and the vast quantity of the guide material which
poured in from the state offices. National headquarters simply would
have been engulfed with useless guidebook copy had it not issued manuals,
instructions and daily letters of advice to both amateur and professional writers on state staffs.[19]

      From the initiation of the guidebook idea, Alsberg had envis-
aged that the District of Columbia entry would be the first to be published, thus serving as a model for all future state guides. Throughout 1936, however, Vardis Fisher, the state director of Idaho, had
worked toward the goal of having his state publish the first guide
book in the nation. Finding no other qualified writers in his state,
Fisher wrote most of the guidebook copy himself and after locating
a private publisher willing to print it with no expectation of profit,
the book was ready for production weeks before the U.S. Government Printing Office was geared up to run off the first copies of
Washington: City and Capital. After an abortive attempt to delay
the Idaho guide, Alsberg relented and agreed to allow it to be published in January 1937, just a few weeks before its District of Columbia counterpart.[20]

      Use of the United States Government Printing Office (GPO)
for production of the District of Columbia guidebook, necessitated
by the fact of Federal jurisdiction, provided an experience which resulted in a decision to use private publishers for all future state

guides. Because the GPO was not set up for book production, its
effort to publish the D.C. guide was both slow and costly. Restrictions as to format, colour, binding, typography, ink and paper resulted in a bulky, dreary-looking production. In addition, the GPO
did not offer, as a commercial publisher would have, discounts to
volume buyers and did not spend money for promotion. This experience prompted Alsberg to try to find a way to permit commercial
publication of all remaining guidebooks. A method whereby sponsors
(usually public officials such as the secretary of state) signed agreements transferring all royalties earned on the sale of a guidebook to
the United States Treasurer (thereby circumventing the Federal law
which required that material produced at government expense be
printed by the GPO) was adopted by the writers' project. Thus all
remaining guidebooks were produced by Hastings House, Houghton
Mifflin, Oxford University Press and other well-known commercial
publishers.[21]

     The fifty-two volumes of the American Guide Series, published
between 1937 and 1941, certainly can be considered collectively as
the single most significant achievement of the Federal Writers' Project.
However, many other notable publications were produced, a number
of which deserve at least token mention. City and local guidebooks,
produced concurrently with and often somewhat to the detriment of
the state guides, helped gain grassroot support for the FWP. Some
of the more significant titles in this category included a two-volume
guide to New York City (1939), U.S. One: Maine to Florida (1938),
Cape Cod Pilot (1937), Intercoastal Waterway (1937) and Los Angeles:
A Guide to the City and its Environs (1941). While most state guidebooks included some discussion of the contributions of blacks, the
Federal Writers' Project also initiated several separate studies dealing
with this topic. Sterling Brown, a black academician from Howard
University who had written a forceful section of the District of Columbia guidebook detailing the lot of the Washington Negro, became an
editor in the FWP national office charged both with overseeing all
black-related copy for state guidebooks and with co-ordinating the
separate studies.[22] Significant titles in the latter category included
The Negro in Virginia (1940), Drums and Shadows: Survival Studies
among Georgia's Coastal Negroes (1940) and Cavalcade of the American Negro (1941). While not published by the FWP, hundreds of
interviews with former black slaves were undertaken by project personnel and, after being deposited in the Library of Congress served
as the basis for several later scholarly works (e.g. Eugene Genovese's
Roll Jordan, Roll, published in 1974).[23] Working closely with the
American Folklore Society, the Federal Writers' Project published
some important collections of folk tales, the best of which came from
the South. Included were Bundle of Troubles and Other Tarheel
Tales (1943), These Are Our Lives (1939) and God Bless the Devil!:
Liars Bench Tales (1940). Social-ethnic studies published under
FWP auspices included Armenians in Massachusetts (1937), The Jewish
Landsmannschaften of New York in Yiddish (1938) and The Swedes
and Finns in New Jersey (1938).[24]

Many of the writers employed by the FWP, particularly those who had achieved some pre-project success writing novels, short stories or poetry, felt strongly that their talents were being wasted on the writing of tour copy and ceaselessly urged, usually through the Writers' Union, that they be given the opportunity to produce creative works on project time. Permission was never granted for this activity, Alsberg feeling that the 30-hour work week demanded of most project employees allowed sufficient time for private creative effort. However, one anthology of writings by FWP personnel completed during off hours was published by the Viking Press in 1937 (American Stuff: an Anthology of Prose and Verse by Members of the Federal Writers' Project) and several novels based upon project experiences were written and published by former employees after 1943.[25]

In spite of much public acclaim, the Federal Writers' Project did not escape the harsh criticism of anti-New Deal and conservative elements of both the press and Congress. Two characteristics of the writers' project which the other art projects did not share--the facts that the programme was not specifically geared to professional talent and that it was not suitable for immediate performance before a public audience--made it particularly susceptible to attack. The term 'boondoggle' became a popular press description of the FWP and other WPA projects that were felt to be of little value to the public.[26] Early in the project, the New York Times erroneously reported a writers' project plan to produce a 2,689,000-word national guidebook on an allocation of $2,689,000 with the headline 'Nation Described at Dollar a Word.'[27] Press charges of 'made literature as made work' and of using project-sponsored publications to promote politcal beliefs were commonplace.[28]

While Congressional criticism of the FWP was for the most part no laughing matter, project activity did receive some attention which from a distance of nearly half a century appears almost comical. Representative Frank Keefe, a Wisconsin Republican, in a House speech on 6 April 1939 that had as its general theme the Communist and 'Nazi-Fascist' propaganda threat to America, lambasted a reference in the District of Columbia guidebook chapter on 'The Negro in Washington.' Calling attention to a 'vicious statement' in the guidebook which contended that George Washington Parke Custis, foster son of the first President, had willed a tract of land in Arlington to a black daughter, Keefe went on to refute this 'libelous indictment' which had been 'disseminated by the Works Progress Administration through the instrumentality of the Federal Writers' Project, a project that has cost the taxpayers of this nation since the summer of 1935 ... $15,016,632, and the net result of the effort is the dissemination of libelous misstatements and untruths that are continually found in these volumes, which are produced at your expense and mine.'[29]

Criticism of the literary merits of the many FWP publications, on the other hand, was generally favourable. As the first volume

in the American Guide Series, the Idaho guidebook naturally received
much attention when it was published in 1937. Reviewed by such
well-known American scholars as Bruce Catton and Bernard De Voto,
the volume was described as 'not merely a comprehensive and readable guide to the state of Idaho, but also a bit of literature worth
reading for its own sake' by the former, and as 'an almost unalloyed
triumph' which would 'not only vindicate the Writers' Project but
also heighten our national self-consciousness ... and facilitate our
knowledge of ourselves' by the latter.[30] Washington: City and
Capital, the second guidebook to be issued, did not receive quite
as favourable a response from critics, partly because of its physical
bulkiness and turgid writing style. To one reviewer, its massive
size (1,141 pages) was clear evidence that 'nobody in the Government
Printing Office, not yet the W.P.A., knows much about the book
publishing business.'[31] The New York Times Book Review, however, while also decrying the heftiness of the book ('It weighs nearly
5½ pounds. Samson himself would hesitate to go sightseeing with
such a burden.'), gave a generally positive rating to the D.C.
guide.[32]

    While definitely mixed, most of the ensuing state and local
guidebooks issued under the auspices of the FWP were approved by
both the public and the press throughout the nation. This included
the group of New England guidebooks, all produced at approximately
the same time by the same publisher. One exception which deserves
some special attention, however, was the guide to Massachusetts, published in August 1937. Initially accepted with enthusiasm at public
ceremonies by Governor Charles Hurley, who announced that he would
recommend that every school and library in the state receive a copy
of the title, the book later came under attack from both public officials and the press. Sections of the volume dealing with the Sacco-
Vanzetti case, the Boston police strike, the 1912 strike by textile
workers and the state's record on child labour were charged as being
injurious to the Commonwealth's reputation. A Boston newspaper
article pointed to the fact that forty-one lines in the book were devoted to the Sacco-Vanzetti case, while only nine were given to the
Boston Tea Party and just five to the Boston Massacre.[33]

    Accusations were made that the book, and thus the entire state
project, had been influenced by radicals bent upon the issuing of
'subversive communistic propaganda.' Governor Hurley, apparently
after a closer inspection of the volume than he had given prior to
the above-mentioned ceremony, issued a statement calling for burning
the book on Boston Common; Senator Henry Cabot Lodge, Jr. and
Congressman John McCormack both called for an investigation as
well as a delay of the book's second printing.[34] While neither suggestion was acted upon, and while the Massachusetts guide did have
many defenders among literary critics of the day, this negative reaction caused the top officials of the Federal Writers' Project to look
more closely at possibly controversial sections of all future guidebooks.
An official censor, or 'policy editor', was added to Alsberg's staff

to 'spot and delete material in the state guidebooks that might be
politically biased,' and the FWP director announced formally that
state directors should try to 'curb extreme outbursts of indignation
at social injustice.'[35] If the national director thought that such
steps would eliminate any possible future furor over his project, his
hopes eventually were to be blasted by a Texas congressman's con-
suming passion for identifying Communist sympathizers working under
government sponsorship.

That many Federal Writers' Project employees did indeed har-
bour a deep interest in and commitment to Marxism was a well-known
fact that no one in authority, Henry Alsberg included, tried to deny.
Several project offices, New York City's in particular, gave employment to many avowed Communist Party members who blatantly used
their work time to engage in party activities. The New York City
project often resembled a comic opera, with sitdown strikes called
by the Communist-front Writers' Union because of reductions in project employment and with Trotskyites and Stalinists constantly battl-
ing, sometimes with fists but more often with pen and typewriter.
'The Stalinists circulated a publication among project workers called
Red Pen, which invariably attacked as Trotskyite anyone who opposed
their policies. The Trotskyites, who often were not so much pro-
Trotsky as they were anti-Stalin, counterattacked with leaflets that
lambasted the Stalinists.'[36]

Sympathy for the Marxist doctrine was not an unusual phenomenon in America during the 1930s, particularly among the intellectual
element of society. Many of the individuals who were employed by
the Federal Writers' Project were deeply concerned about the country's
economic woes brought on by the Depression and about such international misfortunes as the civil war in Spain. The standard Marxist
line was appealing as the answer to all problems domestic and foreign,
and it was taken up by many, most of whom would disavow such
leanings in later years.

Prior to 1939, WPA regulations prohibited discrimination in
hiring based upon political ideology, so even card-carrying members
of the Communist Party were hired on all four of the Federal Number
One units, as well as on other projects.[37] But while their activities were often disruptive, they were never a threat or much of an
influence upon the overall work of the FWP.[38] Their participation
was used by the conservative, anti-New Deal press to bring discredit
to the WPA generally, but this in itself had little impact. Of much
more significance were two Congressional investigations which attempted to prove that the Federal Writers' Project was a prime example
of subversive activity in the government.

In the late summer of 1938, the House of Representatives'
Special Committee on Un-American Activities, under the chairmanship
of Martin Dies, a Texas Democrat, opened an investigation into 'the
extent, character and objects of un-American propaganda activities

in the United States.'[39]   The original reason for the establishment
of the Dies Committee was to examine the activities of the German-
American Bund.[40]   However, the huge amounts of publicity given
the supposed subversion emanating from both the FWP and the Federal Theater Project acted as the catalyst for the committee's selection of these organizations as initial targets during public hearings
which began in early August.   Calling the two projects 'hotbeds of
Communists ... infested with radicals from top to botton,' Representative J. Parnell Thomas (Republican--New Jersey) used his membership on the committee as an opportunity to discredit the entire
New Deal and became the primary attacker of these two art projects.[41]

    While a number of persons connected with the Federal Writers'
Project testified during the Dies Committee hearings, four were of
particular significance.   Two were writers employed by the New York
City writers' project--Edwin P. Banta and Ralph De Sola--and two
were top project officials--Alsberg and his immediate superior, Ellen
S. Woodward, assistant administrator of the Works Progress Administration.

    Banta, then 70 years old, testified that he had joined the Com-
munist Party shortly after he began working for the FWP in October
1935 and admitted being introduced to De Sola at the first meeting
of the party's 'Unit 36-S', or Federal Writers Unit.   Banta told Dies
Committee members, 'At this meeting, I was surprised to find that
fully 40% of the people I was associated with in the Federal Writers
were in attendance', and he submitted his membership book as evidence of his party participation.[42]   As further 'proof of the vali-
dity of his charges, Banta submitted to the committee what eventually
became the prize exhibit--a copy of Earl Browder's The Peoples'
Front, purportedly given to him as a birthday gift by his fellow
project workers 'in recognition of his devotion and untiring efforts
in behalf of our party and Communism' and signed by 106 FWP employees.   Banta concluded his testimony by describing how, while a member of the Communist Party, he had secured advertising for the
Red Pen and had collected dues for Unit 36-S during work hours
until officially resigning from the party in September 1936.[43]

    De Sola, who had worked as zoology editor for the New York
City project and had helped to produce its first major publication,
Who's Who in the Zoo (1937), testified that he too had severed his
ties with the Communist Party, but that between 1935 and 1938 he
had, like Banta, been actively involved in working for Unit 36-S
during project time.   However, unlike Banta, De Sola defended the
writers' project against charges that the guides and other FWP publications served as vehicles for left-wing propaganda.   In front of the
committee, he testified that 'on the contrary, we were given very
explicit instructions from the Washington people not to class-angle
anything that went into the guides, and we were very careful to be
sure to do this.'[44]

Woodward appeared before the committee in December and attempted to defend both the writers' and theatre projects by pointing
to their many accomplishments. With Representative Thomas constantly
interrupting her testimony, Mrs. Woodward praised the American
Guide Series as 'the first attempt to picture American life in its
entirety' and as 'the largest and most comprehensive editorial enterprise ever carried out on the continent'. The committee, however,
was more interested in American Stuff, the anthology of writings
done by project workers during their free time. Committee member
Joseph Starnes (Democrat--Alabama) reading out of context from
Richard Wright's autobiographical contribution to this volume, de-
plored it as 'the most filthy thing I've ever seen'. Later, when in
a part of her prepared testimony Mrs. Woodward questioned the re-
liability of Banta as a witness because of his documented treatment
for mental illness, Dies angrily countered with the illogical argument
that Banta's mental stability was proven by the fact that he had been
praised by his fellow workers who had signed the Browder book.
'Don't you think that the best way to check it [Banta's mental con-
dition], when the witness is presented with a book by Earl Browder
signed by 106 of the 300 employees? Don't you think that is a very
definite check upon the accuracy of his statements?'[45]

Upon Mrs. Woodward's suggestion, the heads of the two projects
being investigated were invited to testify before the committee. While
Hallie Flanagan, director of the Federal Theater Project, performed
in a magnificently feisty manner, Alsberg appeared in a deferential
attitude. A large part of his testimony dealt with his personal opposition to 'the tyrannical ... situation' in the Soviet Union. Regarding the problems with Communist Party Members working on the
New York City project, the FWP national director admitted that the
central office had 'cleaned up the mess as best we could' and that
certain 'class-angled' copy submitted by the New Jersey and Montana
projects had also been worrisome to him. The latter material, however, had been carefully edited by the central staff in order that
the final copy would not be 'censorable for being unfair'. In the
end, the committee thanked Alsberg for his co-operation and Dies
personally commended him for his 'frankness'.[46]

During the Dies Committee hearings, the nation's press did
not neglect the proceedings. Following Banta's testimony, headlines
on page one of the New York Times proclaimed 'Anti-Red Writers
Barred from WPA, Witness Declares ... Former Writer Tells of Communist Grip on 40% of Project Workers.'[47] Later, the same newspaper headlined that Chairman Dies 'Sees Red Wording Put in WPA
Books'.[48] Woodward's appearance elicited a report of her denial
of Communist influence in the writers' and theatre projects with headlines centering upon the 'filthy book' statement of Representative
Starnes.[49] And, finally, Alsberg's condescending testimony produced headlines reading 'WPA Writers' Head Hits Communists ...
Alsberg Tells Dies Committee It Took Two Years to "Clean up Mess"

in Project'.[50] These and other stories gave the Dies Committee
such widespread exposure that a Gallup Poll release in December
1938 indicated that 'three out of five voters in the nation were familiar with the work of the committee and ... 75 percent were in
favor of having the committee continue its investigation'.[51]

It is difficult to weight the impact the Dies Committee probe
had upon the fate that befell the Federal Writers' Project just one
year later. While it would be tempting for one seeking cause-and-
effect reasoning for the FWP demise to award a major role to the
negative image produced by these public hearings, other factors--
such as the overall shift of Roosevelt Administration attention away
from domestic programmes towards matters of international concern--
probably contributed more to the lack of support for the arts projects that was about to be exhibited in Washington.

The final report of the Dies Committee concluded that 'the evidence is very clear that certain employees carried on communistic
activities openly in the Federal Writers' Project', but made no specific recommendations as to how to deal with such activity. Its sole
recommendation was that the House of Representatives adopt a resolution to continue the committee for an additional three years.[52]
This was done, and some further investigation of the FWP was carried
out by the committee's employees, but little testimony was received
regarding the project after 1938.

One other Congressional investigation concerned itself to a
much less intense degree with the Federal Writers' Project. Although
the project originally had been intended to last just six months and
had received its original appropriation based upon this targeted time
frame, it had been funded since 1935 out of continuing WPA appropriations as the American Guide Series had begun to bear fruit and
other publications helped to prove the value of this innovative relief
effort. In 1939, a subcommittee of the House Committee on Appropriations began an investigation of the WPA in order to ascertain the
need for future funding of New Deal relief activity co-ordinated by
this agency. Popularly known as the Woodrum Committee (not after
the committee's chairman, who was Edward Taylor of Colorado, but
rather after Clifton Woodrum of Virginia, who gained the most notoriety from his activity on the committee), hearings were held which
cast additional criticism on all Federal relief programmes.

Once again, the Federal Writers' Project was accused of being
under heavy Communist influence. Many of the same charges levied
during the Dies investigation were once again brought up, including
the indictment that members of the Communist Party were in control
of the New York City writers' unit.[53] Indeed, Ralph De Sola repeated the gist of his earlier testimony, adding an accusation that
Alsberg had previously advised him to say as little as possible at
the Woodrum hearings and had, after the Dies investigation, 'severely
reprimanded [him] for giving voluntarily information not called for.'[54]

While these hearings did not generate anywhere near the amount of publicity that came out of the Dies Committee investigation, they came at a time when all of Federal Number One was under attack and frequently rumoured to be scheduled for dismantling.

In mid-June of 1939, the House Appropriations Committee reported its recommendation that the theatre project be eliminated and the other three arts projects be permitted to continue only under full state sponsorship. By July, the necessary WPA appropriations bill reflecting this strategy had passed both the House and Senate, and President Roosevelt, although sympathetic to those then making last-minute efforts on behalf of the Federal arts projects, reluctantly signed the measure in order to keep the 2½ million workers on other WPA projects employed.[55]

Hence the Federal Writers' Project, as it had been known, came to an end. Under only token control from Washington, the newly-designated WPA Writers' Program continued in existence until 1943. Alsberg was fired by Colonel Francis Harrington, who had replaced Hopkins as WPA administrator in 1938. John Newsom was appointed director of the writer's programme in August 1939, and thereafter worked primarily at securing sponsorship for the guidebooks in those states where they had yet to be published. This was accomplished and the still highly acclaimed series was completed in 1941 with the completion of the Oklahoma guidebook. Other titles begun during the four-year life of the Federal Writers' Project were completed, and as war clouds gathered many of the state units began to shift their work to material relating to the defence effort. Military histories, a guidebook to the U.S. Naval Academy and guides to various military bases for new servicemen typified the new thrust of the programme. Finally, on 30 June 1943, after a life of over seven years and an expenditure of $27,189,370, the writers' programme was liquidated. A final disposition of all unpublished materials was made at the Library of Congress where future scholars would later delve into these records in an attempt to interpret this unique attempt at governmental patronage of the arts.[56]

Looking back from a prospective of almost half a century, the achievements of the Federal Writers' Project clearly stand out as the most enduring of the many New Deal relief efforts. In Franklin Roosevelt's 1935 State of the Union address to Congress, the framework of the emergency relief programme which was later to become the Works Progress Administration was announced. The President, in listing seven 'practical principles' of his envisaged programme, proclaimed that the most essential ingredient was the assurance that the 'work undertaken should be useful, not just for a day or a year, but useful in the sense that it ... creates future new wealth for the Nation.'[57]

The work of the Federal Writers Project definitely gave new wealth to the country. Despite the participation of many unqualified

persons, charges both true and false of subversive political influences, as well as administrative and technical problems too numerous
and detailed to be discussed in this paper, the Federal Writers' Project was able to achieve results that few other New Deal-era relief
efforts could match. The American Guide Series has endured over
the years, with most volumes having been reprinted or revised and
with many still being used in libraries throughout the country. But
perhaps more important than its material contributions is what the
project did for the lives of over 5,000 people. Because of it, the
dignities of many highly educated and very creative individuals survived the harsh punishment of economic deprivation. FWP participants who became well-known and successful writers--Nelson Algren,
Richard Wright, Saul Bellow, John Cheever, Frank Yerby and Studs
Terkel to name just a few--were able to nurture their creative talents
rather than shift their efforts to other areas where writing ability
was not needed and which consequently could have caused the permanent abandonment of their gifted attributes. In the end, this encouragement of the nation's resource of literary talent is undeniably
the crowning achievement of the Federal Writers' Project.

BIBLIOGRAPHY

Books

Browne, Ray B., Landrum, Larry N. and Bottorff, William, eds,
    Challenges in American Culture, Bowling Green (Ohio) 1970.
Dies, Martin, Martin Dies' Story, New York, 1963.
Goodman, Walter, The Committee: the Extraordinary Career of the
    House Committee on Un-American Activities, New York, 1938.
Hopkins, Harry L., Spending to Save: the Complete Story of Relief,
    New York, 1936.
Howard, Donald S., The WPA and Federal Relief Policy, New York,
    1943.
McDonald, William F., Federal Relief Administration and the Arts,
    Columbus (Ohio), 1969.
Mangione, Jerre, The Dream and the Deal: the Federal Writers'
    Project, 1935-1943, Boston (Mass.), 1972.
Penkower, Monty Noam, The Federal Writers' Project: a Study in
    Government Patronage of the Arts, Urbana (Ill.), 1977.
Roskolenko, Harry, When I Was Last on Cherry Street, New York,
    1965.
Yezierska, Anzia, Red Ribbon on a White Horse, New York, 1950.

Journals

Billington, Ray A., 'Government and the Arts: the W.P.A. Exper-
    ience,' American Quarterly, Vol. XIII, Winter 1961, pp. 466-79.

Canby, Henry S., 'Should Writers Go On a Salary?', Saturday Review of Literature, Vol. IX, 26 November 1932, p. 270.
Fox, Daniel M., 'The Achievement of the Federal Writers' Project,' American Quarterly, Vol. XIII, Spring 1961, pp. 3-19.
Kellock, Katherine, 'The WPA Writers: Portraitists of the United States', The American Scholar, Vol. IX, Autumn 1940, pp. 473-82.
Saunders, D.A., "The Dies Committee: First Phase', The Public Opinion Quarterly, Vol. III, April 1939, pp. 223-38.
Weeks, Edward, 'Hard Times and the Author', Atlantic Monthly, CLV, May 1935, pp. 551-62.

Newspaper

New York Times

Government Documents

U.S., Congress, Congressional Record.
U.S., Congress, House, Special Committee on Un-American Activities, Investigation of Un-American Propaganda Activities in the U.S.: Hearings on H. Res. 282, 75th Cong., 3rd sess., 1938.
U.S., Congress, House, Special Committee on Un-American Activities, Report of the Special Committee on Un-American Activities Pursuant to H. Res. 282, 75th Cong., 3rd sess., 1938, H. Rpt. 2.
U.S., Congress, House, Subcommittee of the Committee on Appropriations, Investigation and Study of the W.P.A.: Hearings on H. Res. 130, 76th Cong., 1st sess., 1939-40.

NOTES

1. Edward Weeks, 'Hard Times and the Author', Atlantic Monthly, CLV, May 1935, pp. 555-7.
2. Monty Noam Penkower, The Federal Writers' Project: a Study in Government Patronage of the Arts, Urbana (Ill.) 1977, pp. 5-6.
3. Ibid., p. 6.
4. Henry S. Canby, 'Should Writers Go On a Salary?', Saturday Review of Literature, 26 November 1932, p. 270.
5. William F. McDonald, Federal Relief Administration and the Arts, Columbus (Ohio) 1969, pp. 31-3.
6. Penkower, pp. 15-16.
7. U.S., Congress, Senate, Congressional Record, 74th Cong., 1st sess., 1935, 79, pt. 1: p. 95.
8. McDonald, p. 104.
9. Harry L. Hopkins, Spending to Save: the Complete Story of Relief, New York 1936, p. 174.

10. Penkower, pp. 26-7.
11. Jerre Mongione, The Dream and the Deal: the Federal Writers' Project, 1935-1943, Boston (Mass.) 1972, p. 46.
12. McDonald, pp. 138-40.
13. Mangione, pp. 97-8.
14. Penkower, pp. 58-9.
15. McDonald, p. 672.
16. Daniel M. Fox, "The Achievement of the Federal Writers' Project', American Quarterly, Vol. XIII, Spring 1961, p. 6.
17. Penkower, p. 86.
18. Ibid, p. 85.
19. Mangione, pp. 168-9.
20. Penkower, pp. 125-6.
21. Mangione, pp. 221.
22. Ibid, p. 210.
23. Penkower, pp. 144-5.
24. Mangione, pp. 375-96.
25. Penkower, p. 165.
26. Ibid, p. 70.
27. New York Times, 27 January 1936, p. 4.
28. Mangione, p. 187.
29. U.S., Congress, House, Congressional Record, 76th Cong., 1st sess., 84, pt 4: pp. 3930-3.
30. Mangione, pp. 206-7.
31. Esther K. Birdsall, 'The FWP and the Popular Press', in Challenges in American Culture, ed. Ray B. Browne, Larry N. Lundrum and William K. Bottorff, Bowling Green (Ohio) 1970, p. 104.
32. 'All Around the Capital: [Review of Washington: City and Capital by the Federal Writers' Project]', New York Times Book Review, 25 April 1937, p. 12.
33. Mangione, p. 217.
34. Penkower, p. 102.
35. Mangione, p. 220.
36. Ibid, p. 175.
37. Donald S. Howard, The WPA and Federal Relief Policy, New York 1943, pp. 118-20.
38. Penkower, p. 193.
39. U.S., Congress, House, Special Committee on Un-American Activities, Report of the Special Committee on Un-American Activities Pursuant to H. Res. 282, 75th Cong., 3rd sess., 1938, H. Rpt. 2, p. 1.
40. D.A. Saunders, 'The Dies Committee: First Phase', The Public Opinion Quarterly, Vol. III, April 1939, p. 224.
41. Walter Goodman, The Committee: the Extraordinary Career of the House Committee on Un-American Activities, New York 1968, pp. 25-6.
42. U.S., Congress, House, Special Committee on Un-American Activities, Investigation of Un-American Propaganda Activities in the U.S.: Hearings on H. Res. 282, 75th Cong., 3rd sess., 1938, pp. 982-3.

43. Ibid, pp. 998-1005.
44. Ibid, p. 1024.
45. Ibid, pp. 2734-5.
46. Ibid, p. 2886.
47. New York Times, 16 September 1938, p. 1.
48. Ibid, 22 November 1938, p. 15.
49. Ibid, 6 December 1938, p. 17.
50. Ibid, 7 December 1938, p. 2.
51. Mangione, p. 321.
52. H. Rpt. 2, p. 123.
53. U.S., Congress, House, Subcommittee of the Committee on Appropriations, Investigation and Study of the W.P.A.: Hearings on H. Res. 130, 76th Cong., 1st sess., 1939-40, pp. 249-55.
54. Ibid, p. 260.
55. McDonald, p. 705.
56. Penkower, pp. 230-7.
57. U.S. Congress, Senate, Congressional Record, 74th Cong., 1st sess., 1935, 79, pt. 1: p. 96.

DOUGLAS McMURTRIE AND THE
AMERICAN IMPRINTS INVENTORY,
1937-1942*

Beth Kraig

The American Imprints Inventory (AII) received little attention during its years of operation. Set amid the unprecedented experiments
of the New Deal, buried in the broad panorama of a nation struggling
against social and economic upheaval, and ultimately upstaged by the
tragedies of World War II, how much acclaim could a government-
sponsored survey of early American printed materials be expected
to win? Lack of contemporaneous appreciation should not be equated
with lack of worth, however. Under the astute, energetic leadership of its founder, Douglas McMurtrie, the AII initially functioned
with admirable scholarship and organization. Unfortunately, Mc-
Murtrie faced numerous obstacles as director of the AII and discord
concerning the aims of the project eventually led to his forced resignation in 1941. America's entry into World War II ended the troubled
program before its ultimate goals could be reached, yet the turbu-
lence of its final years did not erase the substantial accomplishments
of the AII during McMurtrie's tenure as its leader. The legacy of
the AII continues to influence and contribute to the study of bibliographical history in America; certainly the AII deserves to share
the spotlight that has long been directed toward other projects and
products of the New Deal era.

The deceptively simple desire that prompted the intellectual
birth of the AII evolved from the work and ambitions of Douglas
McMurtrie in the decades prior to the Great Depression. Although
he graduated from MIT in 1909 with a degree in engineering, Mc-
Murtrie's enthusiasm for typography and the press led him into a
career as a printer. For fifteen years, he practiced his craft in the
New York area.[1] In 1924 he designed and built his own printing
plant, incorporating many innovative concepts into its construction.
But McMurtrie's lifelong penchant for detail and perfection cost him

*Reprinted by permission of the author and publisher from Library
Quarterly 56:1 (January 1986) 17-30; copyright © 1986 by The University of Chicago Press.

dearly in financial terms, and he was forced to sell the firm to Conde Nast Publications.[2] After briefly supervising the plant under its new ownership, McMurtrie moved to Chicago in 1926, where he soon settled into a comfortable position as director of typography for the Ludlow Typograph Company. McMurtrie's renown as a speaker and expert on the press let him serve as a kind of public relations spokesman for Ludlow, and in return, the company gave him a great deal of control of his time and activities.[3]

During his years in New York, McMurtrie devoted considerable effort to his avocational interest in the history of printing and typography. His reputation as a scholar of the press reached its zenith shortly after he moved to Chicago, with the publication of his massive history of bookmaking and printing, The Golden Book.* McMurtrie's approach to research reflected the beliefs of his mentor, Wilberforce Eames, the "dean" of American bibliographers. Eames stressed the importance of using actual imprints as a historical resource, and McMurtrie followed The Golden Book with a series of detailed checklists and brief studies based on his ongoing investigation of American bibliographical history. McMurtrie hoped eventually to compile a four-volume history of the American press, but he collated and published raw data as he worked, a practice he termed "progressive bibliography." Ironically, problems concerning "progressive bibliography" later developed in relation to the goals of the AII, and McMurtrie found himself speaking out against aspects of his own professional principle.

As McMurtrie assembled materials for his history of American printing, he became acutely aware of many flaws in existing bibliographies of American imprints. In 1876, publisher Frederick Leypoldt began production of the American Catalogue,[6] which began the still-continuing practice of listing American publications on an annual basis--but catalogs of works produced prior to 1876 were few and inadequate. Specific failings included omission of location information for some imprints, chronological gaps in coverage, omission of works held only by small or remote institutions, and scant attention given to imprints produced by western and southern presses.

McMurtrie recognized that he could not hope to remedy the flaws by working alone; accordingly, he began to develop plans for a nationwide survey employing hundreds of workers. A network of surveyors would stretch across the country, visiting libraries, archives, and historical institutions. Using a standard form, each surveyor would record bibliographical, descriptive, and location information for every early American imprint found. Completed forms would then be forwarded to a central location for collation. A huge,

---

*The Golden Book was originally published in 1927, a revised edition, published in 1943, was entitled The Book: The Story of Printing and Bookmaking.[5]

comprehensive index file of imprint slips would result, from which
individual bibliographies could be assembled. McMurtrie envisioned
a comprehensive series of such checklists which would eventually en-
compass the entirety of America's printed heritage.[7]

In any decade but the 1930s, McMurtrie's notions might have
been nothing more than pipe dreams, but the development of work
relief programs under the administration of Franklin Roosevelt offered
a means of breathing life into such schemes. Under the New Deal,
a series of federal agencies developed projects that provided jobs
and paychecks for unemployed Americans. Initially, programs like
the Civil Works Administration offered work primarily to construction
workers and laborers, but with the creation of the Works Project
Administration (WPA) in 1935, opportunities developed for white-
collar workers as well. Congress empowered the WPA to create
3,500,000 jobs, of which 10 percent were to be white-collar in nature.[8. p. 121]

One branch of the WPA devoted to the employment of white-
collar workers, Federal Project One, administered four programs designed to enrich the nation's cultural heritage by hiring artists,
actors, musicians, and writers. As Project One began operations
toward the end of the summer of 1935, plans already were underway
to add a fifth program to the agenda. WPA chief Harry Hopkins
asked a young college professor, Luther Evans, to outline a plan for
a national inventory of historical records and documents.

As a result of Evans' work, the Historical Records Survey
(HRS) was formed early in 1936 as a division of the Federal Writers'
Program, one of the four original sections of Project One. Luther
Evans headed the HRS, which assumed equal status as a full section
of Project One in October 1936. Initially, the project trained workers
to inventory public records held in state, county, and municipal depositories. The ease with which the program proceeded encouraged
Evans to seek proposals for additional related projects, and in the
summer of 1936, a survey of manuscript collections began under HRS
supervision.*

Douglas McMurtrie watched the development of the HRS with
enthusiastic interest and recognized that the agency offered a means
of bringing his imprints inventory to life. Encouraged by his good
friend Herbert Kellar, director of the McCormick Historical Association and principal architect of the HRS manuscript survey, McMurtrie
presented his ideas to Luther Evans. Evans responded positively
to the plans, and in early 1937, official approval was granted to
begin the American Imprints Inventory under the administration of

---

*The origins and operations of the Historical Records Survey are
examined most thoroughly in two unpublished studies.[9, 10]

the HRS. Concurrently, Evans appointed McMurtrie a National Consultant to the HRS, with the express duty of supervising the AII.

Prior to official acknowledgment of the AII, McMurtrie took an informal poll of scholars and librarians to determine their reactions to the proposed survey. Responses began to arrive as the AII took shape. "Almost unanimous approval" greeted the project, according to official assessments of the responses.[11, 12] However, several years later McMurtrie confessed that initially "the program was regarded very skeptically by the leaders in the library world."[13, 14] The caustic comments of Joseph Gavits, senior librarian at the New York State Library, reflected the most commonly expressed concerns of his peers: "The first reaction is to wonder what experience you have had with the genus WPA worker that warrants your belief that such a task as you outline could be handled with a result of all dependable for accuracy and completeness.... I suppose the essential reason for lack of faith in such an enterprise is the knowledge that real trained bibliographers have spent lifetimes trying to do completely small parts of what you propose to do in a relatively short time with untrained people."[15] Certainly McMurtrie recognized the merit of criticisms like those offered by Gavits, but he remained convinced that, with proper training and supervision, WPA workers could produce accurate and complete results. He also realized that the drawbacks of using unskilled workers were offset by the benefits of having a staff that could inventory collections across the nation. Objections like those raised by Gavits continued to haunt the program in its early stages, but even Gavits responded favorably to the inventory as the value of its work became apparent.

The AII proceeded slowly and on a very limited scale in its first year of operation. State directors of the HRS were permitted to phase in AII operations as they saw fit; most did not initiate any AII activities at all in 1937.[12] Small projects began in Ohio, Massachusetts, California, Kansas, and Wyoming, states that had efficient HRS programs; later in 1937, units formed in Pennsylvania, New York, Colorado, New Jersey, and the Carolinas.[16] These fledgling projects had closely circumscribed assignments. Although McMurtrie hoped ultimately to extend the inventory to include all imprints produced before 1876, he initially set an end date of 1820 for most of the first AII surveys.

To form a foundation for the inventory, McMurtrie directed a crew of workers to copy all entries from the existing major bibliographies onto standard filing slips. These formed the nucleus of the card catalog which took shape under McMurtrie's immediate supervision in Chicago. To those slips were added the records created by AII workers in the field. McMurtrie designed a special standard form for use by AII surveyors; entitled "Form Number 22 for Historical Records," abbreviated to 22HR, the form had spaces for place and date of publication, title, author, location of the work, and description. Standardized Union Catalog holding symbols were used to

note locations. As the AII expanded and surveyed small institutions
without Union Catalog symbols, it used the Union Catalog code to
create new locations symbols.[12]

After a given institution had been surveyed, slips from that
site were forwarded to McMurtrie in Chicago. There, master cards
were made for each imprint. The Chicago staff added more locations
of an imprint to the master cards as necessary. Workers filed the
master cards first in geographical order, by place of publication (by
state and then within each state, by community). Next, works
printed in a given community were filed in chronological order by
date of printing. Thus, as slips accumulated, files developed that
represented the imprints produced in every community in America.
[17, p. 11]

The AII grew consistently during the last months of 1937, and
extremely encouraging results began to filter in to Chicago. In a
report to Luther Evans written early in 1938, McMurtrie jubilantly
described some of the more important finds:

> The earliest literary composition and the third earliest pam-
> phlet of any character known to have been printed in Ten-
> nessee were recorded as "not located" in the standard bib-
> liography of Tennessee printing. A few weeks ago, a worker
> of the HRS, working in a little-known religious library far
> off the beaten track, in the mountains of North Carolina, re-
> ported the discovery of a perfect copy of "Gospel Liberty,"
> by Hezekiah Balch, printed at "Knoxville, (Territory South
> of Ohio) in 1794...." And just a few days ago, there were
> discovered in another out-of-the-way library, by a Survey
> worker engaged in listing imprints, six documents of great
> importance to North Carolina's pre-Revolutionary history.
> [18]

Such results stimulated expansion of the survey to the degree originally devised by McMurtrie. Projects began in every state and
end dates were extended to 1876 (and to even later dates for western
and southern imprints).

With an influx of over one thousand new workers expected as
the AII expanded in 1938, the need for better training procedures
became critical. The HRS had long utilized simple manuals to advise
its workers, and Luther Evans had urged McMurtrie to follow suit
since the earliest days of the AII. Finally McMurtrie responded, producing the first edition of the American Imprints Inventory: Manual
of Procedure in June 1938.[19]   State directors and workers welcomed
the Manual with delight.

Indeed, the Manual was a masterpiece of instructional literature. McMurtrie presented the purpose and procedures of the AII
in simple, straightforward prose. He prefaced the guide with a brief

history of the project which explained the uses to be made of the
final catalog and checklists by scholars and historians. Workers
generally entered the AII knowing little or nothing about bibliographical research and historical methods; they needed to understand
the value of the project and their part in it. Additionally, work
relief programs (and workers) suffered under the epithet "busy work,"
and it was vitally important to convince employees that their duties
were constructive and necessary. By insuring that AII workers
would recognize the merits of and rationale behind their own tasks,
McMurtrie increased the probability that they would apply themselves
diligently to their jobs. The Manual served to diminish the chances
that AII workers would develop the careless attitudes of the "genus
WPA worker" to which Joseph Gavits had so slightingly referred.

In the many pages of instruction following the introduction,
McMurtrie outlines the AII structure and its component operations.
He included definitions of bibliographical terms and presented an
extremely thorough delineation of the actual recording process. Additionally, he proposed a set of "selling points" that could be used
to gain access to host institutions. Librarians often echoed the
skepticism expressed by Joseph Gavits and had to be convinced to
permit AII workers to use their facilities. Since most libraries were
woefully understaffed during the Depression, McMurtrie advised the
AII worker to make his presence as unobtrusive as possible. He
cautioned that if an AII worker interrupted the activities of a library
unnecessarily, or failed to explain necessary interruptions, ejection
of the worker and refusal of the institution to cooperate with the
survey might be the result.

The most complicated portion of the Manual dealt with recording
information about uncataloged materials. If an imprint had been
cataloged by the host institution, the recording process was much
simplified; however, many older imprints were not cataloged and had
to be examined by the workers. Two recording styles were outlined.
Style A was highly detailed and included features of typography and
layout; Style B involved listing only the type of information usually
included on a standard catalog entry.

McMurtrie mandated use of Style A for all imprints produced
prior to 1801 and noted that it would be used in the final AII checklists. His dedication to the more detailed listings reflected McMurtrie's
role as a historian of typography; for any scholar excepting one concerned with the physical history of the press, Style B was fully adequate. The time and energy needed to record entries in Style A
were considerable, and conflicts would ultimately surface concerning
the need for so complex a listing.

As 1938 drew to a close, the AII formed an integral part of the
HRS and could point proudly to its second year of growth and success. Workers continued to find noteworthy imprints, many of which
were located in institutions far removed from their places of origin.

In a report to the American Library Association, McMurtrie noted
that the earliest known Illinois imprint resided in New Jersey, while
the earliest New Mexican publication could be found in the District
of Columbia, and California held the earliest known Alabama imprint.
[7, pp. 315-16] Results also confirmed McMurtrie's belief that many
imprints could be located in smaller, lesser-known institutions and
that western and southern imprints existed in greater numbers than
had been recognized previously. By locating so many materials in
sites distant from their points of origin, McMurtrie demonstrated
clearly that local printing history could rarely be assembled accurately using only locally held imprints.

The AII also continued to succeed in its fundamental role as
an employer of relief workers; by the end of 1938, approximately
two thousand employees had provided assistance to the AII. Mc-
Murtrie never lost sight of the role his project played as a mechanism for employment. In a radio interview in June 1938, he commented
on his feelings concerning the AII staff: "Idleness is a specially
acute misfortune to anyone used to mental activity. Many of our
workers come to us after long periods of unemployment, during which
they have tried every expedient to land a job. When we put them
to work at a useful task, suited to their abilities and experience,
they gain a new interest in life."[20, p. 41]. McMurtrie's support
concern for his staff paid benefits in the form of more involved, enthusiastic workers. One regional director reported to McMurtrie that
her workers expressed gratitude concerning the many steps taken to
involve them in the project and even pursued new interests in American history and printing by studying the subjects in their spare
time.[21]

At the start of its third year of operations, the AII looked
forward to continued expansion and increased success. Additional
efforts were made to inventory broadsides and broadsheets; also,
McMurtrie promoted a complicated new project under which workers
would read old newspapers and note information about imprints advertised therein. McMurtrie wrote and distributed manuals outlining
these new activities and promoted them with gusto.

However, Luther Evans viewed expansion of the AII with reser-
vations. A backlog of over 200,000 slips clogged the central headquarters in Chicago, and production of final checklists was extremely
slow. Only one substantive checklist based primarily on AII records
appeared by 1939; the need to recheck many slips and the time taken
to register Style A recordings hindered more rapid production. Evans
suspected that McMurtrie's enthusiasm and energy had misled him
into believing that the AII might accomplish more than it actually
could.

McMurtrie chafed at Evans' wary attitude, but unexpected changes
in the administration of the AII confirmed Evans' cautious approach.
In the summer of 1939, Congress reorganized the WPA, mandating that

any states wishing to maintain WPA programs would have to provide
sponsors for 25 percent of the costs.[8, pp. 312-13] This thrust
on the states the responsibility for continuing WPA projects--or
canceling them.

Evans's caution had led him to anticipate possible cutbacks,
and the HRS adapted quite well to the new guidelines; McMurtrie
also responded to the situation with equanimity and managed to secure
state sponsors for many of his AII units.[22] By the end of August 1939, every AII and HRS unit had located state sponsorship.
In many cases, fieldwork never ceased. Nevertheless, the changes
demonstrated how deeply and suddenly economic and political fluctu-
ations might affect the programs. The events of 1939 served as an
omen of more serious problems to come.

Early in 1940, Luther Evans resigned from the leadership of
the HRS to head the Division of Legislative Reference at the Library
of Congress (a post from which he graduated in 1945 to replace Ar-
chibald MacLeish as Librarian of Congress). His successor, Sargent
Child, had been a regional supervisor for the HRS. McMurtrie and
Child were acquainted prior to Child's promotion and by all accounts,
their relationship was amicable. Indeed, Child's philosophy concerning HRS operations resembeld McMurtrie's early views on "progressive bibliography." Child supported rapid, piecemeal production of
checklists and inventories as soon as materials had been surveyed.
[23, p. 4-5] According to one insider, McMurtrie's support of Child
helped secure him the advancement to the directorate of the HRS.[24]

To his new job, Child brought a keen appreciation of the changing direction of the Roosevelt administration. The outbreak of war
in Europe in 1939 had prompted increased attention to military matters
in the White House and Congress. By 1940, funds expended for aid
to Britain and American defense were considerable. Child realistically
assumed that federal support for historical inventories might soon
become quite scarce. If the HRS and AII hoped to survive, Child
reasoned, both agencies would have to prove their worth through
increased productivity.[23, p. 4]

In his first discussion with McMurtrie concerning editorial and
publication activities, Child mildly suggested that inventories of major
libraries could be published in checklist form. He noted that the
AII had recently completed a survey of materials in the Bancroft
Library and might profitably release a simple bibliography of the
results.[25] McMurtrie chose not to accede to this request, but
Child would not abandon lightly his dedication to increased publication.

In fact, pressure from host institutions and sponsors grew
heavy; many supporters of the AII were anxious to see some tangible
product. There was widespread agreement that editing and publishing checklists now constituted the most important task facing the HRS

and AII, as inventory work in many states was nearing or had
reached completion. By the summer of 1940, fieldwork for the AII
was more than 85 percent complete and approximately 6.5 million
slips had already been shipped to Chicago.[26]

Since fieldwork had slowed, many state offices were far less
busy than had been the case earlier. To make use of state workers,
Herbert Kellar, McMurtrie's old friend and founder of the HRS manuscript survey, proposed that the AII return slips to the states for
collation into checklists. He suggested the plan would make good
use of state staff workers and would also hasten production of bibliographies.[27, p. 47] However, McMurtrie disagreed and refused
to relinquish control of the checklist process. Instead, he petitioned
the American Council of Learned Societies for a grant to hire trained
editors to support the Chicago headquarters as it processed slips.[26]
Unfortunately, the grant was denied, and without extra funding, the
AII managed to produce only two checklists in 1940.

The outside pressures that had concerned Sargent Child in
March 1940 grew enormously during that year. During the spring
and summer, Hitler's armies overran Denmark, Norway, the Nether-
lands, Belgium, and France in the terrifyingly short time span of
two and a half months. When Roosevelt asked Congress for funds
to accelerate further his programs of military mobilization, he received more money than had been requested. In response to the
national drive toward defense, WPA leaders began to introduce programs designed to assist in the war effort. With such changes in
priorities, the status of the AII grew more precarious each month,
each week.

Sargent Child began the second calendar year of his leadership of the HRS convinced that drastic change had to be made if
the HRS and AII were to survive. Without fail, in 1941 he would
force an increase in the production of checklists. Throughout 1940,
his administration had developed a strong character based on efficiency and speedy production. Early in 1941, Child addressed the
logjam in the AII operations and concocted a plan specifically designed
to remove obstacles to increased production.

In the outline Child forwarded to McMurtrie, he noted that
only 7,929 titles had been listed in checklists published by the AII,
although millions of record slips had been collected. Sponsors were
growing "exceedingly restive" and some had threatened to discontinue support of the program. To resolve the problems, Child proposed six steps, all of which revolved around two central principles:
decentralization of the editorial process and elimination of Style A
descriptions. In suggesting the latter move, Child correctly observed
that the vast majority of scholars interested in early imprints would
be perfectly satisfied with Style B formatting.[28]

Child unwittingly criticized the two areas of the existing

program that most reflected the personal interests of Douglas Mc-Murtrie. As a historian of typography, McMurtrie valued highly the detailed Style A entries; as a bibliographer and editor, he proudly cherished the personal control he wielded over the centralized editorial system. Although McMurtrie could not disagree with the underlying goal of Child's proposal, since it so nearly approximated his own philosophy of "progressive bibliography," he did not agree that the Child plan offered the best means of using the AII records. Under the circumstances, McMurtrie was willing to overlook his ideals concerning "progressive bibliography," believing that the cost of speedier production would be too high.[29]

Child was in no mood or position to honor McMurtrie's objections and announced that Style A would henceforth be abandoned. He ordered McMurtrie to revise the manual accordingly.[30] McMurtrie bristled at this mandate and produced a revision that Child found wholly inadequate. In response, Child jabbed at McMurtrie with veiled hints that his behavior was unpatriotic. McMurtrie, fervently anti-Nazi in his politics, resented the insinuations.[31] It became clear that the once amiable relationship between McMurtrie and Child had deteriorated drastically.

Operations of the AII could not move forward with its two leaders at odds. Exercising his power as director of the parent agency, Child took the initiative and on July 9, 1941, McMurtrie received notice that his job had been terminated.[32] He was apparently allowed to "resign," perhaps as a final courtesy from Child reflecting earlier, better relations between the two men. McMurtrie's dismissal meant nothing to him in terms of career; he had continued his representation of Ludlow Typograph while heading the AII and never received more than a nominal salary and expenses from the HRS. Nevertheless, the dismissal was a heavy blow emotionally to the man who had fathered the AII and guided it for so long.

McMurtrie's replacement, Don Farran, moved quickly to enact Child's program. By September 1941, seventeen state offices were preparing checklists and eleven more mobilized their resources to begin local editing.[33] Certainly such results indicated that, while the Child plan might not result in an immediate flood of checklists, it seemed likely to step up the production pace. However, events abroad determined that no valid comparison of the McMurtrie plan to the Child program would ever be possible, for the latter was to be cut short. On December 7, 1941, Pearl Harbor changed the course of American history and ushered in the final days of the AII. Just hours after the Japanese bombs fell, the commissioner of the WPA sent a telegram to all state supervisors ordering deferment of projects not connected to defense.[8, p. 318] A later directive mandated cessation of all Federal Project One programs by April 1942.

One final burst of publication accompanied the last days of the AII, even as preparations were underway to relocate the final catalog of 15 million slips from Chicago to a safe haven in Wisconsin. Sixteen checklists, most of which had been near completion by the end of 1941, appeared in 1942. Another seventeen checklists near completion in April 1942 were left unpublished.[34]

Amazingly, despite the unpleasant ending of his association with the AII, Douglas McMurtrie made one last attempt to complete the project in the manner he had originally envisioned. In 1943, he petitioned the Rockefeller Foundation for funds to continue production of checklists. To his delight, he received a grant to complete the three volumes that had been closest to completion in 1942.[35, pp. 1940-41] McMurtrie organized the new program with typical vigor. Then, in February 1944, he contracted a severe case of influenza which damaged his heart. The condition worsened, and on September 19, 1944, Douglas McMurtrie died. With his death, plans for any full-scale revivification of the AII also died.

The AII legacy after 1944 falls into two categories reflecting the two phases that constituted the program. The first part of the legacy consists of the entry slip catalog. By the end of the project, over 15 million slips representing perhaps 8 million different imprints had been collected. A good measure of the value of this file involves comparison of AII records to those already held at the time of the survey by the National Union Catalog (NUC) division of the Library of Congress. A very high percentage of AII records were new to the NUC; estimates made during the years of AII operations ran as high as 90 percent. Imprints produced in the west and south constituted the greatest proportion of new entries. Of all the Mississippi imprints reported by the AII, only 8 percent overlapped entries already recorded by the NUC and just 2 percent of the reported Arizona entries had been on file with the NUC.[35, p. 1941] Such high percentages demonstrated the richness of the AII file. Certainly the slips constituted the single most comprehensive collection of information about early American imprints ever assembled.

The second part of the AII legacy involved publication of the material contained in the file of slips. Less than forty checklists were produced by the project by April 1942. Such a poor record of publication may be explained partially by the obstinacy of Douglas McMurtrie concerning proposals like those made by Child and Kellar; certainly production could have been hastened by adopting such plans. However, the advent of World War II must be blamed, also. It is doubtful that the Child plan could have finished the AII successfully without years in which to do so. Lack of time most effectively prevented publication of AII records.

Yet the publication of AII material did not end with the project in 1942. Since the 1950s, Scarecrow Press has published a series entitled originally the American Bibliography and continued currently as the Checklist of American Imprints. Based on careful collation of AII records, this series listing all American imprints produced in the

years 1800-1834 will continue to bring AII material to the attention
of the scholarly community. In the process of assembling the National
Union Catalog Pre-1956 Imprints series, the Library of Congress also
made use of AII records. Additionally, a series of local bibliographies
produced by library students at Catholic University during the 1950s
and 1960s relied on AII materials almost exclusively. With time, it
is possible that most of the entries created by AII workers will be
made accessible in some manner.

As a project designed to make bibliographical and historical
materials available for study, the AII must be judged an overall success. As part of the WPA, the project also contributed to the nation's
efforts to alleviate the ravages of unemployment through constructive
work relief programs. Douglas McMurtrie must be praised for his
conception of the program and his unfailing dedication to its full
realization. His errors were the result of enthusiasm and scholarly
integrity, not ill will or carelessness. It is difficult to fault Mc-
Murtrie for his excess, since they stemmed for the same attention to
detail and penchant for perfection that contributed so much to the
outstanding results of the American Imprints Inventory.

References

1. Towne, Jackson, "Douglas C. McMurtrie, 1888-1944." Stechert-
    Hafner Book News 16 (October 1961): 17-19.
2. Kellar, Herbert A. "Douglas Crawford McMurtrie: Historian of
    Printing and Bibliographer." In Douglas C. McMurtrie: Bib-
    liographer and Historian of Printing, edited by Scott Bruntjen
    and Melissa Young. Metuchen, N.J.: Scarecrow Press, 1979.
3. McCaffrey, Frank. An Informal Biography of Douglas C. Mc-
    murtrie. San Francisco: Privately printed, 1939.
4. McMurtrie, Douglas. The Golden Book. New York: Covici-
    Friende, 1927.
5. McMurtrie, Douglas. The Book: The Story of Printing and Book-
    making. New York: Oxford University Press, 1943.
6. Leypoldt, Frederick. The American Catalogue. New York:
    A.C. Armstrong & Sons, 1880.
7. McMurtrie, Douglas. "A Nationwide Inventory of American Im-
    prints under WPA Auspices." Public Documents, pp. 301-16.
    Chicago: American Library Association, 1938.
8. McDonald, William F. Federal Relief Administration and the Arts.
    Columbus: Ohio State University Press, 1969.
9. Wellshear, Elizabeth Jean. "Historical Records Survey." M.S.
    thesis. University of Illinois, 1948.
10. Barrese, Edward Francis. "The Historical Records Survey:
    A Nation Acts to Save Its Memory." Ph.D. dissertation. George
    Washington University, 1980.
11. Records of the Works Progress Administration, Record Group
    69. National Archives, Washington, D.C.

12. Preliminary Statement of Plan for the American Imprints Inventory. In [11].
13. Douglas McMurtrie Collection, Michigan State University Library.
14. Evans, Luther, to McMurtrie, Douglas. December 1936. In [13].
15. Gavits, Joseph, to McMurtrie, March 2, 1937. In [13].
16. Evans circular letter to State HRS Directors of New York, Pennsylvania, Colorado, New Jersey, North Carolina, and South Carolina. In [13].
17. American Imprints Inventory: Manual of Procedure. In Source Documents for American Bibliography: Three "McMurtrie Manuals," edited by Scott Bruntjen. Halifax. Nova Scotia: Dalhousie University, University Library, School of Library Service, 1978.
18. McMurtrie to Evans, January 24, 1938. In [13].
19. File, "AII Manual of Procedure, WPA," McMurtrie Collection.
20. McMurtrie, Douglas, "A Nationwide Search for Early American Printing." In Douglas C. McMurtrie: Bibliographer and Historian of Printing, edited by Scott Bruntjen and Melissa Young. Metuchen, N.J.: Scarecrow Press, 1979.
21. Ziemer, Thelma, to McMurtrie, July 30, 1938. In [13].
22. McMurtrie to Evans, June 2, 1939. In [13].
23. Child, Sargent. Status and Plans for Completion of the Inventories of the Historical Records Survey. Washington, D.C.: Historical Records Survey, 1940.
24. Evans to Kellar, Herbert, March 13, 1940. Luther Evans Collection. Library of Congress Manuscript Division.
25. Child, Sargent, to McMurtrie, June 25, 1950. In [13].
26. Report of the National Advisory Committee of the HRS to Waldo Leland. Director. American Council of Learned Societies. August 18, 1940. In [13].
27. Kellar, Herbert, "An Appraisal of the Historical Records Survey." In American Library Association Papers Presented at the 1940 Conference of the ALA Representing the Joint Program of the Committee on Archives and Libraries of the ALA ... edited by A.F. Kuhlman. Chicago: American Library Association, 1940.
28. Child to McMurtrie, February 20, 1941. In [13].
29. McMurtrie to Kellar, February 21, 1941. In [13].
30. Child to McMurtrie, April 5, 1941, Box 215.5, RG 69. In [11].
31. Child to McMurtrie, May 2, 1941, Box 215.5 RG 69. In [11].
32. Kerr, Florence, to McMurtrie, July 9, 1941, Box 215.5, RG 69. In [11].
33. "Status of the AII, September, 1941," RG 69. In [11].
34. Farran, Don, "Final Report of the AII." RG 69. In [11].
35. McMurtrie, Douglas, "The Bibliography of American Imprints." Publishers Weekly 144 (November 20, 1942): 1939-44.

THE PROMISE OF FRUIT ... AND LIGHT†*

Lucretia W. McClure

Janet Doe represents the finest in medical librarianship. She was not only a superb librarian, but a leader in the development of medical librarianship and tireless worker for this association. She served as its president in 1948/49 and was presented the association's highest honor, the Marcia C. Noyes Award, in 1954. In addition, she is a scholar in her own right. Her publication A Bibliography of the Works of Ambrosie Paré brought her worldwide recognition.

Many of us had the privilege of meeting Miss Doe at the 1971 annual meeting of the Medical Library Association in New York. It was my pleasure to visit her earlier this month at her home just outside Katonah, New York. She is a warm and inspiring woman, vitally interested in the world's events and in our profession. I bring you greetings from her.

This lectureship is a tribute to Janet Doe, for all she has stood for and contributed to the profession of medical librarianship. This is her 90th year, and I know you will join me in sending her our collective best wishes. My words today are dedicated to her.

As a member of the medical library profession for twenty years, I have had the opportunity to observe the enormous changes in medical librarianship. Many of you work with databases through automated systems in cataloging, acquisitions, or reference and, in your experience, they had always been available. But it is a relatively short time, some fifteen years, since these advances began to change the nature of our profession. In the early 1960s, there were librarians who had to stand in line with others at the institution's one photocopier to make a copy. Hours were spent searching indexes and

†Janet Doe Lecture in History or Philosophy of Medical Librarianship, presented May 28, 1985, at the Eighty-fifth Annual Meeting of the Medical Library Association, New York City, New York.
*Reprinted by permission of the author and publisher from the Bulletin of the Medical Library Association 73:4 (October 1985) 319–329; copyright © 1985 by the Medical Library Association.

abstracts to compile, by hand, a bibliography. Cataloging was done
according to standards set by a library, not necessarily with regard
to national standards.

Today we stand on the threshold of new advances and new
techniques which will enhance our ability to fulfill our responsibilities.
We have at our fingertips an array of databases and data files; we
have microcomputers, electronic mail, telefacsimile, optical disks, and
video and audio resources, as well as books and journals. How do
we plan to harness these resources? What is the future for our profession?

We use words to describe our work--words such as reference,
information, knowledge--and I believe I can add the word wisdom.
What is their meaning within the context of librarianship? And how
did all of this come about? The purpose of my lecture is to review
the beginnings of reference and/or information services, to note the
development of these services as reflected in medical librarianship,
and to speak of the future of reference and information services.

We use the terms reference and information loosely. Is there
a difference? And how do they relate to the word "knowledge?"
Finally, can we determine, for all of this, a philosophy of service
to our users in the future? You will hear my philosophy in what
follows.

The privilege of being a Janet Doe lecturer brings both joy
and anxiety. The anxiety is eased when one finally arrives at a
satisfactory topic. The joy comes from delving into the subject and
discovering the many ideas and writings of many thoughtful authors,
and this experience far outweighs the anxiety.

One of the significant works I found is Fritz Machlup's
Knowledge: Its Creation, Distribution, and Economic Significance.
In this work, he cites a statement by the economist Arthur C. Pigou
from which comes the title of this paper and around which my theme
is developed. Pigou says: "When a man sets out upon any course
of inquiry, the object of his search may be either light or fruit--
either knowledge for its own sake, or knowledge for the sake of
good things to which it leads." He concludes by saying: "It is the
promise of fruit and not of light that chiefly merits our regard."[1]

But Machlup comments that he believes that fruit can grow only
"where there is enough light."[2] Being a librarian and a seeker
of knowledge, and speaking for our profession, I am certain it is
essential that we have both.

Development of the Library

Let me start with the development of the library in America.

It parallels the development of research and the growth of universities. The second half of the 19th century saw the development of
scholarship, the scholarly associations, specialization, and scientific
and professional education. Daniel Coit Gilman, then president of
Johns Hopkins University, outlined the four functions of a university in an address given in 1893. The first function, of course, is
the education of youth. The other three could also apply to librar-
ianship--to conserve knowledge, to extend the bound of knowledge,
and to disseminate knowledge.[3]

By the end of the century the statement "the library is the
heart of the university" was common and the idea already in the
public domain. Louis E. Martin, Cornell University librarian, may
have put this trite statement to rest, pointing out that the faculty
is the true heart of the university. He is willing to cede that piece
of anatomy to the faculty because the "university library is the mind,
even the soul of the university. The library is as close to being the
vital principle of the university as anything can be."[4]

In earlier times the scholar had been expected to accumulate
his own library; now the universities were under pressure to provide
books and libraries. That the research library was not yet a reality
was clear when the library resources of this country totaled only a
million volumes. Harvard's collection included 72,000 volumes, while
the Library of Congress had but 50,000. The literature suggests
there was some interest in classification and cataloging at this time,
but the librarian's chief function was to build collections.

And build they did. By 1876, Harvard's collection had grown
to more than 227,000; the Library of the Surgeon-General's Office
held some 40,000 volumes. By 1891 the Surgeon-General's library
had increased to more than 100,000 and Harvard's holdings amounted
to nearly 300,000.

Throughout this time, emphasis was on the collections and their
protection, not their use. The first explicit statement for a program
for personal assistance to readers was made by a public librarian,
Samuel Swett Green, in 1876. His article on "personal relations"
between librarians and readers concludes with this comment: "A
librarian should be as unwilling to allow an inquirer to leave the
library with his question unanswered as a shopkeeper is to have
a customer go out of his store without making a purchase."[5]

Otis Robinson, librarian at the University of Rochester, agreed
with Green, adding that the librarian should be much more than a
"keeper of books; he should be an educator." This was a new concept, that the library could be the laboratory of the college. Certainly it is moving away from the idea of the passive librarian whose
only role was to guard the books.[6]

Robinson was professor of mathematics when he was appointed

librarian at Rochester in 1869. He was concerned that students should
become intelligent readers, going so far as to encourage them to take
books freely from the shelves. He may have regretted this enlightened
practice, for he could no longer account for the whereabouts of each
volume. It also inspired the custom of "sub-coat tailing" or conceal-
ing a book under one's coat without checking it out.[7]

In 1886, Frederick Crunden of the St. Louis Public Library
collected data from 108 libraries and found a growing sentiment in
favor of personal assistance by the librarian as the most effective
aid to the reader.[8] Public libraries were moving faster than most
academic libraries in offering help to the reader.

One of the first academic libraries to offer assistance was the
Columbia College Library under the dynamic leadership of Melvil
Dewey. Although many think of him only in terms of classification,
he was secretary of the American Library Association, manager of
the Library Bureau, and editor of the Library Journal. Dewey had
been at the forefront of the public library movement and was ready
to carry this "modern library idea" of individual assistance to the
reader to the university library. In his first Circular of Information published at Columbia in 1884, he outlines the library's responsibilities for "reference service" and he lists two members of the
"reference department" in the annual report for that year.[9]
Clearly the idea of personal assistance by a librarian was becoming
acceptable. Dewey goes so far as to call it the "most important single
department" in the library.[10]

By the end of the 19th century, many scholarly libraries were
utilizing staff in reference, and from that time on, a vast literature
discussing what a librarian should or should not do has appeared.
Should the librarian provide answers? Should the librarian instruct
users in how to obtain information? This discussion is still raging
today, and in the medical field are the added questions of how much
medical information should be provided to the lay public and how
qualified we are to answer health-related questions.

I am concerned with the way medical librarians viewed their
responsibilities in reference and information services. To trace this
development, I used the medical library publications, particularly
the Medical Library and Historical Journal, published from 1903 to
1907, and the Bulletin of the Medical Library Association, beginning
in 1911. Let us look at what is found in these sources.

The Medical Library

The first volume of the Medical Library and Historical Journal
for 1903 contains a short article by John S. Brownne, librarian at
the New York Academy of Medicine. He writes that the cataloger
is the "best person for the main reading room, as being the one

most familiar with the books." This individual, incidentally, opens
the mail and catalogs during the morning and attends to the wants
of the readers in the afternoon.[11]

The next year, Dr. James Macfarlane Winfield, dermatologist
and directing librarian of the Medical Society of the County of Kings
in Brooklyn, addressed the Seventh Annual Meeting of the Association of Medical Librarians in Atlantic City in the "Medical Library as
a Factor in Medical Education." He begins with a disclaimer that,
not being a "trained librarian," he fears that what he has to say
will not be of interest. However, that does not deter him from saying it, and he proceeds to suggest that students should be taken to
a large medical library, be given a topic, and "after winnowing
out the great mass of chaff, get down to the real kernel of the subject." He could have spoken these words at any recent meeting of
medical educators and been wildly cheered.[12]

In the discussion after Winfield's address, Dr. William Osler
indicated his own practice of instructing senior students in medical
literature, getting them to read and discuss important journals.[13]
Dr. A Jacobi of New York immediately challenged this, concluding
that "drawing of the students' attention to medical literature [is] a
very dangerous practice." Students who read neglected the clinics
and left college ill-equipped for practice. Moreover, he said, reading a mass of unimportant medical literature tempted the student to
rush into print with something "puerile and utterly valueless." It
should be noted that only physicians entered into this discussion.[14]

It is also interesting to note that throughout the early years
of these publications, physicians were speaking and writing on the
role of the librarian as often as librarians. Dr. David I. Wolfstein,
a Cincinnati physician, spoke to his colleagues at the Academy of
Medicine in that city in 1905. He does not hestitate to tell his audience about medical literature and libraries. He states that "nine-
tenths of the ordinary journalistic productions is practically worthless a few years after it has been written," and he adds, "I am confident that five-tenths is certainly worthless the day it appears."
Despite this, he declares that the first essential for the library is
to have complete series of the best archives and journals! He goes
on to speak of the librarian:

> To make a library truly serviceable there must be in charge
> a librarian who can serve. He must be something more than
> a book shepherd. True, he must love his flock of books, as
> books, but more for the meat that is in them than for the
> hide in which they are bound.[15]

From his disdain of medical publishing, one might have expected
something similar concerning the librarian. However, he recognized
the importance of service. Another physician who was a strong sup-
porter of our profession was Sir William Osler. Speaking at the opening

of the Summer School of Library Service at the University of Wales
in 1917, he suggests that librarians are not "fiery dragons interposed
between the people and the books." The librarian, he continues,

> ... is the badly salaried intellect of the community and, if
> fortunate enough to be able to suffer fools gladly, he leads
> a life of surprising usefulness. And let us not forget other
> important qualifications--an ability to manage a business as
> complicated as a department shop, and a knowledge of men
> and a gift of manners that will enable him to drive his Com-
> mittee or Council without strain on bit or rein.[16]

Whatever words they chose, these physicians understood and recognized the value of service to readers in the medical library. Their
support of the librarian and the library should not be underestimated.
It is vital that we have equally strong support for the librarian and
the library today.

The Medical Librarian

One of the early articles written by a medical librarian appeared
in the 1919 Bulletin of the Medical Library Association. The author,
Laura E. Smith of the New York Academy of Medicine, makes this
amazing statement: "The doctor is the great wizard, at the wave of
whose wand his drug imps work the wonders of the modern world....
To minister to and assist this wonderful wizard is, then, the privilege of the medical librarian."[17]

Smith makes the point that librarians must be familiar with the
sort of books to consult for specific kinds of material, a theme which
is found repeatedly in library literature. She also cites the need
for library schools to give training in medical librarianship. And this
is only 1919.[18]

During the next decade, the 1920s, there were four articles
which emphasized the importance of the librarian to the medical library. Frank Place, Jr., of the New York Academy of Medicine
Library, suggests that the faculty take the new librarian on a sort
of "motor or airplane trip" and point out the principal points of interest in anatomy, physiology, and bacteriology. He also recommends
an exchange for librarians, along the lines of the exchange for professors, as another way to start the library worker on his way through
"Terra Medica Incognita."[19]

Margaret Brinton of the Mayo Clinic discusses the need to
train students to quote references exactly, adding that the Mayo
Clinic has graduate fellows from all parts of the world and it is the
"exceptional" man who knows how to give a reference correctly.[20]
Brinton cited a 1924 article in JAMA by Donald B. Gilchrist, University of Rochester librarian, in which he states bluntly: "It is a

matter of grave concern to many research workers in medicine that
papers on medical subjects are so poorly and so inaccurately buttressed with bibliographic references. A case occurred recently in
which a misquoted reference was traced through five different papers
written by five different medical men."[21]   Unfortunately, we can
cite many of the same today.

Gilchrist has more to say about medical librarians. Certainly
as head of the library in a university planning a new medical school,
he was interested. Medical librarians should be well enough informed
to select books, to take an active interest in the research undertaken
by the faculty, and to instruct students in use of the library as an
aid to research and in the preparation of a proper bibliography.
Gilchrist adds that he is not aware of a single medical school in which
these last two professional services are demanded of the medical
librarian. He strongly urges that formal instruction in medical bibliography be given by the librarian just as it is in the law library.[22]

Then in 1925 Metta M. Loomis of the College of Medicine of the
University of Illinois wrote specifically about reference services.
She urged that the arrangement of current journals and new books
be such that they could be consulted without the librarian's aid.
Her statement of what is important in reference is right on target--
and it was written sixty years ago:

> Of first importance in maintaining a reference service is the
> librarian, who is not supposed to know things so much as
> to know where to find things. Just as newspaper men de-
> velop a nose for news, reference librarians develop a nose
> for references--a sense that leads then to out-of-the-way
> sources of information. This faculty grows by use, and while
> librarians pretend to no complete knowledge of a subject they
> should know bibliography, be able to evaluate printed matter,
> be familiar with authorities in various lines, know the sub-
> jects being discussed in print, the scope and value of various
> periodicals, and besides all else, they should understand
> handling the public--a public whose spoken requests are so
> often misleading that it requires all the librarian's intuition
> and experience to interpret. Efficient reference work requires
> psychology as well as service.[23]

That succinct paragraph could be published in a current journal and
we would applaud it, for it stands as a remarkable goal for the reference librarian of today.

It should be noted that the papers by Brinton and Loomis were
the first of these reference articles in the medical library journals
to contain bibliographies. Their publication date: just sixty years
ago.

It was not until 1927, however, that an article appeared in the

Bulletin of the Medical Library Association with the term "information" in the title. There had been many discussions concerning what
librarians do, how to deal with the problems of the day, the joy of
having the Index-Catalogue of the Library of the Surgeon-General's
Office and the Index Medicus, and the need to teach students about
medical literature. But it was James F. Ballard of the Boston Medical Library who finally said it in print: "Information, reference and
bibliographic services, while closely related and overlapping each
other, and combined in most libraries, are essentially different."

Information service is defined as answering inquiries which
may be solved by consulting ready reference sources, and under
this heading he would place queries about:

--The name of a bloodless surgeon to treat a growth in the
  neck due to trauma;

--The Address of a good dentist;

--The most widely read medical journal of the U.S.A.; and

--Information on sex and common sense by "a woman."

Reference questions may be answered "by giving the reader a definite
book or article" and the questions he listed as reference or research
included inquiries about:

--After-treatment of low Caesarean operation: Emergency:
  patient dying;

--Student at Harvard: Fixed idea of "Fear of Death." To be
  used in a novel entitled "The Man Who Cannot Die"; and

--The year Osler changed his statement regarding pneumonia
  as a self-limited disease.

Bibliographic research is described as the assembling of the relevant
data.[24] If all this sound familiar, it is. We receive these kinds
of questions in our libraries and we would consider them in this same
framework today.

Physicians in the decade of the 1920s continued to decry the
practice of "spoon feeding" students, and complained that recent
graduates admitted they were hopelessly ignorant of literature and
how to use the library. It was advocated by these physicians that
students be taught the proper use of Index Medicus and the Surgeon-
General's Catalogue as well as an appreciation of "good" journals
and how to analyze articles.

Several articles on reference service appeared in the 1930s.
Florence L. Wickes of the Lane Medical Library describes a problem

still with us: "The reference librarian turns regretfully from thoughts of a blissful state where the written word may be searched for the truth therein, freely, for all who care to come. She turns mercenary; for library bills must be met, and the library budgets decrease; and librarians persist in growing and demanding either an increase in staff or a curtailment of service." Wickes calls this a time to review the library's "frozen assets," those "icy souls" who never dream of giving in return for help lavishly given. These are the doctors, lawyers, and others who make demands upon the library without thought of financial support.[25]

It was the article by Thomas E. Keyes of the Mayo Clinic which provided the definitive description of the reference function in the 1930s: preparation of medical bibliographies, abstracting materials, verification of references, translating, recording of references to the literature as journal issues appear, and formal lectures to teach readers how to use bibliographic tools.[26]

During the 1940s and 1950s, there were fewer articles focusing on reference service or the use of information in the medical library. There were a number on reference resources such as the comprehensive list of reference books included in the chapter on reference work by Eileen R. Cunningham, librarian at the Vanderbilt University School of Medicine, which was published in A Handbook of Medical Library Practice in 1943. This landmark publication was edited by Janet Doe.[27]

Estelle Brodman studied the citation process, that means of evaluating journals by counting the number of times they had been cited. Her critical review of this method was based on an investigation of physiology journals in 1944.[28] This method, first suggested by Gross and Gross in 1927 in a study of journals in chemistry, was soon adopted by librarians in other disciplines.[29] Jennie Gregory carried out a study on the frequency of citations of medical journals, an enormous undertaking by hand, in 1937.[30]

During the period of World War II, other problems came to the fore. It was next to impossible to obtain foreign periodicals, journal costs were sky-rocketing, and American Librarians devoted much time to the changes in their own institutions brought about by the war. Much effort was devoted to helping European colleagues obtain materials. It is not surprising that emphasis turned away from writing about reference services.

What does this brief history of medical reference work tell us? From 1876, when Green outlined his description of service as the link between the reader and the literature, to the end of the 1950s, there had been little change. In reviewing the profession of medical librarianship over the first half of the 20th century. Estelle Brodman stressed that the changes which took place resulted from the growth in size of medical libraries. In the small library, the librarian

might know each book, index each journal issue, and work side by
side with the physician to find exactly what was needed. Growth
of the collections meant more cataloging, more time for selection,
more specialization for the librarian. Until that growth, the responsibilities of the reference librarian and the problems in obtaining
information varied little over the fifty years.[31]

John Shaw Billings, who made so many countributions to librarianship, including the Index-Catalogue of the Library of the
Surgeon-General's Office and the Index Medicus, draws this picture
of the librarian in 1887:

> And while the librarian is in one respect only a sort of hod-
> carrier, who brings together the bricks made by one set of
> men in order that another set of men may build therewith,
> he is apt to take quite as much pride and satisfaction in the
> resulting structure, provided it be a good one, as if he had
> built it himself; and he has constantly unrolling before him
> a panorama which, though at times a little monotonous, con-
> tains as much wisdom, humor, and pathos as any other pro-
> duct of the human intellect with which I am acquainted.[32]

If you would know how we arrived where we are today and
where we are going tomorrow, read the history of our profession
and study the struggles and contributions of our colleagues. During the first half of this century, librarians could find information
on every facet of their work in the medical library literature. There
were articles about:

--The care of fine bindings;

--Cataloging and classification;

--The disinfection of books;

--Association meetings and news of the members;

--The exchange of materials;

--Lists of books and journals;

--Library budgets;

--Mutilation of volumes and theft of materials; and

--Training of librarians, in addition to reference and informa-
    tion.

This was the way it was, and what is so revealing is that much
of it is the same today. You realize the dedication of many, the
number of true giants who have practiced in this field of medical

librarianship, and how hard they fought for their libraries, for improvements, and for the future. The scope of their interests was astonishing, for it ranged from the most scholarly of historical works to one of my favorites--called simply "Dusting the library."[33]

What you do today would not be possible without the work of our predecessors who laid the foundations for these achievements. I believe it is evident from their words, which I have repeated here. We owe tribute to those colleagues upon whose work we are building. A statement on the cover of the 1906 issues of the Medical Library and Historical Journal says it very well: "The foundation stones of the whole modern structure of human wisdom have all been laid by the architects of yesterday. Thrice wise is he who knows the quarries and builders of bygone ages and is able to differentiate the stones which have been rejected from those which have been utilized."[34]

The New Era

And now we come to a new era, for during the 1960s there is a distinct change in the literature. There is an air of excitement, for the computer stands on the horizon, with all that suggests for the library and information access. In 1961 the Bulletin of the Medical Library Association published a full report of the National Library of Medicine's index mechanization project.[35] Even the index to the Bulletin directed one from the term "information" to "mechanization." Changes were coming which would forever revolutionize reference service and how we view and deal with information. Two of the major achievements were computer access to bibliographic data bases and in the publication of citation indexes in the sciences.

If you entered the profession recently, you will have to imagine what it was like to be a reference librarian in the early 1960s. Think, if you will, about compiling a bibliography by consulting indexes and abstracts by a single subject or keyword. If the search was to be relevant to infants or adolescents or to hamsters or frogs, you had to read the articles to determine that. Try doing this in the 1964 to 1965 Index Medicus, which had no subheadings! If you wanted to follow a cited paper, you located articles by a cumbersome method of guesswork and intuition. When you can now produce hundreds of bibliographies each month, realize that ten or twelve produced manually in a month were considered a triumph.

Since the SUNY Biomedical Communication Network went online in 1968, we have never looked back. You may wonder at our primitive beginnings, for there was only one database, the system ran at thirty characters per second, and we learned by trial and error. The development of this computer searching was outlined in last year's Janet Doe Lecture by Irwin Pizer and does not need to be repeated here.[36] Suffice to say that to those of us who experienced it,

it was a revolution. The impact on reference service was as significant to us as was the discovery of antibiotics to the practice of medicine.

This is called the Information Age. We hear that from every
source. Derek de Solla Price's classic description of the exponential
growth of scientific literature during the past three centuries clearly
outlines the problem.[37] Early in this century there were some
1,000 biomedical periodicals; today more than 20,000 exist worldwide.
David T. Durack chose to illustrate this growth in the literature by
weighing the volumes of Index Medicus. For sixty years after it
was founded in 1879, the weight remained the same at two kilograms.
Between 1946 and 1955 the weight doubled. Since that time the
weight of Index Medicus increased more than seven times.[38]

The growth of information and our concern about how a professional can assimilate what is needed are not phenomena of this
time. Early scientists established the journal in order to speed up
the process of sharing information with colleagues. The encyclopedia
was an attempt to collect relevant information in a compact format.
Many methods have been tried. You may remember Vannevar Bush
director of the Office of Scientific Research and Development, for
example, whose solution in 1945 was a desk with the individual's books
and records stored on microfilm, to be called up when needed. He
called the device the "memex."[39] When the literature explosion
seemed ready to engulf us, the computer became our lifeline. And
so it is.

Our experience in utilizing the computer to capture and store
vast amounts of information and to retrieve it in a variety of ways
is a major milestone in reference librarianship. As much as it has
developed in the past twenty years, forecasters point to even more
exciting events ahead. The Matheson Report, Academic Information
in the Academic Health Sciences Center: Roles for the Library in
Information Management, outlines one way of the future for libraries,
incorporating the uses of technology to broaden the library's role
and impact within the institution, to take the library outside the
walls and to link it with other units to establish the library's place
in the institution's information program.[40]

The scientist, not of the future, but of today, can save, file,
and create information to build his own databases. He can communicate with his colleagues via electronic mail, review or referee articles
and comment online, retrieve bibliographic citations from national
databases. There are knowledge bases and data files in addition to
word processing. Suppose he has a disk library containing the literature of the great libraries, such as the National Library of Medicine
or the Library of Congress. Looking at this scenario, one wonders
if a professor could not do all his work at home, and further, why
he would ever have need of the library.

Does the solution to the information overload bring with it the diminution of the librarian? Many declared that the advent of OCLC would put catalogers out of work. There are those today who fear that end-user searching programs will take away our great and wonderful status as "the searcher" of literature.

We cannot turn back to simpler days. I, having been there, do not want to. Information has become an industry. Library schools have become schools of information science. The electronic library is no longer something which will happen in the year 2000; it is a reality. When a laser optical disk can carry up to two billion characters, it is clear that we cannot and must not stand still. Writing in an Aslib publication, The Transition Years: New Initiatives in the Education of Professional Information Workers, Blaise Cronin suggests the following:

> With the growth in distributed processing and end-user access; with the growing importance of effective information flow to organisational performance, and the increasing complexity of the information sources and resources used and created by organisations, particularly large organisations, there has come about an awareness that a new type of information specialist, or "supremo" is needed to pull together existing systems and to plan for future information requirements.[41]

The Way of Knowledge

Perhaps we can find an answer if we look at the word "knowledge." This word is not much used in the library literature; certainly we do not hear that we are in an Age of Knowledge. There are volumes written on information, where to access it, how to transfer it, and how to manage it. It is not described as good information or true information. It is the finding of information which seems to delight us, not the quality of its content.

Daniel J. Boorstin, the Librarian of Congress, spoke eloquently on this subject at the White House Conference on Library and Information Services. He distinguishes between information and knowledge and warns of the danger in failing to recognize that distinction.

> While knowledge is orderly and cumulative, information is random and miscellaneous. We are flooded by messages from the instant-everywhere in excruciating profusion. In our ironic 20th-century version of Gresham's law, information tends to drive knowledge out of circulation. The oldest, the established, the cumulative is displaced by the most recent, the most problematic. The latest information on anything and everything is collected, diffused, received, stored, and retrieved before anyone can discover whether the facts have meaning.[42]

This is my answer to those who fear that the librarian will
no longer have a function or a purpose. We are experts in the field
of information, but we must offer more. As Boorstin says:

> Of course we must be repositories of information. But some-
> how we must also remain places of refuge from the tidal waves
> of information--and misinformation. Our libraries must be
> conspicuously the treasuries of news that stays news.[43]

I believe that we must turn our attention to the acquisition of
knowledge. Who knows better than librarians how to sift through
the vast stores of information for the truth? Dr. Winfield said it
eighty years ago this way: "winnow out the chaff and get to the
real kernel of the subject." Yes, we must use all the technologies
and devices at hand to access our resources, but we cannot stop
with just the transfer of information.

In his book The House of Intellect, Jacques Barzun said "We
forget that every age has carried with it great loads of information,
most of it false or tautological, yet deemed indispensable at the time"
[44] We see examples of this every day. How often do we see a
student take a list of citations, convinced that she has found all
the information available? That fact that the article she chooses
to read comes from a mediocre journal or that she takes the first one
with a good-sounding title should give us cause for concern. How
often do we see a user select material from a questionable publisher
and reject material from a more reliable source?

Our experience in the field of literature and the knowledge
we have acquired concerning publishers, books, authors, journals,
databases, and other sources of information give us the responsibility
to make this experience available to our users. Years ago Loomis
stated that librarians should "be able to evaluate printed matter, be
familiar with authorities in various lines ... and the scope and value of
various periodicals." Certainly we can and do carry out the latter
two suggestions. Whether we are qualified to judge the content of
medical literature is a question we need to consider. Most of us
are neither chemists nor statisticians nor physicians, and the professionals in those diciplines may look askance at our boldness in
claiming this ability. If we expect to become experts, we will need
different training. Before we can say this is the "best" book or
the most accurate article or choose between two conflicting clinical
reports, we must have the knowledge to do it with authority as well
as have the confidence of our scientific colleagues. This issue will
not disappear. It may well become the next level of reference service, and as such will be the challenge of the future.

A friend of mine, in the hospital recovering from surgery,
asked her resident what he thought of Sir William Osler's writings
on diagnosis. His reply shocked her, for he said, "Oh, I never read
that old stuff in medical school. And anyway we have the CAT-scan
for diagnosis today."

This resident may have had loads of information, but he certainly did not have the knowledge of his discipline, medicine. The purpose of medical education is to give the student the "understanding of the accepted truths, the disputed problems, the rival schools and the methods now in favor."[45] This becomes his knowledge base.

A resident who could not be bothered to read Osler has not the foundation of knowledge on which to build in medicine. Osler said "Post-graduate study is a habit of Mind only to be acquired, as are other habits, in the slow repetition of the practice of looking at everything with an inquiring spirit."[46]

The report Physicians for the Twenty-first Century, prepared by the Panel on the General Professional Education of the Physician and College Preparation for Medicine of the Association of American Medical Colleges, gives clear warning to medical educators: students must become active, independent learners and problem solvers, not just passive recipients of information. Two additional recommendations from this report also have impact on our services--that scholarly endeavor requiring originality, research, and the ability to write should be employed in basic medical education and that the ability to learn independently should be evaluated.[47]

The signal to librarians is clear. We can assist in developing these areas of education for our students. There is more than one way to learn: we must continue to encourage the study of the history of medicine and the health professions: we must make available a variety of resources so that a student will not be content with the first piece of information available. We need to recognize the value of serendipity, of the excitement of discovery in seeking knowledge. There is no reward equal to learning that a student has "stumbled" upon an old book or journal and found unexpected wonders, or watching the awe on the face of one who holds a Vesalius or Hunter in his hands for the first time. More wondrous even, if the student comes to share it with you!

Dr. Harvey Cushing said at the dedication of the William H. Welch Medical Library in 1929 that the true function of a library is to "quicken the dormant book so that it may speak again; and with those who treat it lovingly and compassionately, its spirit enters eagerly into communion. To these a library becomes a laboratory for the crystallization of ideas perhaps long expressed, out of which process new ideas have their birth."[48]

We need to be as alert for our own learning as we are for our users. We may be so enamored of the technique that we forget the content. An incident which took place recently may serve to illustrate. The administrator of a medical center asked the librarian for biographical information about a scholar coming to visit. The librarian promptly turned to the computer and handed the administrator a list of publications. This librarian could not see beyond the machine.

Just as we want to ensure that our students and practitioners are
surrounded with the knowledge of the ages, have the opportunity
to learn in as many ways as there are individuals, and to develop
a basis for continuing their own growth throughout years of practice,
we as librarians must do the same.

It is said that with the computer we have the potential for instant distribution of all information to anyone, anytime. Ann Eastman, of the University Faculty Book Publishing Office at Virginia
Polytechnic Institute and State University, says "Surely intelligent
information scientists and other computer experts realize that if every
word written, each bit of scientific data processed, is made available, the wealth of dross would collapse the system." She asks good
questions: "How could we survive if even every book manuscript
were available? How could one find the books one wanted or needed
to read in all that chaos?" And further, "Why should library users
pay ... to maintain a system that includes so much ill-conceived and
ill-written work, work that doesn't deserve to be made public."[49]

How can we help the people we encounter in our libraries--the
students, the researchers, the physicians, nurses, scientists, the
lay public? How do we steer them through this "wealth of dross"
to the answer? Our knowledge of medical literature gives us the advantage. We know about publishing and publishers, we understand
the process of quality filtering of the medical information, we know
which journals are refereed and on what basis journals are selected
for Index Medicus. Every day we make judgments in the selection
of books, journals, media, and databases for our collections. When
we come to select and recommend publications or databases to our
users, this knowledge is invaluable. In this sense, we can become
a filter for the user.

With the advent of each new innovation in communication--the
radio, television, the computer, electronic learning--we have heard
that the death of the book is imminent. It has not happened, and
in fact, I think the printed word is stronger than ever. The book
or journal can be read and reread, wept over, marked with yellow
pen, carried about and enjoyed over lunch or in bed. I have not
heard of anyone taking a piece of microfilm to read in bed or weeping over the beauty of a computer program. And I believe that the
reference librarian, far from being phased out, is at but the beginning. We are the link between the individual and the world's store
of knowledge and/or information. We have skills and techniques to
access, sort, transfer and disseminate information. We also have the
knowledge to evaluate journals, to explore the vast array of resources
and to share this knowledge with our users. We have this unique
place in the educational process and we must not relinquish it to
others.

As my lecture draws to a close, I want to speak about wisdom.
If our literature infrequently discussed "knowledge" as opposed to

"information," it did not seem to discourse on "wisdom" at all. Perhaps because of our innate modesty, or perhaps it is that while wisdom appears in our lives, we have not consciously sought to cultivate it or write about it. That we have it, I am sure, for there are
wise people in our profession. But I must leave that for another
lecturer to discuss.

There is a story told in our family, handed down through
several generations. My ancestors came as pioneers in the 19th century, along with other immigrants, homesteading in the West. They
encountered incredible hardships, gruelling work, and stark poverty.
They ate what they could raise, for theirs was an almost cashless
society.

It was a period of deprivation, but the one thing they would
not let themselves and their fourteen children be deprived of was
an annual subscription to a magazine. It was their only release from
drudgery, the only touch of culture, and it was eagerly awaited each
month. On winter evenings it was read aloud to the family and after
it had been thoroughly covered and discussed, it was lent to various
neighbors. Nine or ten families read it, and when it finally was returned, it was often in tattered condition, but each page was carefully preserved for future enjoyment.

How far have we come from that time, little more than one
hundred years ago? From that simple way of sharing knowledge
we have developed the most sophisticated ways of making ideas and
facts "known."

We can build on the past, for we have the knowledge and wisdom of our librarian forerunners. Our foundation is sound. With
all our resources and our abilities we can, perhaps, change the
designation "Keeper of the Printed Book" to "Keeper of Knowledge"
and pursue the promise of both fruit and light.

References

1. Pigou, A.C. The economics of welfare. 2d ed. London: Macmillan, 1924:3-4.
2. Machlup, F. Knowledge and knowledge production. In: Knowledge: its creation, distribution, and economic significance. Vol.
   1. Princeton, N.J.: Princeton University Press, 1980:11.
3. Gilman, D.C. Higher education in the United States; address
   of the president of the International Congress on Higher Education, held in connection with the Columbian Exposition, Chicago,
   1893. In: University problems in the United States. New
   York: Century, 1898:294-7.
4. Martin, L.E. Excellence and the university library. In: The
   fourteenth and fifteenth annual alumni-in-residence programs.
   Ann Arbor, Mich.: School of Library Science, University of
   Michigan, 1983?:11-2.

5. Green, S.S. Personal relations between librarians and readers.
    Am Libr J 1876 Nov. 30:1:79.
6. Robinson, O.H. Librarians and readers. Am Libr J 1876 Nov.
    30;1:123-4.
7. Hayes, C.D. The history of the University of Rochester Li-
    braries, 120 years. U Rochester Libr. Bull 1970 Spring;25:73.
8. Crunden, F.M. Report on aids and guides, August, '83 to
    June, '85. Libr J 1886 Aug-Sep;11:310.
9. Circular of information. 1884, Columbia College Library and
    School of Library Economy. Reprinted in: School of Library
    Economy, Columbia College, 1887-1889. New York: School of
    Library Service, Columbia University, 1937;31-2.
10. Columbia College Library. Second and third annual reports of
    the chief librarian, June 30, 1886:39.
11. Brownne, J.S. A few hints on medical library administration.
    Med Libr Hist J 1903 Jan;1:33.
12. Winfield, J.M. The medical library as a factor in medical edu-
    cation. Med Libr Hist J 1904 July;2:184.
13. Osler, W. Discussion of Winfield's remarks. Med Libr Hist J
    1904 July; 2:185.
14. Jacobi, A. Discussion of Winfield's remarks. Med Libr Hist J
    1904 July; 2:186.
15. Wolfstein, D.I. Value of a medical library to the community,
    Med Libr Hist J 1905 July;3:204-5.
16. Osler, W. The science of librarianship. Bull Med Libr Assoc
    1917 Jan;7:70,73.
17. Smith, L.E. A suggestion to the medical librarians. Bull Med
    Libr Assoc 1919 Oct;9:31.
18. Ibid.
19. Place, F., Jr. First steps in medical library work. Bull Med
    Libr Assoc 1921 Jan;10:46-7.
20. Brinton, M. Medical librarianship; some of its present day
    problems. Bull Med Libr Assoc 1924 July;14:37.
21. Gilchrist, D.B. A modern medical school library. JAMA 1924
    April 19;82:1289.
22. Ibid.
23. Loomis, M.M. Reference service. Bull Med Libr Assoc 1925
    Oct;15:34.
24. Ballard, J.F. Information, reference and bibliographic service.
    Bull Med Libr Assoc 1927 July;17:19-20, 26-7.
25. Wickes, F.L. Library reference service. Bull Med Libr Assoc
    1934 Jan;22:138.
26. Keys, T.E. Newer developments in medical reference work.
    Bull Ned Libr Assoc 1938 May;26:218-21.
27. Cunningham, E.R. Reference work, including an annotated
    list of reference books. In: Doe J, ed. A handbook of medical
    library practice. Chicago: American Library Association, 1943:
    371-544.
28. Brodman, E. Choosing physiology journals. Bull Med Libr
    Assoc 1944 Oct;32:479-83.

29. Gross, P.L.K., Gross E.M. College libraries and chemical edu-
    cation. Science 1927 Oct 28;66:385-9.
30. Gregory, A. An evaluation of medical periodicals. Bull Med
    Libr Assoc 1937 Feb;25:172-88.
31. Brodman, E. Medical librarianship, a mid-century survey: a
    symposium. Bull Med Libr Assoc 1957 Oct;45:480-5.
32. Billings, J.S. Methods of research in medical literature. Trans
    Assoc Am Phys 1887;2:64.
33. Myers, G.W. Dusting the library. Med Libr Hist J 1903 Apr;1:
    135-6.
34. Med Libr Hist J 1906;4:cover.
35. The National Library of Medicine index mechanization project.
    Bull Med Libr Assoc 1961 Jan;49 (part 2):1-96.
36. Pizer, I.H. Looking backward, 1984-1959: twnety-five years
    of library automation--a personal view. Bull Med Libr Assoc
    1984 Oct;72:335-48.
37. de Solla Price, D.J. Little science, big science. New York:
    Columbia University Press, 1963:8-19.
38. Durack, D.T. The weight of medical knowledge. N Engl J.
    Med 1978 Apr 6;298:773-5.
39. Bush, V. As we may think. Atlantic Monthly 1945 July;176:
    101-8.
40. Matheson, N.W., Cooper, J.A.D. Academic information in the
    academic health sciences center: roles for the library in infor-
    mation management. J Med Educ 1982 Oct;57(10, pt. 2):1-93.
41. Cronin, B. The transition years: new initiatives in the educa-
    tion of professional information workers. Aslib Occasional Pub-
    lication No. 29. London: Aslib, 1983:24.
42. Boorstin, D.J. Gresham's law: knowledge or information.
    AB Bookman's Weekly 1982 Feb. 22; 69:1382.
43. Ibid., p. 1386.
44. Barzun, J. The house of intellect. New York: Harper, 1959:
    11.
45. Ibid., p. 12.
46. Osler, W. Remarks on the medical library in post-graduate
    work. Br Med J 1909 Oct 2;2:926.
47. Physicians for the twenty-first century; the GPEP report.
    Report of the Panel on the General Professional Education of
    the Physician and College Preparation for Medicine. Washington,
    D.C.: Association of American Medical Colleges, 1984:7-13.
48. Cushing, H. The binding influence of a library on a subdivid-
    ing profession. Science 1929 Nov 22;70:486.
49. Eastman, A.H. Books, publishing, libraries in the information
    age. Libr Trends 1984 Fall;3:123.

A HERITAGE DISMISSED:
LIBRARIANS IN SEARCH OF THEIR PLACE
IN AMERICAN POPULAR CULTURE, 1876-1950*

Rosalee McReynolds

"Should librarians be glamour girls?" That was the question a librarian posed to a popular journal of her trade in 1953.[1] She
wasn't being facetious and hinted at an anxiety that had existed
within the profession since the 19th century. Even Melvil Dewey
expressed concern with image when he declared in LJ's maiden issue
that the days of the librarian as a mouser in musty books were past.
Had he put the matter to rest then and there, his hope that the new
American librarian would be "in the highest sense a teacher" might
have been realized.[2] But the "image problem" proved to have a
life of its own, often obsessing librarians to the point that they
could not clearly separate the importance of their personal mien from
that of their professional achievements.

Preposterous Caricatures

Long before the middle-aged spinster came to symbolize their
image, librarians were sensitive to the opinions of others. It was
to literature that they most often turned to find portraits of themselves and they were usually unhappy with what they found. As
early as 1909, a librarian used the word "stereotype" in objecting
to the portrayal of her profession in fiction. She complained that
librarians were depicted in extremes, either as "old fogy bookworms"
or as unreasonably efficient and attractive young people. "Both
types must go down," she insisted, "before the downtrodden, average, ordinary, human librarian can have a fair change."[3]

Another turn-of-the-century librarian, Edmund Lester Pearson,
agreed that librarians had a legitimate quarrel with writers of fiction.

*Reprinted by permission of the author and publisher from Library
Journal 110:18 (November 1, 1985) 25-31. Published by R.R. Bowker,
a division of Reed Publishing, U.S.A.; copyright © 1985 by Reed Publishing, U.S.A., a division of Reed Holdings, Inc.

In his column for the <u>Boston Evening Transcript</u> he suggested that novelists took perverse delight in "making us buy, catalog, and issue books containing the most preposterous caricatures of our calling and of ourselves."[4] Such caricatures included a closet alcoholic, a chief librarian with moth-eaten whiskers, and a "fluffy girl who told you when you asked her for the <u>Phaedo</u> that it was advertised but not published yet!"[5] Inevitably, lamented Pearson, these librarians were outwitted by more astute characters in the novels, even small boys.

Real life relations with the public were equally troubling, especially in public libraries where the population served was often heterogeneous and unpredictable. It was not only the ill-disciplined school child or the laboring poor by whom librarians were frustrated but the educated, middle-class citizen as well. The library assistant, who was usually a female, by the turn of the century was reminded that she had to endure with grace the complaints of the most unreasonable patron. The ideal assistant was expected to emanate qualities of kindness, dignity, and selflessness. At the same time, she was told not to have high expectations of her patrons, yet to restrain any impulse to second-guess their needs.[6] The pressure to attain this ideal was considerable for it was believed that the women who served the public would establish a library's reputation, and subsequently, the image of the entire profession.[7] In very little time, then, the image problem became the women's problem.

The reputation that early library leaders wanted to establish was as noble--and vague--as the definition of the ideal assistant. Bettering humanity through books was a utopian aim couched in the 19th-century notion that life was progression to an ever-improving state. By the end of World War I this idea had been largely rejected, and librarians realized that their power to reform through uplifting literature was limited. As the primary role of the public library shifted from education to recreation, a different, more up-to-date image was required for librarians.

The popular concept of women during the Twenties is, of course, that of the flapper: uninhibited, vivacious, and living life at breakneck speed. It may not have been entirely realistic, but it was appealing and perpetuated through the popular media, particularly film. Movies affected the self-image and personal goals of women everywhere. However rigid the Victorian ideal of womanhood may have been, its advocates never possessed this powerful medium which demanded conformity to a rather narrow definition of beauty and style.

Despite some real and some perceived changes in the lives of the American woman, library journals during the 1920s contained little about her, and no subject heading devoted to her information needs is to be found in the 1921-32 volume of Library Literature.[8] This is at least mildly remarkable given the high proportion of public library patrons, not to mention librarians, who were women, but the omission may actually have had some positive connotations. It may imply that female librarians during this period felt confident in the quality of service they provided to women patrons and possessed a healthy indifference for prevailing models of femininity.

Surgeons of the Mind

This is less true of their male counterparts. For the same period, Library Literature contains more than 60 citations under the headings "Businessman and the Library" and "Professional Man and the Library." Such articles, ostensibly about the contribution that libraries could make to various professions, had a way of descending into comparisons between librarianship and the other fields being discussed. Thus, the librarian became the "surgeon of the mind" and the library an allegory for a bank or a detective agency.[9]

These comparisons were often made by male librarians who seemed particularly anxious to sublimate the feminine side of librarianship and to stress its similarities to male-dominated professions. But try though they might, they simply could not shake their image, or their own belief in their image, as mousy people who "move gently ... (and) don't slam doors."[10]

Such meekness seemed like the direct antithesis of the ambitious businessman who represented the masculine ideal of the decade. He

may have been the butt of the literati but he was the hero of a generation riding an exhilarating, if false, wave of prosperity. Some
librarians were contemptuous of entrepreneurs, feeling themselves
superior to the Babbits, but understood that their budgets lay in
the hands of the Rotarians and Elks who were often library trustees. [11]

Therefore, the library had to be sold to the community as
"Fordishly efficient" and the head librarian, so often a male, as a
businessman in his own right. [12] This impression and its attendant
rewards could never be realized so long as male librarians were as-
cribed passive feminine traits. Because the image of the profession
was so strongly tied to the women who dominated it, the situation
seemed irreversible since the last thing anyone expected or wanted
was for females to display masculine characteristics like aggression
or ambition.

Hopes of early library leaders like Melvil Dewey and Justin
Winsor that women would provide the new science of library economy
with an equally new and positive image were largely unfulfilled, or
at least unshared, by the 1920s. It was only a matter of time before tension between the sexes became an issue. Prospects of this
conflict may be found in an essay by Charles Compton, director of
the St. Louis Public Library, in the October 1927 South Atlantic
Quarterly:

> This is addressed to all writers of modern fiction. Why can
> you not occasionally make use of a librarian for a heroine? ...
> A few modern writers have taken librarians as main or minor
> characters, but they have usually failed in depicting them
> as typical librarians. [13]

On the surface, it seemed like a mere echo of earlier complaints
when he referred to specific literary pieces with librarian-heroines
and explained why these characters were not like their real life
counterparts. This apparently noble gesture had negative under-
tones, however, for Compton quickly revealed that his own vision of
the typical female librarian was quite unflattering:

> Librarians are rank individualists, optimists in practice though
> most of them would not admit that they are; true Simians,
> bookish, if only superficially. Fifty percent have a sense
> of humor (my estimate), are enthusiastic in their work,
> tolerant of ideas but not of people, especially not of other
> librarians, generally not sentimental, sufficiently wicked to
> be interesting. [14]

It is worth stopping for a moment to look at the literature that
Compton and other librarians found so untrue and so unbeautiful.
Between 1886 and 1930 at least 18 novels, plays, or short stories
were produced by American writers in which librarians were major

or minor characters. The authors represent a spectrum of talent
and notoriety from Henry James and Edith Wharton to those now forgotten women who felt they had to disguise their identities under
noms de plume. What emerges from this collection is not a composite
stereotype of a spinster librarian but the absence of one (an annotated bibliography of these works appears in the   appendix).

Fictional Librarians

Although most of the fictional librarians are women they are
a varied lot. The majority are not middle-aged but range instead
between late adolescence and the verge of retirement. Their marital
status includes never-married, married, widowed, and divorced.
Every imaginable temperament is represented from the independent
Carol Kennicott of Sinclair Lewis' Main Street (1920) to the melancholy
and rather dim Charity Royall of Edith Wharton's Summer (1917) to
the exhuberant young cataloger in Henry James's The Bostonians
(1886).

Far fewer male librarians are depicted and they have considerably less dimension. In the Golden Fleece (1903) by David Graham
Phillips the chief librarian is described as a busybody and a gossip-
monger with a fat, pasty face. In Silas Weir Mitchell's mystery,
The Mind Reader (1920), a young medical assistant goes to work in
a library for the purpose of solving crimes. The real librarian,
his supervisor, is a fussy, bespectacled man of indeterminate age.
Unattractive characters, perhaps, but hardly stock literary devices
and hardly cause for alarm.

There may be elements of truth in stereotypes but that of the
librarian is puzzling. Until the 1930s it seems that librarians believed
in it more deeply than the authors who were accused of creating it.
The solution to this puzzle will not be found in the popular literature.
If it is to be found anywhere it is within the profession itself and
within social attitudes held about, and by women.

By the end of the Twenties, American male librarians clearly
felt ambivalent about being members of a female-dominated profession,
but a visiting Englishman (in whose country the mobility of women
librarians had been consciously limited) got straight to the point:
"I do think it regrettable that the profession in America is so largely
in the hands of the 'gentler sex,'" he wrote to the editor of Wilson
Library Bulletin in 1933, "to my mind, this is incorrigible."[15]

Intrigued, the editor published the letter and asked his readership to respond on the theme "Should the Preponderance of Women
in the American Library Profession Be Considered an Evil?" A nerve
had been struck. There followed a chorus of agreement from male
American librarians who, like the Englishman, expressed the belief
that innate feminine traits immediately disqualified women from per-

"How stiffly Miss Lucretia sat in her chair."

L ucretia Penniman, the librarian in popular novelist Winston Churchill's **Coniston** (Macmillan, 1906) as depicted for the book by artist Florence Scovell Shinn, was "one of the first to sound the clarion call for the intellectual independence of American women"

forming at a superior level. The intellectual pursuits of women are usually frivolous, it was contended, certainly not up to the needs of a scholarly male patron. Worst of all was the sentimentality with which women had infused the image of librarianship.[16] In the end, suggested one letter writer, this emotional bent made women more susceptible to "Cupid's bow" and hence to marriage which took them out of the profession. This, he mused, was the greatest ally of male librarians as they "set forth to battle the Amazons."[17]

A Polite Battle of the Sexes

Throughout the decade a polite but genuine battle of the sexes was fought on the pages of the profession's journals. Not all men were so amused by the power of Cupid's bow, feeling that women had a tendency to regard librarianship as a stopgap to marriage. Such an attitude could only contribute to the impression that librarianship

was not a serious, or to paraphrase another Englishman, virile occupation.[18]   Advocates of the masculination of librarianship saw only
one course of action: recruit more men through promises of rapid
promotion and the best salaries.

Women librarians responded briskly and knew that they had
to take positive action on their behalf, but there was no consensus
on what form it should take.   Radical solutions such as unionization
were shunned by the majority.   One librarian summed up the problem
when she said that women were reluctant to protest for fear of being
labeled feminist.   Without a doubt, they did not wish to appear un-
womanly or freakish.[19]

Just one thing effectively joined the radical, moderate, and
conservative librarians of the Thirties.   This was the belief that
they were old-fashioned and out of step with the times.   Where the
radicals felt that this impeded group action, moderates and conservatives worried about the impression it gave outsiders of the profession
and of librarians as people.

A Heritage Dismissed

In this there was unity: if librarians were to acquire a positive image and a promising future they had to make a clean break
with the past.[20]   It was probably one of the most misbegotten ideas
to ever beset the profession and possibly the beginning of an internal
prejudice against older women.   In their effort to leave behind the
persona of a genteel and unwordly lady, librarians rejected an important part of the their own history.

Librarians of the Thirties began to describe their predecessors
as inadequately educated women who went into librarianship as a
"solace for a broken heart or thwarted desires ... " and those who
"could be kept immaculate from contact with the world."[21]   This
assessment may have described some who made their way into the profession in the late 19th and early 20th centuries, but it dismissed
a vital heritage with the same wand.

When Melvil Dewey established his school of library economy
at Columbia College in 1887, 17 women enrolled, much to the consterna-
tion of the administration at the all-male institution.   These women
may have been of genteel background but their behavior was hardly
conventional.   The very idea of them attempting a course of study
at a college which could not admit them because of their sex should
be enough to make the most militant feminist take notice.   They also
seem to have done an admirable job of hiding their emotions for one
finds no traces of broken hearts scattered about the pages of the
early volumes of library journals.

During his directorship of the Denver Public Library in the

1890s, John Cotton Dana also gathered about him a staff of young
female assistants who looked to him for guidance in the pursuit of
their new profession. It may then be said that these women, like
those associated with Dewey, were indeed typically Victorian, sub-
limating their own judgment to rely on that of a male figure. However, like the Columbia group, these women demonstrated the ability
to circumvent social codes and to even poke fun at them.

In Dana's biography there is related an incident when, on a
trip, he sent his staff a picture of a female in trousers which he
labeled "latest librarian uniforms in the East." The biographer continues:

> In the words of a staff member, "This was in the Nineties
> when generally speaking, a lady's anatomy was shadowy....
> The next week when the women staff members met at the
> Dana home for book reviews, they remained upstairs so long
> that Mr. Dana lost patience. When they appeared, Dana
> gasped ... all were in loosely made trousers, some of which
> were tied at the ankles with red bows. Gales of laughter
> followed, after which came the book reviews."[22]

Adventurous and New

Even apart from the more celebrated women who followed Dewey
and Dana, it should not have been forgotten that middle-class women
entering librarianship in the late 19th century were doing something
new and adventurous. They were also anything but shy about discussing sex discrimination. The early volumes of LJ and Public Libraries contain ample protest over unequal working conditions and
salary differentials.[23] The failure to sufficiently appreciate this
legacy may have contributed to the librarians' furstration in establishing a positive identity, not just for outsiders but for themselves.
If nothing else, it betrayed librarians' ignorance of, or disinterest
in, their own past.

Eroding faith in the women of the profession made Depression
era librarians, male and female, more sensitive than ever to their
public image, a sensitivity accentuated by moving pictures. Evidence
that librarians were conscious of the cinema and of movie stars emerges in this period. Until then, the only interest that they publicly
demonstrated in film was in the effect that it would have upon reading habits and its possible use as an educational medium.[24] Eventually, they began to complain about the way they were depicted in
the cinema just as they had complained about their image in literature. It was only a matter of time before they began to compare
themselves to what they saw on the screen.

In response to yet another article lamenting the image of the
profession in fiction,[25] a librarian stated that her colleagues ought
to just accept their meager characterizations since it seemed that

Carol Kennicott, the independent, even revolutionary librarian in Sinclair Lewis's **Main Street**, captured in "The Perfectionist," a drawing by artist Grant Wood to illustrate a special, limited edition of the book published by the Limited Editions Club in 1937

they would never be depicted in even a minor film role.[26] She was mistaken--a film version of Main Street was made in 1923--and soon would be disproven again, for in 1937 Variety reviewed a film called Navy Blues which contained a scenario that has become a standing joke in American folklore: a sailor meets a drab librarian and charms her into taking off her glasses and letting down her hair, thus revealing the beauty that lies beneath.

A librarian who had seen the movie dashed off an angry letter to the editor of Wilson Library Bulletin and called upon her profession to "Stop worrying about increases in salary, better working conditions, and liberalism and devote all our energies to divorcing by legislation, if necessary, the word 'mousy' from librarians."[27]

It was rather ironic that this call to arms should come more than half a century after Dewey had written the obituary of the mouser in musty books. Even more ironic is that in the 1930s, when librarians wanted to be viewed as young moderns, the negative stereotype became more entrenched than ever before. If anything, the popular portrayal of female librarians lost the breadth it previously had.[28]

Sentiment grew that librarians shouldn't expect to find themselves depicted in good, certainly not vivacious, roles. Poet Stanley Kunitz, editor of Wilson Library Bulletin during the Thirties and recipient of a considerable amount of mail on the subject of the librarian image, suggested that the profession simply lacked drama.[29] An anonymous contributor wrote in agreement with Kunitz, pointing out that there was nothing that librarians did that would make any difference in a life- and-death situation, that as people they were too cautious, reluctant to "play really beautifully slashing tennis," or throw dishes.[30] Resignation to drabness, for some, had bitter recriminations:

> What's the matter with us! ... We're just too genteel to live--that's all. Our people generally go into library work "because it's such nice lady-like work" (where did they get that idea!)--and by golly--they'll keep it lady-like or die in the attempt.... We're wishy-washy, namby-pamby, scared of our lives, scared of our Boards, scared of our shadows-- poor, weak sisters.

The letters and articles in a handful of library journals may not present a true picture of the entire profession,[32] but if they are any indicator at all, librarians by the late Thirties were demoralized, looking to outside models not only for clues of how to look and act, but how to actually "be." Celebrities seemed to have meaningful lives. Personality tests held clues to the mystery of whether or not librarians were "real" people.[33]

The observations of nonlibrarians, including the raving of obvious malcontents, were often published in library journals.[34] Even the most vicious attacks on the profession were taken to heart by those librarians who believed that everybody except themselves possessed an innate sense of what it was to be human and to live a full life. It was hardly surprising, then, that in 1942 a librarian named two books as required reading for her colleagues: Joan Bennett's How to Be Attractive and Harry Emerson Fosdick's On Being a Real Person.[35]

Recruiting the Glamorous

The fighting spirit exhibited by at least some librarians during the Thirties had all but evaporated by the war years. Actually, it was the issues that had changed. No longer was it important if women were capable administrators. The major question of the Forties was whether or not librarians were or ever could be glamorous. The most extreme theorists had it that librarians would receive higher

budgets and salaries if they could erase the image of the love-starved
spinster.[36] "Let's put it this way," said one promulgator of this
idea, "wall eyes, buck teeth, a lumpy bust, and a voice out of a
nutmeg grinder should have no more place on a library staff than
in a threatrical cast."[37]

Luring attractive young women into the profession was regarded
as no less valuable than the recruitment of men of any age or description. It was assumed, self-defeatingly, that any pretty female
worth her mettle would eventually want to get married and give up
her career. To interest this element an emphasis was placed on the

The "library cover girl" on the cover of the
September 1943 issue of **Mademoiselle**. The
article inside "talked of
the fun of working in
the modern library,
not to be confused
with the old-fashioned
library 'staffed with re-
jects from **Godey's La-
dy's Book**'"

social side of librarianship, opportunities to meet interesting people,
including eligible bachelors. Libraries on or near army bases were
considered especially good in the latter respect. It was even pointed
out, a mere two years after the bombing of Pearl Harbor, that an
assignment in a library in the Hawaiian Islands was usually synony-
mous with a marriage proposal.[38]

There can be little doubt that librarians of the Forties were affected by images of women projected in the popular culture, particularly those purveyed by Hollywood. On first consideration, movie heroines of the Thirties and Forties seem like grand role models. Certainly, this was the era of women in film and they were often portrayed as being devoted to their work.

As strong as these characters may have been, though, it was common for a movie plot to end with the heroine deserting her job for a man, the implication being that love and marriage were true measures of success for a woman. The further implication was that only failure in love would prompt a woman to pursue a career. Along with this ambivalent working woman, Hollywood in the Forties gave America the pinup, the unembarrassed celebration of sexuality and youth.

For those who believed that good looks meant more than intellect, it seemed like nothing short of a coup when an attractive young woman appeared on the cover of the September 1943 Mademoiselle under the guise of a "reader's adviser." In an accompanying article the library cover girl, as she was called by Wilson Library Bulletin, talked of the fun of working in the modern library, which was not to be confused with the old-fashioned library "staffed with rejects from Godey's Lady's Book."[39]

Reveling in the belief that librarianship was at last on its way to acquiring a glamorous image, another librarian declared that the Mademoiselle article had done more for the morale of young librarians than a carload of professional papers.[40]

There were other hopeful signs for the youth and beauty squad. In the 1945 movie Wonder Man, Virginia Mayo played a voluptuous, blond librarian without glasses. Despite her addition of spectacles, no less delight was expressed over the phenomenon of Greer Garson portraying an attractive librarian in a movie with Clark Gable as the lead (Adventure, 1945). As if this weren't enough, Helen Hayes appeared in a Broadway play, Happy Birthday (1946), as a librarian who gets her man despite her dipsomania and lapses into the delusion that she is Betty Grable. It still seemed like sufficient cause for celebration: the death of brains, breeding and barrenness; the birth of gams, glamour, and Gable.[41]

Yet, for every apparent triumph there seemed to be a corresponding defeat. There were those brief moments in It's a Wonderful Life (1947) when Donna Reed, wearing a mannish suit, closes up the library and heads for a lonely night at home. There was the aged librarian in Human Comedy (1943) and the authoritarian who meted out novels to the young heroine in A Tree Grows in Brooklyn (1945). Then, too, there were the editorial assaults of casual observers, often bitterly critical: housewife, sociologist, lawyer, professor, ex-librarian, businessman, "anonymous." No one seemed unqualified to generalize about librarians in the pages of the profession's own journals.[42]

Of course, it wasn't just any garden variety librarian who was the object of scorn. It was the "Head Harpy," the old maids who "lived no lives"; in short, the invective was directed at the single older woman. Between librarians themselves and their "friends," she became a veritable punching bag. When she wasn't being lambasted, she was being patronized as a great American tradition whose time had come and hopefully gone.[43] She was always spoken of symbolically. It was of little concern that this prejudice against "her" extended to real women--those who had acquired the years of experience to qualify them for responsible positions. Inevitably, this worked against the aspirations of all women entering librarianship.

There is also the discomfiting thought that concern with their personal image distracted librarians from timely events or genuinely professional concerns. At the height of the World War II, Wilson Library Bulletin published an anonymous article suggesting that all female librarians be removed from public service positions after they turned 40.[44]

In a tone wavering between breezy and deadly serious, the writer suggested that only a flock of pretty faces would ever gain the library profession its desperately needed respect. So many letters, pro and con, were received by the journal in response to this article that they had to be published over a period of months.

It cannot be mere conjecture that this intense image consciousness had a certain deadening effect on the profession. "This really must be a millennium or something," wrote a librarian in 1951 on the absence of lively discussion in library journals, "I recall only two real controversies in recent years. One had to do with the glamour or lack of it in our feminine colleagues. Another was

A deline De Walt Reynolds, then 82 years old, played the librarian in the MGM movie version of The Human Comedy. This still photo was used to illustrate how librarians were "negatively" portrayed as older women in "Sweetiepies for Sourpusses" by Gracie Boldstroke [pseud.] in the December 1943 Wilson Library Bulletin

concerned with the desirability or otherwise of men in the profession."[45]

"Something Distasteful ... "

In a sense, 1951 was a millennium for librarianship. For the next 20 years the number of men entering the field soared; correspondingly, the number of women in library administration, weak as it already was, declined significantly during the Fifties and Sixties.[46] It was a trend that went largely unremarked until the women's movement in the Seventies. The realization that women had so little control of the library profession resulted in a great deal of anger, but a shortage of historical data made explanations for the situation difficult to produce.

The easiest and most common assumption was that women were simply victims of sex discrimination, and this is undoubtedly the major reason that women librarians still do not hold more administrative positions. Yet, among those insidious secondary causes, there still lingers librarians' heightened sensitivity to their public image. In the late-19th and early-20th centuries, this manifested itself in an over eagerness not just to serve, but to please.

By the mid-1930s, the most significant product of this sensitivity was chagrin over the stereotype of the middle-aged spinster. In their crusade to disavow this image, librarians, male and female, betrayed a belief that there was something distasteful about women growing old, being plain, never marrying. It may not have been a concept that librarians invented, but the zeal with which they embraced it surely hindered the profession and the women in it.

References

1. Roantree, Dorothy, "Should Librarians Be Glamour Girls," Wilson Library Bulletin, March 1953, p. 521.
2. Dewey, Melvil, "The Profession," Library Journal, September 1876, p. 6.
3. Helen, Rex Keller, "The Old-Fashioned Virtues Versus the Ideal Librarian," Library Journal, July 1909, p. 295.
4. Pearson, Edmund Lester, "The Library in Fiction," reprinted in the Library and the Librarian, Woodstock, Vt.: The Elm Tree Pr., 1910, p. 3.
5. Ibid.
6. Ibid.
7. Pearson, Edmund Lester, Library Journal, May 1907, p. 504.
8. Library Literature, 1921-32, American Library Assn., 1934.
9. Bostwick, Arthur, "The Librarian, the Surgeon of the Mind," Library Journal, March 1, 1925, p. 217-219; Drury, Francis K.W., "The Library as a Detective Agency," Public Libraries, April 1922, p. 205-209.

10. Kaiser, John Boynton, "As Others See Us," Library Journal,
     February 15, 1921, p. 169; "The Unaggressive Librarian,"
     Library Journal, March 15, 1925, p. 262-263; Phelps, William
     Lyon, "Extremely Happy People," Scribner's, July 1923, reprinted
     in Library Journal, August 1921, p. 668. In her book, Stereo-
     type and Status (Greenwood, 1983) Pauline Wilson examined 77
     articles written between 1920 and 1975 by librarians about their
     image. She found that male librarians produced far more of
     these articles than was proportionate to their numbers and this
     was certainly true in the Twenties (p. 20).
11. Thomson, O.R. Howard, "Hold Your Head Up," Public Libraries,
     July 1923, p. 355-357.
12. Thompson, C. Seymour, "Librarianship--A Profession or a
     Business?" Library Journal, December 15, 1922, p. 1063-66.
13. Compton, Charles H., "The Librarian and the Novelist," The
     South Atlantic Quarterly, October 1927, p. 392-403.
14. Ibid., p. 392.
15. Sanders, S.H., letter in "Problems: A Monthly Department of
     Discussion," Wilson Library Bulletin, December 1933, p. 230-
     231.
16. "Problems: A Monthly Department of Discussion," Wilson Library
     Bulletin, March 1934, p. 403-407, 409.
17. Borden, Arnold K., "Should the Preponderance of Women in
     Librarianship Be Considered an Evil?" Wilson Library Bulletin,
     March 1934, p. 403-404.
18. Wellard, James H., "Old Problems and Young Men in English
     Librarianship," Wilson Library Bulletin, February 1934, p. 346-
     347, 371.
19. Tyler, Alice S., "In Reply to the Weaker Sex," Library Journal,
     April 15, 1938, p. 294; Daniels, Marietta, "In Reply to the
     Weaker Sex," Library Journal, April 15, 1938, p. 296.
20. Tyler, op. cit., p. 294; Hyatt, Ruth, reply to "Should the
     Preponderance of Women in the American Library Profession Be
     Considered an Evil?" Wilson Library Bulletin, March 1934, p.
     407.
21. Coleman, Margaret, "Are Librarians People?" Wilson Library
     Bulletin, December 1933, p. 235-236.
22. Hadley, Chalmers, John Cotton Dana: A Sketch. American
     Library Assn., 1943, p. 29.
23. See for example: M.E. Sargeant, "Women's Position in Library
     Service," Library Journal, August 1892, p. 92-94; Annon.,
     "The Case of the Desk Assistant," Library Journal, October
     1902, p. 876-878; "The Desk Assistant: An Imaginary Conver-
     sation," Library Journal, May 1902, p. 251-253; Mary McMillan,
     "Some Causes of Ill Health Among Library Workers," Public Li-
     braries, November 1903, p. 412-414; M.S.C. Fairchild, "Women
     in American Libraries," Library Journal, December 1904, p.
     157-162.
24. Library Literature, 1921-32. American Library Assn., 1934.
25. Danton, J.P., "Unhonored and Unsung," Wilson Library Bulletin,
     May-June 1934, p. 523-525.

26. Craigie, Anna Louise, "No Movie of Our Own," Wilson Library Bulletin, November 1934, p. 35.
27. Block, Maxine, "Arise and Shine!" Wilson Library Bulletin, May 1937, p. 626.
28. For more recent depictions of librarians in popular culture, see Neal Edgar, "The Image of Librarianship in the Media" in A Century of Service, edited by Sidney L. Jackson et al. American Library Assn., 1976, p. 303-320.
29. Kunitz, Stanley J., "The Roving Eye," Wilson Library Bulletin, May-June 1934, p. 520.
30. Anon., "The Roving Eye," Wilson Library Bulletin, September 1934, p. 30.
31. Hugentugler, Mary T., "The Roving Eye," Wilson Library Bulletin, April 1937, p. 544.
32. Pauline Wilson found that most of the 77 articles on the librarian stereotype that she examined were concentrated in a few, albeit major, library journals, particularly Wilson Library Bulletin and LJ, Wilson, op. cit., p. 17. Research conducted for this article led to the same conclusion.
33. "Are Librarians People?" Wilson Library Bulletin, December 1936, p. 248-252.
34. Examples from the 1930s include, "As Others See Us from Coast to Coast," ALA Bulletin, February 1937, p. 131; Sue English, "Confessions of a Timid Soul," Wilson Library Bulletin, May 1935, p. 506; Anon., "Librarians," Wilson Library Bulletin, September 1933, p. 60; Jane D. Wise, "What's Wrong with Librarians," Wilson Library Bulletin, December 1939, p. 304-305.
35. Eckart, Dorothy, "Con't Librarians Be Human Beings," Illinois Libraries, January 1944, p. 63-64.
36. Boldstroke, Gracie [pseud.], "Sweeties for Sourpusses," Wilson Library Bulletin, December 1943, p. 312.
37. Ibid., p. 313.
38. Warren, Althea H., "Vocation Without Regrets," Wilson Library Bulletin, September 1943, p. 25-27.
39. Wilson Library Bulletin, September 1943, p. 75; Charles, Margaret Howser, "Passing the Book," Mademoiselle, September 1943, reprinted in Illinois Libraries, December 1943, p. 373-377.
40. Schunk, Russell J., "Utopian--Maybe!" Library Journal, December 15, 1943, p. 1026.
41. Rothman, Mary Yust, "There's Figures in Those Dewey Decimals," Wilson Library Bulletin, December 1946, p. 296, 298. The alliterations are Rothman's.
42. See, for example, Irving Dilliard, "The Kind of Librarian I Would Like for My Town," Wilson Library Bulletin, May 1941, p. 724-725; Nina Hayes, "Highbrow Hokum," Wilson Library Bulletin, March 1945, p. 477, 481; Anon., "Why I Don't Like Libraries," ALA Bulletin, June 1943, p. 184-185; William H. Form, "Popular Images of Librarians," Library Journal, June 15, 1946, p. 851-855; S.N. Schuman, "What's Wrong with Libraries," Library Journal, May 1, 1946, p. 649-651.

43. See, for example, Virginia Himebaugh, "Miss Beasel and the
    Sank-Choo-Ary," Wilson Library Bulletin, November 1950, p.
    227-232; Josephine Austin, "Miss Cynthia's Last Night," Wilson
    Library Bulletin, November 1945, p. 221-223.
44. Boldstroke, Op. cit., p. 313.
45. Mackenzie, Armine, "The Soft Answer," California Librarian,
    June 1951, p. 195.
46. Schiller, Anita, "Aware: Report on Women in Librarianship,"
    American Libraries, December 1971, p. 1215-16.

Appendix: Librarians in Popular Literature, 1889-1930

Biggers, Earl Derr. The Black Camel. Bobbs, 1928. In this
    Charlie Chan mystery, a librarian is described as a bright young
    woman. (Greer)

Burr, Anna Robeson. The Jessop Bequest. Houghton, 1907. The
    librarian is a harried man, assisted in his work by a young boy
    and a pretty, scatterbrained girl. (Pearson)

Canfield, Dorothy [pseud. of Dorothea Fisher], "Hillsboro's Good
    Luck," Atlantic Monthly, July 1908, p. 131-139. An enthusiastic
    librarian brings culture to a small town. The library burns down
    and the librarian marries a local. (Keller)

Churchill, Winston. Coniston. Macmillan, 1906. The librarian in
    this book is Lucretia Penniman, "One of the first to sound the
    clarion note for the intellectual independence of American women."
    (Greer)

Daskam, Josephine Dodge [psued. of Josephine Dodge (Daskam)
    Bacon], "Little Brother of the Books," in Whom the Gods De-
    stroyed, Scribner's, 1902. A lame boy wins the heart of the towns-
    people and three rigid librarians. (Keller)

James, Henry. The Bostonians. London: Macmillan, 1886. Includes
    a description of a Harvard cataloger as young, ringletted, and
    refined.

Lewis, Sinclair. Main Street. Harcourt, Brace, 1920. Miss Villets
    represents the older, rigid librarian. Carol Kennicott represents
    her antithesis.

Lincoln, Joseph C. Galusha the Magnificent. New York: Appleton
    & Co., 1921. "A thoroughly estimable man, a scholar, author of
    two or three books which few read and almost nobody bought,
    and librarian of the acropolis, a library that Bostonians and the
    book world would know and revere." (Greer)

Merwin, Samuel. Anabel at Sea. Houghton, 1927. "Anabel pools all her resources in a round-the-world cruise in search of a husband." (Book Review Digest, 1927)

Mitchell, Silas Weir, "The Mind Reader," in The Guillotine Club.
New York: Century Co., 1920. A medical student goes to work
in a library for the purpose of solving mysteries. His supervisor,
the real librarian, is a fussy, bespectacled man of indeterminate
age. (Pearson)

Moeller, Philip, "Helena's Husband," in Five Somewhat Historical
Plays. Knopf, 1918. "Analytikos, the King's librarian, is over
70 years old, full of wise sayings and clever speeches but withal
somewhat of a doddery fool." (Greer)

Nicholson, Meredith. "The Susiness of Susan," in Best Laid Schemes.
Scribner's, 1922. "A sprightly tale of a young librarian who by
clever dissembling, to which she afterwards confesses, wins the
friendship of Brown Pendleton, explorer and archeologist, the
guest of honor at a dinner party where Miss Susan Parker revels
in being 'Susie' again." (Book Review Digest, 1922)

Norris, Kathleen. Martie the Unconquered. Doubleday, 1917.
Martie Monroe, "a girl of strong individuality and much ambition,"
escapes the constraints of a small California town by marrying an
unsuccessful actor by whom she later has a son. Martie returns
home and works for the public library. Eventually, she returns
to New York to resume a life independent of her family. (Book
Review Digest, 1917)

Phillips, David Graham. Golden Fleece. New York: P.F. Collier,
1903. Library attendants are described as polite and obliging.
One librarian, discussed at length as a busybody and a gossip-
monger has a fat, pasty face with a drapery of soft, scant, gray
whiskers. (Pearson)

Tully, Jim. Emmett Lawler. Harcourt, Brace, 1922. Expresses
gratitude to women librarians for their help to young writers.
(Library Journal)

Van Vechten, Carl. Nigger Heaven. Knopf, 1926. In this novel
about the rich culture of the Harlem Renaissance, Mary, a young
black woman, works in the library. (Greer)

Wharton, Edith. Summer. New York: Appleton & Co., 1917.
Charity is a melancholy young woman who works in the local library. Eventually, she is reconciled to her narrow future and
marries her guardian.

Widdemer, Margaret. The Rose Garden Husband. J.B. Lippincott
Co., 1915. "She was a tired-out little assistant librarian working
on a salary of 50 dollars a month, and she wished, as many a

tired-out working girl has wished for a home and a husband and
plenty of money--in her case she added a rose garden." (<u>Book
Review Digest</u>, 1915)

Where indicated, plot descriptions are from the following sources:

<u>Book Review Digest</u>, 1915, p. 497.
<u>Book Review Digest</u>, 1917, p. 414.
<u>Book Review Digest</u>, 1922, p. 391.
<u>Book Review Digest</u>, 1927, p. 500.
Greer, Agnes, "The Librarian in Fiction," <u>Wilson Library Bulletin</u>,
    February 1935, p. 317-318.
Keller, Helen Rex, "The Old-Fashioned Virtues Versus the Ideal
    Librarian," <u>Library Journal</u>, July 1909, p. 295-298.
<u>Library Journal</u>, June 1, 1922, p. 502.
Pearson, Edmund Lester, "The Librarian in Fiction," in his <u>The
    Library and the Librarian</u>. Woodstock, Vt.: Elm Tree Pr.,
    1910, p. 1-6.

THE DOORS AND WINDOWS OF THE
LIBRARY: LEIGH HUNT AND SPECIAL COLLECTIONS†*

David H. Stam

My thesis is that Leigh Hunt missed his calling, or to put the case more modestly, that the essential purposes and raison d'être of Hunt's life and work were the same as those of librarianship. After Hunt died in 1859, with the revised version of his Autobiography not yet completed, his eldest son Thornton saw the 1860 edition through the press, and was able to add a preface which in effect summarized the author's life and work in explicitly bibliothecal terms:

> To promote the happiness of his kind, to minister to the
> more educated appreciation of order and beauty, to open
> more widely the door of the library, and more widely the
> window of the library looking out upon nature,--these were
> the purposes that guided and animated his labours to the
> very last.

Earlier in the preface Thornton speaks of Hunt's 'trick of playing with a certain round of quotations [as] among the traits of his character most conspicuous even to casual visitors. In the routine of life, it may be said, he almost thought in a slang of the library.'[1]

For the purposes of this bicentennial essay in honor of Leigh Hunt, I would like to employ that same trick by quotations from Hunt's own writings, published and unpublished, to explore his attitudes toward and relations to libraries and special collections.

Hunt's earliest experience of libraries, as recorded in his Autobiography, was not a particularly pleasant one, for it was behind 'the dreadful door of the library' that the students of Christ's Hospital were flogged for whatever misdemeanors, real or imagined. Hunt remarked that 'They did not invest the books with flowers, as

†This article is adapted from an address given at the Leigh Hunt Symposium at the University of Iowa, 13 April 1984 and is printed here by permission of the "Friends" of the University of Iowa Libraries.
*Reprinted by permission of the author and the publisher from The Book Collector, 35: (Spring 1986) 67-75.

Montaigne recommends.'[2] But later in the Autobiography Hunt
says that 'I had subscribed, while at school, to the famous circulating library in Leadenhall Street [The Minerva Library], and I have
continued to be such a glutton of novels ever since, that, except
when they repel me in the outset with excessive wordiness, I can
read their three-volume enormities to this day without skipping a
syllable....'[3]

In earlier autobiographical musings Hunt says that few of his
fellow scholars at Christ's Hospital 'cared for any of the books that
were taught,' but that his own books were a never-ceasing consola-
tion. 'When the master tormented me, when I used to hate and loathe
the sight of Homer, Demosthenes, and Cicero, I would comfort myself with thinking of the sixpence in my pocket, with which I should
go out to Paternoster-row, when school was over, and buy another
number of an English poet.'[4] His later retrospective view of Christ's
Hospital is a gently charitable one, gratitude for not hindering his
growing mind and allowing him to 'get novels to my heart's content
from the circulating libraries.'[5]

After Issac Hunt published his son's verses as the Juvenila
in 1801, Leigh Hunt became known to many in London literary circles, including the Rev. Thomas Maurice, an oriental scholar who
was Assistant Keeper in the Department of Manuscripts in the British
Museum Library. Maurice befriended the teenaged Hunt, arranged
permission for Hunt to read in the Museum (where he began his study
of Italian), and also provided many a dinner of roast fowl and wine
in his rooms at the Museum where Hunt and Maurice discussed authors
and books, and I imagine Library gossip. Through that connection,
Hunt was also able to arrange reading privileges for some of his
friends.[6]

Other references to libraries in Lord Byron and Some of His
Contemporaries and in the Autobiography are infrequent, but many
observations in his other writings attest to his dependence on libraries of all sorts, as well as his critical views of library service
and practice. Probably most famous is his essay called 'My Books,'
written in Italy where he had few books easily accessible but from
where he could recollect his experience of London libraries critically,
and especially his experiences as a frequent user of the Museum
Library:

> I dislike a grand library to study in, I mean an immense
> apartment, with books all in Museum order, especially wire-
> safed. I say nothing against the [British] Museum itself,
> or public libraries. They are capital places to go to, but
> not to sit in; and talking of this, I hate to read in public,
> and in strange company. The jealous silence; the inability
> to help yourself; the not knowing whether you ought to
> trouble the messengers, much less the gentleman in black,
> or brown, who is perhaps, half a trustee; with a variety

of other jarrings between privacy and publicity, prevent one's settling heartily to work.[7]

Hunt was not alone in his dissatisfaction with the British Museum Library. His near neighbors in Chelsea during the 1830's, Thomas and Jane Carlyle, were particularly critical of libraries and librarians. Jane, for example, wrote to Thomas from Oxford that 'the Bodleian Library must be a most perverse place to study in; for this reason above all, that the numerous private libraries left to it in donation ... are and must be kept apart and entire; so that instead of one great Library arranged under general heads, you have as it were a great many little libraries arranged under one general roof. They told me the inconvenience of this was obviated by the perfection of the catalogues, to which I can only say the perfection of the catalogues must be much beyond the perfection of the Librarians. One of whom, grown grey in the service, I made as red as a lobster with asking him simple questions which he could nowise answer.'[8] Thomas Carlyle often complained of the Museum Library, criticized the catalogues, claimed that the Reading Room gave him "museum Headache,' and particularly resented Panizzi's refusal as Librarian to provide him with a private study.[9] All of Carlyle's carpings were not, however, without good effect for they caused him, with Hunt's support, to lead the movement toward the establishment in 1842 of the London Library, a circulating subscription library on which Hunt came to depend heavily during the later part of his life. Hunt was more supportive and responsible in his comments about the British Museum Library than Carlyle, but nonetheless he welcomed and used the London Library extensively. The Preface to his Stories from the Italian Poets, published in 1846, acknowledged his debt:

> I cannot, in gratitude for the facilities afforded ... , dismiss this Preface without congratulating men of letters on the establishment and increasing prosperity of the London Library, an institution founded for the purpose of accommodating subscribers with such books, at their own houses, as could only be consulted hitherto at the British Museum. The sole objection to the Museum is thus done away, and the literary world has a fair prospect of possessing two book-institutions instead of one, each with its distinct claims to regard, and presenting in combination all that the student can wish; for while it is highly desirable that authors should be able to have standard works at their command, when sickness or other circumstances render it impossible for them to go to the Museum, it is undoubtedly requisite that one great collection should exist in which they are sure to find the same works unremoved, in case of necessity,--not to mention curious volumes of all sorts, manuscripts, and a world of books of reference.[10]

Hunt continued to rely on borrowed books from the London Library

for his later work, especially for his bowdlerized selections from
Beaumont and Fletcher. Hunt was included in the printed list of
subscribers to the London Library for 1846 and in later years, as
was eventually his son Thornton. One can cynically speculate on
where Hunt found the funds for the £6 entrance fee and the £2
per annum, but as he himself said, 'Let him who is without one,
cast the first sarcasm' (Autobiography, p. 38).

Several of Hunt's later printed works, primarily those of local
history and description, are studded with passages on libraries.
The Old Court Suburb, or Memorials of Kensington (1855), praises
the library of Holland House and enumerates some of its prize books
and manuscripts, including three autograph letters of Petrarch and
three autograph plays of Lope de Vega. Hunt's A Summer through
the West End, posthumously published in 1861, but written during
the 1850s, reiterates his praise of the London Library, 'its lending
policies being an incalculable advantage to most people, but especially
to authors not in good health....'[11] The same work gives a more
mixed review to the Record Office:

> The care and neatness, nay elegance, in which its venerable
> documents were kept by their intelligent supervisors, formed
> a singular contrast with the homeliness of their lodging.
> You literally went up and down among them by ladders, as
> if in a veritable stable, passing along alleys of lofts, and
> looking down into a gulf beneath.... It is a pity to see
> such interesting memorials, the last proofs of the existence
> of hundreds of old houses and monasteries, and often coloured
> as if with a remnant of their painted windows, huddled hither
> and thither for want of a proper resting-place.[12]

Hunt had a particular personal reason to be concerned about
the Record Office because one of his sons, Percy Bysshe Shelley
Leigh Hunt, started serving as a junior clerk there in 1841. In a
letter now in The New York Public Library, Hunt wrote in 1841 to
Alaric Watts that the Whigs had 'put one of my sons in the Registra-
tion Office, and another in the Record Office; and though the salary
of the elder of the two is the only one that is sufficient for more
than bare subsistence, yet the relief to myself in regard to the dear
lads was very great.'[13]

Such is some of the evidence I have found in his printed works
about Hunt's views on libraries, public and private. Even more revealing, however, are the traces that remain of his own personal
collection and in his extensive surviving correspondence. It would
be impossible today to reconstruct the entire history of Leigh Hunt's
own library, though a great number of his annotated books are extant and work in progress is revealing many others. But in the
essay on 'My Books' cited above, Hunt also said that 'I may affirm,
upon a moderate calculation, that I have lent and lost in my time
(and I am eight-and-thirty), half-a-dozen decent-sized libraries--I

mean books enough to fill so many ordinary book-cases, I have never complained; and self-love, as well as gratitude, make me love those who do not complain of me,'[14] meaning of course that he had helped deplete other personal collections.

Hunt never had enough money to collect extensively, but his daily routine included extensive sessions of imaginary collection development: 'he opens a new catalogue of old books with all the fervour and ivory folder of a first love, often reading them at tea and dinner, and practicing a fictitious book-hunt, by putting crosses against dozens of volumes on the list, out of the pure imagination of buying them, the possibility being out of the question.'[15]

In his own books, and in some owned by his friends, Hunt like Coleridge and Carlyle was prone to prolific markings and annotations. Many of his books are in the Luther T. Brewer Collection at the University of Iowa; others are scattered in East Coast libraries (from Dartmouth to Virginia), and several survive at the British Library. In looking at these volumes, what is most remarkable to me is the consistency with which Hunt marked passages dealing with books, collectors and libraries. Whether the passage be about development of collections, the preservation or decay of books, or even book retrieval, Hunt is apt to have some annotation showing his interest in the concerns common to librarians. His surviving correspondence also reveals the same interests and shows that many of his friends, such as John Forster, Charles Ollier, Vincent Novello, and Egerton Webbe, tended to use him as their personal reference librarian to locate references, provide citations, and to lend them books. In the slang of today's library profession, Leigh Hunt was a gatekeeper, one who opened up doors to information resources for a wide variety of friends. The correspondents in his 'invisible college' included Charles Dickens, Thomas Carlyle, Alfred Lord Tennyson, and a wide circle of editors and publishers, many of whom exchanged information and books among each other. Amy Lowell's description of Hunt as the 'great introducer' can be extended well beyond his printed works of literary essays, selections of famous authors, and translations of Italian classics.[16]

There is time for only a few examples from Hunt's correspondence and marginalia. For example, on 13 July 1837, Tennyson wrote to Hunt that:

> I was obliged to leave town on the day after that when I was to have drunk tea with you, seen Carlyle, & tumbld your books, I did not like to put you to an expense of postage or I would have written you from the country ... I only arrived here the other night & lit upon your parcel. It was very good of you to get all those poems written out for me & I can never be sufficiently grateful for the Paganini full as it is of the most graceful & thickcoming fancies.[17]

A letter of Hunt's to his wife, Marianne, also indicates his
mode of work, his reliance on libraries, his quest for profitable publishing ventures, and the chaos of his household:

> I have hit upon a matter of compilation, or selection rather,
> which I really think the bookseller's will buy of me offhand.
> It is a thing that has never been done before, and which
> the extraordinary nature of the authors,--their unreadable-
> ness in general and their great beauty in passages--has long
> rendered a want among the lovers of books:--to wit, the
> Beauties of Beaumont and Fletcher. I have already read,
> and picked, from plays, partly out of one of the numbers
> I brought here with me, and partly from a couple of their
> volumes out of the London Library; and I want you to send
> me, from the room above stairs, all the other numbers of
> them which you can find. They were near the door, in a
> lump on the floor ... [18]

Hunt also knew the librarians' desperation to recover a missing
and needed book. On 8 October 1829, he wrote to his wife to help
find some books he needed:

> I have not Pinchard in town & I never lent the vol. of the
> Parnasso, Pray hunt extensively for that vol. Ask Ellen;
> ask the girl--what's her name?--that used to hide things.
> I daresay the picture of Redi tempted her. Offer a reward--
> do any thing:--dance in public.[19]

Anyone familiar with Mrs Hunt will appreciate the ludicrousness of
the last suggestion.

From Hunt's marginalia it is difficult to convey his concern for
libraries and book collecting but it is omnipresent. For example,
Sismondi's Historical View of the Literature of the South of Europe
contains a passage about Cuarino de Verona, teacher and manuscript
in a shipwreck. The loss 'had the effect of turning the hair of
Guarino grey, in one night.' Hunt's marginal note calls this 'A
truly reverend agony,' one with which he easily identified.[20] Other
passages on the collections of the Royal Library of France, the decline of libraries in Fez and Morocco, the Catalonian archives of unpublished Troubadour poetry, and the archival discoveries by Petrarch and Boccaccio, are carefully marked by Hunt.

In a copy of Thomas Campbell's Life of Petrarch,[21] now in
the Houghton Library at Harvard University, Hunt again marked
many passages dealing with libraries and archives. References to
manuscripts in the 'Parisian library,' the vast treasures of the Flor-
entine library, a Paduan Bibliotheca Petrarchesca bought by the King
of France for the Louvre, and many other notes command Hunt's
attention. He admires Guglielmo da Pastrengo of Verona who

was a gay and gallant man, fond of the ladies, as well as
the muses--and wooed neither of them without success; yet
his erudition was so great that he conceived, even in that
obscure age, the bold design of a universal library ...
(Vol. I, p. 151).

Throughout Hunt's annotated books there are countless other
passages marked to show his interests in libraries and archives.
From the same Life of Petrarch let me give a final example where
Campbell relates that Petrarch was very concerned about the preservation of his library after he presented his books to the Venetian
Republic. In a section which Hunt both checked and lined, Campbell says that 'nevertheless, they are not now to be seen at Venice.
Tomasini tells us that they had been placed at the top of the church
of St Mark, that he demanded a sight of them, but that he found
them almost entirely spoiled, and some of them even petrified.' (Fol.
II, p. 249).

I fear I have outdone Hunt in his trick of quotation and his
slang of the library, so I will conclude this evocation of Hunt with
a few of his comments about bibliomania, a disease which he could
well have invented. He says he especially admired the Holland House
library and its collector, Lord Holland, who unlike many collectors
really enjoyed his books. Thomas Frognall Dibdin he damned with
faint praise by saying 'He was not a mere bibliomaniac. He really
saw, though not very far, into the merit of the books which he
read.'[22] But Hunt's favourite was surely Petrarch's peasant. In
the Beinecke Library at Yale is a volume of Ugo Foscolo's Essay on
Petrarch in which Hunt made his usual markings and annotations.
In this edition Foscolo includes one of Petrarch's familiar letters about
a servant who waited on Petrarch in Vaucluse:

He knew not how to read, yet he was also the guardian of
my library. With anxious eye he watched over my most rare
and ancient copies, which, by long use, he could distinguish
from those that were more modern, or of which I myself was
the author. Whenever I consigned a volume to his custody,
he was transported with joy; he pressed it to his bosom with
sighs; with great reverence he repeated the author's name;
and seemed as if he had received an accession of learning
and happiness from the sight and touch of a book.[23]

At the bottom of the page Hunt has added this footnote: 'The memory of this good man ought to be drunk at the anniversaries of the
Bibliomaniacs.' In that same spirit we can celebrate Hunt's bicentennial by proposing a toast in memory of Petrarch's peasant, of Leigh
Hunt, and lovers of books and libraries everywhere.

References

1. The Autobiography of Leigh Hunt. A New Edition, Revised by

the Author; with further revision, and an introduction by his eldest son (London, Smith, Elder, 1860), pp. xvi, xiv.

2. The Autobiography of Leigh Hunt, edited by J.E. Morpurgo (London: The Cresset Press, 1949), p. 71.

3. Ibid., p. 142. On the Minerva Library, founded in 1770, see Richard D. Altick, The English Common Reader (Chicago: University of Chicago Press, 1957), passim.

4. Lord Byron and Some of His Contemporaries; with Recollections of the Author's Life ... Second ed. (London: H. Colburn, 1828), Vol. II, pp. 165, 174, 170.

5. Ibid., p. 83.

6. Ibid., Vol. II, pp. 190-197. For additional information on Maurice, who eventually was appointed Chief Superintendent of the Reading Room, see Edward Miller, That Noble Cabinet: A History of the British Museum. (Athens, Ohio University Press, 1974), p. 93.

7. The Indicator, Part II, Essay LXIII, Reprint ed. (London: Edward Moxon, 1840), p. 49.

8. Jane Carlyle to Thomas Carlyle, 11 August 1837. Published in I Too Am Here. Selections from the Letters of Jane Welsh Carlyle, ed. by Alan and Mary Simpson (Cambridge: Cambridge University Press, 1977), p. 167.

9. Edward Miller: Prince of Librarians: The Life and Times of Antonio Panizzi. (Athens: Ohio University Press, 1967), pp. 178, 214.

10. Stories from the Italian Poets. In Two Volumes, (London: Chapman and Hall, 1846), pp. xv-xvi.

11. A Saunter Through the West End, (London: Hurst and Blackett, 1861), p. 160.

12. Ibid., pp. 210-11.

13. 19 July [1841?], Anthony Collection, Rare Books and Manuscripts Division, The New York Public Library.

14. The Indicator, op. cit., p. 50.

15. Holbrook Jackson, The Anatomy of Bibliomania, (New York: Avenel Books [1981]; first published 1950), p. 466.

16. Amy Lowell: John Keats (Boston: Houghton & Mifflin, 1925), Vol. I, p. 136.

17. British Library, Ashley MS. 2078.

18. British Library, Ashley MS. 3398.

19. Leigh Hunt to Marianne Hunt, Thursday, 8 October 1829. A.L.S. in Berg Collection, The New York Public Library.

20. J.C. Simonde de Sismondi, Historical View of the Literature of the South of Europe. Trans. by Thomas Roscoe. Four volumes (London: H. Colburn, 1823), Vol. II, p. 29. Hunt's copy is in the Rare Books and Manuscripts Division, The New York Public Library.

21. Thomas Campbell: Life of Petrarch, Two volumes, (London: Henry Colburn, 1841).

22. The Old Court Suburb, or Memorials of Kensington, Two volumes, (London: Hurst and Blackett, 1855), Vol. I, p. 226.

23. Ugo Foscolo: Essays on Petrarch, (London: John Murray, 1823), pp. 140-41.

THE ACHIEVEMENT OF FREDSON BOWERS*

G. Thomas Tanselle

In November of 1936, a book appeared with a preface stating that
the author had tried to "balance the theory gained from extended
reading" with "practical experience." This announcement, though
sensible, was hardly remarkable; but it is of interest because the
book was The Dog Owner's Handbook, written by Fredson Thayer
Bowers. It was his first book, and its prefatory statement serves
as a fair characterization of most of his later work: for his writings,
to a striking degree, combine the theoretical and the practical. Much
of what he has written, as we all know, has been of great significance for editorial and bibliographical theory and methodology; but
it is nearly always buttressed by telling examples drawn from his
own wide experience. Who else could have written the essay on
textual criticism in the second edition of the MLA Aims and Methods
pamphlet (1970) or the paper on eclectic texts presented at the Villa
Serbelloni in 1973, citing--without recourse to the discoveries of
others--illustrations from Shakespeare, Fielding, Hawthorne, and
Crane? Who else could have written the recent review of the New
Arden Hamlet and also have been the author of the textual essay in
the Wesleyan Tom Jones? Who else writing on editorial theory has
had the experience of editing, in addition to these writers, such an
array as Marlowe, Dekker, Beaumont and Fletcher, Dryden, Whitman,
William James, and Nabokov? And who else could have enriched a
treatise on descriptive bibliography with such a capacious repertory
of apposite references as one finds in the Principles? Throughout
his work, examples flood in. He has outdistanced his great predecessors in the range of detail at his command to support general observations.

If, as befits this occasion, one tries further to define his achievement, one would have to begin by recognizing that his range is impressive in another way as well: his breadth is manifested not only
in the number of authors, from five centuries, with whom he is familiar but also in the variety of kinds of scholarly and critical work

*Reprinted by permission of the author from the Papers of the Bib-
liographical Society of America 79:2 (1985) 175-190; copyright ©
1985 by The Bibliographical Society of America.

to which he has made fundamental contributions.   No one with the
slightest exposure to descriptive bibliography, analytical bibliography,
or textual criticism can fail to have come across his name, and no
one can expect to make much progress in those fields without ponder-
ing what he has had to say.   He has also produced a series of critical essays on Shakespearean plays (particularly on Hamlet), and his
first book on a literary subject, Elizabethan Revenge Tragedy, remains a basic critical history of the genre; but I think it is fair to
say that this body of work, commendable as it is, has been overshadowed by his unparalleled contributions to the other three fields.
The central position of his work across the whole spectrum of bib-
liographical-textual studies is what places him in direct succession
to the great triumvirate of Pollard, McKerrow, and Greg.   One can
name other first-rate bibliographical scholars between Bradshaw and
Bowers, but none of them matches those three for the size and quality
of an oeuvre that encompasses bibliographical description and analysis
and critical editing.   Professor Bowers is their rightful heir in the
double sense that he has built on their achievement and that what
he has built ranks with their achievement in range and distinction.
The link is exemplified in the dedication of the Principles of Bibliographical Description in 1949 to Greg.   Although Greg lived for ten
years after that and although "The Rationale of Copy-Text" and
much of his bibliography of the Renaissance drama remained to be
published, there is no question that the Principles, and the nearly
concurrent establishment of Studies in Bibliography (where, not surprisingly, the "Rationale" was published), signaled Professor Bowers
as the figure to watch in the ensuing decades.   Just as Greg pre-
sided over the first half of the century (sharing the position with
Pollard and McKerrow for three-quarters of the time), so Professor
Bowers has been the leading force in the second half of the century.

     This shift of leadership also brought the center of bibliographi-
cal development to the United States.   If the so-called "new bibliography," emphasizing the place of physical evidence in literary study,
can be designated--as it often now is--an Anglo-American approach,
we must recognize that Professor Bowers played the pivotal role in
causing "American" to be a part of this epithet.   What had been essentially an English movement became an active field in American
scholarship through the force of his published work and through his
personal influence on students at the University of Virginia (where
not coincidentally a bibliographical society flourishes).   In this shift,
the role of his annual, Studies in Bibliography, cannot be overesti-
mated.   Whereas during the first half of the century The Library,
the organ of The Bibliographical Society in London, was the journal
that conveyed the excitement of being at the center of a developing
field, Studies in Bibliography became the place after the autumn of
1948 where one witnessed most dramatically the maturing of a discipline.   Pioneering essays by American scholars on the analysis of
paper, headlines, and press figures (among other subjects) appeared
in the early volumes, along with a burgeoning body of work on com-
positor determination.   The contributors, however, were by no means

exclusively American: SB soon became, and has remained, an international forum. To create a journal that is indispensable to a field,
and to maintain its vitality and stature over an extended period, is
a rare achievement. Professor Bowers has accomplished this feat
with SB, having nearly completed forty years as its editor (a term
surpassing Pollard's long editorship of The Library and McKerrow's
of the Review of English Studies). In the process he has proved
himself to be a great editor, in an additional sense to the one usually
thought of--for editing a journal is different from editing the text of
a classic work of literature. Yet one of the distinguishing marks of
his handling of SB is his understanding of the connections between
the two. His experience in thinking about textual matters surely
lies behind his sensitive treatment of contributors' manuscripts--
allowing, for instance, British scholars to retain their British spell-
ings. His recognition that formal consistency from article to article
is unimportant--indeed, difficult to justify--sets an enlightened example for journal editors to emulate. In other ways as well his practice has been exemplary: he is known for working with authors to
help them improve their articles, and he is receptive to a variety
of points of view. He has in fact published articles he is not in sympathy with, and clearly he has struggled with the perennial editorial
question of distinguishing responsible work one happens to disagree
with from work that is simply unacceptable. I can think of only
one instance in which I disagree with the decision; assuming that
each of us could do the same, I am confident that the resulting list
of such pieces would be quite small. It would be a record of the
price one gladly pays for the sense of exploration and openness that
is a hallmark of the remarkable run of SB.

    In the mid-century years, Professor Bowers's name quickly
established itself as the one that symbolized the whole field, as the
name one thought of first in connection with bibliographical study.
But one also thought of bibliographical study more often as a result
of his presence. SB and the Principles were sufficient to earn him
the respect of bibliographical scholars, but they alone do not account
for the special position he soon came to occupy in the minds of many
people outside the small circle of committed bibliographical scholars.
Their picture of him was more likely to be that of the advocate, the
publicist, the polemicist, for it was he who often, and insistently,
called their attention to the field and forced them to consider its
indispensability for their own work. In a series of talks and papers,
he tirelessly pressed the claims for the bibliographical approach to
the texts of all fields; his perennial theme is aptly epitomized in the
title of his 1958 Kansas lecture, "The Bibliographical Way." The
earliest of such talks, at the University of Pennsylvania in 1949,
began with the point that the general principles to be set forth were
of wide application, for "No matter what the field of study, the basis
lies in the analysis of the records in printed or in manuscript form,"
and the same attention must be given in every field to "establishing
the purity and accuracy of the materials under examination." The
justice of this view, though not recognized--then or now--by everyone,

cannot be questioned. But advocates are sometimes inclined, through temperament or the repeated necessity of being assertive, to overstate their cases, or to irritate some of their audience through too blunt a depiction of the follies requiring correction. One has to recognize that Professor Bowers, despite the incontrovertible logic of his basic position, has been a controversial figure, and part of the reason is his acceptance of the role of active advocacy, with all the opportunities it affords for giving offense. We all no doubt can remember favorite examples of his scorn. "First let me," he once said, "utterly cast aside the kind of gossiping about books which is written by and published for amateur collectors and which reaches its nadir in some so-called bibliographies of modern authors or in book-collectors manuals." On the same occasion he asserted that library schools "do not know enough to teach analytical bibliography as I understand it, and this deficiency sometimes also means, unfortunately, that books cannot be recorded accurately in libraries." And we recall the curator who was an "outworn cataloguer" deposited in the rare-book room "as a reward for faithful service where the world will pass her peacefully by and no extraordinary demands will interfere with her equable latter years." These snippets suggest why his talks do not always win him new friends; but they also hint at why Philip Young--no admirer of his editorial practice--conceded that he "writes rather well."

The language of such discourse can also give rise to more serious problems, and Professor Bowers has not entirely escaped the danger. For example, he used to speak of "definitive" editions. Those who already understood the nature of critical editing knew that he was using the term in a special sense and that the word was rhetorically effective in helping him emphasize the rigor, discipline, and thoroughness of the bibliographical way. They knew, and realized he knew, that no product of critical judgment can ever be definitive. But not everyone knew: some people have been put off by what they regard as an excessive claim and others (less criticalminded) have come away believing bibliography and textual criticism to be more definite and factual than they are. Professor Bowers's skill in the rhetoric of persuasion has not allowed this kind of situation often to develop; but any characterization of his work must recognize the polemical element and acknowledge the tension that sometimes results, in a single piece, between the charged language of advocacy and the calmer and more precise discourse of the scholarship being advocated.

The dominant attitude that always comes through, however, is one of uncompromising rigor, and that in itself has been enough to bring his work under attack from those who were made to feel defensive of their own less rigorous ways. Even the Principles, which is indeed both polemical and uncompromising (among other things), has thus been controversial. Four years after its publication, Geoffrey Keynes, in his presidential address before The Bibliographical Society, complained of "the shadow which seems in recent years to

have descended over our amiable bibliographical discipline": "we
have been chastised with scorpions because we are not all Gregs."
In his autobiography nearly three decades later, Keynes described
his remarks as "a friendly attack on the Bowers school of analytical
bibliographers." Friendly it may have been on the surface, and
Professor Bowers's reaction to it was courteous: Keynes reports,
"It chanced that Professor Bowers was present at the occasion. I
was glad that he accepted the address in the spirit in which it was
meant, complaining only that he had not thought of the title ['Religio
Bibliographici'] himself." But beneath the pleasantries there was
the sad fact that Keynes viewed the debate as one between amateurs
and professionals and that he saw himself as upholding "humanity"
over "pedantry." He had the issues all wrong; but this is not the
place to examine Keynes's position. I cite the episode only to illustrate how Professor Bowers came to symbolize, following the publication of the Principles, all that was advanced in bibliographical work
and how, for that reason, he was also regarded by some as the great
adversary. Certain reviewers ever since have alluded to the "Virginia school" or the "school of Charlottesville" in a sarcastic tone,
attempting to show--in an effort doomed to failure--their superiority
to the pedestrian routines of Bowersian bibliography. Professor
Bowers has been praised, and he has been attacked, but no one
denies that he stands for an entire field. The graduate students
of 1963 who read The Pooh Perplex no doubt saw something of him
in the supposed contribution of "Smedley Force"; at any rate one
can maintain that without his presence it is not likely that there
would have been a chapter of that book asking "why are there no
watermarks in Winnie the Pooh? Why are there no chain lines? Why
no colophon? Why no catchwords? No signature? No cancelland or
cancellans?" Whether in satire or in more direct commentary, Professor Bowers has been the object of considerable attention in the
scholarly world, because he has himself waged such a broad campaign
to direct attention to his field.

But he has also of course attracted notice because of the in-
trinsic significance of his scholarly discoveries and his observations
on them. One is tempted to say that this kind of attention is the
more important; but then one realizes how intertwined in him are the
publicist and the scholar, and how interrelated are the reactions
each has aroused. The value of securing for the field a larger place
in the scholarly public's consciousness is undeniable, and Professor
Bowers's success in this regard is directly related to his stature as
a productive scholar: we listen more attentively, if not always with
agreement, to the publicist who is not a popularizer but who has
actually produced some of the work that makes the field important.
If Professor Bowers had not chosen to play this larger role, the
state of bibliography today would be less vital and populous, even
though he had made his scholarly contributions. It must be added,
however, that there is a less fortunate side to these connections:
temperament and feelings influence scholarly judgement, and some
scholars who--for whatever reason--have been offended by, or who

disapprove of, the stance of the polemicist may criticize the scholarship without having been open-minded to what it had to say and
without fully understanding it. This personal element surfaces now
and then in the commentary on Professor Bowers's scholarship; we
need not concern ourselves with it, but it must be noted as one of
the side-effects of his unique position. What we should focus on
instead is the productive criticism of his work. I think it can be
said that in descriptive bibliography, in analytical bibliography, and
in textual criticism an understanding of his treatment of the basic
issues is an essential ingredient of future progress: his work may
need, here and there, some revising and extending, but to proceed
without recourse to it would be folly. In matters of consequence,
the last word can never be said; the highest praise is not that one's
work has ended debate but that it is indispensable for further discussion. Reciting Professor Bowers's accomplishments is therefore
only the beginning of a proper tribute; our debt to him is adequately
acknowledged only when we understand that our discussions, now
and in the future, must build on his. To find that some of his practices or conclusions require rethinking or amplification is not to
diminish his achievement; indeed, it is the best way to underscore
his accomplishment, because it reveals that whatever we say takes
its bearings from what he had already said.

     Descriptive bibliography is the area in which he made his
earliest extended contribution, and it is probably true that the Principles is even now his most widely known and influential work. He
may have some misgivings on this score: he may feel--as I do--that
his editorial work, both the theoretical and the practical, is more
subtle and ultimately more significant. But the Principles is a great
book, and one of the reasons is that it makes clear the intellectual
excitement of its subject. Writing about descriptive bibliography
may be somewhat confining, but the book shows that the practice
of descriptive bibliography is a form of history, with all the same
challenges and rewards. Although this point is not discussed explicitly at length, it in fact is the most fundamental and striking insight conveyed by the book--conveyed by its author's practice of
treating bibliographies as pieces of writing (not as compilations), by
his emphasis--in describing how bibliographers work--on the analysis
and interpretation of physical evidence, and by the habit of mind he
displays in working through particular examples. That descriptive
bibliography is a demanding form of historical scholarship underlies
every sentence of the book. There were earlier writers, of course,
who understood these points, but none of them produced a detailed
manual of practice, though some of them did put forward in print
suggestions for reporting certain details, particularly signature col-
lations. At the time the Principles appeared, an English tradition
existed, going back nearly three-quarters of a century, for the recording of signatures; but the authoritative systematic exposition of
it amounted essentially to three articles by Pollard and Greg (in 1906,
1907, and 1934) and a chapter in McKerrow's Introduction to Bibliography (1927). The Principles draws heavily on this tradition, es-

pecially on the work of Greg, whose long introduction to A Bibliography of the English Printed Drama to the Restoration (which did
not appear in print until a decade after the Principles) had been
drafted in 1942 and with whom Professor Bowers carried on an extensive correspondence regarding the Principles. But the Principles,
though it sensibly builds on this foundation, moves well beyond what
had previously been written, in two directions: it refines the for-
mulary of collation by examining it in greater detail than had ever
before been attempted, reinforcing the discussion with an extraordinary array of examples; and it places the collation in a larger context,
offering a comprehensive plan for describing all features of books.
The thoughtfulness of the exposition, which seems to cover nearly
every contingency that might arise, remains impressive, even to readers who have gone over it many times. Those who have had occasion
to work carefully through every statement of the book have emerged
with some minor amendments but have also gained renewed respect
for the quality of mind that produced such a structure of argument.
The book's great achievement is to have made readily accessible, for
the first time, a detailed and comprehensive practical guide to bibliographical procedure that reflects a thoroughly considered rationale.
It became standard upon publication, and will remain so.

Such an accomplishment is not diminished by noting that it
left some work undone, in matters both of detail and of principle.
In treating the details of typography and paper, for example, the
book was charting far less explored territory than was the case with
signature collation, and there is correspondingly more that one now
might feel needs to be added to those discussions. On some larger
theoretical issues, a few questions might also be raised: whether,
for instance, the traditional approach to signature collation sufficiently distinguished an account of physical structure from a record
of printed signatures; and whether the concept of issue could justifiably exclude binding if the binding was the publisher's. When the
Principles was published, Professor Bowers (like nearly everyone
else) was less experienced in handling books after 1700 than earlier
ones, and the Principles therefore needs more supplementing in its
later parts. On certain broad questions of rationale, Professor
Bowers himself has extended the discussion of the Principles, most
notably in two major addresses before The Bibliographical Society,
one soon after the publication of the book (1952) and the other (entitled "Bibliography Revisited") fifteen years later. A dominant theme
that repeatedly emerges in these discourses is the question of "de-
gressive bibliography"--and not surprisingly, for any decision one
makes to abridge the quantity of detail in bibliographical entries
reflects one's sense of priorities regarding the purposes served by
those entries. Thus whether the emphasis of a bibliography is on
literary history and biography (in which case the description of impressions and editions after the author's death may be shortened)
or on printing and publishing history (in which case such impressions
and editions are no less interesting than those of greater textual
significance) is a basic issue to be considered. However this matter

is decided, Professor Bowers leaves no doubt about another: the
length of an entry cannot be allowed to determine the amount of investigation performed.   The space one devotes to reporting the results of research, in other words, has no bearing on the effort required to determine what one is willing to assert are the facts.   There
can be no question that he is right on this score; but the propriety
of proportions in published bibliographical accounts will always be
a subject of debate, for it can no more be settled finally than the
emphasis in any other kind of historical account can be prescribed.
Whether descriptive bibliographers should be expected to collate texts
or whether textual scholars have surpassed bibliographers in sophistication are perhaps finally rather unimportant jurisdictional disputes:
what matters is that the work be done, by those who understand how
to do it, not how much of it is reported in bibliographies and how
much in editions.   Professor Bowers's efforts to distinguish these
scholarly genres may in the long run seem dated; but his cogent
explanation of the relationships between the two provides a ground-
ing of perennial value.   And his own career offers an instructive
example of the basic role of descriptive bibliography in scholarship;
for his work toward a bibliography of Restoration drama has been a
continuous thread in the fabric of his endeavor, surfacing at appropriate points in many of his theoretical essays and now coming once
again to a dominant position among his demanding agenda.   It was in
connection with this bibliography that he once described the rewards
of bibliographical work, which overshadow the drudgery, as "a genera-
tive excitement of exploring the unknown" and of "drawing some
maps of terra incognita."

Even before the Principles appeared and made "Bowers" a household word, Professor Bowers had established himself as a master of
bibliographical analysis in a series of articles, beginning in 1938,
on the use of running-titles and headlines as bibliographical evidence
and on the reconstruction of early proofreading practices from such
evidence.   When he and Charlton Hinman each presented papers on
headlines at the English Institute in 1941, they were--as matters
turned out--offering a preview of how analytical bibliography would
develop after they returned from war duty four years later.   There
is a historical neatness in the fact that the fiftieth anniversary of
The Bibliographical Society occurred in 1942 and that for the occasion
F.P. Wilson wrote his now-famous account of "Shakespeare and the
'New Bibliography,'" for these events proved to mark the close of
one phase of the development of analytical bibliography.   What was
prophetic about the prewar Bowers and Hinman articles was not simply
that they presaged the shift in leadership to American but that they
emphasized new techniques for extracting from physical evidence
details of the printing procedures underlying particular books.   As
Helen Gardner remarked in her revised edition of Wilson's essay,
nearly three decades later, the greatest activity in the intervening
years had been in the study of the printing of Shakespeare's plays,
and she spoke of this work as the product of "what we must call
the 'newer bibliography.'"   The earlier development of the field, from

Pollard (who was himself a link with the analytical study of incuna-
bula) through McKerrow and E.E. Willoughby to Greg (whose magis-
terial writings were the climax of the prewar phase), resulted of
course from the continued exploration of physical evidence, and the
"newer bibliography" represents no turning away from this trend; its
distinctiveness lies largely in its more intense focus on minute physical details, particularly on damaged types, and in its repertory of
techniques (which expanded rapidly in the postwar years) for organizing these details into page-by-page case histories. Professor Bowers
played a critical role in this renewal of vitality in the field both
through his early articles, several of which remain classic pieces of
bibliographical detection, and through his encouragement of analytical
work in SB, which resulted in an efflorescence of compositorial study,
produced by an impressive assembly of able young scholars.

Although his later, editorial undertakings have naturally involved bibliographical analysis, he has not concentrated on this kind
of work, as Hinman did. He has not produced an equivalent of the
Principles for this aspect of bibliographical investigation; but he did
in effect write the prolegomena for such a book in his 1959 Lyell
Lectures, published as Bibliography and Textual Criticism. He took
up there the nature of bibliographical reasoning, assessing the role
in it of inductive argument and defining the various degrees of certainty obtainable by it. The book is subtle, rigorous, and absolutely
fundamental, aiming at nothing less than a characterization of the
habit of mind required for recognizing, and then responsibly employing, bibliographical evidence. One might perhaps take from it (once
again) the conclusion that bibliographers are historians, confronting
the same problem that all historians face: how to weigh the preserved evidence in order to reconstruct past events. These points
would seem to be unexceptionable and uncontroversial, and indeed
the book has not aroused a great deal of controversy; yet I believe
it has a role to play at the center of a debate now attracting considerable (and possibly excessive) attention in the bibliographical
world. Five years after the book appeared, D.F. McKenzie published,
in the pages of SB, his celebrated essay "Printers of the Mind,"
which showed that some of the conclusions drawn by analytical bibliographers had prematurely attained the status of fact, when at best
they were no more than tentative hypotheses, to be tested deduc-
tively. Although this essay is often considered to cast doubt on
analytical bibliography as a field, what it actually exposes is the
improper use of evidence, and it consequently serves to reinforce
with illustrations what Professor Bowers was saying more abstractly
in his Lyell Lectures. Obviously the scrutiny of physical evidence
in books cannot be abandoned. Yet McKenzie did express "a feeling
of mild despondency about the prospects for analytical bibliography";
and some historians who do not understand bibliography have readily
taken this judgment to spell the doom of the field--particularly some
of the new historians of the book, working in the tradition of the
French school of histoire du livre and stressing the role of books in
society. Recourse to archives, as these writers maintain, is certainly

important; but they have difficulty in accepting the great store of
existing books as an archive itself, containing primary evidence of
printing processes. Underlying this difficulty is a failure to perceive
bibliography as historical research and interpretation; therefore Professor Bowers's book --which has not been cited often enough in
this connection--ought to be required reading for those engaged in
such discussion and ought to become increasingly prominent in future
methodological controversy.

When one thinks of Professor Bowers at the heart of controversy, however, it is his editorial scholarship that is most likely to
come to mind. The volumes he has edited (some four dozen of them)
and the general discussions of editorial principles he has written
(two volumes and some two dozen major essays) constitute an enormous body of work, which has in return been commented on volumin-
ously. He emerges from this work as the preeminent authority of
his generation on the textual criticism of post-medieval writings; he
is also--and does not automatically follow--the most influential as
well. His advice and his practice have not, it is true, been universally accepted; but they have been so widely analyzed that even
those who take a different line can scarcely be unaware of how their
own views have been affected by the debate. Some criticism inevitably
refers to specific textual decisions in particular editions: since any
critical edition--by Professor Bowers or anyone else-- rests on critical judgment, there will always be grounds for legitimate disagreement
on individual cruxes. Some of these editorial decisions are linked
to one another and as a class call attention to broader issues. For
instance, some of Professor Bowers's emendations in the text of Hawthorne raise questions, I believe, about the wisdom of regularizing
spelling and punctuation. But this matter is not one on which certainty can be attained, and more than one approach can be defended.
This situation bothers only those critics not mature enough to see
that one can disagree with certain judgments in a work--whether a
critical edition or a critical essay--and still have respect for the
work as a whole. The magnitude of Professor Bowers's achievement
in elucidating the textual histories and providing critical texts of
such a large number of important writings is not lessened by dis-
agreements about some categories of emendations, or by the realization that no critical text can ever be the only defensible one.

Professor Bowers's editions represent a working out in practice
of an approach to editing set forth in detail in his theoretical pieces.
His first substantial essay on editorial principles--which came in 1950,
when he had already established his reputation in analytical and descriptive bibliography--was the first analysis to appear of Greg's "The
Rationale of Copy-Text" (which had been read the previous year at
the English Institute). It was a sympathetic assessment, suggesting
among other points that the rationale was appropriate for Restoration
drama as well as for the earlier drama cited by Greg; it thus set
the stage for what was to follow, for Professor Bowers continued
both to champion Greg's approach and to extend it. (He was also

the first person to put it into practice, in his edition of Dekker.)
Through the 1950s his theoretical statements, like his editing, dealt
largely with Elizabethan drama, but they have a broader applicability.
For example, his Rosenbach Lectures of 1954 (published as On Editing Shakespeare and the Elizabethan Dramatists) contain an admirable basic introduction to modern critical editing; and his Sandars
Lectures of 1958 (published as Textual and Literary Criticism) include, in the opening lecture, what is still one of the best general
accounts of the need for textual criticism, with an extensive range
of illustrations. His most widely circulated introductory essay, however, came early in the next decade, in the form of his contribution
to the MLA Aims and Methods pamphlet (1963), which in its two editions sold 45,000 copies. More students and editors over the last
two decades have probably begun their systematic thinking about
editing with this essay than with any other. And their ranks surely
include many of the editors of what came to be called "CEAA editions,"
for the Center for Editions of American Authors was getting under
way at the same time. (Indeed, a shibboleth among them was the
concluding sentence of the essay, in which each editor was exhorted
to "place all his textual cards on the table--face up.")

      Professor Bowers can be regarded as the architect of CEAA
editorial policy in another way as well: it was a paper of his, read
at the 1962 South Atlantic Modern Language Association meeting, that
explained how Greg's rationale could provide a basis for producing
unmodernized critical texts of nineteenth-century American literature,
and in the first volume of the Ohio State Hawthorne edition the same
year he furnished a practical model to follow. Short as it is, that
paper (published in the 1964 SB) is thus one of the most influential
he has ever produced--and of the most controversial, too, for the
justifiability of extending Greg's reasoning to post-Renaissance material has been a central theme of recent editorial debate, which has
often focused on the products of the CEAA. Adapting Greg to the
nineteenth century requires considering the status of authors' manuscripts, since they do not survive for the dramatists Greg was concerned with. The paper implies that Greg's reason for preferring
an early to a late edition as copy-text (the likelihood that, being
closer to the lost manuscript, it contains more instances of the author's spelling and punctuation) would generally lead to the choice
of a fair-copy manuscript itself, when it exists. Whether one accepts
this conclusion depends on what aspect of authorial intention one
decides to emphasize; those who conceive intention to include expectation, or view authorship as social and collaborative, prefer a first
edition to a manuscript. This issue will never be settled, nor should
it be; but Professor Bowers, in his writings on the eclecticism of
critical editing, has set a standard of argument and eloquence that
those taking other positions must attempt to equal, and he has therefore been a powerful force for raising the level on which editorial
discussion must be conducted.

      Two other essays, from his two dozen of real consequence on

editorial matters, demand mention. The 1972 piece on "Multiple Authority" provides a necessary supplement to Greg's rationale, offering a practical plan for dealing with situations in which two or more
texts stand in the same relationship to a lost ancestor and are thus
of theoretically equal authority. Six years later his remarkable paper
called "Greg's 'Rationale of Copy-Text' Revisited" set forth the most
trenchant examination of Greg that has been written and the most
thorough consideration of the applicability of Greg's thinking to later
periods. Professor Bowers here is perhaps too ready to believe that
changed printing and publishing conditions after the seventeenth
century can support a more generous assessment of the authority
of variants in revised editions; but at least one can say that the
critics who have accused him of dogmatism in pushing the claims of
Greg have not taken this important essay to heart. At the beginning of his Rosenbach Lectures a quarter-century earlier he had remarked on the "comparatively little discussion" of the principles for
editing printed, rather than manuscript, texts; they have now of
course been very much discussed, and the sophistication of his
essay revisiting Greg, emerging as it does from a long line of his
own essays and reactions to them by others, is a measure of the
extent to which he is responsible for the profoundly changed environment in which editors of modern writings work.

    This view of the achievement of Professor Bowers makes clear,
I believe, why any serious conversation on a bibliographical theme,
whether it occurs in celebration of his eightieth birthday or at some
more distant date in the annals of bibliography, cannot fail to involve
issues on which he has taken an illuminating and provocative stand.
His centrality was signaled in 1969 when The Bibliographical Society
in London awarded him its Gold Medal. On that occasion John Carter,
recognizing Studies in Bibliography as one of Professor Bowers's
great accomplishments, linked its qualities with those of its founder:
"Its chronological range, its catholic scope, its uncompromising seriousness of purpose, the professional intensity of its contributors--
all these characteristics reflect the quality of the man who this year
celebrates his twenty-first birthday as its editor." We must now
change that figure to "thirty-seventh," but otherwise the statement
requires no emendation: in the interval Professor Bowers has pursued the same course with unabated energy and undiminished distinction, producing another gold-medal's-worth of work. In Nancy Hale's
beautiful book The Life in the Studio, we read, "With their instinct
for making something, artists tend to respect the past as something
also made." The bibliographical way, like all other paths to the
past, requires the shaping vision of the scholar-artist. Bibliographical clues, like the objects she found in the studio, serve as "keys
to release the life that trembles behind them in the void," a life that
one "otherwise would never have suspected was there." She might
have been describing her husband's work. The effort to establish
what a printer did, or what an author thought, at a particular moment in the past is not essentially different from any other exercise
of the historical imagination. There are responsible ways, and ir-

responsible ways, of marshaling the preserved evidence to create
a picture of the past. What we have cause to celebrate in Professor
Bowers's work, whether or not we agree with every detail of it, is
his responsible and imaginative fashioning of bibliographical evidence
into a coherent view of certain kinds of past events. He has made
the bibliographical way of thinking a presence in our lives through
the artistry of his creative scholarship.

Part IV

THE SOCIAL PREROGATIVE

THE DEZ PROCESS AND
THE LIBRARY OF CONGRESS*

Karl Nyren

The search for a solution to the problem of the deterioration of books due to the acid in the paper upon which they are printed spans several decades. A number of chemical processes to deacidify a volume have been developed in that time, and currently at least two are claimed to have potential as "industrial" processes for use in applications that can deacidify thousands of volumes at a time.

The Library of Congress has opted to use a process involving the volatile chemical diethyl zinc (DEZ), and for several years has been engaged in experiments and projects to develop a prototype plant for massive applications of the DEZ deacidification process, with the aim of developing a prototype process for world-wide adoption of the DEZ-based method for the mass deacidification of books. The process would be used on both old books already deteriorating on library shelves and new ones being added to library collections.

In statements made public over a number of years, the Library of Congress has:

- Asserted that the diethyl zinc (DEZ) process is safe;

- Proposed that it be a model or prototype for deacidification plants to be build around the country;

- Reported steady progress in achieveing a successful process; and, inadvertently or not,

- Allowed the impression to be created that 13 million older books now disintegrating on LC shelves are the prime reason LC has proposed building an $11.5 million deacidification plant at Fort Detrick in Maryland.

*Reprinted by permission of the author and publisher from Library Journal 111:15 (September 15, 1986) 33-35. Published by R.R. Bowker, a division of Reed Publishing, USA; copyright © 1986 by Reed Publishing, USA, a division of Reed Holdings, Inc.

The Danger of DEZ

The inherent danger of the basic chemical involved, diethyl
zinc, has been known all along. LC has claimed for years that it
has successfully harnessed DEZ for mass deacidification.

Early in the LC effort to move the DEZ process from minia-
ture scale in the laboratory to an industrial process, a project was
contracted to an engineering team from Northrop Services, Inc.
Working at the NASA Goddard Space Flight facility, the team went
to great pains to educate themselves about DEZ, spent several days
at the plant of the Stauffer Chemical Company, the Houston manu-
facturer of DEZ, and worked out ways to transport and handle the
chemical.

DEZ is too dangerous to ship except in sealed steel cylinders,
in a dilute solution with oil, and then not in any vehicle carrying
passengers or traveling by air. It can be shipped by UPS.

The Northrop Services team designed a process which they
considered safe, one in which the risks of any serious mishap were
rated as close to zero. That rating was disputed by one member
of the engineering team who felt that the hazards of DEZ had not been
fully explored. As safety engineer for the job, he sounded the alarm
and was allowed to resign. The project proceeded without him.

Success in harnessing DEZ has been regularly announced by
the Library of Congress:

In 1980, LC Research Scientist George Kelly said that "The
process now appears ready for commercial use," with the warning
that it should not be set up in a library or residential neighborhood.

In the LC Information Bulletin of April 23, 1984, it was said
that "The safety aspects of [DEZ] have been completely defined and
the handling of diethyl zinc by trained operators has been reduced
to a routine matter. The process is entirely safe to personnel and
the environment and presents no damage to the books being deacidified."

On May 7, 1984, on the basis of LC testimony, the House Committee on Public Works and Transportation said that "The Library of
Congress has successfully demonstrated that DEZ can be safely used
and the element of risk connected with its use substantially minimized
if not eliminated."

On August 2, 1984, Congress was told that "The Library of
Congress, in cooperation with NASA and an independent safety consultant, undertook a detailed, step-by-step analysis of the equipment
used in the process to evaluate risks in the engineered design. This
analysis resulted in numerous changes in the design to eliminate any

potential hazards, and these changes will be incorporated in the facility at Fort Detrick. As currently engineered, the Library of Congress states that there will be absolutely no safety risks to personnel or books with the Library of Congress process."

On the basis of reports like these, Congress appropriated $11.5 million to build a plant for the Library of Congress process at Fort Detrick. On February 20, 1986, although there had already been two fires and an explosion, all unexplained, at the Goddard installation, and LC was admitting that one of them "may be due to incompatibility of materials in the piping system," the Library of Congress was admitting to no more than a delay. On the following day, February 21, 1986, the plant at Goddard was ordered demolished by NASA, which found the safety factors unacceptable, despite a previous study, noted above, which had set the risk factor at close to zero. According to a draft report by NASA personnel, due to be released in late July, but not yet available, the demolition, it was learned, may have averted a truly massive explosion.

Neither Congress nor the library community has been told of the preponderance of evidence for the danger and unmanageability of DEZ. In an address delivered May 19, 1986 at Oxford, England, LC Scientist Donald Sebera did not even mention the fires, explosions, and final demolition of the LC pilot plant, although it was alluded to by at least one other speaker.

The DEZ Process as Prototype

The Library of Congress has repeatedly claimed that its process would provide a prototype, not only for deacidification plants in this country, but for the world. Congress likes to have the money it grants bear fruit, and accepting LC's assurances that it had tamed DEZ, it listened to Librarian of Congress Daniel Boorstin, at the April 11, 1984 U.S. Senate Committee on Rules and Administration, saying that "The facilities for which we seek authorization can be a prototype for others in the United States and so encourage economies of preservation and acquisition for all our nation's libraries."

The downplaying of the safety risks that would be associated with placing facilities using this volatile, and still not fully understood, process has made the notion of "prototype" facilities seem credible to both Congress and the library community.

Progress Claimed

Details of the DEZ process have never been released by the Library of Congress, although they have been requested. It may be that full information to convert the process to an "industrial" one simply doesn't exist, since the development of the DEZ process has proceeded only as far as the chemical engineering involved. Development of an industrial process is still not accomplished, although it would seem to have been a reasonable expectation of the Congress when it appropriated $11.5 million for the facility.

Past LC reports made it seem that, even years ago, the process was sufficiently developed to be described in detail and considered a finished product.

In September 1980, George Kelly told the Society for Archives and Institute for Paper Conservation that "After five years of development, we now believe the diethyl zinc process is ready for commercial use. Large-scale trials of this process have been described in a paper presented at the sixth AIC Annual Meeting in Fort Worth, Texas in June 1978. At that time, some problems remained, but they have now been resolved." Kelly also predicted, in the first of many target dates, that LC would "possibly begin treatment of the collections in 1982."

In the footnotes to his paper, Kelly gave the first public report of a 5000-book test of the DEZ process, claiming that, "The books were thoroughly tested by the Library of Congress for complete effectiveness of the treatment...."

Not reported to Congress and the library community was the fact that nearly 50 percent of the books which were put through the process were not fully deacidified and many were actually damaged. These two facts have been left out of almost all reports, although LC officials have shared with nonlibrary audiences on more than one occasion.

Donald Sebera, speaking at the 1983 American Institute for Conservation Annual Meeting of the Book and Paper Specialty Group on the results of the 5000-book test, also referred to it as a "success," although he admitted that of the 5000 books treated, "we were estimating somewhere on the order of 50 to 55 percent were fully treated." Sebera's remarks were transcribed from an unedited tape of the meeting.

In August 1983, Peter Sparks, director for preservation at LC, told an IFLA audience that the DEZ process had been "successfully demonstrated ... at the large plant level with about 6600 books [formerly referred to as 5000] treated." He predicted an operational plant for late 1985 at the earliest and claimed: "We are in the home stretch of making [the DEZ process] available for production treatment."

On March 17, 1986, after the pilot plant had been blown up by NASA order, the Library moved its timetable ahead again, but in wording that made it appear that no change had been made, referring not to the "scheduled completion of the project within a time frame close to the original one of 1988."

What Books to Save?

On the occasion cited above, Sebera said that the Fort Detrick plant was designed primarily to handle new acquisitions. According to Sebera, "We're concerned only with, in this development stage, new nonrare books. These books will be processed by the DEZ process before being put on the shelf for use in the collection. Later than it may well be, and we expect there will be, some application to older materials. Perhaps manuscripts, perhaps older books in the collection. But, the design is for new books, of a nonrare type."

Further on, Sebera says that "within 20 years we expect that this process will not need to be used to any great extent. We will be in the secondary format, will be either optical discs or some others, and the new books coming out, probably many of them will already come in these secondary formats."

Various figures have been cited, but new acquisitions at LC are expected to number 350,000 a year. With a capacity of 500,000 books a year, Fort Detrick, at best, would be able to deacidify 200,000 of the 14 million older books in the LC stacks each year. In 20 years that would be four million books.

Much of the support for mass deacidification has been in response to appeals based on the potential loss through deterioration of millions of volumes of irreplaceable treasures. While new acquisitions will be preserved for the ages, books now on LC shelves will be "systematically" treated. The choice of the term "systematic" suggests that LC does not plan to deacidify all its older books or to preserve them in their original form.

Appeals for support of the DEZ process have usually been made in the name of these older books. In 1971, LC Scientist John C. Williams, in a paper on the chemistry of deacidification, said "Libraries today are hospitals for sick books ... the Library of Congress ... has six million volumes too brittle to circulate."

In 1974, Williams and Kelly in a joint paper noted that "the Library of Congress has six million books which are already in such a condition that they should not circulate and ... the whole collection should be neutralized and buffered to halt the degradation ... [in the United States] there must be 100 times this or 300,000 tons in the emergency class."

Again in September 1980, Kelly said, "The Library of Congress has six or seven million books which are so deteriortated that they should not circulate and with some exceptions, the whole collection should be neutralized and buffered." The diethyl zinc process, he said, is ready to solve the problem.

According to the <u>Washington Post</u> on February 21, 1986,
Sparks, joining Boorstin at a House budget hearing in testimony on
the effect of the Gramm-Rudman-Hollings budget cuts, referred to
the deacidification project as one intended to "remove acid from most
of the library's 13 million books."

Alternatives to DEZ

Alternatives to the use of DEZ and other zinc compounds exist,
and even now are being used successfully and safely, both at Princeton and at the National Archives of Canada, where one process, based
on magnesium rather than zinc, has been working since 1971. The
British Library is reported actively developing a somewhat similar
chemical approach, as is France's Bibliothèque Nationale.

LC's Response

A letter in the August issue of <u>LJ</u> (p. 12, 14) by Sparks
claimed that there were several inaccuracies in the April 1 <u>LJ</u> news
story (p. 12) on the demolition of LC's test facility at the Goddard
Space Center.

Key Questions

One purpose for this review of the DEZ information above is
to provide further documentation for statements in that April 1 <u>LJ</u>
report. The issue of whether the Congress or the library community
have been properly informed regarding the DEZ process hinges on
such matters as the danger involved in the DEZ process, the likelihood of the system being a useful prototype for similar plants to be
built around the country, the accuracy of reports of progress made
toward a successful process, and the primary objective of the mass
deacidification plant to be built in Maryland.

The key question, of course, is why the Library of Congress
has persisted in backing the DEZ process when the expenditure of
years of effort and untold funds to make it work have come to so
little. Congress and the library community should expect a credible
response.

FIRST AMENDMENT PROTECTION FOR THE
HIGH SCHOOL PUNSTER AND WILLIAM SHAKESPEARE*

Haig Bosmajian

On April 26, 1983, seventeen-year-old high school senior Matthew
Fraser presented at a student-run assembly at Bethel High School
near Tacoma, Washington, the following short speech to nominate a
friend of his for student body vice-president:

> I know a man who is firm--he's firm in his pants, he's firm
> in his shirt, his character is firm--but most of all, his belief
> in you, the students of Bethel, is firm. Jeff Kuhlman is
> a man who takes his point and pounds on it. If necessary,
> he'll take an issue and nail it to the wall. He doesn't attack
> things in spurts--he drives hard, pushing and pushing until
> finally--he succeeds.
>   Jeff is a man who will go to the very end--even the
> climax--for each and every one of you.
>   So vote for Jeff as ASB vice-president--he'll never come
> between you and the best our high school can be.

School authorities suspended Fraser for three days for violating the
school's disruptive conduct rule which prohibited the use of "obscene,
profane language or gestures," and even though he was subsequently
elected a graduation speaker by his classmates, school officials denied
him permission to speak.

Fraser, a member of the Honor Society who had won statewide
honors as a debater, took his case to the U.S. District Court, and
Judge Jack Tanner,

> issued a declaratory judgment that the School District vio-
> lated Fraser's rights under the First and Fourteenth Amend-
> ments under the United States Constitution and the Civil
> Rights Act by subjecting him to a three-day suspension and
> removing his name from the list of candidates for the gradua-
> tion speaker.... Judge Tanner also enjoined the District

*Reprinted by permission of the author and publisher from English
Journal (March 1986) 67-71; vol. 75, issue 3.

from refusing to allow Fraser to participate in Bethel High
School's commencement exercises as a graduation speaker.[1]

The U.S. Court of Appeals, Ninth Circuit, agreed with Judge
Tanner's decision and decided against the School District which had
appealed. In deciding for Fraser, the Court of Appeals concluded
that the School District had "failed to demonstrate that the speech
had a materially disruptive effect on the educational process." The
court held that "the First Amendment prohibited the District from
punishing Fraser for making a speech that school officials considered
to be 'indecent.'" Further, the court rejected the District's argument that it could "discipline Fraser for using language considered
to be objectionable because the speech was made at a school-sponsored
function and was an extension of the school program." The School
District appealed to the U.S. Supreme Court, and on October 7,
1985, the High Court agreed to hear the case during its 1985-1986
term.

Since what had upset the school officials was Fraser's use of
the double entendre and "indecent" puns, it would have been appropriate and valuable to have included in the Court of Appeals' otherwise persuasive opinion a brief discussion of the pun and double
entendre as figures of speech which have had a long and honorable
history in the literature of Shakespeare, Jonathan Swift, Lewis Carroll, James Joyce, and others. While the court did say that "high
school students voluntarily attending an assembly to hear student
campaign speeches surely do not expect the same measure of privacy
and protection from unwelcome language and ideas that they obviously
do at home" and while the court did cite from Cohen v. California
to assert that "we have at the same time consistently stressed that
we are often 'captives' outside the sanctuary of the home and subject to objectionable speech," the Court of Appeals did not, unfortunately, cite the following from Cohen:

> ... we cannot overlook the fact, because it is well illustrated
> by the episode involved here [Cohen had been arrested for
> wearing in a Los Angeles courthouse a jacket on the back
> of which were the words "Fuck the Draft"], that much lin-
> guistic expression serves a dual communicative function:
> it conveys not only ideas capable of relatively precise, de-
> tached explication, but otherwise inexpressible emotions as
> well. In fact, words are often chosen as much for their
> emotive as their cognitive force. We cannot sanction the
> view that the Constitution, while solicitous of the cognitive
> content of individual speech, has little or no regard for that
> emotive function which, practically speaking, may often be
> the more important element of the overall message sought to
> be communicated. Indeed, as Mr. Justice Frankfurter has
> said, "one of the prerogatives of American citizenship is the
> right to criticize public men and women--and that means not
> only informed and responsible criticism but the freedom to
> speak foolishly and without moderation."[2]

In Cohen the Supreme Court recognized the relationship between banning offensive words and the censorship of ideas.

> ... we cannot indulge in the facile assumption that one can forbid particular words without also running the risk of suppressing ideas in the process. Indeed, governments might soon seize upon the censorship of particular words as a convenient guise for banning the expression of unpopular views.

The censorship of any kind of discourse in our schools must concern all teachers, especially English teachers, who have a stake in protecting the First Amendment rights of students and teachers to express themselves freely without fear of punishment. While Fraser was being punished by school officials for his punning and his use of the double entendre, textbooks used in English classes and books found in the school library contained language more "indecent" than that heard in Fraser's speech. Of course, school officials were practicing a kind of selective enforcement.

The same students who listened to Fraser's speech may have read Hamlet in which there appears the following dialogue.

> Hamlet: Lady, shall I lie on your lap?
> Ophelia: No, my lord.
> Hamlet: I mean, my head upon your lap?
> Ophelia: Ay, my lord.
> Hamlet: Do you think I meant country matters?
> Ophelia: I think nothing, my lord.
> Hamlet: That's a fair thought to lie between maids' legs.
> Ophelia: What is, my lord?
> Hamlet: Nothing.

As Eric Partridge has pointed out in Shakespeare's Bawdy, "Perhaps less aesthetic were his [Shakespeare's] never unaesthetic references to the female lap, the mons Veneris, the pubic hair, the thighs. For Shakespeare, the work lap seems to have always borne a sexual connotation."[3] Hilda Hulme concludes in Explorations in Shakespeare's Language that the above passage from Hamlet "leaves no doubt as to the obscene meaning of lap."[4]

Some of the same students who listened to Fraser's speech may have even been exposed to Shakespeare's Venus and Adonis in which the following lines appear.

> Fondling, she saith, since I have hemm'd thee here
> Within the circuit of this ivory pale,
> I'll be a park, and thou shalt be my deer;
> Feed where thou wilt, on mountain or in dale:
>   Grace on my lips; and if those hills be dry
>   Stray lower, where the pleasant fountains lie.
> Within this limit is relief enough,

> Sweet bottom-grass and high delightful plain,
> Round rising hillocks, brakes obscure and rough,
> To shelter thee from tempest and from rain:
> Then be my deer, since I am such a park;
> No dog shall rouse thee, though a thousand bark.

Park, deer, feed, moutain, dale, fountain, and other words are all used figuratively by Shakespeare. Of dale, for example, Partridge writes:

> Venus, inciting (and trying to excite) Adonis to roam in that park which is her fair body, says, "Feed where thou wilt, on mountain or in dale" (v. 232)--on the enimences or in the valleys: the valley between her breasts; the vulva-valley; and perhaps the rearward ravine.[5]

S.S. Hussey has pointed out in The Literary Language of Shakespeare,

> The Hostess addresses Pistol as "Good Captain Peesel," 2 Henry IV, II, iv, 156, and the spelling indicates a pun on pizzle ("bull's penis"), a word which Falstaff uses elsewhere (I Henry IV II, iv, 241); the same pun occurs when Falstaff says "She (the hostess) is pistolproof" (112).[6]

Whether high school students have read Hamlet, Othello, The Merchant of Venice or other Shakespearean plays, they will have been exposed to puns and the double entendre which are equal in "indecency" to those used by Fraser.

The same students who listened to Fraser's nominating speech hardly can escape the use of the pun and double entendre outside the school. The same week the United States Supreme Court agreed to hear the Fraser case, TV Guide (October 5-11, 1985) described in a Close Up a "Kate and Allie" show:

> As the show opens, Allie learns that the local paper has put her classified ad for employment in the personals column, giving a new and decidedly unintended meaning to the words "energetic woman seeks imaginative and innovative new positions."

Students, young and old, were being invited to view a show on national television revolving around a double entendre which, one would assume, Fraser would have been punished for using in his nominating speech.

A few weeks later, the December 1985 issue of MAD magazine appeared with a cover featuring Rambo (alongside Ronald Reagan) with his huge rocket launcher phallically protruding at hip level. Inside the magazine the "Dumbelles Dept," featured a salute to "all

the ladies who pump iron," the salute in the form of several stanzas
to be sung to Madonna's "Material Girl." One of the stanzas read:

> No lard on the superior girl!   (Superior!)
> Skin hard on a superior girl!
> Flesh rough on a superior girl!   (Superior!)
> "Ram-Tough" on a superior girl!

In fact, the entire MAD magazine is one big pun. The same students
who listened to Fraser's speech in 1983 were brought up on MAD.
As Richard Reeves has half-jestingly observed in his 1973 essay "Mad
Magazine--Witness for the People,"

> He [Reeves' eleven-year-old son] doesn't just read Mad--
> he memorizes, quotes, collects, and fondles it. So, he tells
> me, do all but one of the boys in Miss Piper's sixth-grade
> class at Main Street School in Denville, New Jersey.... Mad
> may be the most influential magazine in the United States....
> Assume it or not, Jeffrey Richard Reeves gets his information
> from television and his viewpoint from Mad, and he and his
> friends will start voting and doing other things in 1980.[7]

Jeffrey, while watching television, no doubt heard the woman in the
advertisement alluringly declare through her double entendre that
all her men wear English Leather or they wear nothing at all.

The high school student, like Fraser, who sees puns, irony,
and the double entendre used effectively in the literature assigned
in English classes and used as a basis for humor in some of the most
successful television programs and used widely in popular magazines
and used effectively in advertisements--that student easily could come
to the conclusion that the use of these rhetorical tropes are equally
appropriate in a high school political campaign.

As the Court of Appeals pointed out,

> Fraser was not talking to children too young to read; he was
> speaking to young adults, many of whom as high school
> seniors on the eve of graduation would have already reached
> voting age. Realistically, high school students are beyond
> the point of being sheltered from the potpourrie of sights
> and sounds we encounter at every turn in our daily lives.

The difficulty with placing a ban on the expression of "indecent" puns and the double entendre is that the "meaning" of the
words may be harmless; the "meaning" is "indecent" to "indecent"
minds. As Frankie Rubinstein has indicated in A Dictionary of
Shakespeare's Sexual Puns and Their Significance, "A ROSE is a
rose is a rose--but it is also a maidenhead, a pudendum and a whore;
it depends on where it is and whose it is."[8] The Court of Appeals
recognized the relative nature of "indecent" language and the danger

of giving school officials "discretion to apply the amorphous standard of 'indecency' to restrict the First Amendment freedoms of high
school seniors making campaign speeches for student office":

> We fear that if school officials had the unbridled discretion
> to apply a standard as subjective and elusive as "indecency"
> in controlling the speech of high school students, it would
> increase the risk of cementing white, middle-class standards
> for determining what is acceptable and proper speech and
> behavior in our public schools. Language that may be con-
> sidered "indecent" in one segment of our heterogeneous
> society may be common, household usage in another. Free-
> dom to be different in our individual manner of expression
> is a core constitutional value; the First Amendment reflects
> the considered judgement of our Founding Fathers that govern-
> ment officials, including public school administrators and,
> for that matter, judges, should not be permitted to use their
> power to control individual self-expression.

While the Court of Appeals decided for punster Fraser, it did
not include in its opinion any discussion of what it means to make
a pun. The United States Supreme Court in its deliberations on this
case might note that The American Heritage Dictionary of the English
Language says of the origin of "to make a pun":

> Probably short for obsolete pundigrion, perhaps variant of
> Italian puntiglio, fine point, quibble, diminutive of punto,
> point, from Latin punctum, pricked hole, point, from pugere,
> to prick.

What is one to do with the student who criticizes the construction of a controversial school building as "the school board's erection?"
Are such words as position, laid, prick, trick and equally "suggestive" words to be banned from high school campaign speeches? Is
the student to be suspended from school for declaring that his or her
opponent "knows all the tricks in the trade" and that "we know what
his favorite position is?"

Since there existed no clear school guidelines to warn Fraser
that he was not free to use puns, irony, or the double entendre in
his speech, he had no way of knowing that he faced punishment if
he incorporated the pun and double entendre into his nominating
speech. The school's disruptive conduct rule stated: "Conduct
which materially and substantially interferes with the educational
process is prohibited, including the use of obscene, profane language
or gestures." In the legal sense, Fraser's speech contained nothing
which was obscene of profane. Of the constitutionality of this rule,
the Court of Appeals said in footnote 12 to its opinion:

> It follows from our First Amendment analysis that we must
> also affirm Judge Tanner's declaration that the school's mis-
> conduct rule is constitutionally infirm, because on its face it

permits a student to be disciplined for using speech considered to be "indecent" even when engaged in an extra-
curricular activity.

Unfortunately, the court did not elaborate on the idea that
teachers and students who have been punished by school officials
for the expression of controversial and "indecent" speech have often
received protection from the courts because the school authorities
had not established clear criteria or guidelines defining what was precisely prohibited and punishable. For example, the United States
Court of Appeals, Fifth Circuit, decided in 1972 for high school
students who had been suspended for distributing near school prem-
ises an "underground newspaper" they had authored and published.
In deciding for the students, the court said,

> We conclude that the regulation [regarding distribution of
> materials], is overbroad: (1) because it purports to estab-
> lish a prior restraint on any and all exercise of expression
> by means of the written word on the part of high school
> students at any time and in any place and for any reason;
> and (2) because it contains no standards whatsoever by
> which principals might guide their administrative screenings
> of "petitions or printed documents of any kind, sort, or
> type."[9]

Another United States Court of Appeals, Fourth Circuit, decided in 1973 for high school students who had challenged the constitutionality of school regulations involving prior restraint on the
distribution of non-school literature. In deciding for the students,
the court said that its decision rested, in part, on the legal proposition that "such prior restraints must contain precise criteria sufficiently spelling out what is forbidden so that a reasonably intelligent
student will know what he may write and what he may not write."[10]

In deciding for a teacher who had been dismissed for assigning
Kurt Vonnegut's Welcome to the Monkey House to her eleventh grade
English classes, a United States District Court stated in 1970,

> Our laws in this country have long recognized that no per-
> son should be punished for conduct unless such conduct
> has been proscribed in clear and precise terms.... When
> the conduct being punished involves First Amendment rights,
> as is the case here, the standards for judging permissible
> vagueness will be even more strictly applied.

As for the effects of unclear guidelines, the court declared,

> When a teacher is forced to speculate as to what conduct is
> permissible and what conduct is proscribed, he is apt to be
> overly cautious and reserved in the classroom. Such a re-
> luctance on the part of the teacher to investigate and exper-

iment with new and different ideas is anathema to the entire
concept of academic freedom.[11]

What these courts, and numerous others, have said about the
need for school authorities to establish clearly what is being pro-
scribed has to be applied to Fraser's case. Without clear guidelines,
Fraser, "a reasonably intelligent student," was forced to speculate
as to what was permissible. Without clear guidelines, students who
saw Fraser being punished for his use of the pun and the double
entendre may indeed become cautious and reluctant to experiment
with language. When one must guess what utterance is going to be
punished, one may become timid and steer clear of any imaginative
language which school officials would condemn as "indecent."

If we expect teenagers in high school to develop a respect for
our First Amendment freedoms, school officials have to demonstrate
that those freedoms apply to both students and teachers. As the
United States Supreme Court put it when it decided in Barnette in
1943 that students of the Jehovah's Witness faith could not be compelled by the state to salute the flag, the First Amendment rights
need to be practiced in our schools "if we are not to strangle the
free mind at its source and teach youth to discount important principles of our government as mere platitudes."[12] Thirty years after
Barnette, United States Court of Appeals Judge Irving Goldberg,
after declaring in Shanley that "it is most important that our young
become convinced that our Constitution is a living reality, not parch-
ment preserved under glass," admonished the school authorities:

> Perhaps it would be well if those entrusted to administer the
> teaching of American history and government to our students
> begin their efforts by practicing the document on which that
> history and government are based. Our eighteen-year-olds
> can now vote, serve on juries, and be drafted; yet the board
> fears the "awakening" of their intellects without reasoned
> concern for its effect upon discipline. The First Amendment
> cannot tolerate such intolerance.[13]

The same year Fraser was told by school officials at Bethel
High School that his language was "inappropriate," a Brunswick High
School senior in Maine was told the quotation she had chosen for inclusion in the school yearbook was "inappropriate." The quotation
she had selected was from the January 24, 1983, issue of Time magazine: "The executioner will pull this lever four times. Each time
2000 volts will course through your body, making your eyeballs
first bulge, then burst, and then broiling your brains." This anti-
capital punishment message was rejected by school officials because
it was "not appropriate for the yearbook." The United States District Court in Maine issued a preliminary injunction which required
"the Defendants [school officials] to do nothing save to hold their
hand with respect to final publication until the rights of both parties
to this litigation may be finally adjudicated." Some of what that

District Court said in its opinion clearly is applicable to the Fraser
case.

> We need not shrink from the hazards of a free people saying
> without restraint what they believe. We have a sufficient
> security in the Framers' profound conviction that the decency
> and sound judgment of an informed citizenry will, in good
> time, winnow the rash statement from the reasonable one,
> reject the foolish proposal for the principled one, discern
> the zealot from the diplomat, and distinguish the demagogue
> from the democrat. That conviction is our substitute for the
> more immediately attainable safety provided by government
> control, in the name of "taste" and "appropriateness," of
> what we as individuals may be and write.[14]

References

1. Fraser v. Bethel School Dist. No. 403, 755 F. 2d 1356 (1985).
2. Cohen v. California, 403 U.S. 15 (1971).
3. Eric Partridge, Shakespeare's Bawdy (New York: Dutton, 1948),
    p. 22.
4. Hilda Hulme, Explorations in Shakespeare's Language (London:
    Longmans, 1962), p. 119.
5. Partridge, p. 98.
6. S.S. Hussey, The Literary Language of Shakespeare (London:
    Longmans, 1982), p. 139.
7. Richard Reeves, "Mad Magazine--Witness for the People" in High
    Rank (ed.), Language and Public Policy (Urbana, Illinois:
    NCTE, 1974), pp. 84-85.
8. Frankie Rubenstein, A Dictionary of Shakespeare's Puns and
    Their Significance (London: Macmillan, 1984), p. xi.
9. Shanley v. Northeast Ind. School Dist., 462 F. 2d 960 (1972).
10. Baughman v. Freienmuth, 478 F. 2d 1345 (1973).
11. Parducci v. Rutland, 316 F. Supp. 352 (1970).
12. West Virginia State Bd. of Ed. v. Barnette, 319 U.S. 624 (1943).
13. Shanley v. Northeast Ind. School Dist., 462 F. 2d 960 (1972).
14. Stanton v. Brunswick School Dist., 577 F. Supp. 1560 (1984).

ISSUES IN YOUTH ACCESS TO LIBRARY SERVICES:
A COMMENTARY ON PROFESSIONAL
ATTITUDES AND PRACTICES†*

Mary K. Chelton

There is an unresolved question in librarianship over the relationship between access and intellectual freedom, engendered in part by
the way in which intellectual freedom is discussed as something people
other than librarians are trying to do away with. This view is institutionalized in the separation of access and intellectual freedom concerns within the priorities of the American Library Association. Priority number one, which is Access to Information says, "ALA will
promote efforts to assure every individual access to needed information at the time needed and in a format the individual can utilize,
through provision of library and information services." Priority number three, which is Intellectual Freedom says, "ALA will promote the
protection of library materials, personnel, and trustees from censorship, the defense of library personnel and trustees in support of
intellectual freedom and the Library Bill of Rights; and the education
of library personnel, trustees, and the general public to the importance of intellectual freedom."[1] The relationship is further clouded
by the exclusive use of the term "access" to index articles on the
"problem patron" in Library Literature.

   Finding neither ALA nor Library Literature particularly helpful,
I turned to several dictionaries and discovered that a common syno-
nym for access was "approach." In one dictionary, access was "The
act of approaching,"[2] and in another the "way by which a thing
or place may be approached."[3] This was a lot closer to my own
philosophical orientation and that of the organizers of this conference.
In library terms, then, access would describe the conglomeration of

†This presentation was delivered on July 31, 1984, at the conference,
"Access to Information: A Youth's Right--A Community's Responsibility," sponsored by the Southeastern Library Association in cooperation with the School of Library and Information Studies, Florida
State University, and the State Library of Florida.

*Reprinted by permission of the author and publisher from School
Library Media Quarterly 14 (Fall 1985) 21-25; copyright © 1985.

means by which users and potential users are assured the means of
approaching desired information.   Regardless of whether the barrier
is psychological, interpersonal, physical, financial, geographical,
linguistic, or legal, the library can play little role in assuring the
public's intellectual freedom rights to legally protected speech without attention to matters of access.

In youth services librarianship, the overriding access issue
is the degree to which the librarian functions in loco parentis and
the degree to which youth-serving librarians should function that
way. Put simply, the issue is whether the child or the parent is
the primary client, and assuming that can be decided on anything
but an individual basis, exactly what does the decision mean on a
day to day basis? On this subject, ALA is quite clear. In "Free
Access to Libraries for Minors. An Interpretation of the Library
Bill of Rights," ALA says, "Libraries or library boards which would
restrict the access of minors to materials and services because of
actual or suspected parental objections should bear in mind that they
do not serve in loco parentis."[4] It is interesting that this is the
only interpretation in which the word access appears, and it does not
appear in the actual Library Bill of Rights itself. Despite ALA's
clarity, however, and my philosophical agreement with the statement,
the Library Bill of Rights has no legal standing and is far less well
known to the general public than the ever troublesome Motion Picture
Association ratings.

Furthermore, the only legal precedent on the books, Board of
Education, Island Trees Union Free School District vs. Pico, does
not offer much philosophical support for ALA's position in terms of
school libraries. A careful reading shows great ambivalence among
the judges about whether anyone in schools other than the school
board has any First Amendment rights. The Pico decision gives no
clear constitutional protection to the rights of students to receive
information; about the best it does is give us the clout to point out
to censorious school boards that they can be hauled into court to
have their motivations examined--a strategy the National Coalition
Against Censorship has been using effectively since the decision.
In my opinion, there is currently more legal protection for school
newspaper editors to distribute information to students than there
is for school librarians to do so.

Since legal discussions of youth access to information remain
largely hypothetical outside the realm of obscenity legislation--more
properly the subject of another speech--the rest of my comments
will cover a variety of professional attitudes and practices which
inhibit youth access in libraries. Since this may involve a fair amount
of self-flagellation, I need to point out that I know that much of the
following is either inherited policy or tradition for which no one of
us may be totally responsible in our own situation. However, I do
feel that the longer these attitudes and practices remain unexamined
and unchallenged, the longer they will continue to undermine what
we say we are attempting to do.

Attitudes

Beginning with attitudes, I think many librarians feel that they, the adult "gatekeepers," really "own" the library, and that library use is a privilege extended to young people who behave in expected ways. The ideal patron would be someone who comes in person alone, who is quiet and respectful, who loves to read "good books," and who is probably a white female just like most of us. The jargon for this mythical patron is "the special reader." A reading student in my YA class at Rutgers described the attitude this way. She was a special education teacher whose students rarely had ever read any book all the way through, and when she finally got them able to do that, she would take them on a visit to the library. There, she said, two things inevitably happened. Since they were not "library kids," the librarian usually was not happy to have them there, and on top of that, had very little that they could read anyway. She wanted to encourage library use among her new readers, but was increasingly frustrated at the attitude of the librarians they encountered.

Our telephone reference policies in public libraries have consistently erected barriers to needed information for kids attempting to do homework. Kids calling for homework help get hit with a double bias. First, they are calling and should come in person to the library, despite the fact that most kids do not control their own transportation. Secondly, they are calling about homework which we think they should be doing themselves with barely minimal librarian assistance; homework being somehow less important than reading for pleasure, despite the fact that young people of school age are legally compelled to be in school. These attitudes not only prevent access to needed information; they fly in the face of demographic reality. With the increase in single- and two-parent working families, the availability of adults to provide transportation and homework help is diminished, and we should probably be expanding telephone reference service to kids, not getting them off the phone and into the library as fast as possible. Someone once said that it takes a village to raise a child, and we all have a responsibility to see that our community's children get their homework done.

Everyone laments the fact that more girls than boys seem to use libraries. Usually the lament is followed by comments that nobody is publishing anything of interest to them, but the truth is that we don't really like boys or what they are interested in very much, unless they conform to our expectations of the ideal, well-behaved mythical patron, and usually they don't unless they are terrible social introverts. Then they usually make a beeline for the science fiction, and we are delighted to leave them to their own devices because most of us don't like science fiction very much either. When I read Soul of a New Machine by Tracy Kidder[5] two years ago, shortly after he won the Pulitzer Prize for nonfiction, I was struck by the successive portraits of the electrical engineers in the book as children and adolescents, and wondered if and how a particular

librarian might have helped them.   I think one of the great undone
research projects is an oral history of the youthful library experiences of some of the geniuses in Silicon Valley, but for starters,
here is one from Soul of a New Machine:

>Alsing's childhood did not leave him with an abundance of
>sweet memories. Discovering the telephone was one of his
>fondest. When he was eight and in the third grade, his
>family moved from central Massachusetts to Evansville, In-
>diana. He loathed that place. "I was smaller, paler, weaker,
>less rugged and I had a funny accent. I remember discover-
>ing in third grade that there was a pecking order--Hey,
>there's a pile and I'm on the bottom of it. I was a very de-
>pressed kid in third grade." He vividly recalled the day
>when he skipped recess, usually a painful event for him any-
>way, and instead worked at his desk on the design of a tele-
>phone. He wanted to find out how the thing could possibly
>capture a voice. It seemed to him an improbable instrument,
>one that shouldn't work. He read about telephones in sev-
>eral encyclopedias. Then he took the family phone apart.
>Finally, he figured it out to his satisfaction. "This was a
>fantastic high, something I could get absorbed in and forget
>that I had these other social problems."
>   One day, while at home in Evansville, he was prowling
>the basement and noticed wires running across the ceiling of
>the coal bin. He traced them back to the phone upstairs.
>He got a hold of some batteries, an old microphone and an
>ancient set of earphones, and from the coal bin--sitting there
>all alone in the grime, with the earphones on--he tapped the
>family's telephone. Once in a while, he accidentally short-
>circuited it, but his father, an engineer for Westinghouse
>who designed refrigerators, was indulgent on that score.[6]

I wonder how many Alsings are running around our libraries
being ignored, or worse, how many of them have learned to do without us? I once listened to several members of a library staff complain about two brothers who kept "pestering" them daily for information on the Marx Brothers with the same single-minded ferocity Al-
sing brought to telephone circuitry. In retrospect, I think their
collective annoyance was because the two brothers were not confined
to the children's room collection anymore.

When young male patrons add sex to their interests in adolescence, they not only come up against our general anxiety about subject matter which will get us in trouble, but also our distaste for
developing male sexuality. Even with our mania for preferring any
fiction to any nonfiction (because most of us are English majors,
right?), Summer of '42,[7] Hard Feelings,[8] and Vision Quest[9]
have all been labeled "obscene" by working librarians in my presence.
This was the main reason why Vision Quest did not make YASD's
recent "Best of the Best" list.   When such books are not being called

"obscene" by one set of librarians these days, they are usually being called "sexist" by another, when neither is particularly accurate. I think the real problem is that we look at these titles as outsiders to the adolescent male experience. Having been excluded from the male locker room, we find its language startling and distasteful personally, and troublesome politically. Having been socialized by the possibility of pregnancy to equate sex and commitment, we are personally upset over depictions of adolescent male sexual experimentation, because we see ourselves retrospectively as the potential victims of it. When you add the fear of parental and administrative reprisal to an already crowded emotional agenda, it is a miracle that any of these books ever get bought by libraries, let alone into the hands of male adolescents who need them. I am hoping that Dolores Sweeney's Center Line dos not end up in the same silly cross fire.

Our peculiar ambivalence toward sexual materials does not just occur in the YA area as can be best documented by all the libraries which did not buy Peter Mayle's Where Did I Come From?[10] And we all know the cases where little pants were added to the nude boy in In the Night Kitchen.[11] As Billy Pilgrim would say, "And so it goes."

Before I leave the problem of our not particularly liking certain classes of patrons or what they are interested in if it does not interest us, I need to point out that, demographically, the United States youth population of the future is going to be made up of a majority of kids not like us. White fertility in this and most other "developed" countries is below replacement level, and our future patrons will be mostly black and Hispanic, unless we opt to work in segregated white schools or enclaves.

Having dropped that particular, inevitable time bomb, let me return to the present and examine some of our materials selection attitudes, the most hypocritical of which is the Law of Literary Merit, which says that concern over literary quality rises in direct proportion to alarm over content. Most of the teenage romances are no more poorly written than the average "realistic" teen novel, but objections to the girl-gets-boy stereotypic formula are far more frequent in professional literature than objections to first person problem novels filled with inept adults. Forever is no more badly written than Paula Danziger's books, but you would never know it from the reviews. I've never been sure whether our preoccupation with the quality of controversial materials means that their quality is expected to save us from feared censorship battles, or that we are just looking for a good excuse to reject the item in question. Whichever the rationale, the result is less access for kids to needed materials which happen to be controversial with adults.

I think we prefer hardback books to any other kind of format, and we have institutionalized a reviewing system which makes it easy for us to maintain that bias. This is a holdover from the days in

which libraries were archives rather than information centers, and
also from the days in which fewer format options existed. I suspect
that if you asked librarians their order of preference, hardbacks
would head the list and comics would be last, with kids preferring
just the reverse. Worse still, most of us still display any books we
buy spine out, ignoring all the analogous display wisdom we could
glean from the national paperback and magazine distributing industries.
I thought that the merchandising fad in public libraries might help
us, but our preoccupation with taste and decor makes many merchandising type libraries still look like hardback emporiums. Kids like
paperbacks. If we want to facilitate their access to information, we
collect materials in the formats they prefer, and we scream bloody
murder for review tools to help us do that.

I think the bottom line is that we think what we like is more
important than what they like and we feel betrayed when they don't
like what we think they should. As a profession, we hate the series
romances and programmed choice stories; yet we ignore the fact that
Bantam alone has made $28 million on the Sweet Dreams romances.
That's money that kids have shelled out themselves for books they
wanted, totally bypassing us. Elaine Harper, the Silhouette author
who writes First Love stories, gets twenty to thirty letters a week
from kids who say, among other things, "Yours was the first book
I ever read all the way through." It makes you wonder whether we
want young readers or clones.

I don't think I would mind the almost universal critical damna-
tion of the series books if I saw just a little of that energy going
into information programming for girls and their parents or care givers
about the knowledge and skills it will take to assure a viable economic
future for women in this culture. One of those skills, ironically, is
literacy, but another is an interest in mathematics and science which
does not become shortcircuited in early adolescence. Most of us
chose, for whatever reason, a "girls' ghetto" occupation, which does
not make us particularly well-equipped to help the women of tomorrow
make a different choice. It's a lot easier to yell and scream about
the romances.

Ironically, for all the librarians who feel that the romances
have too many fluffy, simplistic happy endings, there is also a camp
who feel that materials for young people should never be depressing
or upsetting. This is the mandatory innocence group who are presently arguing about the possible harm done by a picture book on
Hiroshima in the letters column of School Library Journal. Given the
number of children growing up in poverty here plus the number in
unsafe schools and families and neighborhoods, plus the historical
recency of the whole notion of an "innocent childhood," I find it
very hard to sympathize professionally with that materials selection
attitude, but it does exist.

I alluded earlier to the attitude that homework was considered

less important than reading for pleasure by many librarians, and
this attitude has created an artificial dichotomy between the readers'
advisory and reference functions which is exacerbated when a library
is large and departmentalized. Kids' questions become categorized
as either one or the other, when in reality, the question may en-
compass both. This is less a problem in school libraries and children's
departments than in public library YA services. Here the dichotomy
usually favors one function at the expense of the other. Either the
YA librarian is excluded by definition from reference collection building and policy setting, or the YA librarian is part of the reference
staff and the enrichment collection suffers from neglect. Information
is usually not exclusively fact finding or book reading, and breaking
down this artificially conceptualized dichotomy between information
and reading would be a major step toward improving access for the
whole young person, as opposed to that function we think is presenting itself.

Services

        Having covered most of the attitudinal barriers to youth access
in libraries, I would like to move on to some of the physical ones.
First of all, if the librarian or the people at the circulation desk behave like the high priest in the Temple of Doom, it doesn't much
matter what else you do. I think people who work in libraries who
come on to kids--anybody, for that matter--that way should be fired.
Nobody wants to go into a place where they are made to feel about
as welcome as the plague, and we have got some real curmudgeons
who hate kids floating around libraries. Since many of them have
permanent civil service status or are tentured, it takes real guts to
start documenting a case against them, but it is possible and it has
to be done. There are psychological and emotional components to
access, and having unpleasant, unaskable people around can just
kill the urge to go any further. I consider it one of my greatest
successes that the second library school student who worked for us
followed my advice on documenting a case against a rotten clerk in
the children's room and got her dismissed.

        The second physical barrier which consistently annoys me is
our idiotic space planning. We plan for the patrons we want, not
the ones who really exist. Kids are not comfortable in many of our
libraries, and the fact that we feel they should be is irrelevant.
The problem was best summarized by Sue Rosenzweig in her ALA
speech on "After-School Programming for Early Adolescents" reprinted
in the Fall 1983 issue of Top of the News:

        ... physical activity. How many of you have worked with
        or been parents of preschoolers (toddlers)? When you se-
        lected nursery schools, would you have considered ones that
        made your children sit in one place all day and didn't let
        them move around and exercise those restless, growing bodies?

Would you have taken them to a library that didn't allow them
to talk or move around in the children's room? Of course
not. We knew they were growing rapidly and needed room
to move, stretch, and test their new capabilities. Why are
we so willing to acknowledge that need in toddlers, but so
often reluctant to recognize the same need in young adolescents? Like pre-school youngsters, young teenagers are
growing rapidly. They are physically incapable of sitting
still for long periods of time. Any program that ignores
that need and relies upon silence, sedate behavior, and im-
mobility is doomed to failure. That is not to say that young
adolescents are never capable of silence, sedate behavior, or
tranquility. Their spurts of boundless energy are as well
known as their periods of dreamy lethargy. But growing
bodies do need frequent opportunities for movement--for
flexing, stretching, changing positions, and working off
bursts of energy. They also seem to need relaxation time,
too, to absorb the fatigue that often accompanies growth.
In a library, this means having a place where talking quietly
with friends is allowed, where one can sprawl out with a good
book (beanbag chairs are wonderful for this purpose), and
where wiggling and moving around is not frowned upon.[12]

It is also nice if the library is open when kids can use it. I
find it not only unconscionable but unethical that many school libraries close their doors to students during the school year for inventory, and that many public libraries have their thinnest staffing
during the after-school period, or no evening hours or weekend
hours.

Signs can be a problem, too. They are generally so tasteful
that they are downright dull. This does not exactly appeal to the
Michael Jackson generation. Worse than tasteful, though, are signs
in libraries which are amateurish and handwritten. Our patrons and
potential patrons are besieged by some of the most sophisticated graphic
designs in the world, and do we really expect to attract them using
signs designed by and for 45-year-olds, or worse, handwritten?

I've always been interested in the fact that very few school
libraries or public library youth collections feel a need for a new
materials shelf, when it is the one thing taken for granted as a PR
necessity for adult services, if nothing else. Having to search
through old stuff for new does not always lead to a rediscovery of
the old, but more often to frustration with the place. I've also had
librarians tell me that they did not have room for a "books into
movies" shelf, when every place I've ever seen with one couldn't
keep it filled.

Growing bodies need nourishment, but I've seen very few libraries which allow eating or drinking, usually to keep peace with
the custodians, but more often because we assume that every kid

is a potential litterer, sucker sticker, or drink spiller. Somehow
we equate serious work in libraries with being uncomfortable. We
could do a great deal of nutrition education with young people by
having healthy snacks available, and we would probably make a few
hungry adults happy too. Discomfort is an access barrier, and there
is a difference between socialization and social control.

"Access" outside library literature generally refers to the
physical means by which those of us who are disabled are helped to
participate more fully in our society. I think every librarian needs
to spend a day in his or her library in a wheelchair to understand
what lack of access really means. We are all potential spinal chord
injuries, so it is not a favor we're doing for anybody but ourselves.
By extension, we should also probably consider the needs of home-
bound or hospitalized kids in our service communities.

The location of the library within a school or the youth sec-
tion(s) within a public library is crucial. It has always amazed me
how many kids have not been able to tell me when I entered a school
where the library was, nor was there any way for me to find out
except to check in the office with one of those office clerks schools
seem to specialize in. They have perfected not noticing people, and
since they treat adults so shabbily and officiously, I've always shud-
dered about what happens to the kids who need them for something.
Switching schools, even within the same system, can be very unsettling for kids, and it seems silly to me for school librarians not
to take advantage of that first week confusion to make the library a
visible haven for new students who are feeling lost and bereft.
When you can't find a place without lots of directions, it hardly becomes a haven--more likely a hurdle.

I hope I don't need to say that bike racks should be a mandatory accoutrement of every public library, and some provision should
be made for kids who have expensive bikes which they don't want
stolen. I used to have the most officious battles with other staff
over letting kids bring bikes into the lower lobby of a branch library
where I worked. There would be nothing in the lobby but the bike
and the switchboard operator, but the bike did not "belong" there,
you see, and by allowing this familiarity, who knows to what use the
building would be put by the next uppity kid?

Why libraries which purport to serve young people buy designer furniture is beyond me. I am so sick of watching librarians
expend energy to keep kids' feet off coffee tables. I could scream.
Don't buy coffee tables if you don't want feet on them, or at least
have the good sense to buy indestructible coffee tables! Having
once worked in one of those god-awful "designer libraries," I used
to compromise by asking the kids to take their shoes off before they
put their feet on the precious tables, cursing whomever chose the
furniture for that library every time. It always interests me that
college libraries don't seem to mind student sprawl and manage to

plan for it, but secondary school libraries and most contemporary public libraries act as if no kids will ever be in the place except for where the picture books are.

I can't figure out whether security systems are a barrier or a challenge in libraries. I sort of considered them a necessary evil, or rather, an evil of last resort, until I recently received a letter from a school librarian who could not figure out how to insert the tattle tapes into paperbacks, so she did not buy any. As far as I am concerned, anything which keeps us from buying paperbacks is an access barrier.

Structural Access Barriers

An important barrier for potential young patrons is the variety of political boundaries placed on library use: nonresident fees, noncontiguous school and public library district boundaries, and the eligibility requirements built into some of our multi-type library networking agreements. It is scandalous that the New York State Interlibrary Loan System still says that those in prison or under the age of eighteen are not eligible for interlibrary loan service. It is ridiculous that some libraries still do not interloan children's materials, period. My partner, Dorothy Broderick, had to have a children's book read to her over the phone long distance for her dissertation on "The Image of the Black in Children's Fiction" because the owning library should not loan it even for on-site use in the borrowing library. It is stupid that some interlibrary loan agreements require borrowing libraries to affirm the "seriousness" of their patrons' requests.

So many of the multi-type interlibrary loan agreements are based on service ethics of college and university libraries which automatically attribute a status hierarchy to patrons. In universities, for example, there are the graduate faculty, the undergraduate faculty, graduate students, undergraduate students, etc. in descending order. This pecking order should not be institutionalized in interlibrary loan agreements, because it should be immediately obvious that, by these rules, children have no status whatsoever.

Even worse than the policies, however, is the fact that many libraries actively discourage interlibrary loans by young people by simply not volunteering that the service is available. The same is true for reserves.

Any fee-based services are problematic for young people, too, whether the service is database searching, videocassette rentals, or "donations" required for programs. In most cases, the policies written for these services exclude those under eighteen automatically from eligibility to use them, which amounts to discrimination by age of an entire class of people. Even in libraries without these services, young people are frequently excluded from being able to borrow or use very expensive materials like 16mm films.

The "parental permission required" shelves or titles in school libraries are clear access barriers, intentional ones, and I am sure that any type of closed shelves are warranted anymore except possibly for rare and irreplaceable items. Even with them, the possibility of microform reproduction exists.

The ways in which we determine "turf" inside and among libraries create some peculiar barriers for kids. I sometimes think that children's and YA librarians in public libraries spend more time arguing about who "owns" the seventh graders than about who is making sure they find what they want. Who "owns" parents--adults services or youth services? Who "owns" kids--school libraries or public libraries? Who "owns" reference work--adult services or youth services? We come almost full circle to the original question--who "owns" the library?

Several years back I visited a library which had a big sign on the front door at eye level as you entered, which said No running. No eating. No loud talking. No loitering. I stood there--furious, like a New York subway graffiti artist--wanting to scrawl in big red across that sign: "No kids wanted!" If youth advocacy means anything in libraries, at the very least it means that we constantly examine everything we do from the perspective of how it facilitates or impedes youth access. I would like to think of all libraries with an imaginary sign the front door which said Kids Wanted, and meant it.

References

1. ALA. Handbook of Organization and Membership Directory, 1983-84. (Chicago: ALA, 1983) p. 195.
2. Webster Illustrated Contemporary Dictionary. (Doubleday, 1982).
3. Webster's Third New International Dictionary of the English Language, Unabridged. Merriam-Webster, 1981).
4. ALA. Intellectual Freedom Manual, 2d ed. (Chicago: ALA, 1982) p. 22.
5. Tracy Kidder, Soul of a New Machine. (Avon, 1982).
6. Ibid., p. 92-93.
7. Herman Raucher, Summer of '42. (Dell, 1978).
8. Don Bredes, Hard Feelings. (Bantam, 1981).
9. Terry Davis, Vision Quest. (Bantam, 1981).
10. Peter Mayle, Where Did I Come From? (Lyle Stuart, 1973).
11. Maurice Sendak, In the Night Kitchen. (Harper, 1970).
12. Sue Rosenzweig, "3-6 p.m.: After-School Programming for Early Adolescents," Top of the News, 40:1 (Fall 1983) p. 37-47.

A SLOW, SUBTLE EXERCISE IN CENSORSHIP*

Elyse Clark

Suppose there was a school board somewhere that came up with a plan to increase reading motivation. Suppose this board also thought it would be beneficial to teach students some real lessons about the democratic process and constitutional rights. Now suppose that members of this board had the cooperation of the administration in making a decision that would further these goals. Together they decided to remove some very popular books from library shelves. Then a controversy erupted and stewed around these books. Despite protests, the board decided to restrict the books and initiated a parental permission checkout policy. Some board members claimed that this policy would encourage parents to become more involved with their children's reading interests.

In the spring of 1984, this decision to restrict books was made by the Hanover Board of Eduation and school administrators, who decided to institute the policy of obtaining parental permission for students who want to borrow five Judy Blume books from the middle school library. But, unfortunately, the boards' intent was not to increase the popularity of Blume's books (although this did happen) nor to make students more aware of their First Amendment rights (this also happened).

It all began when the parent of a third grade student filed a formal complaint against Honey of a Chimp by Norma Klein, which was in the circulating collection of the school library. According to the Evening Sun of October 8, 1984, the parent objected to the book because it "contained strong sexual content, a bias to liberal values and morals, and indecent language. [The] material condones certain values, attitudes and behaviors." At the bottom of the complaint form, the parent has noted, "[I] recommend reviewing all Judy Blume books for similar content."

*Reprinted by permission of the author and publisher from School Library Journal, 32:7 (March 1986) 93-96. Published by R.R. Bowker Division of Reed Publishing, USA. Copyright © 1986 by Reed Publishing, USA, a division of Reed Holdings, Inc.

The parent's complaint was handled at the elementary level by a committee made up of three administrators and the newly appointed elementary school librarian. The school administration ordered the removal of the following books from library shelves of all elementary libraries, serving kindergarten through fifth grade: Honey of a Chimp, and Judy Blume's Blubber, Deenie, Starring Sally J. Freedman as Herself, Tiger Eyes, and It's Not the End of the World.

When students realized that they were forbidden to check out some of their favorite titles, they composed and circulated a petition, dated April 11, 1984, which read: "We understand that there has been some book banning in the Hanover Public School District and we would like to protest this action. Most of the Judy Blume books have been taken out of the library and we feel people should be able to read her books or those of any other author. We would like to have these books put back. Book banning seems to be the opposite of the purpose of education." Despite the democratic efforts of the 115 original signers of this petition, the books were not replaced. The situation got worse. Later, in a closed session held in June of 1984, the board recommended that these titles also be removed from the shelves of the middle school and high school libraries.

I was greeted with news of the book banning on my return to the library that September. Very soon thereafter, within a few days of the opening of school, I received a verbal directive from my building principal ordering me to remove all of the restricted titles that were on the library shelves. As it happened, the middle school library did not have Norma Klein's book, but all the other Blume titles (and some that were not mentioned in the board directive). Two days later I was handed a list of quotations taken from the six titles, compiled by the elementary review committee with the preface, "The committee recommends that the following books be removed from shelves of the elementary libraries. If the board so chooses, these books could be placed in the middle school library, however, the committee feels that completely removing these books from libraries in the district would be the more appropriate action."

I responded by citing district policy requiring that a formal complaint be made at the middle school level, but was told not to expect one. The board relented on its banning of the six books from the high school library.

On September 20, the principal entered the middle school library while children were present and asked if I had removed the books. I said I had not, and he firmly directed me to do so at that time. I offered the shelves to him if he wished to remove the books, But he said he would not, and if I did not remove the books, I would risk being charged with insubordination. He gave me one day to "think about it." I was torn in my obligation to follow a direct order from my administration as well as to uphold the constitutional rights of the students. At this time I sought counsel from the Hanover

Education Association (HEA) representatives; the local chapter of
the National Education Association. HEA advised me to comply only
with a written order to remove the books.

The next day I received a directive labeled "Removal of Library
Books" dated September 20th. This read: "At the June 13, 1984
committee meeting of the Hanover Public School Board, it was decided
that the following books were inappropriate for the elementary and
middle school libraries. Under the school board's decision, I am requesting that you take the books out of circulation immediately and
that they remain out of circulation until further notice." Listed were
the five Blume titles and the single Klein title. Upon receiving this
ominous order, I removed the books from the shelves (several were
checked out) and put them in my desk.

With the support of HEA, I began grievance procedures on
September 28th. The grounds of this grievance was that board policy
had not been followed because there had never been a complaint made
at the middle school level on any of the books in question.

In October, a middle school committee was appointed to review
each of the titles and make a recommendation to the school board.
I was asked by the administration to serve on the committee along
with the principal and four of the middle school's teachers. When
notified of the committee existence, I sent a request to the board
president:

> On October 12, 1984, I was asked to serve on the middle
> school committee to review the following books: Starring
> Sally J. Freedman as Herself, Blubber, Tiger Eyes, Deenie
> and It's Not the End of the World. In order to know on
> what basis these books are to be evaluated, I am requesting
> a complaint at the middle school level to be forwarded to
> the middle school committee as per Hanover School Board
> Regulation 6163.1.

I received a reply on October 17, not from the board, but
from the administration. It stated that, "a complaint has not been
filed at the middle school," and asked that I review the books, looking for "offensive language, pervasive vulgarity, sexual content,
and psychological or intellectual appropriateness for the age group."

At the same time, The Evening Sun contacted me, seeking
details on the censorship of Blume's books. Hopeful that the committee's recommendation would restore the books to the shelves, I
declined to comment publicly at that time. Knowing what I know now,
events might have turned out differently if I had made a statement.

During the intervening weeks, both students and teachers
were visibly upset over the censorship of library books. Teachers
were disallowing the presentation of book reports on the banned titles.

Students were afraid to use the controversial titles in book discussions; teachers were reluctant to use them in displays for reading programs. Some teachers removed these titles from classroom shelves out of fear that the banning directive extended to them as well. Several parents came to me asking what they could do to help. I told them to write letters to both the local newspaper and the board requesting that the ban be lifted. Students constantly asked me "What's wrong with those books?" and demanded that I let them see them or check them out. They reminded me that other books by Blume, such as Then Again Maybe I Won't and Are You There God, It's Me, Margaret, were still on the shelves. (These two titles were not in the elementary library collection, so they escaped being placed on the original list.) Students also brought to my attention books that contained much more explicit details on growing up than any of the books censored, and mentioned other books which also contained strong language. At any moment during the day, I expected to be confronted by a confused or angry student who would sensationalize the issue before a class.

When the review committee met on October 29, they voted, almost unanimously, to restore the books to the shelves. The only dissenting vote came from the principal, who wanted to put them on a restricted shelf. My written comment to the board read, "After reviewing the books by Judy Blume, I feel that all the titles belong on the middle school library shelves. They fall within the guidelines of the Hanover Public School District's Book Selection Policy as being age appropriate for middle school students." This policy followed the guidelines of the American Library Association and had been in effect for years.

*   *   *

To: The School Board of the Hanover Public School District
From: Principal of Hanover Middle School
Re: Book Evaluation

In approaching the task of reviewing these library books, I viewed the material in the role of Middle School Principal and with the responsibility of being accountable for all that happens within the school building. This presented me with some dilemmas. For instance, if the discipline code prescribed penalties for students who write or say dirty words, how can I knowingly allow books with dirty words in the library? Also, a few years ago, some parents were concerned that some health films dealt with sex among teens in a casual way. The films were removed by the health teacher and me. How do I respond to some of these books? I questioned whether the purpose of a middle school library is the same as the purpose of a public library. I feel the public library has a much broader purpose and that the middle school library's purpose should be determined by the needs of the school as directed by the curriculum and approved by the school board. I considered the idea of "age appropriateness"

and compared this standard to the majority of students who are ages
eleven to thirteen. I prefer being cautious in what I provide for
them. I considered the idea of "therapeutic" literature and determined
that not all students need to receive therapy for the sake of a few.
My reaction to these books is, therefore, the result of this question-
ing I gave myself. Ultimately, I will comply with whatever the school
board and community decide.

*   *   *

In November, I contacted Judith Krug, director of the American
Library Association's Office of Intellectual Freedom, who supplied
some badly needed support and asked for documents of the events
that had transpired. Then, on November 14, 1984, the fateful decision was rendered by the school board. In spite of the majority
recommendation of the review committee to return the books to the
the open shelves, the board voted to establish a restricted shelf
policy requiring that students obtain the permission of a parent before checking out any of the banned books. This same policy was
instituted at the elementary level. Parental objections to the restriction were voiced at the November meeting, but were disregarded.

Frustration with the new policy was high among teachers,
parents, other librarians in the district, and among members of the
community. Hanover Public Librarian Priscilla Greco McFerren, who
was then president of Pennsylvania Library Association, openly expressed her disagreement with the restriction of library materials
calling it censorship. She and other members of the Hanover Public
Library's Board of Directors sent a letter to the Hanover School
Board asking that they lift the restriction. With the support of
several parents, McFerren, and librarians from neighboring communities, a committee was formed to look into changing the restriction
policy. Letters were sent to the board from parents distressed at
the decision. Even Krug sent a carefully drafted letter to the Hanover School Board, urging it to consider the Library Bill of Rights,
pointing out that according to ALA policy, "Libraries or library
boards who would restrict the access of minors to materials and
services because of actual or suspected parental objections should
bear in mind that they do not serve In loco parentis." In concluding her letter, Krug said that "Well-written, sensitive books that
address the very real issues, questions and concerns of young people
in our society are few and far between. Judy Blume's and Norma
Klein's books have received widespread critical acclaim and are extremely popular with young people for these very reasons."

On November 21, 1984, I was confronted with another verbal
directive: to compose the wording of the permission slip to be used
by students for the five Blume books. Again I objected, on the
grounds that this should be an administrative task. My objections
were overruled.

One week later I submitted a briefly worded permission slip with an attached memo stating that I was issuing it under protest and requesting that any further directives be made to me in writing. I was prompted to write a guest column for The Evening Sun, entitled "Memoirs of a Well-Beloved Book." The Sun and other news media continued to cover the issue as it developed.

On December 13, 1984, I reinstituted my grievance against the administration and board: "In having to enforce a restriction policy in the middle school library, I feel I am being discriminated against and my academic freedom is being infringed upon. To that extent, my working conditions have changed by requiring me to change my mode of operation. Therefore, I am requesting that the five Judy Blume books be replaced on the regular shelves and that the restriction policy be lifted." That day, I received the response from my principal: "Restructuring the circulation of books does not constitute a change in working conditions. Grievance denied."

On January 7, 1985, the HEA voted to discontinue grievance procedures on my behalf. My final option had been eliminated. Now it was up to parents and students to make the changes they wanted. Students who had petitioned the previous spring were now at the middle school. They wanted to leave a petition against the restriction policy in the middle school library for other students to sign. I was unsure about encouraging them to do this, urging them instead to leave their petition at the Hanover Public Library. Once the HEA had dropped my final course of action, my instinct was to draw back from the front-line battle.

A few parents wrote letters to the board, a few stopped in to offer their support, a few continued to attend the parents' committee McFerren had encouraged. Ultimately, however, these efforts failed. Parents were afraid of reprisals against their children who were then in the middle school. Some children wanted to attend the board meetings, but couldn't muster enough support. After all, the books were available, if only to some students.

Time passed. People forgot. I remembered Judy Krug's remark that censorship is a subtle process, and can invade our institutions slowly but surely. I saw it happening in Hanover. Discouragement and fear had affected everyone. There were other implications resulting from the restriction policy. I was warned by my principal that the administration and school board were considering ways to change the district's book selection policy. I was cautioned to order only "non-controversial" books in the future.

In the last year, the permission slip forms have been changed three times in an attempt to avoid ambiguity, yet there are problems. Over the course of time many people in the community have forgotten that five books are still being restricted in the Hanover Middle School. But, in the school library, the restriction policy has to be dealt with

on a daily basis. Students come in with only one title checked on
the permission form, and want another title instead. New students
must be instructed about the circulation policy. During busy checkout periods, I must search through stacks of permission forms before
a student can check out the book.

A large sign under Blume's books reads, "These books may
not be checked out without your parent's permission, by order of
the Hanover School Board." Yet students question me. They still
show me other books, such as the Unabridged Dictionary, which
contain the same words which were taken out of context from Blume's
books. How do I respond? Do I ignore the student? Ignore the
book? Report the dictionary to the school board? Where is the librarian's duty in matters of this kind?

I feel my job now entails something of the role of police officer.
When students defy the order and try to peek into the restricted
titles, should I report them to the principal for disobeying orders?
Helpers often look through the books, or shelve them by mistake on
the open shelves. The atmosphere of freedom in our library has
been replaced by one of moderate tension and confusion. Students
reading the titles are skeptical about adults who are so threatened
by these books. I can't estimate how many students won't be able
to read the books because their parents don't care enough to sign
the permission forms, or because they don't want to be singled out.
For many students, it's too much of a hassle to bother with the forms.

Ultimately, as has happened in other libraries, the censors will
win as the books fall into disuse. The chill factor has extended to
the present and future ordering of new books. My own professional
integrity has been called into question and, in future, will be scru-
tinized more closely. The way is paved for continued infringements
on academic freedom, not only for librarians, but for teachers and
students as well.

It has been over a year since the five books were removed,
extra-procedurally, from the shelves of the middle school library.
In the 1982 Supreme Court decision of Pico vs. Board of Education,
Island Trees Union Free School District it was found that the First
Amendment to the Constitution of the United States places "limitations
upon a local school board's exercise of its discretion to remove books,"
that the students do not surrender their First Amendment rights
when they enter the school, and that the school library, more than
any part of the school, is an area where those rights should be up-
held. When is someone permitted to place his or her personal value
system into library policy? Where does it stop? The repression of
knowledge sets a dangerous precedent. In the words of Edmund
Burke, "All that is needed for the triumph of evil is that good men
do nothing."

REFLECTIONS ON "THE RIGHT TO BE INFORMED"*

Joe Morehead†

Introduction

Of the many felicitous observations and insights that characterized
Bernard Fry's distinguished career as public servant, researcher,
editor, and library educator, none are more apt than his use of the
phrase "right to be informed." In Government Publications: Their
Role in the National Program for Library and Information Services,
his lucid analysis of issues involving government publications and
public policy, Fry places the words in apposite context:

> The Freedom of Information Act is only half a loaf. The
> "right to know"--upon request--guaranteed by the Act has
> a companion "right to be informed," which, if not implemented
> in an efficient and effective manner, diminishes the citizens's
> knowledge of his government's programs and policies and their
> pervading influence on his everyday life. Indeed, the citizen's
> knowledgeable participation in the democratic process is in
> jeopardy if government information is not made promptly and
> readily accessible to the public. Public release of previously
> withheld information is only the first step. An even more
> important and positive need is to assure that the large volume
> of significant government documents published daily by the
> GPO and other federal agencies is promptly and adequately
> disseminated and becomes effectively accessible to the using
> public.[1]

In this paragraph are found all the distinctive words and concepts that provide a framework for our professional concerns: govern-

*Reprinted by permission of the author and publisher from Government
Publications Review 13: (1986) 39-47; copyright © 1986 by Pergamon
Press, Ltd.

†Joe Morehead has had a long association with Bernard Fry and
Government Publications Review. When Professor Fry began Government Publications Review, he chose a manuscript entitled, "The
Government Printing Office and Non-GPO Publications" by Joe Morehead as the lead article in volume 1, number 1.

ment information, knowledge, effective access, prompt dissemination, the democratic process. To be informed is an inalienable right; the intransitive construction clearly implies the <u>duty</u> of governments to inform; that is, to provide certain kinds of information in order that citizens may become knowledgeable and make appropriate judgements thereupon. Using Bernard Fry's statement quoted above as a point of departure, I will examine several issues of government information policy, matters that I find crucial to libraries and their constituencies. Few would deny that reliable information is a prerequisite for knowledge, but when one addresses the question of the proper role of governments in the provision of information services, consensus is as elusive as stalking the snow leopard to its Tibetan lair. And wisdom, the desired end of knowledge, is beyond the purview of these reflections, but it is a matter concerning which I have only the most lugubrious sentiments.

Information Technologies

In early 1978, the Joint Committee on Printing (JCP) established the Ad Hoc Advisory Committee on Revision of Title 44 to identify the major issues and policy questions involved in revision of the statute. The problem of terminology being critical, the Advisory Committee established working definitions of such key terms as government information and government publication. With the blessing of the library community, the Committee included information stored in electronic format as suitable for distribution as a "government publication." The Committee saw this as encompassing an "affirmative action by the government to make information available which is of broad public interest" regardless of the package in which the information is contained.[2]

Despite the fact that the effort to revise Title 44 failed, librarians had every hope that the federal government would bring depository libraries into the otherwise ubiquitous world of computerized information. Indeed, showing its fondness for Ad Hoc Committees, the JCP named its staff member Barnadine Hoduski to chair a panel on Depository Library Access to Federal Automated Data Bases. This committee was asked to determine, among other things, the costs and benefits of providing information in electronic format and the role despository libraries should play in this significant aspect of information.[3]

Before this committee was established, however, Garrett E. Brown, Jr., General Counsel of the Government Printing Office (GPO), had issued an opinion to the effect that 44 U.S.C. 1901, as presently worded, requires that government information, to be available for depository distribution, must be <u>printed as a publication first</u>. In his implacable syllogism, Brown sought congressional intent from the landmark Depository Library Act of 1962. Citing Senate Report 1547, Brown said: "The Congressional intent is clear, the act requires that only identifiable documents previously published by the Government are to be made available through the depository program. This would logically not include data in a computer that had not been reduced to a published format." In other words, "The Depository Library Act does not direct that [the] Superintendent of Documents make published documents available in all possible formats to the libraries. It was the intent of Congress that only printed publications would be made available to the depositories."[4]

JCP attempted to circumvent this interpretation of 44 U.S.C. 1901 by proposing regulations that would expand the definition of "government publication" to include electronic databases and allow "electronic transfer" not excluding the possibility of free dissemination to Title 44 depositories. The proposed rules were rendered moot, at least for the moment, when a memorandum from the Justice Department's Office of Legal Counsel to the Office of Management and Budget opined that the regulations are "statutorily unsupported and constitutionally impermissible." Citing the famous Supreme Court Chadha[5] decision, the memorandum questions whether the JCP had statutory authority for the proposed rules, whether the rules would "involve congressional performance of executive functions," and whether the JCP "is seeking to exercise legislative power." Counsel held that the proposed regulations failed on all counts.[6]

If all this energy had been spent trying to get the Congress to amend 44 U.S.C. 1901, depository libraries might be providing users with prompt information from excellent databases such as LEGIS, JURIS, or FLITE, instead of paying dearly for systems like ELSS, CRECORD, or VOTES. The Legislative Information and Status System (LEGIS), for example, was designed by the House of Representatives staff of the Committee on House Administration and was based on an earlier computerized service known as the Bill Status System. There are over 250 legislative steps possible in the process by which a bill becomes law, and LEGIS can accommodate this complexity with alacrity. While the best descriptor is the bill or resolution number, searches can be accomplished by item number (for executive communications, messages, petitions, and memorials), name of sponsor or co-sponsors, committee referral, data of introduction, subject of legislation, etc. Bills in both the House and the Senate can be tracked using LEGIS, which also has the capability of making printed reports available within minutes as well as offering many sorting options.[7] If the definition of a government publication at 44 U.S.C. 1901 was amended to include databases like LEGIS, depository libraries would have a powerful source of current status information and legislative histories to complement or replace the printed tools and commercial online services. This however, is the responsibility of the plenary congress, not a crafty artifice by a congressional committee.

If the federal government has been diffident about sharing its information in electronic form with libraries and their public, it has exhibited an almost indecent temerity in imposing its microform program

upon depository institutions. When the GPO and non-GPO documentation tracks were made operational in 1977, officials at first pledged
to proceed slowly in determining the options and conversion categories.[8] But by 1981, pleading "severe budget constraints,"[9] the
GPO abrogated that pledge. For example, the following ukase appeared on Daily Depository Shipping List No. 16,085-M (June 16,
1981): "We will no longer distribute Congressional House and Senate
bills in paper format. Beginning with the 6th microfiche bill ship-
ment, all depositories previously receiving paper will begin to receive microfiche. Shipments containing paper bills will discontinue."
Most researchers find bills and resolutions on fiche more difficult
to manage than accessing them in filing cabinets. Complex legislation is particularly vexing. The Windfall Profits Tax Bill of 1980,
H.R. 3919, represented a total of 983 pieces, including amendments,
scattered among 66 fiche. To save money, the GPO ignored the
wishes of those depository libraries that indicated a desire to continue receiving bills in paper.

Increasingly, information policy is dictated solely by economics.
Microfiche is basically a user-unfriendly medium. Its manifold disadvantages have been thoroughly documented by Saffady[10] and
Schwark and Breakstone,[11] among others. The computer and its
capabilities, on the other hand, constitute the master metaphor of
our age. While the definition of a government publication at 44
U.S.C. 1901 drifts in the inertia of Gutenberg's galaxy, computer
technologies continue to blaze like meteors in the new empyrean.
The growth of light-based systems and equipment in the next decade
will further affect information transfer, making even more manifest
the need for revised legislation. There is no sound reason that
every Title 44 depository should not have the capability of receiving
all bibliographic and full text information transmitted electronically
from the LEGIS and other useful databases. Present policy is cyber-
phobic, a feckless mix that forces upon depository libraries one
technology while denying to them a powerful and effective instrument.

Timely Distribution

In his remarks, Bernard Fry reiterates the importance of prompt
dissemination of government information. In one significant area of
publishing, that of legal information, the federal court system abdi-
cated its responsibility over a century ago. In 1876, John B. West
and Company issued the first of a series of pamphlets that were to
become the National Reporter System. The purpose of this enterprise was "To furnish the legal profession in the State [of Minnesota]
with prompt and reliable intelligence as to the various questions adjudicated by our own courts at a date long prior to the publication
of the regular reports."[12] By 1887, the entire nation was covered
by the well-known regional reporters and the rest, as they say, is
history. The authors of Effective Legal Research point out that
"Before the National Reporter System was instituted, the publication

of the official reports lagged behind the actual decision from one to
three or four years. This played havoc with the rule of stare de-
cisis, because the latest cases were unavailable."[13]

With that kind of time lag it is little wonder that commercial
publishers entered an area of responsibility abandoned by the official provenance. Nowhere is this relinquished duty more pronounced
than in the publishing pattern of the lower federal courts. While
the courts of appeals print and distribute their slip decisions, "these
decisions are not bound for distribution and few libraries have
them."[14] Many federal district court decisions "can be located
only by consulting a looseleaf service covering a narrow subject
area."[15] As a result, libraries are obliged to rely upon commercial series like Federal Cases, Federal Reporter, Federal Reporter
2d, Federal Supplement, and Federal Rules Decisions (West), and
the looseleaf topical reporters issued by Commerce Clearing House,
Prentice-Hall, and the Bureau of National Affairs. That these commercial products are, by and large, excellent finding aids does not
absolve the government from censure.

Despite the exigencies mandated by res judicata and stare de-
cisis, "the literature of legal bibliography is almost barren of discussions concerning the speed with which the data of legal develop-
ment--decisions, statutes, and rules--reach the legal researcher."
Robert Emery's study of legal series received by a law school library
examined and analyzed a number of official and commercial sources
for timely receipt. "Timeliness was measured in terms of days
elapsed from the date items appeared through the date the publications containing them were received by the library" and results
"were calculated in terms of means, medians, and modes."

One group of like materials sampled compared the receipt of
United States Supreme Court opinions issued in their official series
and published commercially in United States Law Week (U.S.L.W.),
CCH Supreme Court Bulletin, West's Supreme Court Reporter, and
United States Supreme Court Reports, Lawyers' Edition. As expected,
the looseleaf services provided the most rapid information, the CCH
Bulletin outperforming U.S.L.W. by a measurable but not significant
margin. While the official slip opinions (Ju 6.8/b; item 740-A) are
distributed somewhat more expeditiously than the West and Lawyers'
Cooperative advance sheets, "they lack continuous pagination, so
cannot be used for permanent reference." The official preliminary
prints (JU 6.8/a; item 740-B) have a condign reputation for notorious
slowness. Emery found that the "preliminary prints for 358 U.S.,
those most recently received by the library, contain opinions, on
the average (mean), 174 days old, three times as old as those in the
most recent unofficial reporters." The ultimate tortoise award goes
to the bound United States Reports (Ju 6.8; item 741), "which must
owe their survival only to the American convention that the Supreme
Court's decisions should be cited to the official reports when available, and to the Court's own rules, which require their publication

(Sup. Ct. R. 48)." Moreover, researchers cannot rely on the official editions since they lack the citations, headnotes, and other
editorial felicities that characterize the commercial sources.

While some Supreme Court opinions appear within two or three
days online through Lexis and Westlaw, a systematic analysis of
computer-based legal retrieval systems was outside the scope of
Emery's paper. As an aside, it was pointed out that these systems
"might rush a few new cases online each day for purposes of sales
demonstrations, while leaving a substantially larger number of opinions
to wait weeks before input." The author, who holds law and library
degrees, and one of his experienced co-workers "tend to suspect
that Lexis can be depended upon to get more cases online more
quickly than Westlaw."[16] What is abundantly clear is that the
official printed opinions of our highest court, which are both GPO
sales and depository series, are virtually useless as current awareness sources. They are reproduced and delivered in annotated editions by enterprising commercial firms. The absence of a responsible
delivery system on the part of the judiciary allows the private sector
to batten on libraries and law firms which are perforce obliged to
purchase these materials.[17]

Abridging Government Information

By the end of 1983, the Reagan Administration claimed that
initiatives set in motion in the Spring of 1981 resulted in the elimination and consolidation of 3,848 federal government publications, or
approximately one-fourth of a total of 15,917 documents identified in
the inventories of federal agencies.[18] The initial effort in this
aspect of Reagan's "War on Waste" was represented by a brief presidential statement published in the April 24, 1981, issue of the Weekly
Compilation of Presidential Documents.[19] Following that declaration
were several Office of Management and Budget (OMB) bulletins, which
set forth details and guidelines for agency compliance. Initial results
were issued as OMB Press Release 82-25, October 6, 1982. Titled
"REFORM '88: Elimination, Consolidation, and Cost Reduction of
Government Publications," the press release proudly announced that
over 2,000 publications had been targeted for termination and consolidation with a promise of further cuts to come. Attached to the narrative portion of OMB 82-25 was a computerized printout entitled
"List of Government Publications Terminated and Consolidated by
Agency," where actual titles were announced. That the number
reached almost 4,000 over a year later affirms the zeal with which
OMB and the agencies pursued this task.

Presidential counselor Edwin Meese told the media that the publications in question were of the frivolous variety. Parading examples
of titles like How to Buy a Christmas Tree and Make Dishwashing
Easy, Meese disingenuously implied that all of the eliminated publications betrayed this frivolity. The media seemed to accept this as

fact, and "press release journalism" prevailed. Indeed, a delighted
administration published a half-inch thick volume of photocopied news
items and articles from prestigious and lesser newspapers and journals attesting to the melancholy truth that Meese's releases were taken
at face value. Sent to me by a sympathetic official in Washington,
this undated and unpaginated volume is entitled Reform '88 Press
Clips and bears the seal of the Office of Management and Budget.

Over a period of months, the numerous serials from the computerized list attached to OMB 82-25 were identified and examined.
Findings demonstrated that series of substantial value were eliminated,
publications that were considered important enough to be included
in basic sources like Price List 36, the Daily Depository Shipping
List, the Serials Supplement to the Monthly Catalog, Ulrich's International Periodicals Directory, The Standard Periodical Directory,
and John L. Andriot's Guide to U.S. Government Publications.[20]
In subsequent research not yet published, I was able to discern a
typology of cost reduction measures by which OMB reached its total
of almost 4,000 publications. The categories include publications
eliminated altogether; consolidated series, those in which two or more
titles were combined into one; series whose frequency were reduced;
and publications once issued free but now priced. Remember that
these measures are in addition to a GPO micro-publishing policy that
increasingly distributes series to Title 44 depositories on microfiche
only.

The OMB 82-25 computerized list of discontinued and consolidated publications was only the beginning. Other notices continue
to appear regularly in the form of press releases, "Dear Colleague"
or "Dear Reader" letters to subscribers, depository library shipping
lists, announcements published in the GPO newsletter Administrative
Notes (GP 3.16/3-2:vol./no.), and those announced in the introductory
pages of Price List 36 and the Serials Supplement. Extirpated series
include HUD Challenge, Pesticides Monitoring Journal, Solar Law Reporter, OMB's own Statistical Reporter, indexing/abstracting sources
like Oil Pollution Abstracts, and a host of other substantive publications too numerous to mention in these pages.

One example of consolidation will suffice. Four separate
series--Petroleum Statement, Petroleum Refineries in the United
States and U.S. Territories, Sales of Liquid Petroleum Gases and
Ethane, and Deliveries of Fuel Oil and Kerosine--were compressed
to form the Petroleum Supply Annual. Reducing the periodicity of
a publication is closely related to consolidation. Indeed, decreasing
the frequency of a series while still continuing to publish it is perhaps
the most insidious strategy in the assault on government information.
Examples of this practice include the Federal Communications Com-
mision Reports, from weekly to monthly; Treasury Bulletin, from
monthly to quarterly; and Spotlight on Affirmative Employment Programs, from monthly to quarterly.

Changing the status of a publication from free to priced is yet
another salvo in the war on waste. Subscribers have been notified
of the elimination of the free distribution of series like the Vital
Statistics of the United States and the quarterly Family Economics
Review. The quarterly Consumer Information Catalog is conspicuously
slimmer these days now that it no longer carries free publications
from the Department of Agriculture. USDA titles in former issues of
the Catalog comprised one-fourth of all titles listed; some of these
have been eliminated while others have become sales items. Even the
renowned Morbidity and Mortality Weekly Report is no longer distributed free save to depository libraries.[21]

Statistical Information

     The dissemination of statistical data, like legal information,
has always been a crucial component of the information policies of
governments. In the Soviet Union, it is difficult even to obtain accurate street maps of cities, and official statistics are severely restricted in scope. Indeed, statistics that do not reflect a favorable
trend have been increasingly elusive over the years. When infant
mortality started to rise, the appropriate statistical tables ceased to
exist. Oil production and other sensitive economic indicators have
been blurred by combining that information with other general production statistics. After several poor harvests, agricultural data were
simply not announced. Crime statistics in the Soviet Union are
never published, despite the fact that the press reports crime diligently and the study of crime is a topic of public debate among sociologists, criminologists, and party apparatchiks. "From almost
his first day in office, [the late] Yuri Andropov ... made the fight
against crime, especially economic crime, the hallmark of his new
regime."[22]

     While the situation in the United States is patently not as dire
as the above description of statistical reporting in the Soviet Union,
the House Legislation and National Security Subcommittee of the Committee on Government Operations found the Reagan Administration's
budgetary retrenchment disturbing enough to publish a report on
statistical programs. Entitled Reorganization and Budget Cutbacks
May Jeopardize the Future of the Nation's Statistical System,[23] the
committee charged the administration with damaging the effectiveness
of the system by reducing or eliminating programs that, among other
purposes, collect data on family budgets, collective bargaining agreements, certain components of the Consumer Price Index, nursing
homes, health, nutrition, and energy consumption. Over the last
decade, but especially during Reagan's tenure, the committee dis-
cerned "an alarming decrease in the resources devoted to overseeing
federal statistical activities," and published as an Appendix to the
report a list of 58 programs that have been eliminated or reduced.[24]
These programs run the gamut of activities hitherto reported faith-
fully by the Bureau of the Census and other data-gathering agencies.

While some funding for these programs was subsequently restored
by the Congress, the administration has shown a grim determination
to abolish, condense, and reduce the periodicity of federal statistical reporting.

In this regard, the 1980 Census merits comment. After having
spent over $1 billion to conduct the census, the Bureau of the Cen-
sus underwent demoralizing budget cuts and employee "furloughs"--
a euphemism for periodic days off without pay. Moreover, a law on
the books to conduct a mid-decade census is in jeopardy because the
administration does not wish to fund the project. In October, 1981,
the administration asked Congress to cancel the 1982 Census of Agriculture and to change the frequency of that important census from
quinquennial to decennial status. Because of reduced funding, some
categories of the 1977 economic census were not updated by the 1982
edition.

At the same time, the 1980 Census, the country's most sophisticated count ever, is said to have generated 300,000 pages of summary
statistics and over 1,500 computer summary pages containing several
billion data items. Perhaps 90% of this information is available only
in machine-readable form. State Data Centers have converted the
Summary Tape Files (STF) and Public Use Sample (PUS) microdata
to computer output microform (COM) at low cost for distribution to
libraries and other institutions. Ever since FOSDIC,[25] the trend
toward the increasing production and dissemination of census information in nonprint formats has assumed an inevitability; it is cost-
effective for the government and it can be distributed to users many
months ahead of the traditional printed series. This phenomenon
and its general acclamation by the library community have been discussed widely in the library literature, and there is no need to be-
labor it here. There are, however, dissenting voices, and, in fair-
ness, those views should be aired. In his review of the five-volume
U.S. Census Population & Housing Characteristics published by National Decision Systems, Andrew Hacker, a distinguished political
scientist, faults the government for not providing this kind of printed
product. National Decision Systems reformatted a "resource owned
by the public" quite legally. "In this case the 'resource' is not a
national forest, but information about themselves which millions of
Americans turned over to their Government." Noting that State Data
Center COM products are "virtually impossible for scanning purposes,"
Hacker concludes his review in a philosophical vein:

> The Gutenberg revolution in printing made publishing pos-
> sible on a mass scale. It advanced democracy by bringing
> information to the general public. Previously, the only books
> had been handcrafted volumes locked in palaces and mona-
> steries. Our own computer revolution may be bringing us
> full circle. Just as once only the wealthy could afford man-
> uscripts, now electronic information is being supplied to elite
> buyers on a first-use basis. If this trend continues, material

that was once truly in the public domain will be harder to
come by. That this is happening with census data, itself
a product of citizen cooperation, is both sad and unsettling.[26]

While many do not share Hacker's sentiments, his misgivings
provide yet another footnote to the "information rich/information poor"
dialectic.

The 1983 mimeographed "Second Annual Report on Eliminations,
Consolidations, and Cost Reductions of Government Publications"
noted that, when the dust has settled, "the number of publications
with some cost-saving action will total over 6,918 titles or over 43%
of all federal publications" at a total saving of $38 million.[27] But
in his presidential statement, Reagan spoke not only of "periodicals
and pamphlets" but also of "audiovisual products."[28] The several
OMB directives that followed also included audiovisual materials as
part of the overall scrutiny. To the best of my knowledge, none of
these reports has addressed the audiovisual matter and no statistics
have proclaimed reductions for this category. However, an OMB
report to the Senate Appropriations Committee on Administrative Expenses revealed that in 1983 federal entities spent over $80 million
on audiovisual products and services, of which the Department of
Defense's estimated total was $53 million.[29]

The Pentagon produces vast quantities of training films and
public relations films for recruitment. Under the Reagan administration, all of its actions seem curiously exempt from the war on waste.
The Navy spends $110 apiece for electronic diodes available for 4¢
from its own supply system. The Air Force purchases a 12¢ Allen
wrench priced at $9,606. The Navy buys $17 claw hammers for
$435 and 13¢ nuts for $2,043. Plastic caps for the legs of naviga-
tor's stools on a radar plane that cost 31¢ are bought by the Air
Force for $1,118 each. And about the same time that the President
ordered Attorney General William French Smith to establish a new
national commission to study the effects of pornography on society,
government auditors investigating the Pentagon's huge telephone bills
discovered that as much as $300,000 had been spent on calls to
"dial-a-porn" services over official phones, in which users call a
number to hear a prerecorded sexually explicit message.[30]

Conclusion

The ultimate irony in any attempt to abridge the "right to be
informed" is that the effort often requires a great deal of paperwork
to stanch the flow of paper. How many internal memoranda and,
indeed, how many public documents are generated in pursuit of the
reduction of other government publications? More dismaying, however, is the demonstrable fact that the war on waste involving periodicals and pamphlets (but not, apparently, audiovisual products)
is a paradigm of that old bromide where the baby is thrown out with

the bath water. While we may never see the likes again of didactic
literature like Simple Plumbing Repairs and How to Clean Floors,
also departed from the shelves and stacks of libraries are Urban Mass
Transportation Abstracts, Women in Action, SEC Docket, Dimensions,
Performance, Job Opportunities, and many more once-useful serials.

But there are countervailing tendencies. For while governments
may endeavor to diminish, abrogate, or even disavow, their documentation, the greater need to create these symbols of governments' presence will endure and prevail. Even in anticipation of nuclear holo-
caust, the Postal Service has stockpiled postage-free emergency
change-of-address cards in order to trace both the quick and the
dead. There is an account of Abraham Lincoln and his entourage,
toward the very end of the Civil War, walking through the mud-
dried streets of ravaged Richmond. "As they passed through the
ruins, a light wind started up and, suddenly, down the street, like
thousands and thousands of large square leaves, government documents swirled. 'What begins in paper,' said Lincoln wryly, as his
ankles were wrapped round with government records, 'ends in
paper.'"[31]

References

1. U.S., National Commission on Libraries and Information Science,
    Government Publications: Their Role in the National Program for
    Library and Information Services, by Bernard M. Fry. Washing-
    ton: Government Printing Office, 1978, p. 115.
2. U.S., Congress, Joint Committee on Printing, Federal Govern-
    ment Printing and Publishing: Policy Issues, Committee Print.
    Washington, DC: Government Printing Office, 1979, p. 31.
3. U.S. Government Printing Office. Public Documents Highlights
    59 (May 1983): 5.
4. American Library Association, Government Documents Round
    Table, Documents to the People 10 (July 1982): 155-56.
5. Immigration and Naturalization Service v. Jagdish Rai Chadha,
    et al., 77 L.Ed.2d 317, 103 S.Ct. 2764 (1983).
6. U.S. Justice Department, Office of Legal Counsel, Memorandum
    for Michael J. Horowitz, Counsel to the Director, Office of Man-
    agement and Budget, April 11, 1984 (mimeographed), pp. 1, 2,
    passim. See also [LeRoy C. Schwarzkopf] "News from Washing-
    ton" Government Publications Review 11 (March-April 1984):
    190-91.
7. U.S., Congress, Committee on House Administration, The Legis-
    lative Information and Status System for the United States House
    of Representatives, Committee Print. Washington, DC: Govern-
    ment Printing Office, 1979, Appendix B, "Legislative Status
    Steps" (pp. 17-41) charts the over 250 defined steps.
8. Public Documents Highlishts 21 (April 1977): 1.
9. Public Documents Highlights 46 (June 1981): 1, 4.

10. Saffady, William. Computer-Output Microfilm: Its Library
    Applications. Chicago: American Library Association, 1978,
    p. 94.
11. Schwark, Sabine, and Breakstone, Barbara R. "Microform Up-
    date: Current Trends for Law Libraries." Law Library Journal
    71 (1978): 133.
12. West's Law Finder: A Research Manual for Lawyers. St. Paul,
    MN: West Publishing Company, 1982, p. 5.
13. Price, Miles O., et al. Effective Legal Research, 4th ed. Boston:
    Little, Brown and Company, 1979, p. 141.
14. Ibid., p. 157.
15. Jacobstein, J. Myron and Mersky, Roy M. Legal Research Il-
    lustrated, 2nd ed. Mineola, NY: The Foundation Press, Inc.,
    1981, p. 37.
16. Emery, Robert, Esp., "Timeliness of the Contents of Certain
    Legal Publications," April 1984 (unpublished paper, School of
    Library and Information Science, State University of New York
    at Albany), pp. 2, 7-9, 18.
17. Some states like New York, which does not have a public printer,
    actually report officially faster than West. Private printers
    under contract with states may perform better, spurred by com-
    petition with a rival or a potential rival.
18. "Second Annual Report on Eliminations, Consolidations, and Cost
    Reductions of Government Publications," (mimeographed), n.d.,
    pp. 2, 4, passim.
19. Weekly Compilation of Presidential Documents 17 (April 24, 1981):
    447.
20. Morehead, Joe. "Federal Government Periodicals: An Endang-
    ered Species," The Serials Librarian 8 (Summer 1984): 35-50.
    Exemplary titles in this account went beyond the computerized
    list issued by OMB.
21. The current Price List 36 announces Morbidity and Mortality
    Weekly Report for $90 a year (priority) and $70 a year (non-
    priority).
22. Binyon, Michael. Life in Russia. New York: Pantheon Books,
    1983, p. 117.
23. U.S., Congress, House, Committee on Government Operations,
    Reorganization and Cutbacks May Jeopardize the Future of the
    Nation's Statistical System, 97th Cong., 2nd sess., 1982, H.
    RPT. 901.
24. Ibid., p. 15. The 58 programs, listed as exemplary and not
    exhaustive, are published on pages 17 and 18 of the report.
25. FOSDIC (Film Optical Sensing Device for Input to Computers)
    converts microfilm images of completed questionnaires into a
    fully formatted record on computer tape.
26. The New York Times Book Review. August 21, 1983, pp. 7,
    19. See also a review of this $395 product by Beverly D. Rails-
    back in Government Publications Review 11 (March-April 1984):
    183-84.
27. Note 18, supra, p. 5.
28. Note 19, supra.

29. Office of Management and Budget, Report to the Senate Appro-
     priations Committee on Administrative Expenses, p. 13.
30. U.S. News & World Report, June 4, 1984, pp. 73, 74, 84, 85.
31. Vidal, Gore. Lincoln. New York: Random House, 1984, p.
     632. Renowned Lincoln scholar David Herbert Donald of Harvard
     University has authenticated the accuracy of this account.

MAJORITIES FOR CENSORSHIP*

Howard D. White

Censorship fights are always local. Librarians involved in them must
deal not only with local groups but with particular persons. The
data presented here are national, not local, and they are abstractions
from surveys, far from the level on which particular personalities
and dramas emerge. Stories of censorship fights are more interesting than statistical abstractions, and probably more fruitful in suggesting how or how not to conduct anticensorship campaigns. Nevertheless, data from national opinion polls have their uses, as every
politician knows.

The data here are offered not least because they have not
been available to librarians before, at least in their own literature.
Existing studies deal mostly with opinions and practices of librarians
rather than with the American public as a whole.[1] A fresh treatment of American public opinion on censorship, even a preliminary
one such as this, may thus be an interesting novelty. It may have
even useful implications for librarians' politics on the local level.

Methodology

The data came from several of the more recent General Social
Surveys (GSS), as cumulated in the 1972-83 file. These surveys
have been conducted in 10 of the past 12 years by the National
Opinion Research Center in Chicago under sponsorship of the National
Science Foundation. Details of the Sampling design and field work
are given in the Codebook.[2] The GSS may be thought of as high-
quality opinion polls, similar to those of Gallup and Harris, each conducted with samples of approximately 1500 noninstitutionalized Americans, 18 and older, in the continental United States.

The present study draws principally on the four GSS conducted

*Reprinted by permission of the author and publisher from Library
Journal, 111:12 (July 1986) 31-38. Published by R.R. Bowker a
division of Reed Publishing, USA; copyright © 1986 by Reed Publishing, USA, a division of Reed Holdings, Inc.

in 1976, 1977, 1980, and 1982. Each contains five questions, identic-
ally worded, on whether the respondent would favor removing a book
from the public library if it is by a controversial type of author
(see Table 1).

TABLE 1:

QUESTIONS CONCERNING CENSORSHIP
OF CONTROVERSIAL AUTHORS

1. There are always some people whose ideas are considered bad
or dangerous by other people. For instance, somebody who is against
all churches and religion. If some people in your community suggested that a book he wrote against churches and religion should be
taken out of your public library, would you favor removing this book,
or not? [ATHEIST]

2. Or, consider a person who believes that blacks are genetically
inferior. If some people in your community suggested that a book
he wrote which said blacks are inferior should be taken out of your
public library, would you favor removing this book, or not? [RACIST]

3. Now, I should like to ask you some questions about a man who
admits he is a communist. Suppose he wrote a book which is in your
public library. Somebody in your community suggests that the book
should be removed from the library. Would you favor removing it,
or not? [COMMUNIST]

4. Consider a person who advocates doing away with elections and
letting the military run the country. Suppose he wrote a book advocating [this]. Somebody in your community suggests that the
book be removed from the public library. Would you favor removing
it, or not? [MILITARIST]

5. And what about a man who admits that he is a homosexual? If
some people in your community suggested that the book he wrote in
favor of homosexuality should be taken out of your public library,
would you favor removing this book, or not? [HOMOSEXUAL]

The ultimate source of these questions is a famous study, made
by the sociologist Samuel Stouffer in the period of Senator Joseph
McCarthy, on American tolerance of nonconformity.[3] By nonconformity Stouffer meant willingness to extend civil liberties, such as
freedom of speech and the press, to persons whose views most

Americans would find "unpopular." His three types of nonconformist
were an atheist and a socialist (neither so named), and an admitted
communist (so named). From questions about these three types, he
created a scale of American attitudes toward civil liberties. The
Stouffer questions were replicated exactly in the GSS of the early
1970s. In the later GSS used here, the socialist was dropped, but
similar questions about a homosexual, a militarist, and a racist were
added to those on the atheist and the communist.

So far as I am aware, persons who write on censorship for
librarians have never reported on the "library-related" questions in
the Stouffer scale, even though they may be the best public opinion
data on censorship ever assembled.

In addition to these data, the GSS (in some years) have other
questions on matters of intellectual freedom: for example, attitudes
toward the distribution of pornography and toward birth control
information for teenagers. Furthermore, the GSS make possible
analyses of these questions in conjunction with a full range of demographic data (such as age, sex, race, and religion) and with data
on scores of major social issues on which liberals, moderates, and
conservatives differ.

My intent is to examine GSS questions related to intellectual
freedom, particularly the Stouffer-inspired ones on library censorship, in light of selected demographic variables, to see which broad
segments of society give majority support to censorship and which
do not. The analysis is not sophisticated methodologically. It does
not seek to explain people's relative liberalism or conservatism with
a multivariate casual model. It merely shows, through a series of
graphs, interesting variation in support for censorship among major
demographic groups.

The GSS permit trend analysis of questions replicated on national samples from year to year. For simplicity of presentation,
however, I have not reported yearly trends. Rather, I pooled the
respondents of the most recent four surveys in which "intellectual
freedom" questions occurred during 1975-83. Each has an N of
about 1500. The total number of respondents in the graphs is thus
more than 6000, and the smallest subgroup on which percentages
are based is in the neighborhood of 200. These sample percentages
yield estimates of the true percentages in the American population
with very small margins of error.

All results were computed with procedures in the Statistical
Package for the Social Sciences (SPSS) operating on a tape supplied
by the Roper Public Opinion Research Center. Bar charts reflecting
percentages were prepared with LisaGraph on an Apple Lisa microcomputer.

The Overall Public

    The American people as a whole do not, in any of the five
cases of controversial author types, give majority support to censorship. This is shown in Figure 1, where none of the bars, indicating those favoring removal of a controversial book, crosses the 50
percent mark. They range from a low of 38 to a high of 43 percent.
(The complements of the bars, not shown but implicit, represent
those opposed to censorship. For example, if 43 percent are shown
in favor, 57 percent by implication are opposed.)

    Data from the four individual surveys, pooled here, reveal the
same thing: during 1976-82, Americans favoring library censorship
of authors with unpopular views were always in the minority. Obviously they were very sizable minorities; and it may frighten parti-
sans of intellectual freedom that over the past several years approximately four in ten Americans supported censorship. In elections,
however, the majorities against censorship--in the range of 57 to 62
percent--would be considered landslides. Since the GSS are simply
opinion surveys and not elections, there is no way of telling how
firm these majorities actually are. But, on the national level at least,
those who are "pro-intellectual freedom" dominated by a considerable
margin.

    Figure 2 allows another look at the overall American public in
this matter. The data here are computer counts of the persons in
the combined samples who would favor censoring all of the five controversial author types, persons who would censor four of them, and
so on, down through persons who would censor none of the five
types. The latter, of course, would be considered the most liberal.
It will be seen that the single largest group (with the bars jointly
adding here to 100 percent) are the liberals who would censor none
of the authors. These make up 37 percent of the sample. In contrast, those who would remove all of the controversial authors are
only 22 percent. The remaining persons--those who would censor
one, two, three, or four of the offending authors--can be sorted
according to which type or types they would censor, but they never
add up to a majority of the American public, as Figure 1 has shown.

    Other evidence of the liberalism of the majority of Americans
can be briefly noted here, based on the questions in Table 2. The
first three were most recently asked in GSS in 1975, 1977, 1982,
and 1983, while the one on pornography was asked in 1976, 1978,
1980, and 1983. Thus the answers again reflect the pooled samples
of four years--more than 6000 Americans. Figure 3 shows overwhelming support for public availability of birth control information
(92 percent in favor), birth control information specifically for teenagers (84 percent in favor), and sex education (82 percent in favor).

    Figure 4, in which the three bars jointly represent 100 percent

FIGURE 1

Proposed Removal from Public Library of Books by Controversial Authors

% Favoring Removal, U.S. National Sample, 1976-82

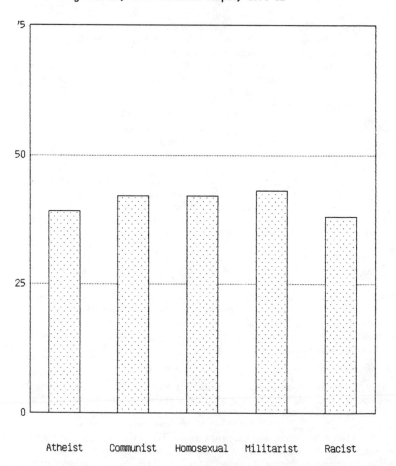

FIGURE 2

Number of Controversial Authors* Americans

Would Remove From Public Libraries

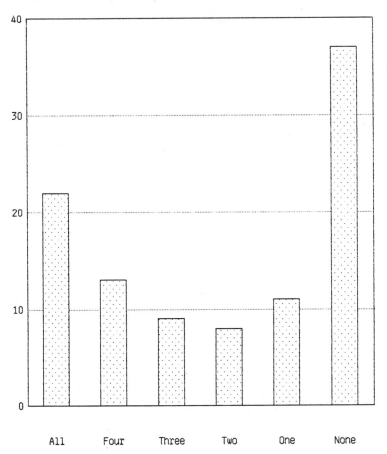

Percentages (Add to 100) U.S. National Sample, 1976-82

*An atheist, a Communist, a homosexual, a militarist, and a racist.

FIGURE 3

U.S. Opinion on Availability of

Sexual Information, 1975–83

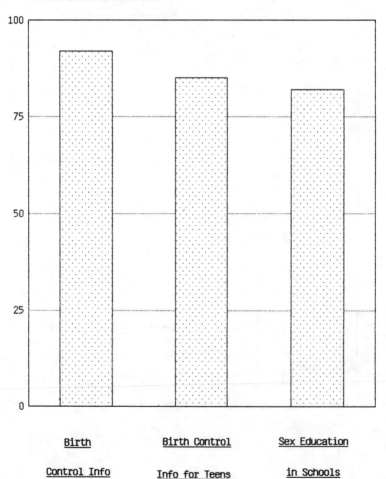

% of Respondents in Favor

FIGURE 4

Attitudes Toward Distribution
of Pornography

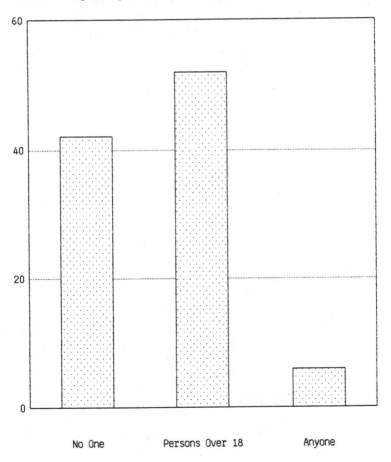

% Believing Pornography Should Be Available to...

U.S. National Sample, 1976-82

TABLE 2:
GENERAL SOCIAL SURVEY

QUESTIONS CONCERNING SEXUAL INFORMATION
AND PORNOGRAPHY

1. In some places in the United States, it is not legal to supply birth control information. How do you feel about this--do you think birth control information should be available to anyone who wants it, or not?

2. Do you think birth control information should be available to teenagers who want it, or not?

3. Would you be for or against sex education in the public schools?

4. Which of these statements comes closest to your feelings about pornography laws?

    There should be laws against the distribution of pornography whatever the age.

    There should be laws against the distribution of pornography to persons under 18.

    There should be no laws forbidding the distribution of pornography.

---

of the sample, breaks down American attitudes toward the distribution of pornography. There is a large minority (42 percent) that would prohibit the distribution of pornography to anyone, regardless of age. (This minority is similar in size to those who would censor each type of controversial author in libraries.) Look, however, at the majority viewpoint: some 52 percent of Americans would allow distribution of pornography to persons over 18, and another six percent would not forbid it to anyone, even young people. Thus a solid 58 percent would not censor pornography, at least for adults.

This does not mean, of course, that most Americans are in favor of library distribution of pornography--an earlier study of mine strongly indicates the contrary.[4] But it does mean that almost six in ten oppose censorship in an area even more controversial than that of sex education or birth control information.

Sex & Censorship

Returning to the matter of controversial authors in libraries, there are indeed majorities in favor of censorship within subgroups of the American public. In the following bar charts, those subgroups whose bars extend above the 50 percent mark can be thought of as giving majority support to censorship. In addition to showing the 50 percent mark, I have superimposed a line graph labeled "U.S. Overall" on each bar chart that represents the percentages favoring censorship in the entire sample. This line, which presents the same data as Figure 1, permits comparison of subgroup percentages with those of the American people as a whole.

As an example of how to read the bar charts, take Figure 5, a breakdown of the samples by sex. Note that the percentages for men and women separately are very close to those for the United States overall--that is, for men and women combined. While the split is very slight, a slightly higher percentage of women than men favors censorship of each of the author types. But neither sex give a majority to censoring any of the five authors; all bars are below the 50 percent marker.

Regional Differences

In contrast, consider Figure 6, in which the United States is broken into four geographic regions. Here we see that the South is always much more "censorious" than the other regions of the country. The South gives clear majorities to censoring four out of five of the authors (the high is 55 percent in favor of removal of the communist's book), and a near majority to censoring the fifth (48 percent in the case of the racist). In some of the annual GSS, the South gives majorities to censoring all five.

It should be pointed out that the South, comprising the Census Bureau's South Atlantic, East South Central, and West South Central states, differs by subregion. In tables in GSS not shown here, the largest majorities for censorship are almost always in the East South Central States--Kentucky, Tennessee, Mississippi, and Alabama. But clearly, the South as a whole is less like the East, Midwest, and West than any of them is like each other.

Stouffer found exactly the same thing 30 years ago,[5] and so have other studies; Southern conservatism is well known. What is striking, however, is the Southern inclination to censor "across the board." Any nonconformist's book meets majority (or near majority) displeasure in the South--the militarist and the racist fare little better than the atheist, communist, or homosexual.

In explanation by sociologists of why this is so will be touched on later. Note here, however, the consistent pattern: the West is generally most liberal, followed by the East. The Midwest is more conservative than either, but not as conservative as the South. This pattern holds across all author types.

FIGURE 5

Proposed Removal from Public Library of Books by Controversial Authors

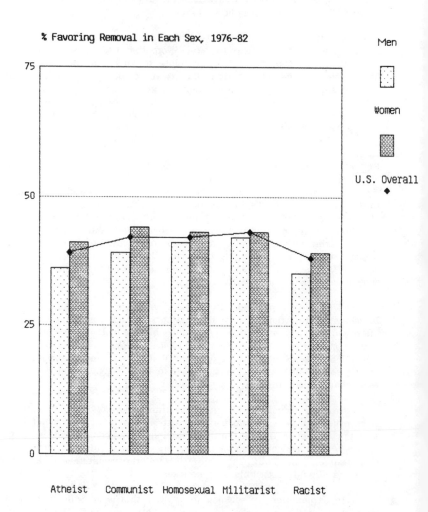

% Favoring Removal in Each Sex, 1976-82

Men

Women

U.S. Overall

Type of Author

FIGURE 6

Proposed Removal from Public Library of Books by Controversial Authors

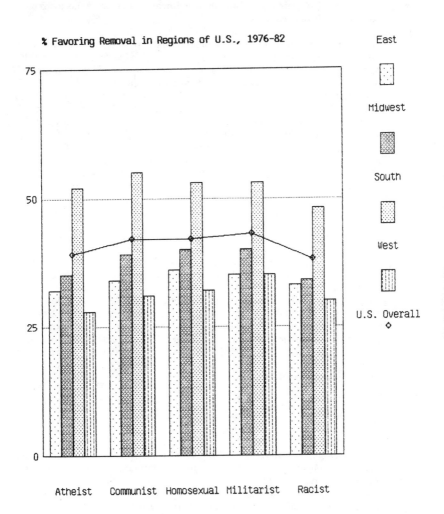

% Favoring Removal in Regions of U.S., 1976-82

Type of Author

The Impact of Age & Education

    Figure 7 presents the percentages favoring censorship in broad
age groups. The data display the oft-noted liberalism of young
people: those in their 30s or younger are least inclined to censor.
With increasing age comes increasing intolerance. Across all authors,
persons 60 and older support censorship by large majorities: almost
two-thirds (64 percent) would ban a library book by a homosexual
advocating homosexuality.

    In many social surveys education is a powerful differentiating
force, and we see its effect in Figure 8. The pattern is extremely
regular: with increasing education come ever smaller proportions of
persons willing to censor. Only those with less than a high school
education regularly give majority support to the banning of library
books. This group constitutes just under a third of the sample--
about 32 percent. Because it is so sizable, it raises the level in
favor of censorship in the United States overall. Americans with a
high school education make up about half the sample, by far the
largest single subgroup. They never come close to majority support
of censorship, and the remaining subgroups with at least some college education (roughly 18 percent of the sample) are even less so
inclined.

Race & Censorship

    The interesting difference between whites and blacks emerges
in Figure 9. Proportionately more blacks than whites are willing to
censor each type of author, and majorities of blacks would censor
the militarist, who argues against elections and for martial law, and
the racist, who claims that blacks are genetically inferior. The black
majority position in the latter case is hardly surprising. However,
consider the full implication: 54 percent of the blacks would ban the
racist's book, but the remaining 46 percent would not. This seems
one of the more dramatic instances of "tolerance" in the GSS, and
calls for considerably more study.

Urban Rural

    Figure 10 displays the contrasts between urban, suburban,
and rural populations. The "top 12 SMSAs" are the 12 largest Standard Metropolitan Statistical Areas in the nation--New York City, Los
Angeles, Chicago, etc. The next 100 largest SMSAs are broken out
separately, and so are the suburbs for the two groups of cities. It
is the suburbs of the top 12 SMSAs that are least supportive of cen-
sorship--the most liberal. Rural regions, on the other hand, give
majorities to censorship in four cases and a near majority in the fifth,
where the author is a racist.

FIGURE 7

Proposed Removal from Public Library of Books by Controversial Authors

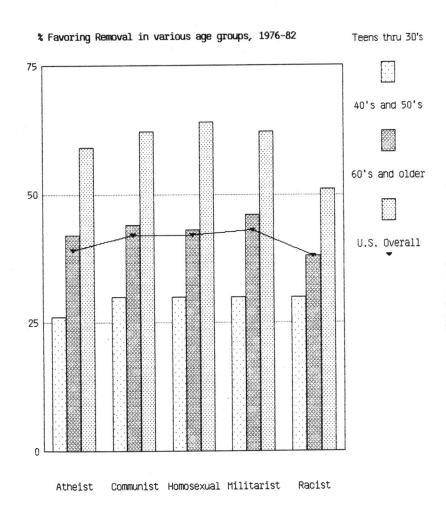

% Favoring Removal in various age groups, 1976-82

FIGURE 8

Proposed Removal from Public Library of
Books by Controversial Authors

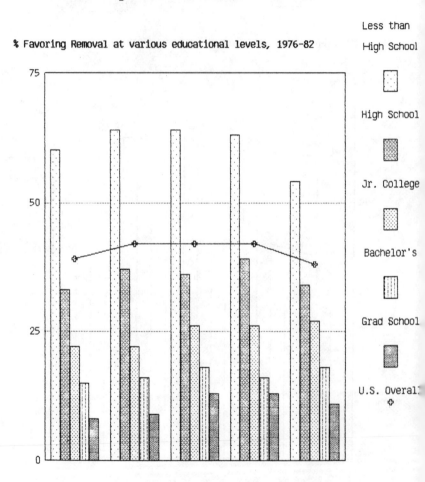

Type of Author

FIGURE 9

Proposed Removal from Public Library of Books by Controversial Authors

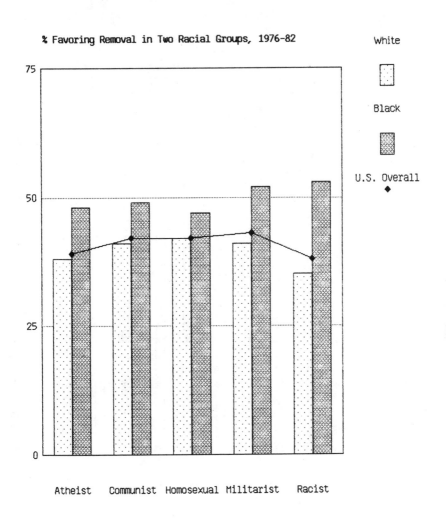

Type of Author

FIGURE 10

Proposed Removal from Public Library of
Books by Controversial Authors

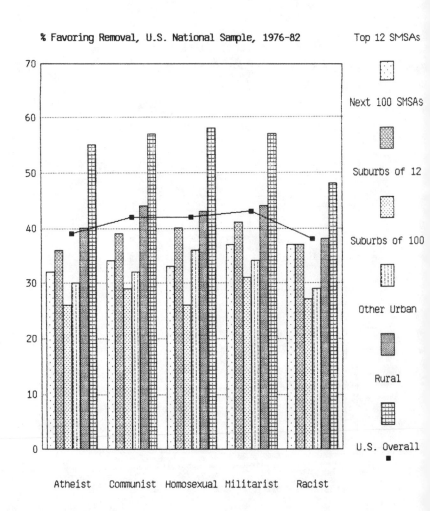

% Favoring Removal, U.S. National Sample, 1976-82

Type of Author

Religion

Figures 11 and 12 present other dramatic contrasts. In Figure 11 we see that none of America's conventional, broad-scale religious groupings favors censorship by a majority, despite the fact that some of the controversial books, as described, go counter to widely held religious beliefs. The Protestants always have the largest proportion of procensorship persons, and the smallest proportion is found among those who profess no religion. (The latter group, which presumably includes atheists, agnostics, and secular humanists, has only a very small porportion--12 percent--in favor of censoring a book by an atheist; 88 percent are opposed.) The Jews are always quite liberal as well. The Catholics, while less liberal than Jews or agnostics, never exceed 40 percent in favor of censorship; to imagine them as monolithically conservative is false.

Baptists & Other Protestants

It would be false, too, to imagine Protestants as undifferentiated in their support of censorship. The term "Protestant" makes a spectrum of denominations with sharply different opinions. Figure 12 is based on the Protestant subset of the sample--about 4000 out of 6000 persons--with Catholics, Jews, etc., omitted. It is the Baptists, the largest single Protestant denomination (and the second largest American denomination after the Catholics), that regularly give censorship majority support.

The next highest level of support for censorship comes from the Protestants labeled "Other" in the GSS. This is a residual category that (unfortunately) includes both conservative and liberal churches--many small fundamentalist and evangelical groups side by side with, e.g., the Unitarian-Universalists. But socially conservative Church members predominate; hence the pattern. (If they can be broken out separately, as I hope to do in a future analysis, they might show even larger majorities for censorship than the Baptists, while the small liberal churches might resemble the Episcopalians or the Jews.)

The third highest level of support--observe the unvarying order in the pattern--comes from the Methodists, who seem here to be the "typical American church." Across all five authors, the percentage of Methodists in favor closely approximates that of the U.S. people overall. The remaining denominations (Lutherans, Presbyterians, Episcopalians) are increasingly more liberal.

Does Diversity Promote Tolerance?

Given ALA's official endorsement of intellectual freedom and the intensive socialization of librarians to combat censorship, it is easy

FIGURE 11

Proposed Removal from Public Library of
Books by Controversial Authors

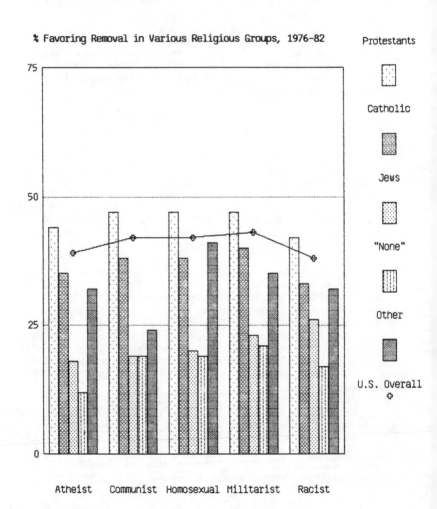

% Favoring Removal in Various Religious Groups, 1976-82

Type of Author

FIGURE 12

Proposed Removal from Public Library of Books by Controversial Authors

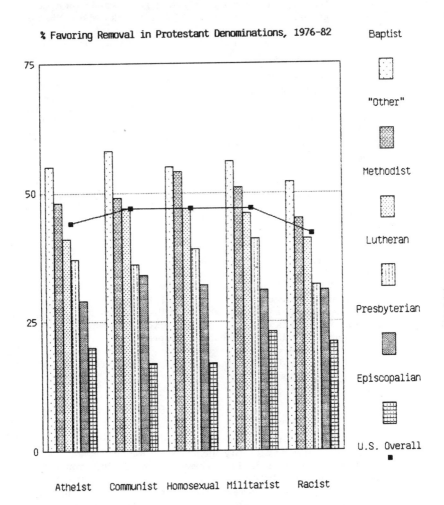

% Favoring Removal in Protestant Denominations, 1976-82

Type of Author

to look askance at the Baptists and the smaller fundamentalist sects
that give majority support to "the other wide." But at least they
censor for a serious reason: If the Bible can change lives for the
better, other books may have the power to change lives for the worse.
And consider, once again, the full implication of the data. A group
like the Baptists must find an atheistic author truly abhorrent and
dangerous. Yet if 55 percent would censor a book by an atheist,
the remaining 45 percent would not. A very sizable minority, in
other words, refuse to censor a book that goes against their deeply
held convictions. This is reminiscent of the blacks who would not
censor a book claiming that blacks are genetically inferior. It is
worth remembering the tolerance of these large minorities when one
is tempted to be cynical about the American people.

The question that emerges from all these demographics, of
course, is that extent to which we are measuring the same people
repeatedly under different headings. For example, an old Alabama
farmer who objects to library books by communists might appear in
one figure as a Southerner, in another as a person with less than
12 years' education, in another as a 60-year-old, in yet another as
a Baptist, and so on.

It is the business of multivariate casual analysis to disentangle
the contributions of each demographic variable in cases such as this,
and I hope to draw on its techniques in a later phase of this study.
Here it may suffice to give Stouffer's explanation of what all the
"pro-censorship" groups seem to have in common: a relative lack
of exposure to diversity.[6] Stouffer and others have hypothesized
that exposure to diversity increases tolerance.

As Williams et al.[7] put it, "At first, individuals exposed to
sociocultural heterogeneity learn that difference per se is not necessarily hamful and that people who act differently are not always
dangerous. This is only a first step, however, because a tolerant
person must be willing to accept nonconformity, within the law at
least, even if it appears to be dangerous. This lesson begins to be
learned when one discovers that his or her own freedom may depend
on a willingness to grant the same rights to others."

Privilege, Class, & Tolerance

Within demographic groups we have examined, those exposed
to relatively greater diversity include men, Westerners and Easterners
(because of high in-migration compared to the South), younger persons, the more highly educated, whites, and suburbanites, particularly those around America's largest cities. To some extent these
catagories go with social and economic privilege--with high standing
in the class structure. It may be that tolerance is associated with
status and privilege, and only appears to be associated with certain
religious denominations because the latter are an indirect or surrogate

measure of socioeconomic status. In any event we have a clear picture of intolerance, measured by willingness to censor, showing up strongly only in certain groups, and these generally not those that, taken nationally, would be considered the most advantaged.

Local Implications

Censorship fights, as I said, are always local; they are ultimately concerned with those values in the community will prevail. It may well be that, in a given place, the majority of the community would favor censorship if a vote could be taken. In such places, or even in places where a strong and vocal minority for censorship exists, it may be useful for the embattled librarian to adduce national criteria, such as the data here provide.

The American people as a whole do not support censorship of library books. Protestants, Catholics, and Jews do not. If the procensorship forces are fundamentalist Christians, it may be worth arguing that the majority of Christians nationally do not share their views; or that, even among fundamentalists, opinions are mixed, with many opposed to censorship.

In the South, where procensorship forces are proportionately higher than elsewhere, it would be folly to make invidious comparisons with the rest of the country, but it might not be amiss to point out that censorship draws its greatest support from the relatively uneducated and the aged. (These groups overlap considerably, since the older generation on the average received less schooling than the newer ones.)

There is no easy formula, in the South or anywhere else; arguments from statistics change very few minds. But they may make the task of those in favor of censorship more difficult, because it is important for them to feel they are in the majority, and admirable because of it, and invincible. These data show that they are not. Even where majorities emerge, they are not in categories universally admired, and large opposing groups are generated in every case.

Most librarians, school or public, would not see the library as a difficult thing to attack. It is, socially speaking, an easy target. Ironically, it may be attacked in censorship fights because it is about the only institution (the schools being the other) against which the censors feel strong enough to stand. Nationally, they are not attacking from a commanding position. If they were stronger, they might take on tougher adversaries. Perhaps librarians ought to be grateful that so often the battle stops with them, painful though it is.

1. See, e.g., Serebnick, Judith, "A Review of Research Related
    to Censorship in Libraries," Library Research, Summer 1975,
    p. 95-118.
2. Davis, James A. General Social Surveys, 1972-83 [machine-
    readable data file]. National Opinion Research Center [producer];
    Roper Public Opinion Research Center [distributor], 1983.
3. Stouffer, Samuel A. Communism, Conformity, and Civil Liber-
    ites: a Cross-Section of the Nation Speaks Its Mind. Doubleday,
    1955.
4. White, Howard D., "Library Censorship and the Permissive Mi-
    nority," Library Quarterly, April 1981, p. 192-207.
5. Stouffer, ch. 5.
6. Ibid.
7. Williams, J. Allen, Clyde Z. Nunn, & Louis St. Peter, "Origins
    of Tolerance--Findings from a Replication of Stouffer's Communism,
    Conformity, and Civil Liberties," Social Forces, December 1976, p.
    394-408. See also the Journal of Social Issues, Spring 1975; the
    entire number is devoted to reexamining civil liberties in Stouf-
    fer's tradition.

NOTES ON CONTRIBUTORS

LARRY AMEY is an Associate Professor at the Dalhousie University School of Library and Information Studies.

HAIG BOSMAJIAN teaches at the University of Washington, Seattle.

MARY K. CHELTON is co-editor of Voice of Youth Advocates (VOYA).

ELYSE CLARK is Middle School Librarian, Hanover Public School District, Hanover, Pennsylvania.

WILLIAM S. CRAMER is Federal Documents Librarian at Oakland University, Rochester, Michigan.

ROSEMARY RUHIG DuMONT is Dean, School of Library Science, Kent State University, Kent, Ohio.

JOAN C. DURRANCE is Assistant Professor at the School of Library Science, University of Michigan, Ann Arbor, Michigan.

MARTIN ERLICH is former director of the Orange Public Library, Orange, California.

JOHN P. FEATHER is Senior Lecturer, Department of Library and Information Studies, Loughborough University, England.

JOHN M. HAAR is History Bibliographer, History and Humanities Department, University of Georgia Libraries, Athens.

THE HENNEPIN COUNTY (Minnesota) Library Task Force on Services to Groups consists of Vicki Oeljen, chair, Lois Anderson, Bill Erickson, Holly McDonnell, Gretchen Wronka, and Julie Ylinen.

EDWARD G. HOLLEY is Professor and former Dean of the School of Library Science at the University of North Carolina, Chapel Hill.

DIANE GORDON KADANOFF is Director of the Norwell Public Library, Massachusetts.

BETH KRAIG is with the department of History, University of Washington, Seattle.

CLARA RICHARDSON LACK is a freelance teacher and resource
leader based in Sacramento, California.

MAURICE B. LINE is Director General, British Library Lending
Division, Boston Spa, England.

LUCRETIA W. McCLURE is the Medical Librarian and Assistant Professor of Medical Bibliography at the University of Rochester School
of Medicine and Dentistry, Rochester, NY.

ROSALEE McREYNOLDS is Serials Librarian, Loyola University, New
Orleans.

LOWELL A. MARTIN is a management and buildings consultant and
Visiting Professor, School of Information Science and Policy, State
University of New York at Albany.

MURRAY S. MARTIN is Director of the Tufts University Library,
Medford, Massachusetts.

JUDITH W. MONROE is a retired librarian and freelance writer who
lives in rural Maine.

JOE MOREHEAD is Associate Professor at the School of Information
Science and Policy, State University of New York at Albany.

KARL NYREN is a Contributing Editor to Library Journal and Editor
of Library Hotline.

CARL F. ORGREN is director, School of Library and Information
Science, University of Iowa, Iowa City.

KATHERINE PATERSON, twice winner of the Newbery Award, received the National Book Award in 1979.

JAMES RICE is Associate Professor at the School of Library and Information University of Iowa, Iowa City.

MARY SELLEN is Library Director, Spring Hill College, Mobile, Alabama.

DAVID H. STAM is University Librarian at Syracuse University,
Syracuse, NY.

G. THOMAS TANSELLE is President of the Bibliographical Society
of America.

HOWARD WHITE is Associate Professor at the College of Information
Studies, Drexel University, Philadelphia, PA.

HOLLY WILLETT is Assistant Professor at the School of Library and
Information Studies, University of Wisconsin-Madison.